BHĀMINĪVILĀSA

OF

JAGANNĀTHA

BHĀMINĪVILĀSA

OF

JAGANNĀTHA

With **Kāvyamarmaprakāśa**

of

LAKSHMAN RAMCHANDRA VAIDYA

Sanskrit text, Study, Introduction, English translation, Prose order, Notes and Appendices.

Edited by

R.K. PANDA

BHARATIYA KALA PRAKASHAN

DELHI (INDIA)

First Edition : 2004

Published by **C.P. Gautam**
BHARATIYA KALA PRAKASHAN
3421-A, IInd Floor Narang Colony, Tri Nagar,
Delhi-110035. Phone : 27153083(O), 27522129 (R)

ISBN : 81-8090-012-6

Laser Type Setting by
A-ONE GRAPHICS
Brahmapuri, Delhi-110053
Phone : 2218 3470

Printed at
Salasar Imaging Systems
Delhi, Ph. 31045804

EDITORIAL

I feel highly satisfied to place this edition of the *Bhāminī-vilāsa* in the hands of students and the lovers of Sanskrit poetry. I have herein made all possible efforts to make this book as useful to the students as possible.

The *Bhāminīvilāsa* is undoubtedly an important work of Paṇḍitarāja Jagannātha. It is the collection of detached verses indepen-dent of each other and so, it may be called a *Kośakāvya*. According to Dr. Keith, this kāvya is admirable in many respects as an erotic poem, an elegy and a store of gnomic sayings. The book is divided into four *vilāsas*—the Prāstāvika, Śṛṅgāra, Karuṇa and Śāntavilāsa. The Prāstāvika-vilāsa is a collection of gnomic and didactic verses. These are very grand in conception and in expression. Every verse is a ready illustration of *anyokti* or *aprastutapraśaṁsā*. The subject matter of these sayings is numerous. Generally philosophy, morals and practical advice to life are suggested through these verses. The second chapter called *Śṛṅgāravilāsa* contains the highest number of verses giving passionate expression to the emotion of love. So this chapter is a good specimen of erotic poetry. Here each stanza is a complete unit of sense, expression and imagery and it presents a daintily finished picture of the emotion or a situation. The poet has depicted the reactions and subtle variations in the moods and fancies of the lover and the beloved. The poet has an extra-ordinary power to describe the abstract thoughts and feelings.

The third Karuṇavilāsa depicts pathetic sentiment and it is an elegiac poetry. This gives expression to poet's serious pathos.

The last vilāsa is entitled *Śāntavilāsa* which contains lyrical verses expressing poet's devotion for God. It seems to be a spontaneous outbrust of the poet's spiritual feeling. The prevailing tone of the verses is one of dedication and surrender to the Lord Kṛṣṇa.

The present edition contains all the four *vilāsas* and therefore it is complete in itself. It contains the thoroughly revised Sanskrit text, a commentary entitled *Kāvyamarmprakāśa* of Lakshman Ramachandra Vaidya, literal English translation, Prose-order, comprehensive introduction, Study, notes and appendices.

The text presented here is mainly based on the edition of the book published by Mr. L.R. Vaidya in Bombay with his own gloss in 1887. The appendix A is also taken from his work. The reason why this book is selected is that it gives the largest number of verses. The Editor has made meticulous efforts in making the work as authentic as possible.

This text was also out of print since long time and the book which I could collect with great difficulty, was as good as a manuscript. Some pages were broken and some letters were missing. Some letters were not even legible. One important point which is worth noting is that in his edition Dr. Vaidya has invariably used the *anuśvāra* sign in those places where usually its corresponding nasal is substituted. But I have changed them and used the nasal signs in the places of *anuśvāras*. Another important point to be noted is that Dr. Vaidya has not noted the variant readings in his edition whereas the present editor has collected them from the various available printed editions so that a critical reader will be well aware of the different readings and will certainly derive pleasure out of reading. Since Vaidya's edition was published long back in 1887 one can easily make out its condition. This work, due to its intrinsic merit, has attracted many learned scholars who have prepared the editions of this work.

We come to know about the following editions :

1. The Paris edition of the poem by M.A. Bergaigne, published in 1872. The edition is a scholarly attempt and gives a tolerable correct text.
2. Professor Taranatha had brought out an edition in 1872.
3. S.M. Paranjape's edition. Poona, 1985.
4. B.G. Bal's edn. Bombay, 1895.
5. Nirnayasagara edn. 11, 1933.
6. Har Dutt Sarma's edition, Poona, 1935.
7. Ed. by Sheshadri Lyer, Hyderabad.
8. Bhāminīilāsa, Karuṇa and Śṛṅgārvilāsa of Jagannātha with Translation in English ed. by H.D. Sarma, Poona Oriental Book Agency, 1938.
9. Paṇḍitarāja Kāvyasaṁgraha, ed. by Aryendra Sharma, 1958.
10. The Bhāminīvilāsa of Paṇḍitarāja Jagannātha edited with The 'Prakāśa' Hindi commentary by Radhey-syam Misra, The Kashi Sanskrit Series, 171, The Chowkhamba Sanskrit Series Office, 1966.
11. Paṇḍitarāja Jagannāthakāvya granthāvalī, Edited and Translated into Hindi by Dr. Hari Narayan Dikshit Eastern Book Linkers, Delhi, 1996.
12. Bhāminīvilāsa of Jagannātha Paṇḍit (Prāstāvikavilāsa and Shamtavilāśa) Edited with a complete Translation into English, Prose order, Introduction, Notes and Appendices by E.V. Dadape and D.G. Apte, pubd. by K.M. Khushalani, Baroda, 1935.

13. Of all these the last four editions are available and I have made use of them for the present edition of this work.

Since the work was popular there are many variant readings. Dr. Vaidya does not note them. He remarks:

As to varioe lectiones, happily they are few, and are mostly too unimportant to deserve notice. I have adopted, generally, the reading of the majority of the copies, and, in a few cases, where such a course appeared necessary, the one that I thought best. But I have not considered it worth while to notice the variants, except in some special cases. It should be remembered in this connection that Jagannātha himself often twists his verse, in a variety of ways, in the *Rasagaṅgādhara* to meet the exigencies of Alaṁkāra, and it is sometimes difficult to determine the version which he subsequently adopted in the *Bhāminīvilāśa* (vide, Vaidya, L.R. Preface, pp. iii-iv.

However, the present editor has spared no pains in making this work more authentic and useful. He has corrected some of the readings which are available in Vaidya's edition in the light of some printed editions. Though they are few, still are no way insignificant. We give here some of the examples.

(1).	तुलना मुखस्यापि	मुखास्याप्ता (II.149)
(2).	हिमाम्बुझंझानिलविह्वलस्य	हिमाम्बुङ्गानिल- (II. 169)

Apart from this, the editor has

(1) Prepared the prose-order of all the verses given in the text.

(2) Revised the English translation of the verses of the *śṛṅgāravilāsa* and *karuṇavilāsa*.

(3) Prepared notes on the verses of the *Śṛṅgāravilāsa* and the *Karuṇavilāsa*.

(4) Prepared two appendices-
(i) Metre (ii) Alphabetical Index of verses.

(5) Prepared a critical study of this poem. Furthermore, he has brought to light many significant aspects of Paṇḍitarāja's creative faculty. He has identified almost all the figures of speech that have figures of speech that have occured in the verses of the Bhāminīvilāsa. It will be very much useful to the students who are interested in the stylistic study of Jagannātha.

The text contains a commentary of Dr. L.R. Vaidya who describes the importance of this work in the following words.

"The Sanskrit gloss which accompanies the text is intended for the ordinary reader as well as for more advanced student. It does not profess to be a full commentary dealing with each word of the stanza according to its place in syntactical construction. It explains the connection of words, wherever that is obscure, and gives the meanings of hard words and unusual phrases, the side-meaning of words and sentences, and the bearing of the whole stanza, when necessary. These things, it is hoped, will be useful to the ordinary reader. Further, it solves, in some cases, difficulties of grammar, often explains the alaṁkāra and rasas, and points out the beauties of the stanza according to the way of native crities." (Preface, p. iv).

The Introduction (pp. 1-23) portion is taken from the edition prepared by E.V. Dadape and D.G. Apte. It covers all information that is available about the great poet Jagannātha and his works. It is comprehensive.

The English translation of the verses in the *Prāstāvika-vilāsa* and *Śāntavilāsa* are of E.V. Dadape and D.G. Apte. The rest i.e. *śṛṅgāravilāsa* and *karuṇavilāsa* are of H.D. Sarma. It is taken from the edition of the Bhāminīvilāsa, (Karuṇa and Śṛṅgāravilāsa) of Jagannātha with Translation in English) ed. by H.D. Sarma, Poona. Oriental Book Agency, 1938. The translation is literal. It is perhaps the only translation in English available on this work. With great difficulty I could collect a copy of this translation. It is out of print.

The notes for the portions of Prāstāvikavilāsa and śāntavilāsa is taken from the edition of E.V. Dadape and D.G. Apte.

In the notes almost every important compound is solved, ample references and parallel quotations are given, and notes on grammar is also added in some important cases. The plan of notes that the learned editors had followed is one based upon the correct application of the principles of psychology and for the ready grasp of students. Ample *Subhāṣita* and other relevant verses are quoted with the intention of widening the knowledge of the students and to simulate self-activity on their part. Almost in all *anyoktis,* central ideas and applications are given to facilitate the understanding of the students. In some verses the learned editors have drawn from Acyutarāya's commentary *Praṇayaprakāśinī* and have also discussed some important readings. The present editor has prepared the notes on the verses of the Śṛṅgāravilāsa and Karuṇavilāsa.

This edition also contains a study of the Bhāminivilāsa. No edition gives such a study which is comprehensive and critical. It has illustrated with appropriate citations the intrinsic merits of Jagannāth's creative faculty. The figures (Alaṁkāras) of all the verses are identified under this study.

I hope that the efforts and difficulties of the present editor in bringing out this edition will be appreciated by the students of poetry for whom it is chiefly intended. I am confident that an edition of this type will be helpful in extending the poetry literature of Jagannātha Paṇḍita who has given us the nectar of poetry.

In preparing this work, I have derived immense help from the works of the previous learned editions, my puvasūris. I gratefully acknowledge the dept, I have to them. I have no hesitation in admiring their efforts and no intention in hiding their contributions. Therefore in the proper places I have their names.

I am very much thankful to my friends, Dr. Harekrishna Panigrahi, Orissa, Sri Gopal Panda who have supplied to me the necessary material (books and zerox copies).

I have also pleasure in thanking my wife Sweta for her help and encouragement.

My thanks are due to C.P. Gautam, the proprietor of Bharatiya Kala Prakashan for publishing this work and extending this valuable source of knowledge to the public.

Baroda **R.K. Panda**
15th, November, 2003

CONTENTS

INTRODUCTION*

—E.V. Dadape and D.G. Apte

Jagannātha Paṇḍita is unanimously considered as one of the most glorious stars in the galaxy of Sanskrit poets and as such has been receiving that incredibly high degree of honour and commendation which no poet perhaps has ever been able to command at the hands of the cultured public, since the comparatively darker ages when कालिदास and भवभूति both invaluable crest-jewels of the goddess Saraswatī-are recorded to have flourished. However, one will be struck to observe that this great edifice of the unrivalled glory of our poet rests on a foundation immensely different from that of his two great predecessors and compeers in his renown. कालिदास and भवभूति built their unparalleled glory on the unprecedented poetic imageries and fascinating diction which appear in dramas like शाकुन्तल and उत्तररामचरित, and in works like रघुवंश and कुमारसम्भव, जगन्नाथ, however, had no such big work which was mainly instrumental in establishing his fame. It is a pleasant mystery that although more popular of his works such as भामिनीविलास गंगालहरी etc. are inaccessible to an ordinary scholar, his real fame rests on them. We think, this is due to his masterly command over language and high class polemics, linked with profound knowledge of the subject in hand, which effectively appeal to the learned scholars. In this respect our poet can be very favourably compared with the great English

---

* Bhāminīvilāsa of Jagannātha Paṇḍita, Pub. by K.M. Khushalani, Baroda, 1935

poet Milton who is unanimously accepted as the best and is read the least. It is hence in the fitness of things that a reader of a famous work like भामिनीविलास should be conversant with some important incidents, forming the outline of the biography of this "sovereign of poets".

पण्डित जगन्नाथराय was born in the year 1550 A. D. in the village मुंगुंडा in the district वेंगिनाडी in the country of आंध्र. His father पेरमभट्ट was one of the most learned Brahmins and had mastered almost all शास्त्रs, which constituted highest learning in those days. His mother's name was लक्ष्मी, who was a very pious and devout lady. जगन्नाथ himself refers to this in verse 52 of his work प्राणाभरण in the following verse,

तैलंगान्वयमंगलालयमहालक्ष्मीदयालालितः।
श्रीमत्पेरमभट्टसूनुरनिशं विद्वल्ललाटन्तपः॥
.............श्रीमत्पण्डितराजपण्डितजगन्नाथो व्यधासीदिदम्॥

In the introduction to his work रसगंगाधर he also gives the names of the विद्यागुरुs of his father in detail as follows,

श्रीमज्ज्ञानेन्द्रभिक्षोरधिगतसकलब्रह्मविद्याप्रपञ्चः
काणादीराक्षपादीरपि गहनगिरो यो महेन्द्रादवेदीत्।
देवादेवाध्यगीष्ट स्मरहरनगरे शासनं जैमिनीयं
शेषाङ्कप्राप्तशेषामलभणितिरभूत्सर्वविद्याधरो यः॥

As a worthy son to a worthy father, जगन्नाथ also, when a mere youth, mastered all these विद्याs from his father. This explains perhaps why he called his father a महागुरु. He was first a गुरु because he was his father and secondly because he was also his विद्यागुरु. In his introduction to the रसगंगाधर he says **पाषाणादपि पीयूषं स्यन्दते यस्य मायया। तं वन्दे पेरुभट्टाख्यं लक्ष्मीकान्तं महागुरुम्॥** After the death of his loving mother, जगन्नाथ

was married to भामिनी, who also, it is said, besides being greatly devoted to her husband, was well-versed in शास्त्रs. But as ill luck would have it, by the death of his beloved wife, जगन्नाथ was thrown into an abyss of sorrow and disgust of the world for a long time. This is perhaps imprinted in the following verse of his **करुणविलास. सर्वेऽपि विस्मृतिपथं विषयाः प्रयाताः। विद्याऽपि खेदगलिता विकलीबभूव।। सा केवलं हरिणशावकलोचना मे। नैवापयाति हृदयादधिदेवतेव।** (भा. वि. ३.३.). But his grief allayed as time passed on, and he once more made up his mind to build a sound reputation and left his country forthwith.

It is said that before he started on his tour he propitiated the goddess बालात्रिपुरसुंदरी and got from her the following boon, आकुरु देशं विचरेः मा कुरु परवादिनिर्जये शंकाम्। स्वीकुरु वरमेकं मे व्याकुरु भो वत्स शास्त्राणि।। In the course of his travels he arrived at Jaipur and was adequately appreciated by the then ruling prince राजा भगवानदास–the brother of भानुमति, the wife of अकबर–and opened a college which in a short time, became famous because of the students of जगन्नाथ, who brought credit to his institution after prosecuting their studies in शास्त्रs like न्याय, वेदान्त, व्याकरण, etc., there. Thus when जगन्नाथ was to raise his reputation and make him known all over the country.

The history of India is replete with stories regarding अकबर's sincere longing for the knowledge of all religions and then of founding one common religion, based on the choicest principles of all of them, to be followed by all persons, irrespective of caste or creed. He was of course not partial towards any religion in particular, and entertained any and every learned man that came to him. Once a काजी approached him and asked him to throw a challenge to the representatives of all religions to come and discuss with him, if their religion was sufficiently systematic to withstand the tests of Islam. In a cosmopolitan spirit, this was broadcasted by the prince, and the Hindus, who constituted the majority of his subjects found themselves in a helpless plight. They searched for a man, who should save their religion and unanimously agreed upon requesting जगन्नाथ to represent their religion which was at stake. Consequently जगन्नाथ had to studying critically the tenets of Islam he started for vanquishing his adversary.

Long and learned were the discussions which took place among the learned representatives of these two antagonistic faiths, but in the end, the काजी had to yield to the logical argument and the wide and deep knowledge of जगन्नाथ. This earned for him an almost India-wide name and fame and consequently of course made him an object of envy. After this success जगन्नाथ became an object of respect and admiration and the king would hardly feel satisfied unless he had conversed with जगन्नाथ at least for some time in a day. This friendship between the prince and the poet waxed stronger and as time passed on, he became one of those fortunate few who were basking in the sunshine of royal patronage and favour.

The king had a daughter from his Rajput wife भानुमति who had a wonderful predilection for Sanskrit learning and hence had studied the language and some scriptures under teachers, expert in that. Although born of a Mahomedan, she betrayed all signs of inclination towards and appreciation for everything that was Hindu and as such admired the पंडित very highly.

On one occasion when the king and the पंडित were sitting together, talking at ease, there appeared before them, the daughter of the king carrying water for her father who was sitting there and had asked her to fetch it for him. The

पंडित was smitten by her bewitching beauty, and all of a sudden uttered the following pictching beauty, in which he very vividly described the paragon of beauty that was standing before him. The verses are.

इयं सुस्तनी मस्तकन्यस्तकुंभा कुसुम्भारुणं चारुचैलं दधाना।
समस्तस्य लोकस्य चेतःप्रवृत्तिं गृहीत्वा घटे न्यस्य यातीव लोकम्॥१॥
यवनी नवनीतकोमलांगी शयनीये यदि लभ्यते कदाचित्।
अवनीतलमेव साधु मन्ये न वनी माधवनी विलासहेतुः॥२॥
यवनी रमणी विपदः शमनी कमनीयतया नवनीतसमा।
'उहि ऊहि' वचोऽमृतपूर्णमुखी स सुखी जगतीह यदङ्कगता॥३॥

He was unable to overcome the passionate love for the lady and made himself bold enough to pray to the king to give her to him as a gift. He had previously known that the princess was also loving to have पंडितराज for her consort, and as the king was favourably inclined to such inter-caste marriages, he would not, in the least, object to his proposals. The verse that he instantaneously uttered runs thus, न याचे गजालिं न वा वाजिराजिं न वित्तेषु चित्तं मदीयं कथंचित्। इयं सुस्तनी मस्तकन्यस्तकुम्भा लवंगी कुरंगी दृगंगीकरोतु॥ according to the desire of the poet and the princess, the marriage was celebrated (about the year 1605 A.D.) in all royal pomp and glory, notwithstanding the opposition of the learned orthodoxy of the town and the king gave the couple costly gifts and annual grants.

The Brahmins in Delhi felt annoyed at this undesirable event and wanted to disunite the pair and break their marriage; and to help in this pious work they sought upon the assistance of one हरदीक्षित, a learned Paṇḍita of Benares, who also felt it a great offence given to the Hindu religion. In about 1006 i.e. immediately after the death of Akbar हरदीक्षित arrived in Delhi. A great meeting was held, in which जगन्नाथ was openly challenged for discussion about the śāstric sanction for his marriage. This was a private function and the result being indecisive people gave a verdict against जगन्नाथ and he was excommunicated.

Being disgusted with constant public opposition and consequent mental and physical seclusion the Paṇḍita started on a sojourn, and passed several years outside Delhi, in a comparatively happier mood, with his learned and loving wife, writing poems, which of course must have been highly instrumental in giving him immense relief from the persecution of his bitter enemies.

During his long absence of about two decades from Delhi, he was once invited by Jehangir, but he refused to go, seeing that the prince was vicious. However later on, in the reign of Shah Jahan, he was again invited to Delhi and a great Durbar was held to honour the पंडित and to bestow upon him, the title of पंडितराज.

Vide मूर्तिमतेव नवावासफखानमनःप्रसादेन द्विजकुलसेवादेवाकि-वाङ्मनःकायेन माथुरकुलसमुद्रेन्दुना रायमुकुन्देनादिष्टेन सार्वभौमश्रीशहाजहान् प्रसादाधिगतपंडितराजपदवीविराजितेन तैलंगकुलावतंसेन पंडितजगन्नाथेनासफ-विलासाख्येयमाख्यायिका निरमीयत। (आसफविलासप्रस्तावना।)

Thus when he was passing his days and had forgotten the enmity of हरदीक्षित, a shock suddenly came to him. While one day, his wife, the Mahomedan princess had gone out for taking a walk, she was kidnapped by some persons who were hired for the same work by हरदीक्षित, and then closed up in an old castle. For a long time the पंडित waited, but भामिनी did not return to him. He managed to send persons in search of her, but after a few days, growing impatient, he himself started, and travelled on and on in the hope of finding his beloved wife until at last he reached Benares, and resigned himself to the mercy of विश्वेश्वर, praying earnestly for his reunion with his wife, now almost lost to him.

भामिनी luckily found helpers when she was imprisoned in the castle and was successful in effecting her escape, and started to Benares where, she determined to burn herself. After some months, she disguised as a mendicantreached Benares. Bent upon self-immolation she was madly wandering when suddenly she came across जगन्नाथ who was also in the same plight. Thus their joy knew no bounds. Since then, the couple used to spend their time in devotion and prayer, following the rites prescribed by the śāstras. On the days of दशहरा (i.e. ज्येष्ठशुद्धप्रतिपद् to दशमी) the couple resolved upon propitiating the Ganges by a hundred repetitions of the famous पीयूषलहरी (later known as गंगालहरी) on each of the ten days. On the very first day the incidental arrival of अप्पयदीक्षित resulted into a short conversation between these two intellectual giants. The story has been described in the notes on Bh. V. IV. 30. Thus nine days passed smoothly. On the tenth, the couple, as usual took their ablutions in the morning and began the repetitions of the गंगालहरी. After the hundred repetitions of that day were completed, he, accompanied by his यवनी wife proceeded to take a bath into the Ganges, but his enemies led by हरदीक्षित were there, who obstructed him, calling him a पतित, and hence unfit to bathe, lest the sacred water be polluted. जगन्नाथ of course was all calm. He retreated and came to the top of the घाट (the steps leading to the river-water) and seating himself there began to repeat his पीयूषलहरी which constitutes fifty two stanzas. Immediately a miracle took place and the waters of the sacred river began to rise, one step for every stanza, on that घाट only, where the पंडित was sitting. When the repetiton of all the fifty-two verses was completed, the पंडित became ready to throw himself into the hands of the Ganges who was beckoning to him to come to her. But the यवनी feared she would be left alone, hence on her behalf the पंडित requested to Goddess to accept यवनी also into her lap and save her. On this occasion the यवनी is said to have addressed the following verse to the Ganges:

सुरधुनि नृपकन्ये पुण्यवन्तं पुनासि
स तरति निजपुण्यैस्तत्र किं ते महत्वम्।
नृपवरकुलजातां यावनी मां पुनासि
तदिह तव महत्वं, तन्महत्वं महत्वम्।।

Immediately the surging billows of the Ganges rose up to their heads and washed both of them away, leaving the people to wonder at the mysterious incident that had taken place before their open eyes and gaping mouths. Thus disappeared from this mortal world, the poet and scholar of immortal fame.

It must, of course, be borne in mind that the above biography is based mainly on anecdotes that are prevalent about जगन्नाथ, there being very few points which have been finally decided, and hence are not aloof from the danger of being called into question in times yet to come. However it is desirable to sound a note of caution in attaching unnecessary importance to any detail and wait for some time in future when more historically authentic facts are available for reference and consequent scrutiny.

The poet's date, though he is comparatively much modern, is also a question which has not been finally settled and shares this misfortune as his worthy predecessors like Kālidāsa do. Only a few sources are open for us for investigating into this matter and almost every statement has to be based more on logical inference than upon first hand material. We have stated before that जगन्नाथ was born in August 1550 A.D. and that he died when he was 92 years of age i.e. in 1642 A.D. If such be the case and there seems no reason why it should be considered improbable—he can possibly have lived in the reigns of all the three emperors, Akbar, Jahangir and Shah Jahan, whose reigns collectively cover the period from 1556 A. D. to 1658 A.D. Calculating mathematically we find this easily possible. Akbar was born on the 14th of October 1542 and ascended the throne of Delhi in 1556 i.e. 6 years after the birth of Jagannātha. Supposing that जगन्नाथ was initiated when he was eight, and that he spent about a dozen years at least in acquiring the vast knowledge he possessed, we may safely infer that he was about 21 when he became Paṇḍita. He was then married and soon after, his wife expired leaving a son behind her. It is after this that Jagannātha started on a sojourn when he was probably 24. Then he is said to have opened a college at Jaypore and his fame spread far and wide. Allowing the period of only a decade as the duration of this college, it won't be exaggerating to infer that he was about 34 when he was sufficiently well-known to be appointed as the representative of Hinduism to take up the challenge of the Muslim Kazi for religious discussion. When he was successful he is said to have been appreciated by the King and it is said that जगन्नाथ on this occasion addressed the following verse to the emperor.

जयत्यकबरः पृथ्वीपतिरूर्जितविक्रमः।
येनारातिवधूवर्गः सर्वोऽप्यकबरीकृतः॥

At this time जगन्नाथ was about 35. This period approaches 1585 A. D. At this time Akbar was about 43 years of age and had ruled for about 29 years. Thus we find that it easily stands in the range of possibility that he was a junior contemporary of Akbar and a senior contemporary of Jahangir and Shah Jahan. Taking this into consideration all his life fits in well with the facts that have been mentioned before. Those who oppose this theory say so merely on the ground of the absence of additional positive evidence, but so long as nothing other-wise is proved, it is better to stick to what is already before us.

जगन्नाथ is a master of vigorous, effective and elegant diction and manifests conspicuously all the characteristics expected of a great poet. His wonderful imagery and unique achievements in polemics are clearly brought out in his works like the रसगंगाधर, which is the crowning work of the poet and unrivalled in its excellence. Unlike many a poet, he handles both prose and poetry with equal ease and grace which undoubtedly adds greatly to his unrivalled fame. In depicting pathos also he seems at his best. In the present verses, he sometimes appears before us as a love-sick man, sometimes as an austere philosopher, stamping all the world as a mirage and a non-entity and on other occasions as a devotee entirely dependent upon the grace of the Lord Krisha. His poems thus exhibit to an observer his majestic self-playing the role of a devotee, a lover, an abstruse-thinker, grammarian, an expert controvertialist, and a versatile scholar. (For an estimate of जगन्नाथ himself about his own poetry read the following from Bh. V. III 6. **निर्दूषणा गुणवती रसभावपूर्णा सालंकृतिः श्रवणकोमलवर्णराजिः। सा मामकीनकवितेव मनोऽभिरामा रामा कदापि हृदयान्मम नापयाति॥** His scholarship also extends over various fields like that of grammar, rhetorics, etc. and everywhere he has surpassed his contemporaries.

The writers on Jagannātha cannot but draw the attention of the readers to the two ignoble and yet unavoidable traits of his character, viz. his uncommon inclination towards egoism and his jealousies and trenchant attacks on his opponents. As the examples of the former we may point out a few verses at the end of the fourth Vilāsa (See verses 37-38-39-40-43 and 44) Also see. "श्रुतमात्रा वाक्यार्थं करतलबदरमिव निवेदयन्ती घटना प्रसादस्य। अयं च सर्वसाधारणो गुण:। उदाहरणान्यत्र प्रायेण मदीयानि सर्वाण्येव पद्यानि (र. ग. आनन I) also see the verse at the introduction to the र. ग. निर्माय नूतनमुदाहरणानुरूपं काव्यं मयात्र निहितं न परस्य किञ्चित्। किं सेव्यते सुमनसां मनसापि गन्धः कस्तूरिकाजननशक्तिभृता मृगेण।। All the learned persons unanimously interpret such verses as insults to others of the same vocation, yet, Jagannātha deserves an indulgent treatment, since a major part of his poetry is indeed what he has described it to be. His is a "over-confident" about his capacity, for which he should be "confident." Yet it would not be unbecoming to recommend that he should be forgiven if at all self-praise is a very serious crime – ; and should not be taken very seriously to task so as to affect his reputation as a poet and a scholar.

The second charge is that of being very trenchant and caustic in his sarcasms as manifested in नेदं रूपकम्। रूपके च बिम्बप्रतिबिम्बभावो नास्तीति केनाप्यालंकारिकमन्येन प्रतारितस्य दीर्धश्रवस उक्तिरश्रद्धेयैव।। (र. ग. रूपकप्रकरण). All persons of good taste will indeed blush at this, but taking into consideration the inborn antipathy of one scholar towards another, this does not seem so condemnable as it is generally considered to be. That his writings smack of indecency in some places is a sorry fact, but can examples of a worse type of acrimony not be quoted in numbers from equally dignified writers and saints? Nay, what great person has ever spared his adversary, in his book, when once he is caught in his sure grip ? It is perhaps, taking this fact into consideration that the great कालिदास has wisely said "प्राय: समानविद्याः परस्परयश:पुरोभागा:।।" Even great saints cannot restrain themselves when they find their adversaries cornered and helpless. It is hence best to look askance at this aspect of the भागवतपुराण viz. "तेजीयसां न दोषाय" which frees the deliquents from all the blames resulting from their insulting words. However this is not to be imitated as the भागवत further explains," नैतत्समाचरेज्जातु मनसाऽपि ह्यनीश्वरः। विनश्यत्याचरन्मौढ्याद्यथा रुद्रोऽब्धिजं विषम्।। (भागवत+-३३-३०)

His views on religion are our next point of consideration. He seems to be a perfect follower of the Advaita philosophy as propounded by Śaṅkaracāryā, inasmuch as he considers कर्मन् as subservient to ज्ञान; and as such these cannot bind a ज्ञानिन्. It is perhaps on account of this, that he refused to undergo the प्रायश्चित्तविधि for marrying a यवनी, since he was far too advanced to resort to any कर्मन्. He many times propounds the doctrines incorporated in the books on philosophy. cf. **निखिलं जगदेव नश्वरं पुनरस्मिन्नितरां कलेवरम्। अथ तस्य कृते कियानयं क्रियते हन्त जनैः परिश्रमः।।** (Bh. V. IV. 24) so alsoश्वपचात्मभुवोर्निरन्तरा मम भूयात्परमात्मनि स्थितिः which is more or less parallel to शुनि चैवश्वपाके च पण्डिताः समदर्शिनः of the Bhagwad Geeta. We also recommend the students here to refer to the verse विष्वद्रीच्या भुवनमखिलं etc. (Bh. V. IV-18) and the notes thereon. This is one aspect where he is seen as a votary of the non-qualified Brahman, longing for the achievement of the identity with the eternal according to the doctrine of the Upaniṣads which lays down that after the bonds of duality are cut asunder, one obtains unity and becomes free from the bonds of worldly actions. This is the ideal stage for an out-and-out Advaitist where everything ceases to exist and where nothing affects his mental equipoise.

As different from this comparatively dry aspect, Jagannātha is engrossed in the qualified ब्रह्म i.e. श्रीकृष्ण; (See Bh. V. IV. 17) on whom, from time immemorial eulogies have been showered like anything by his devotees. Krishṇa is the soother and the saviour of all his devotees and hence is popular among the learned as well as the comparatively ignorant people. जगन्नाथ sees eye to eye with the author of the Bhāgwata, inasmuch as he sees a perfect non-difference between the unqualified Brahman and the qualified कृष्ण of the Bhāgwata—किमपि ब्रह्म कृष्णाभिधानम् (Bh. V. IV. 17). He also bends before that कृष्ण, the performer of various Līlās and the consort of Gopis—cf. श्रितो वृंदारण्यं etc. (Bh. V.IV.5 and कलिन्दनगनन्दिनीतटसुरद्रुमालंबिनी (Bh. V. IV 3). He is merged in his solemn and sincere devotion to the son of Nanda and confidently assures his mind that, in the end Krishna will be his saviour and thus he would get salvation. cf. चेतःसरणावस्यां कि नागन्ता कदापि नंदसुतः।। (Bh. V. IV. 28) and अस्ति मम शिरसि सततं नंदकुमारः प्रभुः परमः (Bh. V. IV 31.) (Also see the notes on the verse 3 of the 4th विलास in this connection.) When in this state of a devotee he disrgards even the कर्मकाण्ड, the ज्ञानकाण्ड and other things calling them all as errors and remarks that none but the contemplation of Viṣnu will save us. (Bh. V. IV. 21). Thus जगन्नाथ as a champion of भक्ति cult is the follower of रामानुज while in the matters of philosophy his verses evince the principles of शंकराचार्य's philosophy.

There is a plurality of जगन्नाथs known to history. One of them is better known to us than the other, being the poet of that name who has written the two dramas वसुमतीपरिणय and रतिमन्मथ. That the authorship of both these dramas is given to only one man, is based on the identity of some verses occurring in the two plays, and that the same stanza is employed in both to give the name and parentage of the author. The prologues point out that he was patronized by a petty chief and that the name of his father was Balkrishna. बालकृष्णसचिवोत्तंसस्य रूपांतरम्...........अस्ति न्यस्तपदोगुणैरिह जगन्नाथाभिधानः सुधीः। and that his plays were acted, in Poona, at the Gaṇapati festival. cf. बाजिरायप्रभुवर्यस्य नंदनेन बालाजिराय-महीसंक्रन्दनेन यथा भोः कलाधर, भवता भगवतः श्रीमहागणपतेरस्मिन् महोत्सवे वार्षिके समवेता इमे रसिकाः .... विनोदयितव्या इति।

—वसुमतीपरिणय Act I

This points out clearly the difference between our present poet and the author of these two dramas in three main important points (1) Difference in descent (2) Difference in time, whereas one was a contemporary of Akbar, the other was a contemporary of बालाजीबाजीराव the third peshwa and finally (3) Difference in place. One lived in the court of Akbar i. e. in the north whereas the other lived in the south. There are also many other जगन्नाथs mentioned as follows.

(१) जगन्नाथ—the author of a Prakrit work शशिसेना

(२) जगन्नाथ तर्कपञ्चानन—the author of विवादभंगार्णव who gives रुद्र as his father's name.

(३) जगन्नाथ—a resident of तैलङ्गण who wrote many works on politics and translated the part of the Mahābhārata dealing with politics.

(४) सम्राट् जगन्नाथ—the writer of a book on Geometry.

(५) जगन्नाथ of मिथिला—the author of अनन्तचन्द्रिकानाटक.

(६) जगन्नाथ, the son of श्रीनिवास, the author of a भाण (a kind of drama) called अनंगविजय.

(७) जगन्नाथ मिश्र—the author of सभातरंग

(८) जगन्नाथ सरस्वती—the author of अद्वैतामृत.

(९) जगन्नाथ सूरि—the author of समुदायप्रकरण.

(१०) जगन्नाथ – the author of शरभराजविलास.

(११) जगन्नाथ–the son of नारायणदैवज्ञ–the author of काव्य-ज्ञानविलास.

(१२) जगन्नाथ – the author of अनुभोगकल्पतरु.

However, none of these can be identified with our present जगन्नाथ and this suspicion need not detain us here.

Now, before giving a detailed list of the works of our author, it is more natural to give a little critical information about our present work-भामिनीविलास. The mere knowledge of the name would lead one to form a wrong idea about the book namely that the book must contain verses in which the love sports of a beautiful passionate lady are described. But the fact here is peculiar. It does not contain a continuous story like the *Meghadūta*, but is a mere collection of verses which the poet composed on various occasions to suit various purposes. Even in the arrangement of the verses as it stands at present there is nothing to vouchsafe the conclusion that there is a thread of meaning inwardly connecting one verse with the subsequent one. One thing, however, must be marked, namely that अच्युतराय, the author of the प्रणयप्रकाशटीका on भामिनी-विलास has made vain attempts to link together the verses, but the attempt at the outset seems ridiculous and the way in which he shows the relation of the subsequent verse with the previous one, would not give the least satisfaction to any body. However one cannot help feeling astonished when one comes across the commentator's own remark in his commentary on the last (IV 32) verse which runs as under: – "एवं च मया अयं ग्रन्थः काव्यग्रंथनबुध्या नैव कृतः। किन्तु तत्तदवसरे लीलामात्रेण तानि तानि पद्यानि कृतानि." His opinion here is clearly expressed and yet he has not desisted from attempting to show an undercurrent of chains behind all those verses.

However, this must not weigh much when we see the poet himself saying in the last verse that it is not a deliberately connected composition but that he has merely collected his verses together and sealed them up in a work. The verse runs as follows. **दुर्वृत्ता जारजन्मानो हरिष्यन्तीति शंकया। मदीयपद्यरत्नानां मंजूषैव कृता मया॥** (IV 45). He clearly remarks that he was forced to do this sort of arrangement lest his verses might be plagiarized by persons who might claim them as their own productions and the name that he gave to his collection was that of his first wife who is probably the chief subject of description of his करुणविलास. Thus this is obviously a collection of miscellaneous stanzas, each stanza, complete in itself, having no context, no definite arrangement and dealing with an independent subject of its own. The work thus resembles the three शतकs of भर्तृहरी. Many of the verses have been composed to present some incidents of his own life as some say, e. g. many of his अन्योक्तिs are infused with personal touches, serving as his memoirs. The first verse, they say applies to his defeated enemies, and his almost supernatural capacities as a Paṇḍita, the 9th verse in प्रास्ता. is said to refer to the occasion when he attempted to bring consolation to his wife यवनी who was lamenting over her low birth and so on. Almost all of these verses occur in the रसगंगाधर in one connection or another and this supports the view that has been expressed above.

Like the composition of भर्तृहरि divided into three शतकs the composition under consideration is divided into four विलासs together making one book भामिनीविलास. They are प्रास्ताविक-विलास–शृंगारविलास–करुणविलास and शान्तविलास. Some editions however read अन्योक्त्युल्लास for प्रास्ताविकविलास and शृंगारोल्लास

for श्रृंगारविलास. The reading उल्लास instead of विलास does not stand to reason. There should be all विलासs uniformly named. Yet the substitution of अन्योक्ति (उल्लास) for प्रास्ताविक needs a more serious attention. Critically looking to the contents of this section there is nothing like प्रास्ताविक (introductory) in it. Nor does any of these sections need any introduction in view of the facts that have been proved above. The probable reason why it was termed प्रास्ताविक seems to be that these verses form the remainder, after those falling under श्रृंगार, करुण, and शांतरसs were taken out from the aggregate number, and were afterwards grouped into one big mass, called as the प्रास्ताविक section and placed at the opening of the book which justifies its name but other things also must be taken into consideration, which will lead us to conclude that although the name प्रास्ताविक not altogether wrong or inappropriate, अन्योक्त्युल्लास is indeed better, since more than half the number of verses are अन्योक्तिs that rest being of the सुभाषित type. So what we would like to propose is that the first part should be named as अन्योक्तिविलास and neither of the present two names that are printed should be given. The second and third विलासs contain verses dealing with subjects connoted by their names—the श्रृंगार dealing with the amorous sentiment and the करुण delineating the pathos probably dealing with his lamentation at the death of his first wife, which indeed creates an earnest feeling of sympathy for the sufferer, the last i.e. शांतविलास indeed is worthy of its name since there is serenity in almost every verse and the poet is very beautifully giving vent to his thoughts on various points, such as कर्मन्s, their utility from the point of the attainment of final bliss and his earnest longing and unfathomable faith in the fact that श्रीकृष्ण—the son of Nanda-is sure to save him in the end (See verses 21 and31). In the closing portion of the विलास he gives free vent to his estimate of his own poetry, presenting to himself the title of पंडितराजराजितिलक (IV. 44]. He also hints at the facts that he had malicious adversaries in this field who deliberately disparaged his poems and that there were others who, though they did not express their jealousy, were reserved in showering upon his poetry the praises which it deserved on account of its extra-ordinary merit (see verses 40 and 41of IV विलास). जगन्नाथ also has not borne patiently these reproaches, he has passed very trenchant remarks upon them calling them as mere dead bodies, nay, he has called them even the beasts in the human form. (See Verses 38, 39 of IV). The last verse of the Vilāsa states in very clear terms his object in composing this book.

No introduction will ever be complete without giving a comprehensive list of the works of the present poet. Many of these names have been referred to by him in his work रसगंगाधर and the others are known as being his productions. The list runs as follows.

The five लहरीs to which he makes a reference in the रसगंगाधरः—मन्त्रिर्मिताश्च पञ्चलहर्यो भावस्य. R. G. *Ānana* I, are these (१) पीयूषलहरी (२) सुधालहरी (३) अमृतलहरी (४) करुणालहरी and (५) लक्ष्मीलहरी.

(१) पीयूषलहरी–It is entitled to appear first in the list becausse it is the most popular and most read and is one of the most beautiful works of Jagannātha. It consists of 52 stanzas in praise of the Ganges, thus accounting for the fact that its popular name is the गंगालहरी. All the verses are full of devotion towards the Ganges which the poet honours as his mother and his sole saviour. The beauty of this work is beggars description and cannot but request the readers to enjoy it for themselves. The popular belief in connection with this work is that this was composed, when जगन्नाथ sat on the Ghat, determined upon bringing his mundane existence to an end and immediately after this was completely sung, he disappeared in the Ganges. But this anecdote does not hold any water because many of the verses from this work have been taken up in the R. G. (See कृतक्षुद्राघौघानथ सपदि सन्तप्तमनस: etc. which is quoted in R. G. अनन्वयप्रकरण), which, if the case were such, would seem ridiculous. The fact is that it was composed several years before his death but he took to singing and repeating it with extra-ordinary devotion, in the ten days of the दशहरा and ultimately was washed away as tradition says. The metre शिखरिणी also tends to heighten the sentiment of devotion.

(२) **सुधालहरी**–This is an aggregate of 30 stanzas all composed with the intention of singing the glories of God Sun, of the type of the सूर्यशतक of मयूर, who is said to have been cured of leprosy by its efficacy. It is a composition which also bespeaks of the rare poetic gift of its author, the stanzas from this also are found in the R. G.

(३) **अमृतलहरी**–Thia is a devotional song addressed to the Yamunā, consisting of only ten verses and composed on the lines of the famous नर्मदाष्टक of Śaṅkaracārya.

(४) **करुणालहरी**–This poem contains about sixty verses which are addressed to Vishnu, the tutelary deity of जगन्नाथ wherein he, very pathetically, beseeches him to save him from the unbearable worldly ills, which he is heir to. It is full of pathos which perhaps accounts for its name. It is also in other places titled as विष्णुलहरी but it is yet better to call it करुणालहरी, because this is the way in which the author himself has referred to it in इदं च पद्यं मन्निर्मितायां भगवद्भक्तिप्रधानायां करुणालहर्यामुपनिबद्धमिति।.................

R. G. *Ānana* I

(५) **लक्ष्मीलहरी**–This is a composition of about 40 verses addressed to लक्ष्मी, the consort of Viṣṇu. The verse 30 of this is almost the same as the verse 137 in the श्रृंगारविलास of the भामिनीविलास, the same verse being also quoted in रसगंगाधर.

(६) **यमुनावर्णनचम्पूः**–This is a compositon partly in verse and partly in prose (गद्यपद्यमयी वाणी चंपूरित्यभिधीयते). This is not much known to the public although it is said that it is printed in काव्यमाला. There are references from this work in the रसगंगाधर.

(७) **रसगङ्गाधर**–This is the most voluminous and the most learned of all the works mainly rests the reputation of our author. It is a treatise on poetics, written in a masterly style, with great ability, sound reasoning and conusmmate judgment after a careful study of the previous works on the subject. Indeed it may be said that जगन्नाथ has done for poetics what भट्टोजी दीक्षित and नागोजी भट्टो after him did for grammar. In this the author discusses every disputed point at great length, fully examines the opinions of the previous writers on it and generally arrives at a satisfactory conclusion.

However, one peculiar thing to be marked about this work is that it is nowhere found complete. It ends after the third quarter of the following Aryã;

किं कुर्वते दरिद्राः कासारवती धरा मनोज्ञतरा।
कः पावनस्त्रिलोक्या..................................॥

The natural explanation in such a case would be that the author must have died leaving the work half-done. But this argument also does not stand when we find जगन्नाथ referring to his own रसगंगाधर in one of his other works viz. चित्रमीमांसाखण्डन which opens with रसगंगाधरे चित्रमीमांसाया मयोदिता:। ये दोषास्तेऽत्र सांक्षिप्य कथ्यन्ते विदुषां मुदे।। Thus one is forced to infer that it has been deliberatety left unfinished. Or there is a third possibility viz. the composition of these two works चित्रमीमांसाखण्डन and रसगंगाधर must have been simultaneous and these two must have been left unfinished due to the author's death. However, nothing can be proposed in this connection which is free from uncertainty.

(८) **मनोरमाकुचमर्दन**–It is a criticism on the book called मनोरमा which is a commentary by भट्टोजीदीक्षित on his own सिद्धान्तकौमुदी. It aims at pointing out some of the many blunders committed by भट्टोजीदीक्षित as the author i.e. जगन्नाथ himself says in the opening of the book ....गुरुद्वेषदूषितमतीनां यद्यपि पुरुषायुषेणापि न शक्यन्ते गणयितुं प्रमादास्तथापि दिङ्मात्रेण कानपि कुशाग्रीयधिषणेषु निरूपयाम:। In the opening here जगन्नाथ salutes शेषवीरेश्वर who was the Guru of his father and thus this seems to be an inconsistency. However, it might possibly have been that जगन्नाथ also must have learnt some books on grammar from his father's Guru. One of the geneological trees as given in an old book, based on the observation of मनोरमाकुचमर्दन, शब्दरत्नमंजूषा etc., mentions जगन्नाथ as the direct pupil of शेषवीरेश्वर whose father's name was शेषश्रीकृष्ण. भट्टोजीदीक्षित was the pupil of this शेष-श्रीकृष्ण. वीरेश्वरगुरुं शेषं नत्वा......the opening verse of मनोरमाकुचमर्दन shows that he was the disciple of शेषवीरेश्वर.

(९) **अश्वघाटी**–This is a composition of about 25 verses and is named after the metre in which it is composed. The last verse runs like this : रामनाम्न: स्वपौत्रस्य कामनापूरणोत्सुक: अश्वघाटीं जगन्नाथो विश्वहृद्यामरीचरत्। This shows that he composed it at the request of his grand son. But none of the verses has been quoted in र. ग. This has been attributed to another जगन्नाथ, the author of वसुमतीपरिणय and रतिमन्मथ, who bears the same name i.e. जगन्नाथ and yet cannot be identified with the present poet. One peculiarity, however, of this is that the 25 verses show the वृत्त्यनुप्रास of all the 25 consonants except the last two and that also with great success.

(१०) **प्राणाभरण**–This a composition consisting of about 50 stanzas addressed to the King प्राणाभरण of Cooch Behar. It was offered to him in the year 1627 A.D. when जगन्नाथ had been there. The first verse in this work is almost identical with Bh. V. IV. 42. Almost all the other stanzas are found in the र. ग. and it may be conjectured that it was composed by culling verses from र. ग. It also bears a short commentary by जगन्नाथ himself, which in many places makes the same remarks as have been once made in the र. ग.

(११) **जगदाभरण**–is a composition of 50 verses addressed to one जगत्सिंह–the son of कर्णसिंह, the Rana of Udaipur. It was offered to the King in 1627. Many of the verses can be traced in र. ग. One peculiarity of this work is that many of the verses in the present poem have been taken verbatim from प्राणाभरण and the change is only in the name of the King e.g. verse 2 in this book is जागर्तु क्षितिमंण्डलोपरि जगत्सिंहो घराधी-श्वरः in प्राणा. verse 2 the line is जागर्तु क्षितिमण्डले चिरमिह श्रीकामरूपेश्वरः।। so also नुतो निखिलभूसुरैर्विजयते जगत्केसरी (जग. २१) is changed to नुतो निखिलभूसुरर्जयति. कामरूपेश्वरः in प्राण. २१. Mr. Bhāmburkar has disproved the belief that this is addressed to Dara Shukoh, Shah Jahan's eldest son; (which is supported by Mr. Vaidya perhaps on the authority of Paṇḍit दुर्गाप्रसाद in his edition of R. G.)

(१२) **आसफविलास**–This work describes the exploits of

one आसफखान who is identified with the नवाब आसफखान of the court of Shah Jahan. This आसफखान was later on given the title of Khan-Khanān in 1634 and he died in 1641- र. ग mentions two verses which treat of one Asaf Khan and it might possibly be that this same आसफखान must have been referred to there. पयोधिकल्पा मतिरासफेंदोर्महीतलेऽन्यस्य न हीति मन्ये र. ग.उ. प्र.। युक्त तु याते दिवमासफेंदौ तदाश्रितानां यदभूद्विनाज्ञ: र. ग. वि. प्र. Herein जगन्नाथ himself says that he composed this work at the instance of one रायमुकुंद of मथुरा. A part of its introduction runs as follows:

मूर्तिमतेव नबाबासफखानमन:प्रसादेन द्विजकुलसेवाहेवाकिवाङ्मन:कायेन माथुरकुलसमुद्रेन्दुना रायमुकुंदेनादिष्टेन सार्वभौमश्रीशहाजहांप्रसादाधिगत-पंडितराजपदवीविराजितेन तैलंगकुलावतंसेन पंडितजगन्नाथेन आसफा-विलासाख्येयमाख्यायिका निरमीयत।

(१३) **भामिनीविलास**–The book was composed with the object that it might serve as a store of illustrations. This is easily disproved however firstly because the last verse effectively militates against it and secondly because it is more than credible that जख could exactly foresee what verses should be composed to serve as examples in his र. ग. There is also another theory which says that the भा. वि was composed by somebody after the death of जगन्नाथ which also may have been a fact.

(१४) **चित्रमीमांसाखण्डन**–This work is composed by जगन्नाथ disproving the opinions that have been expressed by अप्पयदीक्षित in his work चित्रमीमांसा, based on his own remarks made in his र. ग. on that subject e.g. in the introduction to this book he says रसगंगाधरे चित्रमीमांसाया मयोदिता:। ये दोषास्तेऽत्र संक्षिप्य कथ्यन्ते विदुषां मुदे।।

(१५) **पंडितराजशतक**–This is also probably a work of our poet. Nothing more is however known in the matter.

A STUDY OF BHĀMINĪVILĀSA

—*By R. K. Panda*

The *Bhāminīvilāsa* of Jagannātha is one of the best Kāvya-saṁgrahas those are produced in modern Sanskrit literature. It is a collection of free verses (*muktakas*) composed on varied topics in various metres. Some of the scholars are of the opinion that Jagannātha had composed these verses for illustrating the poetic elements like the types of poetry, *guṇas, alaṅkāras* etc. for those which he has explained in his *magnum opus Rasagaṅgādhara*, the work that has brought for him eternal name as a great literary critic. But, all the verses those are available in the *Bhavinīvilāsa* are not given in the *Rasagaṅgādhara* as illustrative verses. This suggests that the author had given a new shape to this work i.e. *Bhāminīvilāsa* in which he had compiled all his free verses and used only some of them for illustrating the alaṅkāras etc. in the *Rasagangādhara*. He has entitled *Bhāminīvilāsa* beacause majority of the verses refer to Bhāminī directly and indirectly probably his wife or beloved. However, some of the writers question-whether he had a wife or not ? Acyutarāya, a commentor on *Bhāminīvilāsa* believes that he had not any wife[1] *(Dharmapatnī)* at all.

But, it is not correct, argues P. Ramachandrudu, "to draw such conclusions on the strength of a stray verse of a doubtful origin, because this verse is included in one of the old anthologies. On the other hand many verses of the *Karuṇavilāsa* which contains more personal element in it, clearly show that PR. had a Hindu wife married according to Hindu custom."[2] The learned scholar cites the following verse which refers to the '*Saptapadī* that is observed in the Hindu marriage.

धृत्वा पदस्खलनभीतिवशात् करं मे
याऽऽरूढवत्यसि शिलाशकलं विवाहे।
सा मां विहाय कथमद्य विलासिनि द्या-
मारोहसीति हृदयं शतधा प्रयाति।।

Karuṇavilāśa, Verse 5

Ramachandrudu conjectures that her (Bhāminī's) name was Kāmeśwarī, a name common in the Telugu families on the strength of the following verse:

मन्दस्मितेन सुधया परिषिच्य या मां
नेत्रोत्पलैर्विकसितैरनिशं समीजे।
सा नित्यमङ्गलमयी गृहदेवता मे
कामेश्वरी हृदयतो दयिता न याति।।

He argues :

"And Mahādevasūri, himself claiming to be the grand son of PR. while commenting on the line 'याते च सम्प्रति दिवं प्रति बन्धुरत्ने' of the first verse of *Karuṇavilāsa*, writes : गृहिण्यां दिवं प्रतियाते, मृतायां सत्याम्। 'Again he gives the meaning of' नित्यमङ्गलमयी गृहदेवता मे (of 12th verse) as 'नित्यमङ्गलः ....पुत्रपौत्राद्युत्सवः, तत्प्रचुरा नित्यमङ्गलमयी गृहदेवता कामेश्वरी' etc. (Paṇḍitarāyajīvitam, p. 42). All these go to prove beyond doubt that PR. had a wife married according to Dharmaśāstra".[3]

"Though the work is named *'Bhāminīvilāsa'*, all the four Vilāsas, into which it is divided, do not seem to have connection with Bhāminī; only the *Śṛṅgāravilāsa* which depicts all phases of love and the *Karuṇavilāsa* have connection with Bhāminī, the second one only indirectly. So it may be conjectured that the poet had planned originally to write only *Śṛṅgāravilāsa* and *Karuṇavilāsa* under the title of *Bhāminīvilāsa* and later on thought it better to add two more vilāsas i.e. *Prāstāvikavilāsa* and *Śāntavilāsa* at the two ends of the poem, originally planned".[4]

The *Bhāminīvilāsa* contains miscellaneous verses. It has neither any plot nor any context. Each stanza has an occasion of its own, and is complete in itself. So there is a diversity of subjects. It is one of its qualities. One can easily mark the poetic beauty of these verses. The poet himself says in the beginning of his *Prāstāvikavilāsa :*

माधुर्यपरमसीमा सारस्वतजलधिमथनसम्भूता।
पिबतामनल्पसुखदा वसुधायां मम सुधाकविता।।

I.1

His nectarlike poems are the utmost limit of sweetness as they are produced by the churning of the ocean of literature. They are made for giving great pleasure to the persons who possess a heart of poetic sensibility.

This shows poet's confidence. He was also well-aware of his poetic calibre and beauty of his compositions. As he had a proper training and profound knowledge of the different śāstras mainly poetics, grammar and logic he could climb the highest peak. He is right in saying:

निर्दूषणा गुणवती रसभावपूर्णा
सालंकृतिः श्रवणकोमलवर्णराजिः।
सा मामकीनकवितेव मनोऽभिरामा
रामा कदापि हृदयान्मम नापयाति।। III.6

Jagannātha's poems are faultless, possess excellences, full of sentiments and emotions, richly embellished and have a grand style in which the proper arrangement of letters are pleasing to the ear.

In the 3rd (last) verse of the *śāntavilāsa* the poet says that he has made this casket of the jewels of his verses lest the bastard poetasters will misappropriate them. It was the main objective of Jagannātha.

मधु द्राक्षा साक्षादमृतमथ वामाधरसुधा
कदाचित् केषाञ्चिन्न खलु विदधीरन्नपि मुदम्।
ध्रुवन्ते जीवन्तोऽप्यहह! मृतका मन्दमतयो
न येषामानन्दञ्जनयति जगन्नाथभणितिः।।

Śāntavilāsa, v. 42.

Bhāmīnīvilāsa is undoubtedly the best work of Paṇḍitarāja Jagannātha. It is a collection of detached verses independent of each other and so, it maybe called a *Kośakāvya.*[5] According to Dr. Keith, this kāvya is admirable in many respects as an erotic poem, an elegy and a store of gnomic sayings.[6] The book is divided into four *vilāsas*-the *Prāstāvika, Śṛṅgāra, Karuṇa* and *Śāntavilāsa*. The *Prāstāvika-vilāsa* is a collection of gnomic and didactic verses. These are very grand in conception and in expression. Every verse is a ready illustration of *anyokti* or *aprastutapraśaṁsā*. The subject matter of these sayings is numerous. Generally philosophy, morals and practical advice to life are suggested through these verses. The second chapter is called *Śṛṅgāravilāsa* which contains the highest number of verses giving passionate expression to the emotion of love. So this vilāśa is a good specimen of erotic poetry. Here each stanza is a complete unit of sense, expression and imagery and it presents a daintily finished picture of the emotion or a situation. The poet has depicted the reactions and subtle variations in the moods and fancies of the lover and the beloved. The poet has an extraordinary power to describe the abstract thoughts and feelings.

The third *Karuṇavilāsa* depicts pathetic sentiment and it is an elegiac poetry. This gives expression to poet's serious pathos.

This work has been published from many places over many times and the number and order of the verses of each publication differ widely. There is some disagreement in its various editions with regard to the number of verses in each vilāsa as the following table will show.[7]

Editions	Anyokti or Prāstāvika	Śṛṅgāra	Karuṇa	Śānta	Total No. of Verses
M.A. Bergaigne's edition, Paris, 1872	127	182	19	46	374
Prof. Taranatha's edition, Calcutta, 1872	126	102	18	46	292
L.R. Vaidya's edition, Bombay, 1887 and Mr. Seshadri's edition, (no date)	129	183	19	45	376
S.M. Paranjape's edition, Poona, 1895.	101	102	19	33	255
B.G. Bal's edition, Bombay, 1895.	101	101	19	33	254
Nirnaya Sagara edition, Bombay, Third edn., 1933.	101	102	19	32	254
Dr. Har Dutt Sarma's edition, Poona, 1935.	101			33	

(Vide L.R. Vaidya's edition of the *Bhāminīvilāsa,* preface, p. 2.) B.G. Bal in his edition gives in addition to 101 verses of the *anyoktisamullāsa,* one verse between the twentieth and twenty-first verses, three verses between the seventy-fourth and seventy-fifth, one verse between the eightieth and eighty-first and twenty-three verses at the end; in the *Śṛṅgāra-samullāsa,* three verses are given as *prakṣiptas* just before the seventy-fourth, sixty verses (as *prakṣiptas*) just before the seventy-fifth and one verse just before the ninety-fifth; in the *Śāntasamullāsa* are given five verses as *prakṣiptas* after the fourth, one stanza after the sixth, four stanzas after the fifteenth and one stanza after the thirtieth, the last *prakṣipta* being found as the opening stanza in the Kāvyamālā edition of the *Prāṇābharaṇa*. S.M. Paranjape also gives in his edition an appendix of verses—twenty-one for Vilāsa I, seventy-nine for Vilāsa II and eleven for Vilāsa IV.

According to Nāgeśabhaṭṭa, the poet composed these verses specially before he wrote the *Rasagaṅgādhara* in order to provide illustration for that work. This view, however, is not correct. The fact of the matter seems to be that Jagannātha made impromptu verses as the need for illustration arose in writing his *Rasagaṅgādhara*. Afterwards he collected them, lest they should be plagiarised—

दुर्वृत्ता जारजन्मानो हरिष्यन्तीति शङ्कया।
मदीयपद्यरत्नानां मञ्जुषैषा कृता मया।। (IV.45)

It is not clear whether this work relates to any particular lady.

S.M. Paranjape advances a different theory:[8] (*a*) the original of the *Bhāminīvilāsa* contains many verses which are not found in the *Rasagaṅgādhara* and are in all probability composed long before the *Rasagaṅgādhara*; (*b*) except three verses found in the *Rasagaṅgādhara*, all verses in the *Karuṇavilāsa* might have originally been written by the poet, long before the compositions of the *Rasagaṅgādhara,* to bemoan the death of his *bhāminī* (probably his wife) and not for the illustrative purposes in the *Rasagaṅgādhara* and the verses in the *Śṛṅgāravilāsa* might have consequently been composed long before the verses in the *Karuṇavilāsa* to describe the various aspects of his love with the *Bhāminī* before her death, and (*c*) the impromptu verses written by the poet for the illustrative purposes in the *Rasagaṅgādhara* might have been later on incorporated. Whether Jagannātha has left it unfinished in the midle of *uttarālaṅkāra*, as the printed text shows, or whether he has continued it, nothing can be decisively said about the correctness of this theory.

Many verses explain the rules of conduct and maxims of truth without any *anyāpadeśa* :

परार्थव्यासङ्गादुपजहदथ स्वार्थपरता-
मभेदैकत्वं यो वहति गुणभूतेषु सततम्।
स्वाभावाद्यस्यान्तः स्फुरति ललितोदात्तमहिमा
समर्थो यो नित्यं स जयतितरां कोऽपि पुरुषः।। I.79

The above verse explains the character of the ideal man who will always be bent upon doing good to others, even neglecting his own work, maintains equality among all and extends charity to the needy.

Some Subhāṣita type of verses :

दूरीकरोति कुमतिं विमलीकरोति
चेतश्चिरन्तनमघं चुलुकीकरोति।
भूतेषु किं च करुणां बहुलीकरोति
सङ्गः सतां किमु न मङ्गलमातनोति।। I. 122

The company of the good people removes (all your) ill-thoughts, purifies mind and destroys the sin that continues from a long time, It also enhances the feelings of mercy. What auspicious thing does it not beget?

Similarly the verse—

अनवरतपरोपकारव्यग्रीभवदमलचेतसां महताम्।
आपातकाटवानि स्फुरन्ति वचनानि भेषजानीव।। I.123

The speech of the great, whose pure mind is always engrossed in the performance of philanthropic deeds and which are bitter only at the beginning, shine like medicines bringing happiness in the end.

The wicked people are experts in putting troubles in the welfare of good people like the snakes who are capable of taking away the lives of innocent persons.

खलास्तु कुशला: साधुहितप्रत्यूहकर्मणि।
निपुणा: फणिन: प्राणानपहर्तुं निरागसाम्।। I. 110

आनन्दमृगदावाग्नि: शीलशाखिमदद्विप:।
ज्ञानदीपमहावायुरयं खलसमागम:।। I. 109

The companionship with the wicked is like a forest conflagration to the deer in the form of joy, a rutting elephant to the tree in the form of character and tempestuous wind to the lamp in the form of knowledge.

व्योमनि बीजाकुरुते चित्रं निर्माति सुन्दरं पवने।
रचयति रेखा: सलिले यस्तु चरति सत्कारम्।। I. 98

He who treats the wicked with respect, as if sows seeds in the sky, draws a beautiful picture in wind and draws lines in water.

हालाहलं खलु पिपासति कौतुकेन
कालानलं परिचुचुम्बिषति प्रकामम्।
व्यालाधिपं च यतते परिरब्धुमद्धा
यो दुर्जनं वशयितुं तनुते मनीषाम्।। I. 95

He who cherishes a desire to win over a wicked man, wishes indeed to drink deadly poison with curiosity, to kiss closely the fire of final destruction or to embrace actually the lord of serpents.

शून्येऽपि च गुणवत्तामातन्वान: स्वकीयगुणजालै:।
विवराणि मुद्रयन्द्रागूर्णायुरिव सुजनो जयति।। I. 90

A good man is successful who transforms a dunce into a person of qualities, by means of his own stock of qualities by hiding his faults immediately like a spider who builds his web in a place which is empty, by his net of thread and covers the openings in the houses immediately.

In the *Śṛṅgāravilāsa* the poet has described the beauty of various parts of his beloved. Her face sheds indescribable lustre. There is no danger of Rāhu's wrath. There is not even any chance of its contamination or fading. The tenderness of her limbs cannot be compared with lotus-garlands because they are extremely rough. Similarly her eyes are like the evening lotusess. Her breasts have surpassed the beauty of bore, myro-bolen, mango and the pomogranat fruit. Her breathing has surpassed the beauty of ciron fruit. The grace of her navel resembles in complexion the interior of the white lotus of dawn. She attains the beauty of a lightening. She is cakora-eyed. She even surpasses the incomparable beauty of Indra's sovereignty. Gold would stand comparison with her body only when it is put into fire. When her heart is distracted with the pangs of separation, in a single moment she feels the Malaya-breezes to be fires, regards the crystal palace to be forest and is reduced to the condition of a fish out of agarugum to be a deadly poison. She is of gold colour. She is not the creation of *Vidhi* since her lowerlip surpasses the beauty of the foliage leaf and the beauty of her face that of the moon. According to our poet, she is not a woman but a beautiful creeper pressed down by swarms of bees. Her smile is not a smile but a charming blooming of a lotus. Her mouth is not mouth; it is a flower which issues fragrance and her breasts are not breasts, they are a pair of gold coloured fruits. In her lotus-like mouth the luster of the rows of beautiful teeth, blended with that of the red lower lip, shines forth like filaments of flower. While that fawn-eyed one was conducting herself like Tilottamā, this mortal world was heaven to our poet. Her face loses its beauty by anger just as a frost beaten lotus wears no charm. Her face with an indescribable black mark tilaka on the forehead appears like a full blown lotus with a bee reposing in it. The face of that deer-eyed one being covered with the hem of her blue garment, appears like the moon reflected in the waters of the Yamunā.

Thus this Vilāsa brings forth a charming picture of feminine beauty. The poet's approach is conventional. He has made use of many symbols which help in creating good images.

The *Karuṇavilāsa* contains nineteen elegiacal verses lamenting the untimely death of Bhāminī. The poet's delineation of pathos in all its elegance is realistic. We cite here some of the verses from the BV :

दैवे पराग्वदनशालिनि हन्त जाते
याते च संप्रति दिवं प्रति बन्धुरत्ने।
कस्मै मनः कथयितासि निजामवस्थां
कः शीतलैः शमयिता वचनैस्तवाधिम्।। Verse No. 1

Our poet excels in delineation of *Karuṇarasa* as is evident from the following verse which contains the feeling of the tragic shock which Paṇḍitarāja has got at the death of his beloved.

प्रत्युद्गता सविनयं सहसा पुरेव
स्मेरैः स्मरस्य सचिवैः सरसाऽवलोकैः।
मामद्य मञ्जुरचनैर्वचनैश्च बाले
हा! लेशतोऽपि न कथं शिशिरीकरोषि।। Verse, III. 2

Alas! O lady, why do you not as before, coming forward to receive me with smiles and loving glances, the ministers of love, sooth me in the least today with pleasing words?

Although there is no scope for the delineation of *Vīrarasa* in the *Bhāminīvilāsa* still we are able to trace out some of the verses which depict *dayāvīra*, *kṣamāvīra* etc. Here is an example of *kṣamāvīra*:

अपि बहलदहनजालं मूर्ध्नि रिपुर्मे निरन्तरं धमतु।
पातयतु वासिधारामहमणुमात्रं न किञ्चिदपि भाषे।।

An example of *dharmavīra :*

सपदि विलयमेतु राज्यलक्ष्मी-
रुपरि पतन्त्वथ वा कृपाणधारा:।
अपहरतुतरां शिर: कृतान्तो
मम तु मतिर्न मनागपैति धर्मात्।। I.1

A finest specimen of *bhaktirasa* is the following :

जगज्जालं ज्योत्स्नामयनवसुधाभिर्जटिलयन्
जनानां सन्तापं त्रिविधमपि सद्य: प्रशमयन्।
श्रितो वृन्दारण्यं नतनिखिलवृन्दारकवृतो
मम स्वान्तध्वान्तं तिरयतु नवीनो जलधर:।। IV.5

An example of Karuṇarasa.

चिन्ता शशाम सकलाऽपि सरोरुहाणा-
मिन्दोश्च बिम्बमसमां सुषमामयासीत्।
अभ्युद्गत: कलकल: किल कोकिलानां
प्राणप्रिये! यदवधि त्वमितो गताऽसि।। III.7

O beloved! ever since your departure from this place, the anxiety of lotuses has absolutely subsided, and the disc of the moon has attained the beauty and the melodious notes of cuckoos have arisen.

In the *Śāntavilāsa,* the poet has brought out the miserable condition of the world. Like his predecessors and the great poets like Śaṅkārācārya, Jagannātha also says that his mind is destressed by the rows of flames spreading around, of the forest conflagration which is burning the circle of the extensive forest in the form of the objects of senses. So Śrīkṛṣṇa, the indescribable row of clouds, is the object of his contemplation which, when merely remembered, removes the terrible anguish through kindness, which is encircled by hundred of lightnings of everlasting glow, which rests on the celestial tree and which is growing on the bank of the daughter of the mountain Kālind. The poet belives that there is no cessation of desires in the Pātāla, in the city of Gods or on the top of the Meru. So there is only one way to be free from all these desires, i.e. Kṛṣṇa which is resort of eternal bliss.

In this Vilāsa the poet has depicted the *Śāntarasa* in all his verses and also tries to show us the road of eternal peace.

"As a poet Jagannātha takes a high rank, and may be classed with Kālidāsa, Bhavabhūti and other writers of celebrity. He is essentially a poet of emotions, and has achieved a high measure of success in his department. Though he belongs to the degenerate times of Sanskrit poetry, he is almost free from the affectation and extravagance of his age. In sweetness of melody and perspicuity of diction he stands on a level with Bilhaṇa and Jayadeva. Praśāda, as he himself tells us, is a special characteristic of his poetry."[9] While talking about *Prasādaguṇa* he declares with great confidence that almost all his compositions can be taken as examples of *Prasādaguṇa*.

Jagannātha was a keen observer of men and manners around him. The sportive movements of beautiful damsels, intent upon drawing the attention of their lovers, which is perhaps a common sight in the capital of the Mughal Empire, devoted to sensual pleasures, does not miss his keen observation and one of such incidents is given a beautiful expression in his following verse :—

भवनं करुणावती विशन्ती गमनाज्ञालवलाभलालसेषु।
तरुणेषु विलोचनाब्जमालामथ बाला पथि पातयाम्बभूव।। II.107

In this verse, the poet brings home the atmosphere of the Mughal-rule.

To rear the pairs of pegions was considered to be the mark of civilization and fine taste in those days, which is devoutly practised even today by some people. This finds a fine expression in the following verse :

निरुद्ध्य यान्तीं तरसा कपोतीं
कूजत्कपोतस्य पुरो दधाने।
मयि स्मितार्द्रं वदनारविन्दं
सामन्दमन्दं नयनाम्बभूव।। II.30

The verses of Jagannātha contain *camatkāra* which, according to him, is the soul of poetry. In his *Rasagaṅgādhara* he lays stress like Kṣemendra, on the principle of *camatkāra* and declares it on many occasions as the soul of poetry. The *camatkāra* is nothing but *ramaṇīyatā* which is capable of giving some extraordinary pleasure to the reader of poetry. He has therefore tried to create this *ramaṇīyatā* in his poetry by means of *rīti*, *guṇa* and *alaṅkāras*. P. Ramachandrudu righty remarks :

"The very important contribution of PR. to Sanskrit Poetics, lies in his unique attempt at bringing in a happy synthesis among the different schools, such as Dhvani school, Alaṅkāra school and Rīti school etc., under the pleasant banner of *Ramaṇīyatā*, otherwise known as '*camatkāra*'."

Jagannātha's verses are highly appreciated and remembered with pleasure as they are dominated with the element of aesthetic rapture. The poet has shown his ingenious talent in the delineation of rasa, mainly Śṛṅgāra and Karuṇa. Here an example from his *Bhāminīvilāsa* is given.

शयिता सविधेऽप्यनीश्वरा
सफलीकर्तुमहो! मनोरथान्।
दयिता दयिताननाम्बुजं
दरमीलन्नयना निरीक्षते।। II. 100

The verse gives a picture of the union of a mugdhā-nāyikā with her husband, whose desires she could not all at once fulfill on account of her modesty, high birth and natural restraint. It is an example of *Rasadhvani* and therefore it is an *uttamottamakāvya. Saṁbhoga-śṛṅgāra* is illustrated by the above verse. Here the *ālambanavibhāva* of the nāyikā's love is the nāyaka, her husband; the *uddīpanavibhāva* is the lonely place indicated by her lying close by her husband; her looks with her eyes closed a bit are the *anubhāvas* and the modesty, eagerness to satisfy her desires, etc., are the *vyabhicāribhāvas*—these help in the suggestion of *Śṛṅgārarasa* of the *saṁbhoga* type. The suggestion of *rati* is the main idea (*Vākyārtha*) of this verse.

Another example of *Saṁbhoga-śṛṅgāra* is given bellow:

केलीमन्दिरमागतस्य शनकैरालीरपास्येङ्गितैः
सुप्तायाः सरुषः सरोरुहदृशः संवीजनं कुर्वतः।
जानन्त्याप्यनभिज्ञयेव कपटव्यामीलिताक्ष्या 'सखि'
श्रान्ताऽसीत्यभिधाय वक्षसि तया पाणिर्ममासज्जितः।। II. 166

Going into the pleasure house and gradually dismissing the female companions by signs while I was fanning the lotus-eyed one who had become angry and had feighned asleep and who though recognised me, still pretending to keep her eyes closed, saying friend, you are fatigued, placed my hand on her own bosom.

Śānta is illustrated by the verse :

मलयानिलकालकूटयो रमणीकुन्तलभोगिभोगयोः।
श्वपचात्मभुवोर्निरन्तरा मम जाता परमात्मनि स्थितिः।। IV. 33

Here the whole phenomenal world is the *ālambanavibhāva,* equality among all is the *anubhāva* and the knowledge, etc., are the *vyabhicāribhāvas* and the combination of these leads to the suggestion of *śāntarasa*.

Alongwith *rasadhvani, bhāva, rasābhāsa, bhāvābhāsa* etc. are also ably delineated by the poet with the consequents or external manifestations and transitory feelings : The *bhāvadhvani* is illustrated by the following verse :

यदवधि दयितो विलोचनाभ्यां सहचरि! दैववशेन दूरतोऽभूत्।
तदवधि शिथिलीकृतो मदीयैरथ करणैः प्रणयो निजक्रियासु।।

II.58

There is a brilliant picture of a newly married lady frightened at the embrace of her husband. This is an illustration of *Śṛṅgārābhāsa*.

भुजपञ्जरे गृहीता नवपरिणीता वरेण रहसि वधूः।
तत्कालजालपतिता बालकुरङ्गीव वेपते नितराम्।। II. 39

Another example :

भवनं करुणावती विशन्ती
गमनाज्ञालवलाभलालसेषु।
तरुणेषु विलोचनालमाला-
मथ बाला पथि पातयांबभूव।। II. 62

An example of *Vipralambha-śṛṅgārābhāsa :*

व्यत्यस्तं लपति क्षणं क्षणमहो मौनं समालम्बते
सर्वस्मिन्विदधाति किं च विषये दृष्टिं निरालम्बनाम्।
श्वासं दीर्घमुरीकरोति न मनागङ्गेषु धत्ते धृतिं
वैदेहीविरहव्यथाविकलितो हा हन्त लङ्केश्वरः।। II. 84

Alas! the lord of Laṅkā (Rāvaṇa) over powered with the pangs of separation from Vaidehī, at one moment speaks incoherently, and in other moment gazes vacantly all round, and in next moment assumes silence and fetches a deep sigh and has no strength remaining in his limbs.

Love in separation is also described in various ways. The conduct of a *mugdhā-nāyikā* portrayed in the following verse is really touching.

वाचो माङ्गलिकीः प्रयाणसमये जल्पत्यनल्पं जने
केलीमन्दिरमारुतायनमुखे विन्यस्तवक्त्राम्बुजम्।
निःश्वासग्लपिताधरं परिपतद्बाष्पार्द्रवक्षोरुहा
बाला लोलविलोचना शिव शिव प्राणेशमालोकते।। II. 15

The *nāyikā* is unable to express her feelings and to exchange words with her husband in the presence of the relatives. She only looks at him through a window with her eager eyes.

पाटीरद्रुभुजङ्गपुङ्गवमुखायाता इवातापिनो
वाता यान्ति दहन्ति लोचनममी ताम्रा रसालद्रुमाः।
एते हन्त किरन्ति कूजितमयं हालाहलं कोकिला
बाला बालमृणालकोमलतनुः प्राणान्कथं रक्षतु।। II. 57

The above verse describes the sad condition of a *nāyikā* in separation which become unbearable to her by the breeze blowing from the sandal woods, by the reddish mango trees and by musical notes of cuckoos. The condition of *gopikās* including the much dignified Rādhā in times of separation is described in the following verse :

आविर्भूता यदवधि मधुस्यन्दिनी नन्दसूनोः
कान्तिः काचिन्निखिलनयनाकर्षणे कार्मणज्ञा।
श्वासो दीर्घस्तदवधि मुखे पाण्डिमा गण्डमूले
शून्या वृत्तिः कुलमृगदृशां चेतसि प्रादुरासीत्।। II. 79

Since the day on which the beauty of Nanda's son was seen, beauty which distils honey and which is adept in the art of attracting the eyes of the whole bevy of deer-eyed ladies, deep sighs began to issue from their mouth, pallor showed itself on their cheeks, and a feeling of restlessness filled their mind.

According to some critics *dhvani* (suggestion) is the soul of poetry. Ānandavardhana is the well-known promulgator of this theory. Paṇḍitarāja Jagannātha has composed many verses which are suggestive. They come under the *uttamottama-kāvya*. Here we are citing few examples to acquint the readers about the nature of suggestive poetry composed by Jagannātha.

Vastudhvani

तदवधि कुशली पुराणशास्त्रस्मृतिशतचागतो विवेकः।
यदिवधि न पदन्दधाति चित्ते हरिणकिशोरदृशो द्दशोर्विलासः।।

II. 14

Oh clever mind! the discernment which arises from fitting meditations of hundreds of Purāṇas, śāstras and Smṛtis, would be able to make a stand only so long as the eyes of the fawn-eyed one has not possessed you.

Alaṁkāradhvani

दयिते! रदनत्विषाम्मिषादयि! तेऽमी विलसन्ति केसराः।
अपि चालकवेषधारिणो मकरन्दस्पृहयालवोऽलयः।।

II. 97

Ah love, these are indeed the filaments that sparkle under the guise of the streeks of the lustre of your teeth, and these are indeed the bees desirous of flower juice which have assumed the form of your hair.

Bhāvābhāsadhvani

सर्वेऽपि विस्मृतिपथं विषयाः प्रयाताः
विद्याऽपि खेदकलिता विमुखीबभूव।
सा केवलं हरिणशावकलोचना मे
नैवापयाति हृदयादधिदेवतेव।। III.3

All objects have been completely forgotten. Even learning over powered with grief has turned away its face. But that fawn-eyed one alone like presiding deity does not leave my heart.

Bhāvasandhidhvani

योवनोद्गमनितान्तशङ्किता: शीलशौर्यबलकान्तिलोभिता:।
सङ्कुचन्ति विकसन्ति राघवे जानकीनयननीरजश्रिय:।। II. 34

The beauty of the lotus-like eye of Jānakī constrained by the advent of youth (in Rāma) and attracted by effulgence, strength, and prowess of Rāma, closed and expanded alternately.

Bhāvaśāntidhvani

मुञ्चसि नाद्यापि रुषम्भामिनि मुदिरालिरुदियाय।
इति सुद्दश: प्रियवचनैरपायि नयनाब्जकोणशोणरुचि:।। II. 88

"O haughty one, behold the line of clouds has appeared in the sky, but still you do not quit your anger." These words uttered by the lover of the fair-eyed one removed the radiant colour from the corner of her lotus-eye.

Bhāvodayadhvani

वीक्ष्य वक्षसि विपक्षकामिनीहारलक्ष्म दयितस्य भामिनी।
अंसदेशविनिवेशितां क्षणादाचकर्ष निजबाहुवल्लरीम्।। II. 21

On the bosom of her lover having observed the impression made by the necklace of a rival woman, the lovely lady at once withdrew her creeper-like arm from his shoulder.

Bhāvaśabalatā

पापं हन्त मया हतेन विहितं सीताऽपि यद्यापिता
सा मामिन्दुमुखी विना बत वने किञ्जीवितन्धास्यति।
आलोकेय कथम्मुखं सुकृतिनाङ्किन्ते विदध्यन्ति मां
राज्यं यातु रसातलम्पुनरिदन्न प्रापितुङ्कामये।। II. 110

Uttamakāvya

दोर्दण्डद्वयकुण्डलीकृतलसत्कोदण्डचण्डाशुग-
ध्वस्तोद्दण्डविपक्षमण्डलमथ त्वां वीक्ष्य मध्येरणम्।
वल्गद्राण्डिवमुक्तकाण्डवलयज्वालावलीताण्डव-
भ्रश्यत्खाण्डवरुष्टपाण्डवमहो को न क्षितीश स्मरेत्।। I. 128

Having observed in the battle field you who destroyed the circle of powerful enemies by the terrible darts from his brilliant bow bent round by the pair of his arms, what king will not remember that indignat Pāṇḍava Arjuna who was standing in the khāṇḍava wilderness which was destroyed by the movement of the series of flames issuing from the circle of arrows discharged from his twanging Gāṇdiva bow.

Madhyamakāvya

It is an exmaple of utprekṣā.

कालिन्दजा नीरभरेऽर्द्धमग्ना बकाः प्रकामं कृतभूरिशब्दाः।
ध्वान्तेन वैराद् विनिगीर्यमाणाः क्रोशन्ति मन्ये शशिनः किशोराः।
II.20

Adhamakāvya

यस्मिन् वेल्लति सर्वतः परिचलत्कल्लोलकोलाहलै-
र्मन्थाद्रिभ्रमणभ्रमं हृदि हरिद्दन्तावलाः पेदिरे।
सोऽयन्तुङ्गतिमिङ्गलाङ्गकवलीकारक्रियाकोविदः
क्रोडे क्रीडतु कस्य कालकलहत्यक्तार्णवो माधवः।। I.55

Jagannātha illustrates *ananvaya-dhvani* in the following verse :

पृष्टाः खलु परपुष्टाः
परितो दृष्टाश्च विटपिनस्सर्वे।
भेदेन भुवि न पेदे
साधर्म्यं ते रसाल मधुपेन।। I.29

'The cuckoos were asked; all the adjoining trees were seen; oh Mango tree! nowhere on this earth was discovered by the honey-drinking bee an object similar to you and different from you'. Here the words *bhedena, na* and *pede* suggest the *ananvaya-alaṅkāra*.

Similarly, the verse :

इदमप्रतिमं पश्य सरः सरसिजैर्वृतम्।
सखे! मा जल्प नारीणां नयनानि दहन्ति माम्।। II. 87

gives us *Smaraṇālaṅkāra-dhvani*.

A example of *Udāharaṇa*

अमितगुणोऽपि पदार्थो
दोषेणैकेन निन्दितो भवति।
निखिलरसायनराजो
गन्देनोग्रेण लशुन इव।। I. 81

In the figure Udāharaṇa the relation of the part with its whole, between the general statement and the paticular statement is expressed by words like *iva, yathā* etc. Words like *iva, yathā* etc. with the help of *lakṣaṇā* indicate the relation of the part with its whole.

An object may possess many good qualities but it become undesirable for one defect, as in the instance of the garlic-the best of elixirs, with its nasty smell. The word *iva* is not used in this verse in the sense of *sādṛśya*. It conveys by *lakṣaṇā* the sense of *sāmānyaviśeṣabhāva*, the relation between the general and the particular. In this example, the predicate 'निन्दितो भवति' conveys the idea of निन्दितत्व in general terms in respect of garlic, while the subject refers to a particular case.

Another important feature of Sanskrit literary style is the use of the *guṇas* (excellences) in poetry. His style may be called Vaidarbhī which is characterised by ten *guṇas*. The most important excellence, which Jagannātha embodies in his poetry is *Prasāda-guṇa*.[11] His diction is characterised by the *prasāda*. An example :

गुरुमध्यगता मया नताङ्गी
निहता नीरजकोरकेण मन्दम्।

दरकुण्डलताण्डवन्नतभ्रु-
लतिकम्मामवलोक्य घूर्णिताऽऽसीत्।। II. 17

Another prominent excellence in Jagannātha's poetry is *mādhurya* which consists in the use of appropriate letters suggesting aesthetic joy in poetry. This *arthaguṇa* is found in the following verse:

तीरे तरुण्या वदनं सहासम्
नीरे सरोजञ्च मिलद्विकाशम्।
आलोक्य धावत्युभयत्र मुग्धा
मरन्दलुब्धाऽलिकिशोरमाला।। II. 20

Guṇas are the essential qualities of the soul of poetry (i.e. *rasa*) and are really inherent in it; they are associated figuratively to the body of poetry just as qualities like valour etc. are associated figuratively to the body though strictly they belong to the soul.[12]

स्वेदाम्बुसान्द्रकणशालिकपोलपाली-
दोलायितश्रवणकुण्डलवन्दनीया।
आनन्दमङ्कुरयति स्मरणेन काऽपि
रम्या दशा मनसि मे मदिरेक्षणायाः।। II. 3

The charming state of her whose eyes are intoxicated produces some unspeakable delight in my mind by its resemblance to the state that deserves praise owing to her earrings dangling on the region of her cheeks having thick drops of perspiration.

The following example will suffice to illustrate *prasāda-guṇa*.

आयातैव निशा निशापतिकरैः कीर्णन्दिशामन्तरं
भामिन्यो भवनेषु भूषणगणैरङ्गान्यलङ्कुर्वते।
मुग्धे! मानमपाकरोषि न मनागद्यापि रोषेण ते
हा हा बालमृणालतोऽप्यतितरां तन्वी तनुस्ताम्यति।। II. 74

The disc of the moon beautiful like umbrella of the king cupid, shone in the sky just at the moment when the lotus-eyed one was revolving in her mind that the night that dispels the sleep of the dear-eyed one has already set in and that now, how will her pride hold its own undaunted.

Another example of *Prasāda-guṇa*.

चिन्तामीलिमानसो मनसिजः सख्यो विहीनप्रभाः
प्राणेशः प्रणयाकुलः पुनरसावास्तां समस्ता कथा।
एतत् त्वाम्प्रति बोधयामि मम चेदुक्तिं हिताम्मन्यसे
मुग्धे मा कुरु मानमाननमिदं राकापतिर्जेष्यति।। II.54

Śrutipeśalatā is one of the *artha-guṇas* accepted by Vāmana. It is found in almost all the verses of Paṇḍitarāja. Because of this, his poetry contains a special flavour and is to be musical. It attracts the hearts of readers easily and gives him some uncommon pleasure.

In the poetry of Jagannātha we mark some strikingness which is called *Vakrokti* by the great critic Kuntaka. Here are examples to bring home the nature of *Vakrokti* that has found place in the stanzas of Jagannātha.

लिङ्गवक्रता

आमूलाद् रत्नसानोर्मलयवलयितादा च कूलात्पयोधेः
यावन्तः सन्ति काव्यप्रणयनपटवस्ते विशङ्कं वदन्तु।
मृद्वीकामध्यनिर्यन्मसृणरसझरीमाधुरीभाग्यभाजां
वाचामाचार्यतायाः पदमनुभवितुं कोऽस्ति धन्यो मदन्यः।।[13] IV. 38

उपचारवक्रता

तृष्णालोलविलोचने कलयति प्राचीञ्चकोरीगणे
मौनम्मुञ्चति किञ्च कैरवकुले कामे धनुर्धुन्वति।
माने मानवतीजनस्य सपदि प्रस्थातुकामेऽधुना
धातः! किन्तु विधौ विधातुमुचितो धाराधराडम्बरः।। I. 3

Another example of *Upacāra-vakratā* :

कस्तूरिकातिलकमालि: विधाय सायं
स्मेरानना सपदि शीलय सौधमौलिम्।
प्रोढिम्भजन्तु कुमुदानि मुदामुदारा-
मुल्लासयन्तु परितो हरितो मुखानि।। II. 4.

Oh love! now at the evening tide go to the top of the palace with a smiling face and light the quarters around and let the lotuses, thereby, enjoy abundantly the highest delight.

In this verse also we get *arthaśakti—mūlaka-rūpaka-dhvani*.

संवृतिवक्रता

तन्मञ्जु मन्दहसितं श्वसितानि तानि
सा वै कलङ्कविधुरा मधुराननश्री:।
अद्यापि मे हृदयमुन्मदयन्ति हन्त!
सायन्तनाम्बुजसहोदरलोचनाया:।। II. 5

Alas! that agreeable smile, those breathings, and that chaste and pleasant beauty of the face of her whose eyes are as the evening lotuses, still maddens my heart.

We give here an example of *Paryāya-vakratā :*

अनिशं नयनाभिरामया रमया सम्मदिनो मुखस्य ते।
निशि नि:सरदिन्दिरं कथं तुलयाम: कलयाऽपि पङ्कजम्।।

II. 162

How shall we compare even to a slight degree, the lotus whose beauty fades by evening with your face which prides itself upon possessing beauty which is even pleasing to the eye.

Poetry differs from ordinary expression by its beautiful form. Emotions and ideas, when expressed in a charming, out-of-the way, striking manner, give delight which is similar to the delight experienced on the realization of Brahman. This element of charm, strikingness and out-of-the wayness is designated alaṁkāra by the ancient rhetoricians. Alaṁkāras very effectively bring out the nicest distinctions of objects, the minutest shades of thought; they endow the style with a charming dignity, render the language picturesque and magnificient.

Jagannātha was a master of poetic figures. He has introduced them in his poetry with perfect skill. His use of them is natural and effortless and so it is graceful. He has employed both types of *alaṁkāras-śabdālaṁkāras* and *arthālaṁkāras*, though, *śabdālaṁkāras* are not very prominent in his poetry. We shall refer here to the prominent figures of speech decorating his poetry.

Alliteration (anuprāsa) is the most favourite of all his verbal figures and Jagannātha has introduced it in his poetry freely with perfect skill and force. The apt use of alliteration has rendered the language of his poetry musical. The use of this figure is not an end itself, but it has served emotions and so it has become the means of realisation of *rasa*. We cite here some instances.

नितरां नीचोऽस्मीति त्वं खेद
कूप! मा कदापि कृथाः।
अत्यन्तसरसहृदयो यतः
परेषां गुणग्रहीतासि।। I. 9

एणीगणेषु गुरुगर्वनिमीलिताक्षः
किं कृष्णसार! खलु खेलसि काननेऽस्मिन्।
सीमामिमां कलय भिन्नकरीन्द्रकुम्भ-
मुक्तामयी हरिविहारवसुन्धरायाः।। I. 49

Jagannātha also makes use of yamaka, another verbal figure for bringing pleasing effect to his poetry.

शयिता सविधेऽप्यनीश्वरा सफलीकर्तुमहो मनोरथान्।
दयिता दयिताननाम्बुजं दरमीलन्नयना निरीक्षते।। II. 182

Of all ideal figures, upamā (simile) finds a supreme position in the scheme of his poetic embellishment.

Here, in the following pages I have followed the statistical method for arrangement of alaṁkāras. It will be very useful to the readers to identify the alaṁkāras.

I

प्रास्ताविकविलासः

1. माधुर्यपरमसीमा	अप्रस्तुतप्रशंसा (सादृश्यमूला)
2. दिगन्ते श्रूयन्ते	''
3. पुरा सरसि मानसे	''
4. तृष्णालोलविलोचने	''
5. अयि दलदरविन्द	''
6. समुपागतवति	''
7. तावत्कोकिल	''
8. कमलिनि	''
9. नितरां नीचोऽस्मीति	'' (श्लिष्टविशेषणं काव्यलिङ्ग)
10. येनामन्दमरन्दे	'' ; परिकर
11. अयि मलयज!	'' ; काव्यलिङ्ग (वाक्यार्थहेतुक)
12. पाटीर! तव	'' ''
13. नीरक्षीरविवेके	''
14. उपरि करवालधारा–	उल्लेख (संकीर्ण)
15. स्वच्छन्दं दलदरविन्द	सादृश्यमूला अप्रस्तुतप्रशंसा
16. याते मय्यचिरा–	'' ; काव्यलिङ्ग
17. आपेदिरेऽम्बरपथं	'' ; परिकर
18. मधुप इव	'' ; काव्यलिङ्ग
19. गुञ्जति मञ्जु	'' '' उपमा

20. यैस्त्वं गुणगणवानपि	'' व्याजस्तुति ; काव्यलिङ्ग
21. गाहितमखिलं	सादृश्यमूला अप्रस्तुतप्रशंसा ; उपमा
22. अपनीतपरिमला-	'' ; व्याजस्तुतिः
23. तटिनि! चिराय	'' ; परिकर
24. पत्रफलपुष्प-	'' ''
25. एकस्त्वं	'' भ्रान्तिमान्
26. तरुकुलसुषमा-	'' परिकर
27. कलभ! तवान्तिक-	'' ''
28. अमरतरुकुसुम-	'' काव्यलिङ्ग
29. पृष्टाः खलु	'' अनन्वयः
30. तोयैरल्पैरपि	'' ; प्रतीपम्
31. आरामाधिपति-	'' ; प्रहर्षणम्
32. न यत्र स्थेमानं	'' ; पर्यायः
33. दधानः प्रेमाणं	'' ; असम्भवः
34. मूलं स्थूलमतीव	''
35. ग्रीष्मे भीष्मतरैः	'' विषमः
36. दवदहनजटाल-	'' परिकरः
37. शृण्वन् पुरः	'' काव्यलिङ्ग
38. सौरभ्यं भुवनत्रयेऽपि	अप्रस्तुतप्रशंसा (विशेषनिव)
39. नापेक्षा न च	'' ; विभावना
40. समुत्पत्तिः स्वच्छे	'' सादृश्यमूला ; समुच्चयः
41. साकं ग्रावगणैः	''
42. किं खलु रत्नैरेतैः	''
43. इयत्यां सम्पत्ता-	''
44. अयि रोष-	''
45. न वारयामो भवतीं	'' ; पुनरुक्तवदाभासः
46. पौलमीपतिकानने	''
47. भुक्ता मृणालपटली	''
48. प्रारम्भे कुसुमाकरस्य	''

49. एणीगणेषु	''
50. जठरज्वलन	''
51. येन भिन्नकरिकुम्भ-	''
52. स्थितिं नो रे दध्याः	'' ; भ्रान्तिमान्
53. गिरिगह्वरेषु	''
54. निसगादारामे	'' ; असम्भवः
55. यस्मिन्वेल्लति	''
56. लूनं मत्तगजैः	''
57. स्वर्लोकस्य शिखामणिः	'' ; मालारूपक
58. स्वस्वव्यापृति-	'' ; विषादन
59. रे चाञ्चल्यजुषो	'' ; उपमा
60. पिब स्तन्यं पोत	'' ; भ्रान्तिमान्
61. धीरध्वनिभिरलं	अतिशयोक्तिः ; काव्यलिङ्ग
62. वेतण्डगण्ड-	अप्रस्तुतप्रशंसा
63. नीरान्निर्मलतो	'' ; विषम
64. लीलामुकुलितनयनं	'' ;
65. विदुषां वदनाद्वाचः	पूर्णोपमा
66. औदार्यं भुवनत्रयेऽपि	अप्रस्तुतप्रशंसा
67. एको विश्वसतां	प्रतीपम्
68. विश्वास्य मधुरवचनैः	काव्यलिङ्ग
69. अन्या जगद्धितमयी	भेदकातिशयोक्तिः
70. आपद्गत किल	प्रातिवस्तूपमा
71. विश्वाभिराम-	''
72. लीलालुण्ठित-	अर्थापत्तिः
73. गीर्भिर्गुरूणां	प्रतिवस्तूपमा
74. वहति विषधरान्	''
75. सत्पूरुषः खलु	दृष्टान्तः
76. कृतमपि महोपकारं	अप्रस्तुतप्रशंसा
77. पाण्डित्यं परिहृत्य	''

78. खलः कापट्यदोषेण	''
79. परार्थव्यासङ्गा-	समासोक्तिः
80. वंशभवो गुणवानपि	प्रतिवस्तूपमा
81. अमितगुणोऽपि	उदाहरण
82. उपकारमेव तनुते	''
83. वनान्ते खेलन्ती	विषमम्
84. पुरो गीर्वाणानां	''
85. युक्तं सभायां	समम् ; अप्रस्तुतप्रशंसा
86. किं तीर्थं हरिपाद-	परिसङ्ख्या
87. निष्णातोऽपि च	''
88. नैर्गुण्यमेव साधीयो	''
89. परोपसर्पणानन्त	''
90. शून्येऽपि च गुणवत्ता–	श्लिष्टोपमा
91. खलः सज्जनकार्पास-	रूपकम्
92. परगुह्यगुप्तिनिपुणं	उपमा
93. यशः सौरभ्यलशुनः	मालारूपक (शुद्ध–परम्परित)
94. धत्ते भरं कुसुमपत्र-	सादृश्यमूला अप्रस्तुतप्रशंसा ;
95. हालाहलं खलु	निदर्शना
96. दीनानामिह	अप्रस्तुतप्रशंसा (सादृश्यमूला)
97. गिरयो गुरवस्ते	सारः
98. व्योमनि बीजाकुरुते	निदर्शना
99. हारं वक्षसि	स्वभावोक्तिः ; अप्रस्तुतप्रशंसा
100. मलिनेऽपि रागपूर्णा	अप्रस्तुतप्रशंसा
101. स्वार्थं धनानि	अर्थान्तरन्यासः
102. जनकः सानुविशेषो	अप्रस्तुतप्रशंसा
103. कस्मै हन्त	पर्यायोक्तम्
104. धूमायिता दशदिशो	अप्रस्तुतप्रशंसा
105. भिन्ना महागिरिशिला:	''
106. गर्जितमकर्ण्य	स्वभावोक्तिः

107. किमहं वदामि — व्याजस्तुतिः
108. रे खल! तव — आक्षेप
109. आनन्दमृगदावाग्निः — रूपकम्
110. खलास्तु कुशलाः — प्रतिवस्तूपमा
111. वदने विनिवेशिता — अपह्नुतिः
112. कृतं त्वयोन्नतं — व्याजस्तुतिः
113. अविरतं परकार्य- — अप्रस्तुतप्रशंसा and रूपकम्
114. एत्य कुसुमाकरो — विषादन
115. निर्गुणः शोभते — विनोक्तिः
116. पङ्कैर्विना सरो भाति — विनोक्तिः
117. तत्त्वं किमपि — प्रतिवस्तूपमा
118. सरजस्कां पाण्डुवर्णां — अप्रस्तुतप्रशंसा
119. यथा तानं विना — मालोपमा ; विनोक्तिः
120. सन्तः स्वतः प्रकाशन्ते — प्रतिवस्तूपमा
121. अयि बत गुरुगर्वं — लेशः
122. दूरीकरोति कुमतिं — कारकदीपकम् ;
123. अनवरतपरोपकार- — पूर्णोपमा
124. व्यागुञ्जन्मधुकर- — गुणहेतूत्प्रेक्षा
125. मृतस्य लिप्सा — तुल्ययोगिता ; दीपकम्
126. उत्तमानामपि — अर्थान्तरन्यासः
127. अयाचितः सुखं — ”
128. दोर्दण्डद्वयकुण्डली- — स्मरणम्
129. खण्डितानेत्र- — ”

II

शृङ्गारविलासः

1. न मनागपि — व्यतिरेकः
2. नितरां परुषा — अप्रस्तुतप्रशंसा

3. स्वेदाम्बुसान्द्र	"
4. कस्तूरिकातिलक-	रूपकम्
5. तन्मञ्जु मन्दहसितं	"
6. प्रातस्तरां प्रणमने	"
7. गुरुजनभय-	उपमा
8. बदरामलकाम्र-	सार:
9. जंबीरश्रियमतिलंघ्य	"
10. कपोलपालिं	उत्प्रेक्षा
11. नीवीं नियम्य	उपमा (आर्थी)
12. आलीषु केली-	"
13. मुधैव मन्तुं	"
14. तदवधि कुशली	उपमा (धर्मवाचकोपमानलुप्ता)
15. आगत: पतिरिती-	पूर्णोपमा
16. अवधौ दिवसा	"
17. वक्षोजाग्रं	"
18. गुरुभि: परिवेल्लिता-	"
19. गुरुमध्यगता-	"
20. विनये नयनारुण-	उपमा
21. अकरुण मृषाभाषा-	"
22. तीरे तरुण्या	ससन्देह
23. वीक्ष्य वक्षसि	"
24. दरानमत्कन्धर-	स्मरणम्
25. रोषवेशार्न्निर्गतं	उपमा
26. हृदये कृतशैवला-	"
27. इत एव	उपमा ; रूपकम्
28. कथय कथमिवाशा	समुच्चय:
29. प्राणापहरणेनासि	"
30. निरुध्य यान्तीं	"
31. तिमिरं हरन्ति	"

32. कुचकलशयुगान्त-	,,
33. विधाय सा मद्वदनाकूलं	पर्यायोक्तम्
34. मुहुरर्थितयाद्य	,,
35. श्रुतिशतमपि भूय:	प्रतीपम्
36. लवलीं तव लीलया	व्यतिरेक:
37. यौवनोद्गमनितान्त-	यथासंख्यम्
38. अधिरोप्य	,,
39. भुजपञ्जरे गृहीता	पूर्णोपमा
40. उपनिषद: परिपीता	विशेषोक्ति:
41. अकरुणहृदय	उपमा
42. लोभाद्वराटिकानां	प्रहर्षण
43. रूपारुचिं निरसितुं	विषमम्
44. किं जल्पसि	प्रतीपम्
45. औत्सुक्यात्परिमिलतां	स्वभावोक्ति:
46. गरिमाणमर्पयित्वा	परिवृत्ति:
47. न्यञ्चति वयसि	तुल्ययोगिता
48. निस्सीमशोभा-	हेतूत्प्रेक्षा
49. गुरुमध्ये हरिणाक्षी	स्वभावोक्ति:
50. नयनाञ्चलावमर्शं	,,
51. मानपराग्वदनापि	,,
52. लोचनफुल्लाम्भोज-	रूपकम्
53. अधिरजनि	स्वभावोक्ति:
54. चिन्तामीलितमानसो	व्यतिकर:
55. अलंकर्तुं कर्णौ	समासोक्ति:
56. आयातैव निशा	,,
57. वाचो माङ्गलिकी:	,,
58. यदवधि दयितो	,,
59. निरवलां रजनीं	,,
60. निपतद्बाष्पसंरोध-	,,

61. यदि लक्ष्मण सा	,,
62. भवनं करुणावती	,,
63. पापं हन्त मया	,,
64. उषसि प्रतिपक्षकामिनी	,,
65. क्षमापणैकपदयो:	,,
66. निर्वासयन्तीं	पर्यायोक्त:
67. राज्ञो मत्प्रतिकूलान्मे	,,
68. मलयानिलमनलीयति	वाचकलुप्ता उपमा
69. कालागुरुद्रवं	,,
70. विधिवञ्चितया	,,
71. विरहेण विकलहृदया	,,
72. दारिद्र्यं भजते	अत्युक्ति:
73. पाटीरद्रुभुजङ्ग-	समुच्चय:
74. आयातैव निशा	समाधि:
75. प्रभातसमयप्रभा	विषम:
76. विदूरादाश्चर्य-	पर्याय:
77. कपोलावुन्मीलन-	उपमा
78. राजानं जनयाम्बभूव	व्यतिरेक:
79. आविर्भूता यदवधि	,,
80. प्रसङ्गे गोपानां	,,
81. कैशोरे वयसि	रूपकम्
82. शयिता शैवलशयने	,,
83. अधरद्युतिरस्तपल्लवा	अनन्वय:
84. व्यत्यस्तं लपति	कारकदीपकम्
85. उदितं मण्डलमिन्दो	समुच्चय:
86. प्रादुर्भवति पयोदे	,,
87. इदमप्रतिमं	स्मरणम्
88. मुञ्चसि नाद्यापि	,,
89. आलोक्य सुन्दरि	भ्रान्तिमान् ; उल्लेख:

90. स्मितं नैतत्	अपह्नुति:
91. संग्रामाङ्गणसम्मुखा-	''
92. श्यामं सितं च	''
93. अलिर्मृगो वा नेत्रं	ससन्देह:
94. सुविरलमौक्तिकतारे	रूपकम्
95. रूपजला चलनयना	सावयवरूपकम्
96. शोणाधरांशुसंभिन्ना-	पूर्णा श्रौती समासगा उपमा
97. दयिते रदनत्विषां	अपह्नुति:
98. तया तिलोत्तमीयन्त्या	उपमा (वाचकोपमानलुप्ता)
99. अङ्कायमानमलिके	लुप्तोपमा
100. शिशिरेण यथा	दीपकम्
101. चलदृंगमिवाम्भोज-	पूर्णोपमा
102. शतकोटिकठिन-	उपमा
103. श्यामलेनाङ्कितं	वाचकलुप्तोपमा
104. अद्वितीयं रुचात्मानं	व्यङ्ग्योपमा
105. नीलाञ्चलेन	श्रौती वाक्यगता पूर्णोपमा
106. स्तनाभोगे पतन्	पूर्णोपमा
107. यथा लताया:	पूर्णोपमा
108. इदं लताभि:	स्मरणम्
109. सा मदागमन-	''
110. अविचिन्त्यशक्ति-	रूपकम्
111. मीनवती नयनाभ्यां	रूपकम्
112. पान्थ मन्दमते	परिणाम:
113. संपश्यतां तामति-	ससन्देह
114. सपल्लवा किं नु-	''
115. नेत्राभिरामं	''
116. कनकद्रवकान्ति-	भ्रान्तिमान्
117. वनितेति वदन्त्येतां	उल्लेख:
118. स्मयमानाननां	''

119.	वदनकमलेन	धर्मवाचकलुप्तोपमा
120.	कलिन्दजानीर-	स्वरूपोत्प्रेक्षा
121.	परस्परासङ्गसुखा-	हेतूत्प्रेक्षा
122.	जनमोहकरं	"
123.	दिवानिशं	फलोत्प्रेक्षा
124.	वियोगवह्नि-	गुणफलोत्प्रेक्षा
125.	निधिं लावण्यानां	उत्प्रेक्षा, उपमा and व्यतिरेक:
126.	स्तनान्तर्गत-	अपह्नुति:
127.	जगदन्तरममृत-	स्वरूपोत्प्रेक्षा
128.	तिमिरशारद-	सम्बन्धातिशयोक्ति:
129.	प्रिये विषादं	तुल्ययोगिता
130.	राज्याभिषेक-	उत्प्रेक्षा
131.	आननं मृगशावाक्ष्या	स्मरणम्
132.	यान्ती गुरुजनै:	निदर्शना
133.	नयनानि वहन्तु	व्यतिरेक:
134.	मृणालमन्दानिल-	स्वभावोक्ति:
135.	विबोधयन् कर-	समासोक्ति:
136.	आनम्य वल्गु-	अप्रस्तुतप्रशंसा
137.	अभूदप्रत्यूह:	प्रतीपम्
138.	विनैव शस्त्रं	विभावना
139.	यदवधि विलास-	"
140.	न मिश्रयति	विषमम्
141.	वडबानलकालकूट-	समम्
142.	लभ्येत पुण्यै-	कारणमाला
143.	प्रभुरपि याचितुकामो	अर्थान्तरन्यास:
144.	जलकुम्भमुम्भित-	मीलितम्
145.	त्वमिव पथिक:	उत्तरम्
146.	किमिति कृशाऽसि	उत्तरम्
147.	तुलामनालोक्य	प्रतीपम्

148. इयमुल्लसिता	अनुमानम्
149. आसायं सलिलान्तः	प्रतीपम्
150. अयि मन्दस्मित–	सम्भावना
151. मधुरतरं स्मयमानः	स्वभावोक्तिः
152. मधुरसान्मधुरं	''
153. शतेनोपायानां	''
154. गुञ्जन्ति मञ्जु	''
155. यथा यथा नाम–	उपमा
156. हरिणीप्रेक्षणा	काव्यलिङ्गम्
157. लोलालकावलि–	उपमा
158. दन्तांशुकान्तर–	व्यतिरेकः
159. सानुकम्पा सानु–	''
160. अलकाः फणि–	''
161. वदने तव	''
162. अनिशं नयना–	''
163. अङ्गैः सुकुमारतरैः	असङ्गतिः
164. खिद्यति सा पथि	''
165. मथुरागमनोन्मुखे	उपमा and रूपकम्
166. केलीमन्दिरमागतस्य	प्रहर्षणम्
167. मान्थर्यमाप	सहोक्तिः
168. श्वासोऽनुमानवेद्यः	आक्षेपः
169. पाणौ कृतः	निदर्शना
170. अरुणमपि विद्रु–	व्यतिरेकः
171. सुदृशो जितरत्न–	अन्योन्यम्
172. परपूरुषदृष्टि–	''
173. अङ्गानि दत्वा	परिवृत्तिः
174. जितमौक्तिकसम्पदां	प्रत्यनीकम्
175. विलसत्याननं तस्या	''
176. निभाल्य भूयो	प्रतीपम्

177. करिकुम्भतुला-	अर्थान्तरन्यास:
178. परिष्वजन् रोषवशात्	प्रहर्षणम्
179. चेलाञ्चलेनानन-	विषादनम्
180. अधरेण समागमा-	पूर्वरूपम्
181. सरसिरुहोदरसुर-	मीलितम्
182. शयिता सविधे-	सन्देहसङ्कर: of Upamā and Rūpaka
183. वदनारविन्द-	भ्रान्तिमान्

III

करुणविलास:

1. दैवे पराग्वदन-	काव्यलिङ्गम्
2. प्रत्युद्गता सविनयं	,,
3. सर्वेऽपि विस्मृतिपथं	धर्मवाचकोपमानलुप्ता उपमा
4. निर्वाणमङ्गलपदं	,,
5. धृत्वा पदस्खलन–	,,
6. निर्दूषणा गुणवती	,,
7. चिन्ता शशाम	काव्यलिङ्ग ; व्यतिरेक:
8. सौदामिनीविलसित-	,,
9. केनापि मे विलसितेन	,,
10. काव्यात्मना मनसि	,,
11. या तावकीनमधुर-	व्यतिरेक:
12. मन्दस्मितेन सुधया	रूपकम्
13. भूमौ स्थिता रमण!	,,
14. लावण्यमुज्ज्वल-	,,
15. कान्त्या सुवर्णवरया	उत्प्रेक्षा
16. कर्पूरवर्तिरिव	मालोपमा
17. स्वप्नान्तरेऽपि	श्लेषोत्थापितविरोधाभास:
18. दयितस्य गुणाननु-	,,
19. रीतिं गिराममृत-	पर्यायोक्त

IV

शान्तविलासः

1. विशालविषयाटवी-	व्यतिरेक:, रूपकम्, धर्मलुप्तोपमा
2. अये जलधिनन्दिनी-	रूपकम्, प्रतीपम्, परिकर:
3. स्मृतापि तरुणातपं-	रूपकातिशयोक्ति:, व्यतिरेक:, रूपकम्
4. कलिन्दगिरिनन्दिनी-	सावयव रूपकातिशयोक्ति:; व्यतिरेक:
5. जगज्जालं ज्योत्स्ना-	,,
6. ग्रीष्मचण्डकर-	वाक्यगता श्रौती पूर्णोपमा
7. अपारे संसारे	परिणाम: (तुल्याधिकरणक)
8. आलिङ्गितो जलधि-	उपमा
9. नयनानन्दसन्दोह-	रूपकातिशयोक्ति:
10. वाचा निर्मलया	काव्यलिङ्गम्
11. पातालं व्रज याहि	रूपकम्
12. गणिकाजामिल-	रूपकम्
13. मृद्वीका रसिता	,,
14. व्रजं पापमहीभृतां	मालारूपकम्
15. रे चेत:! कथयामि	आक्षेप:
16. अव्याख्येयां वितरति	,,
17. सन्त्येवास्मिञ्जगति-	स्मरणम्
18. विष्वद्रीच्या भुवन-	विचित्रम्
19. सेवायां यदि	परिसङ्ख्या
20. भवग्रीष्मप्रौढा-	सावयवरूपकम्
21. बन्धोन्मुक्त्यै	विचित्रम्, काव्यलिङ्गम्
22. प्रथमं चुम्बित-	पर्याय:, समासोक्ति:
23. मलयानिलकाल-	,,
24. निखिलं जगदेव	,,
25. प्रतिपलमखिलाँ-	विशेषोक्ति: (अनुक्तनिमित्ता)
26. सपदि विलयमेतु	,,

27. अपि बहलदहन-	,,
28. तरणोपायमपश्य-	पर्यायोक्तम्
29. श्रियो मे मा सन्तु	तिरस्कार:
30. किं निःशङ्कं शेषे	आक्षेप:
31. सन्तापयामि किमहं	,,
32. रे रे मनो मम	प्रत्यनीक
33. मरकतमणि-	सन्देह:
34. तरणितनया किं	सन्देह: (निश्चयगर्भ:)
35. चपला जलदा-	निश्चयान्तसन्देह:
36. भूतिर्नीचगृहेषु	,,
37. आमूलाद्रत्नसानो-	,,
38. गिरां देवी	,,
39. मधु द्राक्षा	व्यतिरेक:
40. निर्माणे यदि	,,
41. मद्राणि मा कुरु	अवज्ञा (in first part) and उल्लास in second
42. विद्वांसो वसुधातले	,,
43. धुर्यैरपि माधुर्यै-	व्यतिरेक:
44. शास्त्राण्याकलितानि	,,
45. दुर्वृत्ता जारजन्मानो	रूपकातिशयोक्ति: ; रूपकम्

Now, some of the Alaṅkāras are illustrated.

Aprastutapraśaṁsā :

The figure Aprastutapraśaṁsā occurs when the *prastuta* (contextual behaviour) is conveyed by the *aprastuta* behaviour by dint of anyone of the relations like similarity etc. which are to be stated.

दिगन्ते श्रूयन्ते मदमलिनगण्डा: करटिन:
करिण्य: कारुण्यास्पदमसमशीला खलु मृगा:।

इदानीं लोकेऽस्मिन्ननुपमशिखानां पुनरयं
नखानां पाण्डित्यं प्रकटयतु कस्मिन्मृगपतिः।। I. 2

Elephants with their temples soiled with ichor are heard to have fled to the end of the quaters; the female elephants are the objects of pity; while other beasts of prey stand no comparison in nature. Where should then, in this world, this lord of beasts exhibit the skill of his clows, with their ends matchless (in sharpness.)

Sasandeha

Here doubt on the part of the sages whether Rāma from a far looks like a mountain decorated with emeralds or like a young tamāla tree, is poetically represented.

मरकतमणिमेदिनी धरो वा तरुणतरस्तरुरेष वा तमालः।
रघुपतिमवलोक्य तत्र दूरादृषिनिकरैरिति संशयः प्रपेदे।। IV. 33

There (in the Daṇḍakāraṇya) at the sight of the lord of Raghus from a distance, doubt was entertained by the groups of sages as to whether it was a mountain of emeralds or a young tamāla tree.

Vibhāvanā :

In Vibhāvanā, the effect is represented as taking place in the absence of cause. Though an apparent contradiction is apprehended when the effect is represented as taking place in the absence of cause, this contradiction is removed when some other cause, not so well-known is understood as giving rise to the effect.

विनैव शस्त्रं हृदयानि यूनां विवेकभाजामपि दारयन्त्यः।
अनन्तमायामयवल्गुलीला जयन्ति नीलाब्जदलायताक्ष्यः।। II. 138

Victorious are the sports of her whose eyes are pleasing and fascinating like petal of a blue lotus and who without weapon of any sort breaks the hearts even of those youths who possessed discernment.

Here 'tearing off' is the effect. Its cause is a weapon, but as tearing off is represented as taking place in the absence of weapons, Vibhāvanā takes place.

Prativastūpamā

Prativastūpamā is the implied similarity between two sentential meanings which are possessed of a common property under the *vastu-prativastu-bhāva*.

आपाद्गतः खलु महाशयचक्रवर्ती
विस्तारयत्यकृतपूर्वमुदारभावम्।
कालागरुर्दहनमध्यगतः समन्ता-
ल्लोकोत्तरं परिमलं प्रकटीकरोति।। I. 70

The above verse contains the figure *Prativastūpamā*.

The best of the magnanimous, indeed, when fallen into adversity, extends the unpreecedented genorosity; sandal when cast into fire emits all around extraordinary fragrance.

Another example is given bellow.

वंशभवो गुणवानपि सङ्गविशेषेण पूज्यते पुरुषः।
न हि तुम्बिफलविकलो वीणादण्डः प्रयाति महिमानम्।। I. 80

A man is worshipped for his company even if he is of a good family and possessed of qualities. The board of a Vīṇā does not attain greatness without the tumbī underneath it.

Yathāsaṁkhyam

When a reference is made to objects in the same order in which they have been already mentioned, there occurs the figure yathāsaṁkhya.

योवनोद्गमनितान्तशङ्किताः शीलशौर्यबलकान्तिलोभिताः।
सङ्कुचन्ति विकसन्ति राघवे जानकीनयननीरजश्रियः।। II. 37

The beauty of the lotus-like eye of Jānakī, constrained by the advent of youth (in Rāma) and attracted by effulgence, strength and prowess of Rāma, closed and expanded alternately.

Purvarūpa

अधरेण समागमाद्रदनामरुणिम्ना पिहितोऽपि शुक्लभावः ।
हसितेन सितेन पक्ष्मलाक्ष्याः पुनरुल्लासमवाप जातपक्षः।। II. 180

The white colour of her teeth which owing to their contact with the lower lip was for a while shrouded by its red colour, manifested itself by the white smile of her who has long eye-lashes.

Dṛṣṭānta

Dṛṣṭānta as a figure based on similarity where the common property, the *upameya* and the *upamāna* should be reflected in one another by *bimba-pratibimba-bhāva*.

सत्पूरुषः खलु हिताचरणैरमन्द-
मानन्दयत्यखिललोकमनुक्त एव।
आराधितः कथय केन करैरुदारै-
रिन्दुर्विकासयति कैरविणीकुलानि।। I. 75

A good man pleases the whole world without being asked, by his good deeds. By whom entreated, tell me, does the moon open up the right lotuses with his generous rays?

Here, the *upameya* i.e. good man and his good deeds on the one hand is reflected in the *upamāna* i.e. the moon and generous rays on the other. Similarly, the common properties i.e. the actions of pleasing the word and opening the lotuses also reflected each other, so that although they are different, they seem to be identical. It is a perfect example of *bimba-pratibimba-bhāva*.

Parivṛtti

The figure consists in an exchange when it is poetically presented. In Parivṛtti a person gives up something belonging to him to someone and receives in exchange something from that very person.

अङ्गानि दत्वा हेमाङ्गि! प्राणान् क्रीणासि चेन्नृणाम्।
युक्तमेतन्न तु पुनः कोणं नयनपद्मयोः।। II. 173

Oh you! lady of golden complexion! It is proper that you purchase life of the men after giving away the parts of your body; but it is not proper when you purchase the life of the men after giving away your pair of lotus eyes. The former half of the above verse presents a case of *samaparivṛtti* while the latter part depicts *viṣama-parivṛtti*.

Nidarśanā

Nidarśanā occurs when two sentential meanings are stated separately whose identity is cognised by implication and is finally reduced to similarity. In the above verse, the *abheda* of the agents is expressed in words and it implies the *abheda* of actions.

हालाहलं खलु पिपासति कौतुकेन
कालानलं परिचुचुम्बिषति प्रकामम्।
व्यालाधिपं च यतते परिरब्धुमद्धा
यो दुर्जनं वशयितुं कुरुते मनीषाम्।। I. 95

He who cherishes a desire to win over a wicked man, wishes indeed to drink deadly poison with curiosity, to kiss closely the fire of final destruction or to embrace actually the lord of serpents.

Parisaṁkhyā

When an object, generally known, is excluded by some speciality, the figure is Parisaṁkhyā.

सेवायां यदि साभिलाषमसि रे लक्ष्मीपतिः सेव्यतां
चिन्तायामसि सस्पृहं यदि तदा चक्रायुधश्चिन्त्यताम्।

आलापं यदि काङ्क्षसि स्मररिपोर्गाथा तदालप्यतां
स्वापं वाञ्छसि चेन्निरर्गलसुखे चेतः सखे! सुप्यताम्।। IV. 19

Oh friend mind, if you desire to serve, serve the consort of Lakṣmī; if you desire to contemplate, contemplate over Viṣṇu. If you want to converse, sing the verses of Śiva; if you want to sleep, sleep in unlimited joy of Brahman.

Vyatireka :

The vyatikara is defined as the excellence of the upameya over the upamāna due to the possession of a certain property.

अनिशं नयनाभिरामया रमया संमदिनो मुखस्य ते।
निशि निःसरदिन्दिरं कथं तुलयामः कलयापि पङ्कजम्।।

II. 162

How shall we compare even to a slight degree, the lotus whose beauty fades by evening with your face which prides itself upon possessing beauty which is ever pleasing to the eye?

Here, the heroine's face is the *upameya* and the lotus the *upamāna*. The face is superior to the lotus, since it possesses a certain property-that of being beutiful day and night, a property the lotus lacks.

Samuccaya

When a connection among objects occurs simultaneously the figure samuccaya takes place.

उदितं मण्डलमिन्दो रुदितं सद्यो वियोगिवर्गेण।
मुदितं च सकलललनाचूडामणिशासनेन मदनेन।। I. 70

No sooner did the orb of the moon rise then the multitude of separated persons began to weep at once and the god of love, whose command is born like the crestjewel by all women, become delighted.

Here many actions are counted simultaneously with many *dharmis*.

Samādhi

When what is to be accomplished by one cause becomes easy due to accidental operation of another cause the figure samādhi occurs.

आयातैव निशा मनो मृगदृशामुन्निद्रमातन्वती
मानो मे कथमेष सम्प्रति निरातङ्कं हृदि स्थास्यति।
ऊहापोहमिमं सरोजनयना यावद् विधत्तेतरां
तावत् कामनृपातपत्रसुषमं बिम्बं बभासे विधोः।।

The disc of the moon, as charming as the umbrella of the king cupid arose just while the lotus-eyed one was engaged in the thoughts as to how heart pride would fearlessly hold its position in her at a time when the night, which rendered the mind of deer-eyed women void of sleep (i.e. full of love), had actually come.

Here the effect, removal of pride due to the cause, arrival of night becomes easy of accomlishment due to accidental operation of another cause, the rise of the moon.

Apahnuti

In the Apahnuti, the upameya is negated and the upamāna is superimposed on it.

स्मितं नैतत्किन्तु प्रकृतिरमणीयं विकसितं
मुखं ब्रूते मूढः कुमुदमिदमुद्यत्परिमलम्।
स्तनद्वन्द्वं मिथ्या कनकनिभमेतत्फलयुगं
लता रम्या सेयं भ्रमरकुलनम्या न रमणी।। II. 90

Ah! this is not a woman, but a beautiful creeper pressed down by swarns of bees; for this is not a smile but a naturally charming blooming of a lotus; and that which is talked of as mouth, is surely a flower whence fragrance is issuing; and to say that these are breasts is utter falsehood, since they are a pair of gold coloured fruits.

The above is an example of Apahnuti. It *sāvayavā-apahnuti* as both subordinate and principle *apahnutis* are inter-related, adding beauty mutually.

श्यामं सितं च सुदृशो न दृशोस्स्वरूपं
किन्तु स्फुटं गरलमेतदथामृतञ्च।
नो चेत्कथं निपतनादनयोस्तदैव
मोहं मुदं च नितरां दधते युवानः॥ II. 76.

The above is an example of *niravayava* variety of Apahnuti. 'The eyes of the beautiful damsel are not merely blue and white in appearance but they are evidently poison and nectar; otherwise, how do the youth swoon and joy when her eyes fall upon them? Here *śyāmasitatva* (both blueness and whiteness) of the eyes is negated and *garalā-mṛtatva* (both poisonness and nectarness) is superimposed on them, with the explanation of a reason. Hence it is *hetvapahnuti*.

Rūpakātiśayokti

कलिन्दगिरिनन्दिनीतटवनान्तरं भासयन्
सदा पथि गतागतक्लमभरं हरन्प्राणिनाम्।
स्फुरत्कनककान्तिभिर्नवलताभिरावेल्लितो
ममाशु हरतु श्रमानतितमां तमालद्रुमः॥ I. 4

"May the Tamāla tree-brightening the heart of the forest on the banks of (the Jumna), the daughter of Kalinda mountain, reliving the animate world of its faligues while wandering to and fro on its different routes and encircled by new creepers endowed with the splendour of (liquid) gold-remove immediately all my exhaustions." Here the suppression of the *viṣaya* God Viṣṇu—by the Viṣayin -tamāla tree is based on series of suppressed ideas in the first three feet of the verse:

the birth of people in different social ranks, etc., are suppressed by the idea—the wanderings of people resulting in great-exhaustion; and the lovely damsels of cow herds are suppresed by the idea of golden creepers.[14]

Asaṅgati

अङ्गैः सुकुमारतरैः सा कुसुमानां श्रियं हरति।
प्रहरति हि कुसुमबाणो जगतीतलवर्तिनो यूनाः।। I. 163

It is an example of *Asaṅgati*. Here the cause-offence consisting in stealing the beauty of flowers-exists in the lady, and the effect-striking is experienced by the youths. The word *'praharti'* conveys the sense of love torments. This sense is the *viṣaya*. The *viṣaya* is the principal sense-'beating or striking because of fault'. The two senses are identified. The well-known cause of beating is the fault consisting in stealing (the beauty of flowers). An apparent contradiction arises when the cause-fault is represented as existing in the lady and the effect-striking of beating is represented as experienced by the youths. The contradiction is removed when the *viṣaya* (torments), is taken into account and when it is understood that the youths undergo torments of love due to the beauty of the lady which is described as stealing the beauty of the flowers. *Abhedādhyavasāna,* therefore, is essential in *Asaṅgati*.

Pratyanīka

Humiliation caused to one belonging to the enemy when put in a poetic turn is the case of Pratyanīka.

रे रे मनो मम मनोभवशासनस्य
पादाम्बुजद्वयमनारतमानमन्तम्।
किं मां निपातयसि संस्कृतिगर्तमध्ये
नैतावता तव गमिष्यति पुत्रशोकः।। IV.32

"Oh! my mind! would you let me who has bowed down

to the lotus feet of Mahādeva (the chastised of the cupid), fall into the earthly cavity? But even then your sorrow from the death of your son will no be allowed". Here the mind is unable to overcome the enemy i.e. Mahādeva directly. It humiliates a devotee of Mahādeva like myself.

Avañjā-Alaṅkāra

निष्णातोऽपि च वेदान्ते वैराग्यं नैति दुर्जनः।
चिरं जलनिधौ मग्नो मैनाक इव मार्दवम्।। I. 87

The above stated verse is an example of *Avajñā-alaṅkāra* (*tad viparyayo'vajñā*) which is the opposite of the figure Ullāsa. When the virtues and faults of one person do not give rise to the apprehension of another's virtues or faults, the figure *Avañjā* takes place there.

Tiraskāra-Alaṅkāra

Jagannātha is the rhetorician to treat Tiraskāra as a distinct figure. According to him, when an object very much known as good in character is condemned because of its connection with a particular fault, the figure Tiraskāra takes place.

श्रियो मे मा सन्तु क्षणमपि च माद्यद्गजघटा
मदभ्राम्यद्भृङ्गावलिमधुरझङ्कारसुभगाः।
निमग्नानां यासु द्रविणमदिराघूर्णितदृशां
सपर्यासौकर्यं हरिचरणयोरस्तमयते।। IV. 29

In this verse the merit derived out of the royal fortune is condemned lest it should dissuade one from devotion towards the feet of Lord Hari.

Pratīpa

In the first variety of Pratīpa, the object which is well-known as an upameya, is described as the upamāna, and the well-known upamāna is described as the upameya. This shows that the upameya is superior to the upamāna and the upamāna is inferior to the upameya in this figure.

किं जल्पसि मुग्धतया हन्त ममाङ्गं सुवर्णवर्णमिति।
तद् यदि हुताशे तदा हताशे! तुलां तवारोहेत्।। I.44

Alas! what are you saying out of innosence that my body is the fire then only it assumes the colour of your body. Here in the first half of the verse the superiority of the hue of gold is denied and the superiority of the hue of the body of the girl is emphasised in the second half. The use of two words, mugdhā and hatāśā, keeps out upamā here.

Uttara

किमिति कृशासि कृशोदरि किं तव परकीयवृत्तान्तैः।
कथय तथापि मुदे मम कथयिष्यति याहि पान्थ तव जाया।।
I.146

The above verse contains a figure called *uttara* which is defined as *praśnapratibandhakajñanaviṣayībhūto'rtha uttaram. Praśna* is a desire for knowledge. This desire for knowledge comes to an end when knowledge, which is the object of the sentence describing the answer arises. The figure *Uttara* is divided into two varieties: (A) when the question is inferred (b) when the question is mentioned. The above verse falls in the category of second variety.

Vicitra-alaṅkāra

When someone wishing to achieve a desired object, behaves in a way quite contrary to the desired, with a view to achieving the desired object, the figure vicitra takes place.

विष्वद्रीच्या भुवनमखिलं भासते यस्य भासा
सर्वासामप्यहमिति विदां गूढमालम्बनं यः।
तं पृच्छन्ति स्वहृदयमनावेदिनो विष्णुमन्या-
नन्यायोऽयं शिव! शिव!! नृणां केन वा वर्णनीयः।। IV. 18

In this verse it is described that people inquire of others about Viṣṇu who is the substratum of everybody's self and by whose brilliance the entire universe is illumined.

Another example in the same Vilāsa is worthnoting.

बन्धोन्मुक्त्यै खलु मखमुखात् कुर्वते कर्मपाशान्
अन्तःशान्त्यै मुनिशतमतानल्पचिन्तां भजन्ते।
तीर्थे मज्जन्त्यशुभजलधेः पारमारोढुकामाः
सर्वं प्रामादिकमिह भवभ्रान्तिभाजां नराणाम्।। BV. IV. 21

Here performance of sacrifice in order to achieve salvation, giving thought on the doctrines of the sages, taking a dip into the ocean containing inauspicious object indicate contradictory behaviour on the part of the person aspiring for the desired objects like salvation.

Praharṣaṇa

When the desired object is attained without making any effort due for it the figure Praharṣaṇa occurs.

तिरस्कृतो रोषवशात् परिष्वजन्
प्रियो मृगाक्ष्या शयितः पराङ्मुखः।
किं दुःखितोऽसाविति कान्दिशीकया
कयाचिदाचुम्ब्य चिराय सस्वजे।।

A certain lover, treated with contempt in anger by the deer-eyed one when he was going to embrace her and therefore sleeping with his face turned away from her was embraced by her for a long time after kissing him, she being distracted that he was perhaps hurt. Here the desired object is achieved accidentally though no effort is made on the part of the hero.

Kalpitopamā

गुरुजनभयमद्विलोकनान्तः समुदयदाकुलभावमावहन्त्याः।
दरदलदरविन्दसुन्दरं हा हरिणदृशो नयनं न विस्मरामि।। I. 7

The above verse is an example of *kalpitopamā* which is a variety of Upamā. The *upamāna* here is lotus; the upameya is the eye, and the common property is beauty. The upamā here beautifies the memory and through memory it gives rise to the love in separation.

Viṣādana

The attainment of an object quite opposed to what was desired is termed viṣādana.

स्वस्वव्यापृतिमग्नमानसतया मत्तो निवृत्ते जने
चञ्चूकोटिविपाटिताररपुटो यास्याम्यहं पञ्जरात्।
एवं कीरवरे मनोरथमयं पीयूषमास्वादय-
त्यन्तः सत्प्रविवेश वारणकराकारः फणिग्रामणीः।। I. 58

Here the encaged parrot muses upon its happy future when the violent snake enters into the cage.

Milita

When the characteristics of one object are not understood as distinct those of the other which is distintly apprehended.

जलकुम्भमुम्भितरसं सपदि सरस्याः समानयन्त्यास्ते।
तटकुञ्जगूढसुरतं भवगवानेको मनोभवो वेद।। I. 144

Here sweating, trembling etc. due to love are not distinctly apprehended from those which arise the trouble of bringing water.

Leśa

When a good quality is described as a fault because of its being means for an evil and when a fault is described as a quality because of its being a means for achievement of a desired object, the figure Leśa takes place.

नैर्गुण्यमेव साधीयो धिगस्तु गुणगौरवम्।
शाखिनोऽन्ये विराजन्ते खण्ड्यन्ते चन्दनद्रुमाः।। I.88

Here a very good quality of emission of perfume in sandal wood is described as a cause of its destruction.

Rūpaka

Rūpaka is one of the main figures based on similarity. Whereas in Upamā, the idea that one thing is like another is stated clearly in words, in Rūpaka, however, the upamāna is identified with the upameya in order to emphasise the excellence of the latter, although they are actually known to be different.

सुविरलमैक्तिकतारे धवलांशुकचन्द्रिकाचमत्कारे।
वदनपरिपूर्णचन्द्रे सुन्दरि राकासि नात्र संदेहः।। I. 94

It is an example of *Samastavastu-viṣaya Sāvayava-rūpaka*. *Sāvayava-rūpaka* consists of a group of *rūpakas* which are inter-related among themselves. Though the *rūpakas* here are inter-related, the poet intends to present one metaphor as principal because of his potency. The relation between the main and the subordinate metaphors is body-limbs relation. And in the *Samastavastu-viṣaya* all the *rūpakas* get mentioned in words.

Arthāpatti

When an object is known from another object by dint of the same argument, the figure Arthāpatti occurs there.

लीलालुण्ठितशारदापुरमहासम्पद्भराणां पुरो
विद्यासद्मविनिर्गलत्कणमुषो वल्गन्ति चेत् पामराः।
अद्य श्वः फणिनां शकुन्तशिशवो दन्तावलानां शशाः
सिंहानां च सुखेन मूर्धसु पदं धास्यन्ति शालावृकाः।। I.72

Here the idiots display their learning before the denizens of the land of the goddess Sarasvatī. If this is a fact then the wolves will lay their feet on the heads of the lions, the hares on the heads of the elephants and the small birds on the heads of the snakes today or tomorrow. The laying of the feet of the wolves etc. on the heads of the lions and others is apprehended by the force of the same reasoning with which the display of learning by the idiots before the learned is understood.

Pariṇāma

अपारे संसारे विषमविषयारण्यसरणौ
मम भ्रामं भ्रामं विगलितविरामं जडमतेः।
परिश्रान्तस्यायं तरणितनयातीरनिलयः
समन्तात्सन्तापं हरिनवतमालस्तिरयतु।। I. 7

The above verse contains the figure pariṇāma which is defined by Jagannātha as *viṣayī yatra viṣayātmatayaiva pakṛtopayogī na svātantryeṇa saḥ pariṇāmaḥ*. Pariṇāma arises when the *viṣayi (upamāna)* is useful in fulfilling the work of the present context by assuming identity-relation with the *viṣaya* but not independently.

The above verse is an example of *sāmānādhikaraṇa-pariṇāmālaṅkāra* contained in the sentence. In this verse the '*Hari-nava-tamāla* is capable of removing the *tāpa* caused by *saṁsāra,* more on account of the Tamāla's being identical with Hari who alone can alleviate all the troubles. Therefore, it is an instance of *Pariṇāma.*

Paryāya

When one object is represented as residing in many abodes in succession, the figure Paryāya takes place there. For an example:

विदूरादाश्चर्यस्तिमितमथ किञ्चित्परिचयात्
उदञ्चच्चाञ्चल्यं तदनु परितः स्फारितरुचिः।
गुरूणां सङ्घाते सपदि मयि याते समजनि
त्रपाघूर्णत्तारं नयनमिह सारङ्गजदृशः।। II.76

The eyes of the fawn-eyed beloved were steady with wonder when she saw me at a distance; she became tremulous after a partial recognition; afterwards her lustre grew on all sides and when I soon approached the assembly of the elders, her pupils began to roll through shyness.

Bhrāntimān

Jagannātha defines that mistake is said to happen when the certain knowledge of the identity of one object occurs due to similarity, without deliberate force of will, in another object, and the false knowledge of identity is pleasing to the appreciative reader. If such a mistake is used in a sentence where living and animate (being commit that mistake, the poetic desoription of that mistake) constitutes the figure Bhrāntimān.

कनकद्रवकान्तिकान्तया मिलितं सममुदीक्ष्य कान्तया।
चपलायुतवारिदभ्रमान्ननृते चातकपोतकैर्वने।। I. 116

The above is an example of bhrāntimān. "Seeing Rāma joined with his wife whose complexion was like molten gold, young cātakas danced in the forest, mistaking them for rain clouds with lightening.

Kāraṇamālā

It is that chain when the preceding word is the cause of the succeeding one and vice versa constitutes the figure Kāraṇamālā.

लभ्येत पुण्यैर्गृहिणी मनोज्ञा
तया सुपुत्राः परितः पवित्राः।
स्फीतं यशस्तैः समुदेति नित्यं
तेनास्य नित्यः खलु नाकलोकः।। II.142

An attractive wife may be obtained by dint of pious deeds, good sons who are honest in every sphere may be had by her, abiding fame results from them truly and on account of fame obtained the permanently heavenly bliss. In this verse the cause precedes the effect.

Sāra

Sāra-alaṅkāra occurs when the same object attains gradually superior or inferior status due to change of circumstances.

जम्बीरश्रियमतिलङ्घ्य लीलयैव
व्यानम्रीकृतकमनीयहेमकुम्भौ।
नीलाम्भोरुहनयनेऽधुना कुचौ ते
स्पर्धेते किल कनकाचलेन सार्धम्।। I. 9

"O you, your eyes are beautiful like a blue lotus, your breasts, after easily exceeding the beauty of a citron and throwing into the background the beautiful golden jars, are now indeed competing with the golden mountain (Meru)".

Tulyayogitā

In *Tulyayogitā,* either all *prakṛta* objects or all *aprakṛta* objects are connected with one property consisting of a quality or an action etc.

प्रिये विषादं जहीहीति वाचं
प्रिये सरागं वदति प्रियाया:।
वारामुदारा विजगाल धारा
विलोचनाभ्यां मनसश्च मान:।। I.129

When the lover lovingly said to her beloved—oh love, give up dejection, profuse streams of tear ran down from her eyes and pride vanished from her mind.

Anyonya

When two things do the same act in order to add speciality to each other the figure Anyonya occurs. The following are the two examples of its two varieties.

(I) सुदृशो जितरत्नजालया
सुरतान्तश्रमबिन्दुमालया।
अलिकेन च हेमकान्तिना
विदधे कापि रुचिः परस्परम्।। BV. II.171

The line of the drops of perspiration produced in the cause of the love-play, which surpassed a collection of jewels in beauty, and the golden-coloured forehead of the fair-eyed one heightened mutual beauty to an inexpressible extent.

(II) परपूरुषदृष्टिपातवज्राहतिभीता हृदयं प्रियस्य सीता।
अविशत् परकामिनीभुजङ्गीभयतः सत्वरमेव सोऽपि तस्याः।
BV. II.172

Afraid of a stroke of the thunderbolt in the form of glances of persons other than her husband, Sītā entered the heart of her dear husband, and he too entered her at once through the fear of a female serpent in the form of another woman.

In the first example the objects add beauty to each other in the form of quality and in the second the objects bring mutual beauty in the form of action.

Viśeṣokti :

In Viśeṣokti the effect is not represented as taking place though the well-known cause for such an effect is present.

उपनिषदः परिपीता गीतापि च हन्त मतिपथं नीता।
तदपि न हा विधुवदना मानससदनाद् बहिर्याति।। II. 40

The philosophical lore has been completely digested; Gītā, too, was made the object of meditation. But alas! the moon-faced one does not leave my mental abode.

Here the well-known causes like the study of the upaniṣads and the meditation on the contents of the Gītā are present; but their effect, dissociation from women is not represented here as taking place. The cause for non-rising of effect i.e. extreme love for the moon-faced lady is stated here. The verse is thus a case of Uktanimittā Viśeṣokti.

Thus from the above presentation we clearly know that Jagannātha has adopted ornamental style. He has defined poetry in the *Rasagaṅgādhara* as a word conveying charming sense. The charm in the sense arises only when there is some connection with the suggested sense. The alaṅkāras embellish the suggested sense, which thus is the essence of poetry and which consits of *rasa*, *vastu* and *alaṅkāra*. The alaṅkāra should be the cause of delight of the appreciative readers. They should be beautiful and should be flawless. The function of alaṅkāra is to give rise to *camatkṛti* which is defined as peculiar delight and which is experienced by the sahṛdayas, appreciative readers in their hearts. In the BV, we see the nature of *camatkāra*, the poet creates through the proper use of alaṅkāras.

Now, we should consider other features of Jagannāth's creativity.

One notable feature of this work is that there are some *samānārthaka* stanzas which contain one and the same meaning.

We cite here some of the verses:

(I) अपनीतपरिमलान्तरकथे पदं न्यस्य देवतरुकुसुमे।
पुष्पान्तरेऽपि गन्तुं वाञ्छसि चेद् भ्रमर! धन्योऽसि।।

Verse I. 22

has a similar meaning with the following :

अमरतरुकुसुमसौरभसेवनसम्पूर्णसकलकामस्य।
पुष्पान्तरसेवेयं भ्रमरस्य विडम्बना महती।। Verse I. 28

(II) अयि मलयज महिमायं कस्य गिरामस्तु विषयस्ते।
उद्गिरतो यद्गरलं फणिनः पुष्णासि परिमलोद्गारैः।। V. I. II

has a similar meaning with the verse :

पाटीर तव पटीयान्कः परिपाटीमिमामुरीकर्तुम्।
यत्पिंषतामपि नृणां पिष्टोऽपि तनोषि परिमलैः पुष्टिम्।।
V.I. 12

has similarity with

(III) गाहितमखिलं विश्वं परितो दृष्टाश्च विटपिनः सर्वे।
सहकार न प्रपेदे मधुपेन भवत्समं जगति।। V. I. 21

पृष्टाः खलु परपुष्टाः परितो दृष्टाश्च विटपिनः सर्वे।
माकन्द न प्रपेदे मधुपेन तवोपमा जगति।। I. 29

(IV) खलः सज्जनकार्पासरक्षणैकहुताशनः।
परदुःखाग्निशमनो मारुतः केन वर्ण्यताम्। V. 91

यशः सौरभ्यलशुनः शान्तिशैत्यहुताशनः।।
कारुण्यकुसुमाकाशः खलः सज्जनदुःखदः।। V. I. 93

(V) स्वस्वव्यापृतिमग्नमानसतया मत्तो निवृत्ते जने
चञ्चूकोटिविपाटितारपुटो यास्याम्यहं पञ्जरात्।
एवं कीरवरे मनोरथमयं पीयूषमास्वादय-
त्यन्तः संप्रविवेश वाराणकराकारः फणिग्रामणीः।। V. I. 58

एत्य कुसुमाकरो मे सञ्जीवयिता गिरं चिरं मग्नाम्।
इति चिन्तयतो हृदये पिकस्य समधायि शौभिकेन शरः।।
V. I. 114

This kind of indirect reference to things to be described is one of the chief characteristics of Jagannātha's devotional lyrics which is found in the following verse of the BV :

स्मृतापि तरुणातपं करुणया हरन्ती नृणा-
मभङ्गुरतनुत्विषां वलयिता शतैर्विद्युताम्।
कालिन्दगिरिनन्दिनीतटसुरद्रुमालम्बिनी
मदीयमतिचुम्बिनी भवतु कापि कादम्बिनी।। IV. 3

"Let the wonderful line of clouds taking its stand on the

divine trees on the banks of the Jumna, the daughter of Kalinda mountain encircled by hundreds of lightnings of parmanent lustre and removing the fresh troubles of men through compassion even when only remembered be the object of my contemplation"; Similarly in the following verse.

सन्त्येवास्मिञ्जगति बहवः पक्षिणो रम्यरूपाः
तेषां मध्ये मम तु महती वासना चातकेषु।
यैरध्यक्षैरथ निजसखं नीरजं स्मारयद्भिः
चित्तारूढं भवति किमपि ब्रह्म कृष्णाभिधानम्॥ IV. 17

There are many beautiful birds in this world; of them all I am greatly attached to the cātaka; for, it is through him that indescribable Brahman, which goes by the name Kṛṣṇa, finds its way into my mind'. That the very sight of the cātaka bird reminds him of the row of clouds, the saviours of their life, which again calls to his mind the charmful and lovely form of Lord Kṛṣṇa shows the wealth of his poetic fancy, as also his intense devotion to the commonly inaccessible feet of God.

Jagannātha employs a variety of metres. From the table appended at the end (P.) it will be seen.

Jagannātha was a poet of self-confidence. His confidence in his poetical skill is clearly expressed by him on many occassions. In one of his poems, he challenges all the contemporary poets.

आमूलाद् रत्नसानोर्मलयवलयितादा च कूलात्पयोधेः
यावन्तः सन्ति काव्यप्रणयनपटवस्ते विशङ्कं वदन्तु।
मृद्वीकामध्यनिर्यन्मसृणरसझरीमाधुरी भाग्यभाजां
वाचामाचार्यतायाः पदमनुभवितुं कोऽस्ति धन्यो मदन्यः॥ IV. 37

निर्माणे यदि मार्मिकोऽसि नितरामत्यन्तपाकद्रवन्-
मृद्वीकामधुमाधुरीमदपरीहारोद्धुराणां गिराम्।

काव्यं तर्हि सखे सुखेन कथय त्वं सम्मुखे मादृशां
नो चेद् दुष्कृतमात्मना कृतमिव स्वान्ताद् बहिर्मा कृथाः।। IV. 40

Jagannātha had a great command over language and he was a master of ornamental style and beautiful expression. He had composed verses where the sound is an echo to the sense.

Jagannātha shows his love for nature in its beautiful and sublime moods. He was a minute observer of Nature. He was proficient in the treatment of tender human feelings. The BV contains many verses those reach the high-water mark of tenderness and pathos. In his descriptions of Nature and of human feelings Jagannātha is conventional. He had concerned himself with the cooing of the cuckoo, the mango blossom, and the exciting influence of moon light etc.

Footnotes :

1. Acyutarāya's com. on Bhāminīvilāsa, p. 68.
2. Ramachandrudu, P., *The contribution of Paṇḍitarāja Jagannātha to Sanskrit Poetics,* Nirajana Publishers and Book sellers, Delhi, 1983, Vol. I, p. 18.
3. *Ibid.*, p. 18.
4. *Ibid.,* p. 24.
5. कोषः श्लोकसमूहस्तु स्यादन्योऽन्यानपेक्षकः।
   व्रज्याक्रमेण रचितः स एवातिमनोरमः।।
   Sāhityadarpaṇa, VI. 329-30
6. Keith, A.B., A History of Sanskrit Literature, p. 234.
7. Ramaswami Sastri, V.A. Jagannātha Paṇḍita, Annamalai University Sanskrit Series, No. 8 Annamalainagar, 1942, p. 66.
8. See his edition of the *Bhāminīvīlāsa*, 1985, introduction, pp. III-XII.
9. Vaidya, R.L. Ed. Bhāminīvilāsaḥ, 1887, Bombay; Introduction, p. 22.
10. p. 537
    रसभावौ तदाभासौ भावस्य प्रशमोदयौ।
    सन्धिः शबलता चेति सर्वेऽपि रसनाद्रसाः।।
    S.D. Op. cit. 3. 259.60.

शृङ्गार एव मधुरः वरः प्रह्लादनो रसः। DAL. 2.7
This verse is found in the Prāṇābharaṇa/Jagadābharaṇa. Pannṇḍitarāja-Jagannātha—Kāvyagranthāvalī, ed. by Hari Narayan Dikshit, p. 225.

11. श्रुतिमात्रेण शब्दात्तु येनार्थप्रत्ययो भवेत्।
साधारणः समग्राणां स प्रसादो गुणो मतः ।।
KP. 8.76.

12. श्लेषः प्रसादः समता माधुर्यं सुकुमारता।
अर्थव्यक्तिरुदारत्वमभोजः कान्तिसमाधयः।।
Kāvyādarśa I. 41

13. सति लिङ्गान्तरे यत्र स्त्रीलिङ्गञ्च प्रयुज्यते।
शोभानिष्पत्तये यस्मान्नामैव स्त्रीति पेशलम्।।
V.J. 2/22

14. रूपकातिशयोक्तिः स्यान्निगीर्याध्ववसानतः।
Kuvalayānanda.

भामिनीविलासे

(I)

प्रास्ताविकविलासः
(Prāstāvikavilāsaḥ)

I

प्रास्ताविकविलासः

(अन्योक्तिविलासः)

माधुर्यपरमसीमा सारस्वतजलधिमथनसम्भूता
पिबतामनल्पसुखदा वसुधायां मम सुधाकविता॥१॥

अन्वयः—मम सुधाकविता वसुधायां माधुर्यपरमसीमा, सारस्वत-जलधिमथनसम्भूता, पिबतामनल्पसुखदा, (च) (अस्ति)।

निधाय हृदि विश्वेशं नत्वा विद्यागुरून् गुरून्।
नानाग्रन्थान् समालोच्य पाठभेदान् विविच्य च॥१॥
यः पण्डितधुरीणेन जगन्नाथेन निर्मितः।
श्रीभामिनीविलासाख्यः प्रबन्धो भुवि विश्रुतः॥२॥
रसिकाल्हादजननं तं व्याख्यातुं यथामति।
यत्ते लक्ष्मणशर्माहं वैद्यवंशसमुद्भवः॥३॥
त्यज्यते नात्र दुर्बोधं नानपेक्षितमुच्यते।
काव्यमर्मप्रकाशाय परो यत्नो विधीयते॥४॥
दृष्टं किमपि लोकेस्मिन्न दोषपरिवर्जितम्।
तदत्र स्खलितं यत्तत्सहध्वं विबुधोत्तमाः॥५॥

पण्डितराजेन रसगङ्गाधरे

निर्माय नूतनमुदाहरणानुरूपं
काव्यं मयात्र निहितं न परस्य किञ्चित्।
किं सेव्यते सुमनसां मनसापि गन्धः
कस्तूरिकाजननशक्तिभृता मृगेण॥

इति ग्रन्थादौ कृतां प्रतिज्ञां परिपालयता ये सरसा नूतनाः श्लोका निर्मायोदाहरणतया निहिता अन्ये च ये स्फुटश्लोकाः प्रसङ्गवशाद्रचितास्तेषा-

मन्यैरात्मकृतत्वख्यापनपरिहारायैकत्र संकलनेनेदं विलासचतुष्टयात्मकमुत्कृष्टं भामिनीविलासाख्यं काव्यं निबद्धमित्यस्यैव काव्यस्यान्तिमपद्यादनुमीयते। अस्य प्रास्ताविकाख्ये प्रथमे विलासे प्रायोऽन्योक्तय एवैकत्र संकलिताः। अस्य विलासस्यान्योक्तिविलास इति यन्नाम केषुचित्पुस्तकेषु दृश्यते तदप्येतन्मूलकमेवेति भाति। प्रास्ताविकविलास इति नाम त्वन्येषां सुभाषित-श्लोकानामपीह सत्त्वादनुरूपतरम्। शृंगाराख्ये द्वितीये विलासे शृङ्गारप्रचुराणि करुणाख्ये तृतीये करुणरसप्रधानानि शान्ताख्ये चतुर्थे च शान्तरसोद्बोधकानीह पद्यानि निबद्धानि। काव्यस्य भामिनीविलास इति संज्ञा भामिन्याः स्वभार्याया विलासमुद्दिश्य कृतेति तारानाथशर्मणामभिप्रायः। वस्तुतस्तु संज्ञाबीजं न निश्चयेन ज्ञायत इत वक्तव्यम्।

व्याख्याः—पिबतां पानं कुर्वताम्। पिबतामित्यनेनान्यथान्वयासंभवात् सुधा कवितेति विशेषणसमास एव ग्राह्यः।

Eng.Tr.:-My nectarlike poem, the utmost limit of sweetness, produced by churning the ocean of literature, is the giver of great pleasure on this earth, to those who drink (peruse) it.

दिगन्ते श्रूयन्ते मदमलिनगण्डाः करटिनः
करिण्यः कारुण्यास्पदमसमशीलाः खलु मृगाः।
इदानीं लोकेऽस्मिन्ननुपमशिखानां पुनरयं
नखानां पाण्डित्यं प्रकटयतु कस्मिन् मृगपतिः॥२॥

अन्वयः—मदमलिनगण्डाः करटिनः दिगन्ते श्रूयन्ते, करिण्यः कारुण्या-स्पदं, मृगाः खलु असमशीलाः इदानीं पुनः अस्मिन् लोके अनुपमशिखानां नखानां पाण्डित्यं अयं मृगपतिः कस्मिन् प्रकटयतु।

व्याख्याः—इयमप्रस्तुतप्रशंसा यां जना अन्योक्तिं प्राहुः। अप्रस्तुतव्यवहारेण प्रस्तुतव्यवहारो यत्र वर्ण्यते साऽप्रस्तुतप्रशंसा। इयं पञ्चधा भवति। अप्रस्तुतेन प्रस्तुतं गम्यते यस्यामित्येका। कार्येण कारणमित्यपरा। कारणेन कार्यमिति तृतीया। सामान्येन विशेष इति चतुर्थी। विशेषेण सामान्यमिति पञ्चमी। अस्मिन् पद्ये स्ववृत्तान्त एव कविना प्रस्तुतत्वेन विवक्षित इति वदन्ति। करटिनो

दन्तिनः। दिगन्ते श्रूयन्त इत्यनेन तेषां पलायनं ध्वनितम्। कारुण्यास्पदत्वे स्त्रीत्वं हेतुः। असमशीला विषमस्वभावाः। तुच्छा इति यावत्। पाण्डित्यं विदारणरूपस्वकर्मकौशलम्।

Eng.Tr.:-Elephants with their temples soiled with ichor are heard (to have fled) to the end of the quarters; the female elephants are the objects of pity; while (other) beasts of prey stand no comparison in nature. Where should then, in this world this lord of beasts exhibit the skill of his claws, with their ends matchless (in sharpness)?

पुरा सरसि मानसे विकचसारसालिस्खलत्-
परागसुरभीकृते पयसि यस्य यातं[१] वयः।
स पल्वलजलेऽधुना मिलदनेकभेकाकुले
मरालकुलनायकः कथय रे कथं वर्तताम्?॥३॥

अन्वयः–पुरा यस्य वयः मानसे सरसि विकचसारसालिस्खलत्पराग-सुरभीकृते पयसि यातं सः मरालकुलनायकः अधुना मिलदनेकभेकाकुले पल्वलजले कथं वर्तताम्।

व्याख्याः–सारसालिः कमलपंक्तिः। भेको मण्डूकः। मरालो हंसः।

Eng.Tr.:-O, tell (me). How should the leader of the family of swans, who formerly passed his life in the lake, in the water scented by the pollens dropping from the rows of full-blown lotuses, now remain in the water of a puddle full of multitudinous frogs flocked together?

तृष्णालोलविलोचने कलयति प्राचीं चकोरीगणे
मौनं मुञ्चति किं च कैरवकुले कामे धनुर्धुन्वति।
माने मानवतीजनस्य सपदि प्रस्थातुकामे[२]ऽधुना
धातः। किं नु विधौ विधातुमुचितो धाराधराडम्बरः?॥४॥

---

१. 'वीतं' पाठान्तरम्।

२. 'प्रस्थानकामे' इति पाठान्तरम्।

अन्वयः—तृष्णालोलविलोचने चकोरीगणे प्राचीं कलयति (सति), किं च कैरवकुले मौनं मुञ्चति (सति), कामे धनुर्धुन्वति (सति), अधुना मानवतीजनस्य माने सपदि प्रस्थातुकामे (सति), हे धातः, विधौ धाराधराडम्बरः विधातुं उचितः किम्।

व्याख्याः—कलयतीत्यादि सत्सप्तम्यन्तम्। कलयति चन्द्रिकापानार्थं स्वीकुर्वति। मौनं मुञ्चति संकोचं त्यजति। कैरवं चन्द्रविकास्यः सितोत्पल-जातिविशेषः। धुन्वति टङ्कारयति। मानः पुरुषकृतापराध-प्रकाशकश्चेष्टाविशेषः। धाराधराडम्बरो मेघाच्छादनम्।

Eng. Tr.:-When the multitude of birds, with their eyes tremulous on account of thirst, look (eagerly) towards the east, when the assemblage of night lotuses gives up its silence (i.e. blows open), when the God of love shakes his bow (of course of flowers) and when the (amorous) pride of proud ladies is about to disappear, is it then, fit for a mass of clouds Creator! to begin to envelope the moon ?

अयि दलदरविन्द स्यन्दमानं मरन्दं
तव किमपि लिहन्तो मञ्जु गुञ्जन्तु भृङ्गाः।
दिशि दिशि निरपेक्षस्तावकीनं विवृण्वन्
परिमलमयमन्यो बान्धवो गन्धवाहः॥५॥

अन्वयः—अयि दलदरविन्द तव स्पन्दमानं मरन्दं लिहन्तः भृङ्गाः किमपि मञ्जु गुञ्जन्तु। तावकीनं परिमलं दिशि विवृण्वन् अयं अन्यः बान्धवः गन्धवाहः।

व्याख्याः—दलदरविन्द विकसितकमल। किमप्यनिर्वचनीयम्। अति-मधुरमित्यर्थः। अन्यस्त्वदीयरससेवनासक्तभ्रमरापेक्षया विलक्षणः। भ्रमराणां मकरन्दलाभेन कृत्रिमबन्धुत्वं भवेन्नाम। गन्धवाहस्य तूपकारलाभाभावेना-कृत्रिमबन्धुत्वमतिश्लाघ्यमिति भावः।

Eng. Tr.:-O blooming lotus, let the bees licking your trickling honey, hum anything melodiously. (But) this other i.e. the wind diffusing your fragrance in every direction, is your disinterested friend.

समुपागतवति दैवादवहेलां कुटज! मधुकरे मा गाः।
मकरन्दतुन्दिलानामरविन्दानामयं महामान्यः॥६॥

अन्वयः—हे कुटज, दैवात्समुपागतवति मधुकरे अवहेलां मा गाः। अयं (मधुकरः) मकरन्दतुन्दिलानां अरविन्दानां महामान्यः (अस्ति)।

व्याख्याः—मकरन्दतुन्दिलानां पुष्परसपरिपूरितानाम्।

Eng.Tr.:-When the bee approaches you, by chance, O Kuṭaja flower, do not disrespect him. (Because) he is highly honourd by the lotuses corpulent on account of honey.

तावत्कोकिल! विरसान् यापय दिवसान्वनान्तरे निवसन्।
यावन्मिलदलिमालः कोऽपि रसालः समुल्लसति॥७॥

अन्वयः—(हे) कोकिल यावद् मिलदलिमालः कोऽपि रसालः समुल्लसति तावत् वनान्तरे निवसन् (त्वं) विरसान् दिवसान् यापय।

व्याख्याः—विरसान् स्वाभिमतप्रयोजनशून्यान्। कथमपि कालक्षेपं कुर्विति भावार्थः। मिलदलिमालः संप्राप्तभ्रमरसंघः। रसालश्चूतवृक्षः।

Eng.Tr.:-Pass away the uninteresting days, O Cuckoo, dwelling in the heart of a forest (without cooing) until the mango tree with rows of bees flocking together, puts forth blossoms.

कमलिनि मलिनीकरोषि चेतः
किमिति! बकैरवहेलितानभिज्ञैः।
परिणतमकरन्दमार्मिकास्ते
जगति भवन्तु चिरायुषो मिलिन्दाः॥८॥

अन्वयः—(हे) कमलिनि, अनभिज्ञैः बकैः अवहेलिता इति (त्वं) चेतः किं मलिनीकरोषि। ये परिणतमकरंदमार्मिकाः मिलिन्दाः ते जगति चिरायुषो भवन्तु।

व्याख्याः–मलिनीकरोषि सखेदं करोषि। परिणतः परिपक्वः। मार्मिका मर्मज्ञाः। मिलिन्दा भ्रमराः। येषां रसिकत्वमेव नास्ति तेषामवहेलनया न कापि हानिरतो न खेदः कार्यः। ये मार्मिकास्ते चिरायुषश्चेत् त्वया सर्वमेव प्राप्तमिति तात्पर्यार्थः।

Eng.Tr.:-O lotus-plant! Why do you make your mind dejected because you are disrespected by the herons ? May the bees, the appreciators of your fully matured honey, live long in this world.

नितरां नीचोऽस्मीति त्वं खेदं कूप! मा कदापि कृथाः।
अत्यन्तसरसहृदयो यतः परेषां गुणग्रहीतासि॥९॥

अन्वयः–(हे) कूप, नितरां नीचोऽस्मीति त्वं मा कदापि खेदं कृथाः। यतः (त्वं) अत्यन्तसरसहृदयः परेषां गुणग्रहीता चासि।

व्याख्याः–नीचो निम्नो हीनश्च। सरसहृदयः सजलाभ्यन्तरः सरसान्तःकरणश्च। गुणः कलशाकर्षणरज्जुः कलाप्रावीण्यं च। श्लिष्टविशेषणेयमप्रस्तुतप्रशंसा।

Eng.Tr.:-O well, never give yourself up to sorrow with the thought, "I am exceedingly low (नीच)" because you have your bottom (हृदय) full of excessively sweet water (रस) and you accept (ग्रहीता) the rope (गुण) of others (in order to let the water be drawn up.)

येनामन्दमरन्दे दलदरविन्दे दिनान्यनायिषत।
कुटजे खलु तेनेहा तेने हा मधुकरेण कथम्॥१०॥

अन्वयः–येन मधुकरेण अमन्दमरन्दे दलदरविन्दे दिनान्यनायिषत तेन (एव मधुकरेण) हा! कुटजे खलु ईहा कथं तेने।

व्याख्याः–अमन्दमरन्दे परिपूर्णमकरन्दे। हा तेन मधुकरेण कुटजे कथमीहा तेने इत्यन्वयः। ईहा स्पृहा। तेने चक्रे।

Eng.Tr.:-Alas! How did the bee who passed his days in

a full-blown lotus, containing a great deal of honey, cherish indeed a longing for a कुटज flower ?

अयि मलयज! महिमायं कस्य गिरामस्तु विषयस्ते।
उद्गिरतो यद्गरलं फणिनः पुष्णासि परिमलोद्गारैः॥११॥

अन्वयः–अयि मलयज अयं ते महिमा कस्य गिरां विषयः अस्तु, यत् (त्वं) परिमलोद्गारैः गरलम् उद्गिरतः फणिनः पुष्टिं पुष्णासि।

व्याख्याः–कस्य गिरां विषयोस्तु। न कस्यापीत्यर्थः। परिमलोद्गारैगन्ध-विशेषप्रवाहैः। विषं वमतो सर्पानपि स्वगन्धेन तर्पयसीत्यहो ते महिमेत्यर्थः।

Eng. Tr.:-O sandal, who can describe your this greatness? (lit. of whose speech can this your greatness be the subject?), since you nourish the cobras vomitting out poison, by the outpourings of your fragrance.

पाटीर! तव पटीयान्कः परिपाटीमिमामुरीकर्तुम्।
यत्पिंषतामपि नृणां पिष्टोऽपि तनोषि परिमलैः पुष्टिम्॥१२॥

अन्वयः–हे पाटीर इमां तव परिपाटीं उरीकर्तुम् कः पटीयान् यत् पिष्टः अपि त्वं पिंषतामपि नृणां परिमलैः पुष्टिं तनोषि।

व्याख्याः–पाटीरं चन्दन। परिपाटीं रीतिम्। उरीकर्तुं स्वीकर्तुम्। पिषतां चूर्णयताम्। धर्षयतामिति यावत्। अस्य तात्पर्यार्थस्तु (११) पद्यस्येव।

Eng. Tr.:-O Sandal, who is clever in imitating this your conduct, that you gratify with your fragrance even those persons who grind you, although you are ground by them.

नीरक्षीरविवेके हंसालस्यं[१] त्वमेव तनुषे चेत्।
विश्वस्मिन्नधुनाऽन्यः कुलव्रतं पालयिष्यति कः?॥१३॥

अन्वयः–(हे) हंस नीरक्षीरविके त्वमेव आलस्यं तनुषे चेत् अधुना विश्वस्मिन् कः अन्यः कुलव्रतं पालयिष्यति।

व्याख्याः–विवके विवेचने। पृथक्करण इति यावत्। त्वमेवेत्येव-

---

१. 'हंसालमालस्यम्' इति पाठान्तरम्।

कारेणेतरस्य विवेकित्वं नास्तीति सूच्यते। विश्वस्मिन् त्रैलोक्ये। कुलव्रतं तवेति शेषः।

Eng.Tr.:-O swan! if you yourself become lazy in differentiating between water and milk, who else in the world, now, will observe this vow, handed down from generation to generation?

उपरि करवालधाराकाराः क्रूरा भुजङ्गमपुङ्गवाः[१]।
अन्तः साक्षाद् द्राक्षादीक्षागुरवो जयन्ति केऽपि जनाः॥१४॥

अन्वयः—उपरि करवालधाराकाराः भुजङ्गमपुङ्गवात् क्रूराः अन्तः साक्षाद् द्राक्षादीक्षागुरवः केऽपि जनाः जयन्ति।

व्याख्याः—उपरि बहिः। करवालधाराकाराः खड्गधारावत्तीक्ष्णाः। भुजङ्गमपुङ्गवान्महाभुजङ्गमात्। द्राक्षाया दीक्षायाः शीतलत्वमाधुर्यादिरूपाया गुरव उपदेष्टारः। केप्यनिर्वचनीयमहिमानः उल्लेखालंकारोयमुपमाव्यातिरेकाभ्यां तयोः समुच्चयेन च संकीर्णः।

Eng.Tr.:-A victory to persons of indescribable greatness whose external form is like the edge of a sword, and who are more frightful than huge snakes, but who are at heart preceptors, evidently initiating grapes in sweetness.

स्वच्छन्दं दलदरविन्द! ते मरन्दं
विन्दन्तो विदधतु गुञ्जितं मिलिन्दाः।
आमोदानथ हरिदन्तराणि नेतुं
नैवान्यो जगति समीरणात्प्रवीणः॥१५॥

अन्वयः—हे दलदरविन्द ते मरन्दं स्वच्छन्दं विन्दन्तः मिलिन्दाः गुञ्जतं विदधतु। अथ जगति आमोदान् हरिदन्तराणि नेतुं समीरणात् अन्यः नैव प्रवीणः।

व्याख्याः—मिलिन्दा भ्रमराः। हरिदन्तराणि दिगन्तराणि। अयं श्लोकः (५) पद्येन समानार्थकः।

---

१. 'भुजङ्गमपुङ्गवात्' इति पाठान्तरम्।

Eng.Tr.:-O full-blown lotus, let the bees enjoying your honey at their own pleasure make a humming sound. But, in the world, none other than wind is well-versed in conveying (your) fragrance to different quarters.

याते मय्यचिरान्निदाघमिहिरज्वालाशतैः शुष्कतां
गन्ता कं प्रति पान्थसन्ततिरसौ संतापमालाकुला।
एवं यस्य निरन्तराधिपटलैर्नित्यं वपुः क्षीयते
धन्यं जीवनमस्य मार्गसरसो धिग्वारिधीनां जनुः॥१६॥

अन्वयः–निदाघमिहिरज्वालाशतैः अचिरात् शुष्कतां याते मयि संतापमालाकुला असौ पान्थसंततिः कं प्रति गन्ता एवं निरंतराधिपटलैः नित्यं यस्य वपुः क्षीयते अस्य मार्गसरसः जीवनं धन्यम्, धिग् वारिधीनां जनुः।

व्याख्या:–निदाघमिहिरो ग्रीष्मसूर्यः। गन्ता गमिष्यति। आधिर्मानसी व्यथा। जीवनं जीवितं जलं च।

Eng.Tr.:-Blessed is the existence of this lake on the road, whose body is always growing emaciated on account of great constant mental anguish. When I shall be soon dried up by the hundreds of rays of the summer-sun, to whom will this crowd of travellers, oppressed with excessive heat, go? Fie upon the life of oceans.

आपेदिरेऽम्बरपथं परितः पतङ्गा
भृङ्गा रसालकुसुमानि समाश्रयन्ते[1]।
संकोचमञ्चति सरस्त्वयि दीनदीनो[2]
मीनो नु हन्त कतमां गतिमभ्युपैतु॥१७॥

अन्वयः–हे सरः त्वयि संकोचमञ्चति पतङ्गाः परितः अम्बरपथं आपेदिरे भृङ्गाः रसालकुसुमानि समाश्रयन्ते, हन्त दीनदीनो मीनः कतमां नु गतिम् अभ्युपैतु।

---

१. 'समाश्रयन्ति' इति पाठान्तरम्।

२. 'दीनदीने' इति पाठान्तरम्।

व्याख्या:—आपेदिरे पूर्वमेव गता:। पतङ्गा पक्षिण:। रसाल आम्र:। संकोचमञ्चति शुष्कत्वं याति। दीनदीनोत्यन्तदीन:।

Eng.Tr.:-O lake! when you would be dried up, the birds around might have recourse to the aerial path, the bees might resort to the mango-blossoms, but alas! to what plight would the miserable fish be reduced?

मधुप इव मारुतेऽस्मिन्मा सौरभलोभमम्बुजिनि[१]! मंस्था:।
लोकानामेव मुदे महितोऽप्यात्मामुनार्थितान्नीत:॥१८॥

अन्वय:—हे अम्बुजिनि मधुपे इव अस्मिन् मारुते सौरभलोभं मा अमंस्था:, अमुना मारुतेन लोकानामेव मुदे महित: अपि आत्मा अर्थितां नीत:।

व्याख्या:—अम्बुजिनि कमलिनि। महित: श्रेष्ठ:। अर्थितां नीतो याचकतां प्रापित:। लघुत्वं स्वीकृतमिति यावत्। परोपकारायैवायं त्वां सौरभं याचते न लोभादित्यर्थ:।

Eng. Tr:-O Lotus, (1) Don't consider that there is greed for fragrance in this wind like that in the bee. (2) Don't be greedy in giving your fragrance to the wind as you do when you give it to the bee; for though highly renowned, he has stooped to mendicancy for the pleasure of the people alone (i.e. his desire is not selfish).

गुञ्जति मञ्जु मिलिन्दे मा मालति! मौनमुपयासी:[२]।
शिरसा वदान्यगुरव: सादरमेनं वहन्ति सुरतरव:॥१९॥

अन्वय:—हे मालति मिलिन्दे मञ्जु गुञ्जति मौनं मा उपयासी:। एनं वदान्यगुरव: सुरतरव: शिरसा सादरं वहन्ति।

व्याख्या:—मौनमप्रफुल्लीभावं मूकभावं च। वदान्यगुरवो दातृश्रेष्ठा:।

Eng.Tr.:-O मालति flower! do not keep silence (i.e. do not remain closed) when the bee is melodiously humming, (because) the celestial trees, the foremost among the generous, bear him respectfully on their heads.

---

१. 'अम्बुज! निमंस्था:' इति पाठान्तरम्।

२. 'मालति! मानमौनमुपयासी:' इति पाठान्तरम्।

यैस्त्वं गुणगणवानपि सतां द्विजिह्वैरसेव्यतां नीतः।
तानपि वहसि पटीरज! किं कथयामस्त्वदीयमौन्नत्यम्॥२०॥

अन्वयः—हे पटीरज, यैः द्विजिह्वैः गुणगणवानपि त्वं सतां असेव्यतां नीतः तानपि (द्विजिह्वान्) वहसि (एतद्) त्वदीयं औन्नत्यं किं कथयामः।

व्याख्या:—द्विजिह्वैः सर्पैः। पिशुनैरिति च गम्यते। पटीरज चन्दनतरो।

Eng.Tr.:-O sandal tree! what to talk of the nobility of yours, since you give resort even to those very serpents (traducers-backbiters by whom, you though possessed of a host of qualities, are rendered incapable of being resorted to by the good ! (i.e. your nobility is beggars description).

गाहितमखिलं गहनं[1] परितो दृष्टाश्च विटपिनः सर्वे।
सहकार न प्रपेदे मधुपेन भवत्समं[2] जगति॥२१॥

अन्वयः—हे सहकार मधुपेन अखिलं गहनं गाहितं, परितः सर्वे विटपिनश्च दृष्टाः (किन्तु) भवत्समं जगति न (किञ्चिदपि) प्रपेदे।

व्याख्या:—गाहितं विचितम्। गहनं वनम्।

Eng.Tr.:-The whole wilderness was investigated, all the trees around were observed, but, O mango tree ! the bee did not come across one like you in the world.

अपनीतपरिमलान्तरकथे पदं न्यस्य देवतरुकुसुमे।
पुष्पान्तरेऽपि गन्तुं वाञ्छसि चेद् भ्रमर! धन्योऽसि॥२२॥

अन्वयः—हे भ्रमर अपनीतपरिमलान्तरकथे देवतरुकुसुमे पदं न्यस्य पुष्पान्तरेऽपि गन्तुं वाञ्छसि चेत्, धन्योऽसि।

व्याख्या:—अपनीता दूरीकृता परिमलान्तरकथा येन तस्मिन्। धन्योसीत्युपालम्भः। पुष्पान्तरं वाञ्छसि चेद्धिक् त्वामिति भावः।

Eng.Tr.:-O bee! how discriminate (indiscriminate) you are, if you desire to go yet to another flower, after having

१. 'विश्वं' और 'विपिनं' इति पाठान्तरम्।
२. 'तथापि ते समं जगति' इति पाठान्तरम्।

stepped on (enjoyed) the flower of a celestial tree, which has removed the talk of any other fragrance. i.e. whose fragrance is unrivalled.

तटिनि! चिराय विचारय विन्ध्यभुवस्तव पवित्रायाः।
शुष्यन्त्या अपि युक्तं किं खलु रथ्योदकादानम्॥२३॥

अन्वयः—हे तटिनि चिराय विचारय, शुष्यन्त्या अपि विन्ध्यभुवः पवित्रायाः तव रथ्योदकादानं खलु युक्तं किम्।

व्याख्याः—विन्ध्यभुवो विन्ध्यपर्वतप्रसूताया अत एव पवित्रायाः।

Eng.Tr.:-O river! think for a long time (i. e. well) whether it is indeed proper for you, who are sacred because of your rise in the विन्ध्य mountain, to receive street water, even though you are dried up ?

पत्रफलपुष्पलक्ष्म्या कदाप्यदृष्टं वृतं च खलु शूकैः।
उपसर्पेम भवन्तं बर्बुर[1]! वद कस्य लोभेन॥२४॥

अन्वयः—हे बर्बुर पत्रफलपुष्पलक्ष्म्या कदाप्यदृष्टं, शूकैः च खलु वृतं भवन्तं वद कस्य लोभेन उपसर्पेम।

व्याख्याः—शूकैः कण्टकैर्वृतं व्याप्तम्। बर्बुरो बाभली इति प्रसिद्धो वृक्षः।

Eng.Tr.:-O बर्बुर tree ! say with what attraction should we approach you, who are never seen possessed of the beauty of leaves, fruits and flowers, but are covered with thorns.

एकस्त्वं गहनेऽस्मिन्कोकिल न कलं कदाचिदपि कुर्याः।
साजात्यशङ्कयाऽमी न त्वां निघ्नन्ति[2] निर्दयाः काकाः॥२५॥

अन्वयः—हे कोकिल, अस्मिन् गहने त्वं एकः कदाचिदपि कलं न कुर्याः (येन) अमी निर्दयाः काकाः साजात्यशङ्कया त्वां न निघ्नन्ति।

व्याख्याः—कलं मधुररावम्। साजात्यशङ्कया सजातीयोयमस्माकमिति धिया। कलं करोषि चेद् वैजात्यं ज्ञात्वा त्वामिमे हन्युरेवेत्यर्थः।

---

१. 'बर्बर' इति पाठान्तरम्।

२. 'निघ्नन्तु' इति पाठान्तरम्।

Eng.Tr.:-O cuckoo! you, while alone in the forest, should never utter sweet notes so that these merciless crows may not slay you, mistaking you to be one of their own kind.

तरुकुलसुषमापहरां जनयन्तीं जगति जीवजातार्तिम्।
केन गुणेन भवानीतात! हिमानीमिमां वहसि?॥२६॥

अन्वयः—हे भवानीतात तरुकुलसुषमापहरां, जगति जीवजातार्तिं जनयन्तीं, इमां हिमानीं केन गुणेन वहसि?

व्याख्याः—सुषमा शोभा। जीवजातार्तिं प्राणिसमूहपीडाम्। भवानीतात हिमालय। हिमानीं हिमसंहतिम् न तवेदमुचितमिति भावः।

Eng.Tr.:-O father of पार्वती, for what attraction, do you bear this mass of snow, which in this world, mars the beauty of the collection of trees and which inflicts pain on all living beings?

कलभ! तवान्तिकमागतमलिमेनं मा कदाप्यवज्ञासीः।
अपि दानसुन्दराणां द्विपधुर्याणामयं शिरोधार्यः॥२७॥

अन्वयः—हे कलभ तव अन्तिकं आगतं एतं अलिं कदापि मा अवज्ञासीः दानसुन्दराणां द्विपधुर्याणां अपि अयं (अलिः) शिरोधार्यः (विद्यते)।

व्याख्याः—कलभ गजशिशो। द्विपधुर्या गजश्रेष्ठाः।

Eng.Tr.:-O young elephant, never disregard the bee that has approached you, (for) he is to be borne on the head, even by the foremost of elephants, adorned with rut.

अमरतरुकुसुमसौरभसेवनसम्पूर्णसकलकामस्य।
पुष्पान्तरसेवेयं भ्रमरस्य विडम्बना महती॥२८॥

अन्वयः—अमरतरुकुसुमसौरभसेवनसम्पूर्णकलकामस्य भ्रमरस्य इयं पुष्पान्तरसेवा महती विडम्बना।

व्याख्याः—इदं पद्यं (२२) पद्येन समानार्थकम्।

Eng.Tr.:-This resorting to another flower of a bee, all of whose wishes are completely fulfilled by the enjoyment to fragrance of flowers of the celestial trees, is a matter of great ridicule.

पृष्टाः खलु परपुष्टाः परितो दृष्टाश्च विटपिनः सर्वे।
माकन्द न प्रपेदे मधुपेन तवोपमा जगति॥२९॥

अन्वयः—हे माकन्द परपुष्टाः खलु पृष्टाः परितः च सर्वे विटपिनो दृष्टाः (किन्तु) मधुपेन तव उपमा जगति न प्रपेदे।

व्याख्याः—परपुष्टाः कोकिलाः। इदं (२१) पद्येन समानार्थकम्।

Eng.Tr.:-Indeed cuckoos are inquired of, all the trees around are observed, but nothing equal to you, O mango tree, is met with by the bee.

तोयैरल्पैरपि करुणया भीमभानौ निदाघे
मालाकार! व्यरचि भवता या तरोरस्य पुष्टिः।
[1]सा किं शक्या जनयितुमिह प्रावृषेण्येन वारां
धारासारानपि विकिरता विश्वतो वारिदेन॥३०॥

अन्वयः—हे मालाकार अस्य तरोः या पुष्टिः भवता अल्पैः अपि तोयैः भीमभानौ निदाघे करुणया व्यरचि, सा वारां धारासारानपि विश्वतः विकिरता प्रावृषेण्येन वारिदेन जनयितुं शक्या किम् ?

व्याख्याः—अल्पैस्तोयैरर्थात् कूपाद्युद्धृतैः। भीमो भानुर्यस्मिन् तस्मिन्निदाघे ग्रीष्मे। प्रावृषेण्येन वर्षाकालिकेन। विश्वतः सर्वतः।

Eng.Tr.:-Is it possible here for the rainy cloud, which sprinkles down all around, even heavy showers of water, to bring about that nourishment in this tree which is effected by you, O gardener! with tenderness, with even a little water in summer when the sun was scorching ?

आरामाधिपतिर्विवेकविकलो नूनं रसा नीरसा
वात्याभिः परुषीकृता दशदिशश्चण्डातपो दुःसहः।

१. 'किञ्चिन्मात्रम्' इति पाठान्तरम्।

एवं धन्वनि चम्पकस्य सकले संहारहेतावपि
त्वं सिञ्चन्नमृतेन तोयद! कुतोऽप्याविष्कृतो वेधसा॥३१॥

अन्वयः—नूनं आरामधिपतिः विवेकविकलः, रसा नीरसा, दशदिशः वात्याभिः परुषीकृताः, चण्डातपः दुःसहः, एवं धन्वनि चंपकस्य सकले संहारहेतौ अपि, हे तोयद, अमृतेन सिञ्चन् त्वं वेधसा कुतोऽप्याविष्कृतः।

व्याख्या:—वात्याभिर्वातसमूहैः। धन्वनि मरुभूमौ। अमृतेन जलेन।

Eng.Tr.:-Indeed, the keeper of the garden is thoughtless, the earth is void of moisture, the ten quarters are rendered dusty by gusts of wind, and the scorching heat is unbearable, thus even though all these are the reasons for the destruction of the चंपक in the barren land, you O cloud! sprinkling it with water (nectar) are manifested by Brahma, from an unexpected quarter.

न यत्र स्थेमानं दधुरतिभयभ्रान्तनयना
गलद्दानोद्रेकभ्रमदलिकदम्बाः करटिनः।
लुठन्मुक्ताभारे भवति परलोकं गतवतो
हरेरद्य द्वारे शिव शिव शिवानां कलकलः॥३२॥

अन्वयः—यत्र (द्वारे) अतिभयभ्रान्तनयनाः गलद्दानोद्रेकभ्रमदलिकदम्बाः करटिनः स्थेमानं न दधुः (तत्र) परलोकं गतवतः हरेः, (पुरा) लुठन्मुक्ताभारे द्वारे, अद्य शिव शिव ! शिवानां कलकलः भवति।

व्याख्या:—यत्र यस्मिन् द्वारे। स्थेमानं स्थिरत्वम्। गलदानं स्रवन्मदोदकं तस्योद्रेकोतिशयस्तेन भ्रमन्तोलिकदम्बा भ्रमरसंघा येषु तथा विधाः। हरेर्द्वारे शिवानां कलकलो भवतीत्यन्वयः। शिव शिवेति खेदे।

Eng.Tr.:-Alas ! today the female jackals are howling near the door of the dead lion, where myriads of pearls are rolling, where formerly elephants whose eyes were tremulous owing to excessive fear and around whose temples dripping with excessive ichor, the bees were hovering did not dare to stand steadily.

दधानः प्रेमाणं तरुषु समभावेन विपुलां[१]
न मालाकारोऽसावकृत करुणां बालबकुले।
अयन्तु द्रागुद्यत्कुसुमनिकराणां परिमलै-
र्दिगन्तानातेने मधुपकुलझङ्कारभरितान्॥३३॥

अन्वयः–तरुषु समभावेन प्रेमाणं दधानः असौ मालाकारः बालबकुले विपुलां करुणां न अकृत, तु अयं (बालबकुलः) द्रागुद्यत्कुसुमनिकराणां परिमलैः दिगन्तान् मधुपकुलझङ्कारभरितानातेने।

व्याख्या:–तरुषु स्वीयेष्विति शेषः। बालबकुले विपुलां करुणां नाकृतेत्यन्वयः। द्राग् झटिति। उद्यतामुदयं प्राप्नुवतां कुसुमानां निकराः समूहास्तेषाम्। झङ्कारो गुञ्जारवः।

Eng. Tr.:-Loving all the trees impartially, the gardener did not show much (special) compassion towards the young बकुल plant. still, it filled the ends of quarters with the humming of the clusters of bees with collections of flowers quickly springing from it.

मूलं स्थूलमतीव बन्धनदृढं शाखाः शतं मांसला
वासो दुर्गमहीधरे तरुपते! कुत्रास्ति भीतिस्तव?।
एकः किन्तु मनागयं जनयति स्वान्ते ममाधिज्वरं
ज्वालालीवलयीभवन्नकरुणो दावानलो घस्मरः॥३४॥

अन्वयः–हे तरुपते मूलं बन्धनदृढं अतीव स्थूलं, शतं शाखाः मांसलाः, दुर्गमहीधरे वासः तव भीतिः कुत्रास्ति; किन्तु अयं एकः ज्वालालीवलयीभवन् अकरुणः घस्मरः दावानलः मम स्वान्ते मनाग् आधिज्वरं जनयति।

व्याख्या:–शतमित्युपलक्षणम्। तेन बह्व्य इत्यर्थः। मांसलाः पुष्टाः। दुर्गमहीधरे दुर्गमपर्वते। तव भीतिः कुत्रास्ति। यन्निमित्ता भीतिस्तन्न पश्याम इत्यर्थः। एकः केवलः। मनागीषत्। आधिज्वरं चिन्तातापम्। ज्वालाली-वलयीभवनं ज्वालामण्डलरूप इत्यर्थः। घस्मरो भक्षकः।

१. 'विपुलम्' इति पाठान्तरम्।

Eng.Tr.:-The big trunk is firmly strengthened by roots, the many (hundred) branches are massive, your situation is on a mountain difficult to ascend, O lord of trees whence is the danger to you ? But only the voracious relentless conflagration forming circles of the collections of flames, produces a little fever in the form of mental agony, in my mind.

ग्रीष्मे भीष्मतरैः करैर्दिनकृता दग्धोऽपि यश्चातक-
स्त्वां ध्यायन् घन! वासरान् कथमपि द्राघीयसो नीतवान्।
दैवाल्लोचनगोचरेण भवता तस्मिन्निदानीं यदि
स्वीचक्रे करकानिपातनकृपा तत्कं प्रति ब्रूमहे?॥३५॥

अन्वयः—हे घनग्रीष्मे भीष्मतरैः करैः दिनकृता दग्धः अपि यः चातकः त्वां ध्यायन् द्राघीयसः वासरान् कथमपि नीतवान्। इदानीं दैवात् लोचनगोचरेण भवता तस्मिन् यदि करकानिपातनकृपा स्वीचक्रे तत् कं प्रति ब्रूमहे।

व्याख्याः—दिनकृता सूर्येण। द्राघीयसो दीर्घतरान्। करका वर्षेपलः। कृपेति सोल्लुण्ठम्। तेन निर्दयत्वमित्यर्थः।

Eng. Tr.:-O cloud! the चातक bird though scorched with terrible rays in the summer, passed with great difficulty the long days, contemplating on you now that you who have fallen in the range of his sight through his good luck, took to kindness (cruelty) of showering hailstones on him; with whom shall we lodge a complaint ?

दवदहनजटालज्वालजालाहतानां
परिगलितलतानां म्लायतां भूरुहाणाम्।
अयि जलधर! शैलश्रेणिशृङ्गेषु तोयं
वितरसि बहु कोऽयं श्रीमदस्तावकीनः?॥३६॥

अन्वयः—दव....हतानां परिगलितलतानां भूरुहाणां म्लायतां सतां, अयि जलधर शैलश्रेणिशृङ्गेषु बहु तोयं वितरसि, कोऽयं तावकीनः श्रीमदः?

व्याख्याः—जटालः संघीभूतः। ज्वालो ज्वाला। भूरुहाणां म्लायतां सतामित्यन्वयः। इयमनादरे षष्ठी। तेन म्लानीभवतो वृक्षाननादृत्येत्यर्थः। श्रीमदो जलसम्पत्तिमदः। लक्ष्मीमद इत्यपि ध्वन्यते।

Eng.Tr.:-What sort of pride in abundance of water, is this of yours, that you pour, O cloud, a great deal of water, on the summits of the series of mountains although the trees that are struck by the net-work of flames gathering together from the forest-conflagration,—trees, whose encircling creepers are dropped down and which consequently fade away?

शृण्वन् पुरः परुषगर्जितमस्य हन्त
रे पान्थ! विह्वलमना[१] न मनागपि स्याः।
विश्वार्तिवारणसमर्पितजीवनोऽयं[२]
नाकर्णितः किमु सखे! भवताम्बुवाहः?॥३७॥

अन्वयः—रे पान्थ पुरः अस्य परुषगर्जितं शृण्वन् हन्त मनाक् अपि विह्वलमनाः न स्याः। सखे विश्वार्तिवारणसमर्पितजीवनः अयं अम्बुवाहः भवता न आकर्णितः किमु ?

व्याख्या:—विश्वार्तिवारणाय समर्पितं जीवनं येन तथाविधः। जीवनं जलं जीवितं च। भवतायं विश्वार्तिवारणसमर्पितजीवनो नाकर्णितः किमित्यन्वयः। अस्योपकृतय एव गर्जितत्वमिति भावः।

Eng.Tr.:-O traveller, hearing the harsh thundering of the cloud before you, alas ! do not be in the least melancholy, O friend, has not this cloud, who devoted all his water (life) in allaying the distresses of the world, been heard of by you ?

सौरभ्यं भुवनत्रयेऽपि विदितं शैत्यं तु लोकोत्तरं
कीर्तिः किं च दिगङ्गनाङ्गणगता किन्त्वेतदेकं शृणु।
सर्वानेव गुणानियं निगिरति श्रीखण्ड! ते सुन्दरा-
नुज्झन्ती खलु कोटरेषु गरलज्वालां द्विजिह्वावली॥३८॥

अन्वयः—सौरभ्यं भुवनत्रयेऽपि विदितं, तु शैत्यं लोकोत्तरं, किं च कीर्तिः दिगंगनांगणगता, किंत्वेतत् एकं शृणु, हे श्रीखण्ड, कोटरेषु खलु

---

१. 'विस्मितमना' इति पाठान्तरम्।
२. "०जीवितोऽयम्" इति पाठान्तरम्।

गरलज्वालां उज्झन्ती इयं द्विजिह्वावली, सर्वान् एव ते सुन्दरान् गुणान् निगिरति।

व्याख्या:–तु निश्चयेन निगिरत्युद्वमति। लोपयतीति यावत्। श्रीखण्ड चन्दन।

Eng. Tr.:- O sandal tree! your fragrance is known even to the three worlds, extra-ordinary is your cooling power and your fame has reached the courtyard of women in the form of direction, but listen to one thing. This row of serpents, giving out indeed flames of venom in your hollows, swallows up all your merits.

नापेक्षा न च दाक्षिण्यं न प्रीतिर्न च सङ्गतिः।
तथापि हरते तापं लोकानामुन्नतो घनः॥३९॥

अन्वय:–न अपेक्षा, न च दाक्षिण्यम् न प्रीतिः, न च सङ्गतिः तथापि उन्नतः घनः लोकानां तापं हरते।

व्याख्या:–अपेक्षा प्रत्युपकारादिवाञ्छा। दाक्षिण्यमानुकूल्यम्। तथाप्य-पेक्षादितापहरणहेत्वभावेऽपि। उन्नत उच्चदेशस्थित उदारप्रकृतिश्च।

Eng.Tr.:-There is no expectation (in return), no (consciousness of) courtesy, no love (for people) nor acquaintance, yet the high—soaring cloud (the magnanimous person) removes the heat (worries) of the people.

समुत्पत्तिः स्वच्छे सरसि हरिहस्ते निवसति[१]**–**
र्निवासः पद्मायाः सुरहृदयहारी परिमलः।
गुणैरेतैरन्यैरपि च ललितस्याम्बुज तव
द्विजोत्तंसे हंसे यदि रतिरतीवोन्नतिरियम्॥४०॥

अन्वय:–हे अम्बुज (तव) स्वच्छे सरसि समुत्पत्तिः हरिहस्ते निवसतिः, (त्वं) पद्मायाः निवासः, (तव) परिमलः सुरहृदयहारी, एतैरन्यैरपि च गुणैः ललितस्य द्विजोत्तंसे हंसे यदि रतिः स्यात् (तर्हि) इयं तव अतीवोन्नतिः।

---

१. 'निवसनं' इति पाठान्तरम्।

व्याख्या:—हरिहस्ते विष्णुहस्ते सूर्यकरे वा। निवासो वासस्थानभूतत्वम्। ललितस्य मण्डितस्य। द्विजोत्तंसे पक्षिश्रेष्ठे। ब्राह्मणवर इति च ध्वन्यते। अतीवोन्नतिः परं माहात्म्यम्।

Eng.Tr.:-O lotus, you are born in a pure pond, your abode is the hand of Hari, you are the residence of Laxmi, your fragrance captivates the hearts (even) of Gods, if you—who are adorned by these and other qualities-love a swan-the best of brids—it is the zenith of your greatness.

साकं ग्रावगणैर्लुठन्ति मणयस्तीरेऽर्कबिम्बोपमा
नीरे नीरचरैः समं स भगवान्निद्राति नारायणः।
एवं वीक्ष्य तवाविवेकमपि च प्रौढिं परामुन्नतेः
किं निन्दान्यथवा स्तवानि कथय क्षीरार्णव! त्वामहम्॥४१॥

अन्वयः—ग्रावगणैः साकं अर्कबिम्बोपमाः मणयः तीरे लुठन्ति, नीरचरैः समं प्रौढिं अपि च वीक्ष्य, हे क्षीरार्णव, त्वां अहं किं निन्दानि अथवा स्तवानि।

व्याख्या:—महान्तोपिक्षीरार्णवमाश्रयन्त इति तस्यौन्नत्यम्। स तु यथोचितोपचारं न करोतीत्यविवेकिता।

Eng.Tr.:-On the banks, the jewels resembling the orb of the moon are rolling with the multitudes of stones; in the water is resting the भगवान् नारायण, with the aquatic animals; thus seeing, O milk—ocean, your thoughtlessness, and the zenith of your greatness, should I praise or censure you?

किं खलु रत्नैरेतैः किं पुनरभ्रायितेन वपुषा ते।
सलिलमपि यन्न तावकमर्णव! वदनं प्रयाति तृषितानाम्॥४२॥

अन्वयः—हे अर्णव एतैः रत्नैः खलु किम्, पुनः ते अभ्रायितेन वपुषा किम्, यत् तावकं सलिलं अपि तृषितानां वदनं न प्रयाति।

व्याख्या:—अभ्रायितेनाभ्रवन्नीलेन।

Eng.Tr.:-O sea, indeed, what is the use of these jewels? What is the use of your body like the sky, in as much as your water does not reach the mouth of the thirsty (i.e. they cannot drink your water?)

इयत्यां सम्पत्तावपि च सलिलानां त्वमधुना
न तृष्णामार्तानां हरसि यदि कासार! सहसा।
निदाघे चण्डांशौ किरति परितोऽङ्गारनिकरान्
कृशीभूतः केषामहह! परिहर्तासि खलु ताम्॥४३॥

अन्वयः—हे कासार! यदि त्वम् अधुना सलिलानाम् इयत्यां सम्पत्तौ अपि च आर्तानाम् तृष्णां सहसा न हरसि (तर्हि) निदाघे चण्डांशौ परितः अङ्गानिकरम् किरति कृषिभूतः अहह केषां ताम् खलु परिहर्तासि।

व्याख्याः—कासार सरोवर। तां तृष्णाम्।

Eng.Tr.:-O lake, if you do not at once quench the thirst of the thirsty (lit. distressed) even though now you have so much wealth of water, alas ! whose thirst indeed will you remove, being dried up, when in summer the hot-rayed one (the sun) will diffuse around (his rays as hot as) burning charcoal ?

अयि रोषमुरीकरोषि नो चेत्
किमपि त्वां प्रति वारिधे! वदामः।
जलदेन तवार्थिना विमुक्ता-
न्यपि तोयानि महान्[१] न हा जहासि॥४४॥

अन्वयः—अयि वारिधे (त्वं) रोषं नो उरीकरोषि चेत् त्वां प्रति किमपि वदामः हा महान् (त्वं) तव अर्थिना जलदेन विमुक्तानि अपि तोयानि न जहासि।

व्याख्याः—अपिर्भिन्नक्रमः। तेन महानपीत्यन्वयः। हेति खेदे।

Eng.Tr.:-O sea ! we shall speak to you something if you do not get angry. Alas ! you though great do not give up even those waters that have been showered by the cloud, who is your suppliant.

---

१. 'मनाङ्' इति पाठान्तरम्।

न वारयामो भवतीं विशन्तीं वर्षानदि! स्त्रोतसि जह्नुजायाः।
न युक्तमेतत्तु पुरो यदस्यास्तरङ्गभङ्गान् प्रकटीकरोषि॥४५॥

अन्वयः—हे वर्षानदि जह्नुजायाः स्त्रोतसि विशंतीं भवतीं न वारयामः एतत्तु तव न युक्तं यदस्याः पुरः तरङ्गभङ्गान् प्रकटीकरोषि।

व्याख्याः—जह्नुजाया भागीरथ्याः। यस्याश्रयणं कार्यं तेनैव सह विरोधप्रकटनमत्यन्तासमीचीनमिति भावः।

Eng.Tr.:-O river in the rainy season! we do not prevent you from confluenting into the stream of the Ganges, but it is not proper for you that you manifest your breaking of waves, before her.

पौलोमीपतिकानने विलसतां गीर्वाणभूमीरुहां
येनाघ्रातसमुज्झितानि कुसुमान्याजघ्रिरे निर्जरैः।
तस्मिन्नद्य मधुव्रते विधिवशान्माध्वीकमाकाङ्क्षति
त्वं चेदञ्चसि लोभमम्बुज! तदा किं त्वां प्रति ब्रूमहे॥४६॥

अन्वयः—पौलोमी...रुहां कुसुमानि येनाघ्रातसमुज्झितानि (पश्चात्) निर्जरैः आजघ्रिरे, तस्मिन् मधुव्रते अद्य विधिवशात् माध्वीकं आकाङ्क्षति (सति) (हे) अम्बुज, त्वं लोभं अञ्चसि चेत् तदा त्वां प्रति किं ब्रूमहे।

व्याख्याः—पौलोमीपतिकानने नन्दनवने। पौलोमीन्द्राणी। आघ्रात-समुज्झितान्यादावाघ्रातानि पश्चात् समुज्झितानि। येन मधुव्रतेन। अस्याघ्रात-समुज्झितानीत्यनेन सम्बन्धः। गीर्वाणभूमीरुहां कल्पवृक्षाणाम्। मधुव्रतो भ्रमरः। विधिवशाद्दैववशात्। माध्वीकं मधु।

Eng.Tr.:-What shall we say to you, o lotus, if you become greedy, when that bee, who first smelt the flowers of the celestial trees in the garden of Indra and which were then smelt by Gods, is through ill-luck, expecting honey from you?

भुक्ता मृणालपटली भवता निपीता-
न्यम्बूनि यत्र नलिनानि निषेवितानि।

रे राजहंस वद तस्य सरोवरस्य
कृत्येन केन भवितासि कृतोपकारः॥४७॥

अन्वयः—हे राजहंस यत्र भवता मृणालपटली भुक्ता, अम्बूनि निपीतानि, नलिनानि निषेवितानि, वद तस्य सरोवरस्य कृतोपकारः केन कृत्येन भवितासि।

व्याख्याः—मृणालपटली मृणालसंघः।

Eng.Tr.:-O king of swans, with what act will you return the obligation of that lake to you, where the clusters of lotus fibers have been enjoyed by you, waters were also drunk to your heart's content and lotuses have been tasted ?

प्रारम्भे कुसुमाकरस्य परितो यस्योल्लसन्मञ्जरी-
पुञ्जे मञ्जुलगुञ्जितानि रचयंस्तानातनोरुत्सवान्।
तस्मिन्नद्य रसालशाखिनि दशां दैवात्कृशामञ्चति
त्वं चेन्मुञ्चसि चञ्चरीक! विनयं नीचस्त्वदन्योऽस्ति कः॥४८॥

अन्वयः—हे चञ्चरीक कुसुमाकरस्य प्रारम्भे यस्य परितः उल्लसन्मञ्जरीपुञ्जे मञ्जुलगुञ्जितानि रचयन् तान् उत्सवान् आतनोः, तस्मिन् रसालशखिनि अद्य दैवात् कृशां दशां अञ्चति सति, त्वं विनयं मुञ्चति चेत् त्वदन्यः को नीचः ?

व्याख्याः—कुसुमाकरस्य वसन्तस्य।ताननुभूतान्। चञ्चरीक भ्रमर। विनयः कृतज्ञताबुद्धिः। चतुर्थचरणेऽनुप्रासलंकारः।

Eng.Tr.:-O bee, who is meaner than you, if you do not be midest towards that mango-tree, which is at present through ill-luck shorn of leaves etc., and on whose collection of blooming sprouts, you enjoyed festivals by your sweet songs, at the advent of the vernal season ?

एणीगणेषु गुरुगर्वनिमीलिताक्षः
किं कृष्णसार! खलु खेलसि काननेऽस्मिन्।

सीमामिमां कलय भिन्नकरीन्द्रकुम्भ-
मुक्तामयीं हरिविहारवसुन्धरायाः॥४९॥

अन्वयः–हे कृष्णसार गुरुगर्वनिमीलिताक्षः अस्मिन्कानने एणीगणेषु किं खलु खेलसि ! इमां भिन्नकरीन्द्रकुम्भमुक्तामयीं हरिविहारवसुंधरायाः सीमां कलय।

व्याख्याः–एणीगणेषु हरिणीसंघेषु।

Eng.Tr.:-O black antelope ! why do you enjoy in this forest in the herds of female antelopes, closing your eyes through great pride ? Know this to be the boundary of the play-ground of the lion filled with pearls (dropping down) from the temples of the elephants, that have been found open.

जठरज्वलनज्वलताऽप्यपगतशङ्कं समागतापि पुरः।
करिणामरिणा हरिणा हरिणाली हन्यतां नु कथम्॥५०॥

अन्वयः–करिणां अरिणा हरिणा जठरज्वलनज्वलता अपि पुरा समागता अपि हरिणाली अपगतशङ्कं कथं हन्यताम्।

व्याख्याः–जठरज्वलनज्वलता जठराग्निना तप्यमानेन। क्षुधार्तेनेत्यर्थः। अपगतशङ्कं निःशङ्कम्। अनेनानायासप्राप्यता दर्शिता। द्वितीयार्धे यमकं स्पष्टमेव।

Eng.Tr.:-How should a herd of deer, although come in front, be unscrupulously killed by a lion, who is the enemy of elephants, even though he is scorching by the gastric fire (excessive hunger).

येन भिन्नकरिकुम्भविस्खल-
न्मौक्तिकावलिभिरञ्चिता मही।
अद्य तेन हरिणान्तिके कथं
कथ्यतां नु हरिणा पराक्रमः॥५१॥

अन्वयः–येन (हरिणा) भिन्नकरिकुम्भविस्खलन्मौक्तिकावलिभिः मही अञ्चिता तेन हरिणा अद्य हरिणांतिके पराक्रमः कथं कथ्यताम्।

व्याख्याः–अञ्चिता भूषिता। पराक्रमः स्वीय इति शेषः।

Eng.Tr.:-How should that lion who covered the earth with the rows of pearls dropping from the temples of elephants torn open, to-day speak about his valour to the deer ?

स्थितिं नो रे दध्याः क्षणमपि मदान्धेक्षण! सखे!
गजश्रेणीनाथ! त्वमिह जटिलायां वनभुवि।
असौ कुम्भिभ्रान्त्या खरनखरविद्रावितमहा–
गुरुग्रावग्रामः स्वपिति गिरिगर्भे हरिपतिः॥५२॥

अन्वयः–हे सखे मदान्धेक्षण गजश्रेणीनाथ, इह जटिलायां वनभुवि त्वं क्षणमपि स्थितिं न दध्याः, कुम्भिभ्रान्त्या खरनखरविद्रावितमहागुरुग्रावग्रामः असौ हरपतिः गिरिगर्भे स्वपिति !

व्याख्याः–स्थितिं नो दध्या वासं मा कुरु। जटिलायां निम्नोन्नतायाम्। कुम्भिभ्रान्त्या गजोसाविति मत्वा। खरनखैस्तीक्ष्णनखैर्विद्रावितो विदारितो महागुरुग्रामोत्यन्तगुरुशिलापुञ्जो येन तथाविधः। यः करिबुद्ध्या शिलापुञ्जमपि विदारयति सत्वां विदारयेदिति निश्चय एवेति भावः।

Eng.Tr.:-O lord of herds of elephants! whose eyes have been blinded by rut, do not tarry even a moment here in this dense forest. Here in the interior of the mountain is sleeping the best of lions, who has torn asunder with his pointed nails very big mountains (masses of rocks) mistaking them (rocks) for elephants.

गिरिगह्वरेषु गुरुगर्वगुम्फितो
गजराजपोत! न कदापि सञ्चरेः।
यदि बुध्यते हरिशिशुः स्तनन्धयो
भविता करेणुपरिशोषिता मही॥५३॥

अन्वयः–हे गजराजपोत गुरुगर्वगुम्फितः (त्वं) गिरिगह्वरेषु न कदापि संचरेः। यदि स्तनंधयः हरिशिशुः बुध्यते, मही करेणुपरिशेषिता भविता।

व्याख्याः–गुम्फितो वेष्टितः। पूरित इति यावत्। पोतः शिशुः। स्तनन्धयः

स्तनपायी। भविता भविष्यति। करेणुः करिणी। हरिशिशुः सर्वानेव करिणो हनिष्यति। केवलं करिण्य एवावध्यत्वादवशिष्टा भविष्यन्तीति भावः।

Eng.Tr.:-O cub of the lord of elephants, being elated with great haughtiness you should never stir in the caves of the mountain. If the cub of the lion sucking his mother's breast were to be roused, only the female elephants will be left on the earth.

निसर्गादारामे तरुकुलसमारोपसुकृती
कृती मालाकारो बकुलमपि कुत्रापि निदधे।
इदं को जानीते यदयमिह कोणान्तरगतो
जगज्जालं कर्ता कुसुमभरसौरभ्यभरितम्॥५४॥

अन्वयः—तरुकुलसमारोपसुकृती निसर्गात् कृती मालाकारः बकुलमपि आरामे कुत्रापि निदधे। इदं को जानीते यदयमिह कोणान्तरगतः जगज्जालं कुसुमभरसौरभ्यभरितं कर्ता।

व्याख्याः—कर्ता करिष्यति। अस्मिन् मालाकारस्येतरवृक्षसाधारणी बुद्धिरनुचितैवेति भावः।

Eng.Tr.:-A gardener well-versed by nature, ingenious in planting the multitude of trees, planted in his garden even the बकुल tree somewhere. Who knows this that it (though) planted in some corner here will fill the whole world with the fragrance of (its) number of flowers ?

यस्मिन्वेल्लति सर्वतः परिचलत्कल्लोलकोलाहलै-
र्मन्थाद्रिभ्रमणभ्रमं हृदि हरिद्दन्तावलाः पेदिरे।
सोऽयं तुङ्गतिमिङ्गिलाङ्गकवलीकारक्रियाकोविदः
क्रोडे क्रीडतु कस्य केलि[१]कलहत्यक्तार्णवो राघवः॥५५॥

अन्वयः—यस्मिन् राघवे (तन्नामके मत्स्ये) वेल्लति (सति) सर्वतः परिचलत्कल्लोलकोलाहलैः हरिद्दन्तावलाः हृदि मन्थाद्रिभ्रमणभ्रमं (आ)

१. 'काल' इति पाठान्तरम्।

पेदिरे, सः अयं तुङ्गतिमिंगिलाङ्गकवलीकारक्रियाकोविदः केलिकलहत्यक्तार्णवः राघवः कस्य क्रोडे क्रीडतु।

व्याख्याः—वेल्लति चलति। कल्लोलो महानूर्मिः। हरिदन्तावला दिग्गजाः। तिमिङ्गिलो मत्स्यभेदः। कवलीकारो गिलनम्। राघवो मत्स्यभेदः। द्वितीयार्धेऽनुप्रासः स्पष्ट एव।

Eng.Tr.:-In whose side (lit. cavity) may this राघव fish play, (the fish) who is an expert in swallowing the bodies of the lofty तिमिंगिल fish and who quitted the sea due to the quarrel in sport, at whose movements the elephants at the quarters experience the apprehension (once experienced) at the time of the revolving of the churning mountain, because of the loud uproar of the huge waves moving all around ?

लूनं मत्तगजैः कियत्कियदपि च्छिन्नं तुषारार्दितैः
शिष्टं ग्रीष्मजभीष्मभानुकिरणैर्भस्मीकृतं काननम्।
एषा कोणगता मुहुः परिमलैरामोदयन्ती दिशो
हा कष्टं ललिता लवङ्गलतिका दावाग्निना दह्यते॥५६॥

अन्वयः—कियदपि (काननं) मत्तगजैः लूनं, कियदपि तुषारार्दितैः छिन्नम् शिष्टं (काननं) ग्रीष्मजभीष्मभानुकिरणैः भस्मीकृतं, हा कष्टं एषा कोणगता, मुहुः परिमलैर्दिशः आमोदयन्ती, ललिता लवङ्गलतिका दावाग्निना दह्यते।

व्याख्याः—लूनं खण्डितम्। तुषारार्दितैर्हिमपीडाभिः।

Eng.Tr.:-Some part of the forest is (cut) destroyed by intoxicated elephants, some part is chopped by persons oppressed by frost and the rest is reduced to ashes by the terrible rays of the summer-sun. Alas! this charming clove plant (creeper) frequently rendering the directions fragrant now lying in the corner, is being burnt by the forest conglagration.

स्वर्लोकस्य शिखामणिः सुरतरुग्रामस्य धामाद्भुतं
पौलोमीपुरुहूतयोः परिणतिः पुण्यावलीनामसि।

सत्यं नन्दन किन्त्विदं सहृदयैर्नित्यं विधिः प्रार्थ्यते
त्वत्तः खाण्डवरङ्गताण्डवनटो दूरेऽस्तु वैश्वानरः॥५७॥

अन्वयः–हे नन्दन, (त्वं) स्वर्लोकस्य शिखामणिः, सुरतरुग्रामस्य अद्भुतं धाम, पौलोमीपुरुहूतयोः पुण्यावलीनां परिणतिरसि (इति) सत्यम्। किन्तु सहृदयैः विधिः नित्यं इदं प्रार्थ्यते। "त्वत्तः खाण्डवरङ्गतांडवनटः वैश्वानरः दूरेऽस्तु।"

व्याख्या:–पुरुहूत इन्द्रः। सहृदयैर्विधिरिदं प्रार्थ्यत इत्यन्वयः। खाण्डवं कुरुक्षेत्रगतो वनविशेषः। अर्जुनेन खाण्डववनसमर्पणेन वह्निस्तर्पित इति प्रसिद्धमेव।

Eng.Tr.:-O Nandana garden, it is a fact that you are the crest—jewel of the heavenly world, a wonderful abode of the collection of celestial trees and the fulfilment of the series of virtuous acts of Indra and Indrāṇī. But the Creator is being always prayed to by the merciful, thus, "Let fire, the actor, dancing on the stage in the form of the खाण्डव forest, be away from you.

स्वस्वव्यापृतिमग्नमानसतया मत्तो निवृत्ते जने
चञ्चूकोटिविपाटिताररपुटो यास्याम्यहं पञ्जरात्।
एवं कीरवरे मनोरथमयं पीयूषमास्वादय-
त्यन्तः संप्रविवेश वारणकराकारः फणिग्रामणीः॥५८॥

अन्वयः–'स्वस्वव्यापृतिमग्नमानसतया मत्तो जने निवृत्ते चञ्चूकोटिविपाटिताररपुटः अहं पञ्जराद् यास्यामि' एवं कीरवरे मनोरथमयं पीयूषं आस्वादयति अंतः वारणकराकारः फणिग्रामणीः संप्रविवेश।

व्याख्या:–मत्तो निवृत्ते मद्विषयचित्तवृत्तिमकुर्वाणे। अररपुटं कपाटपुटम्। अन्तः पञ्जरमध्ये। वारणकराकारः करिशुण्डादण्डसदृशः। फणिग्रामणीः सर्पश्रेष्ठः। अत्र विषादनालंकारोऽप्रस्तुतप्रशंसाघटकतया स्थितः। विषादनं चाभीष्टार्थविरुद्धलाभः।

Eng.Tr.:-"When (all) men turn away from me being engrossed in their respective occupation, I shall go away (i.e. fly off) from the cage, breaking open the pane of the door (of the cage) with the points of my beak," while thus a parrot was tasting the nectar, in the form of this desire there crept in, the best of serpents, having the shape of the trunk of an elephant.

रे चाञ्चल्यजुषो मृगाः! श्रितनगाः कल्लोलमालाकुला-
मेतामम्बुधिकामिनीं व्यवसिताः सङ्गाहितुं वा कथम्।
अत्रैवोच्छलदम्बुनिर्भरमहावर्तैः समावर्तितो
यद् ग्रावेव रसातलं पुनरसौ यातो गजग्रामणीः॥५९॥

अन्वयः—रे चाञ्चल्यजुषः श्रितनगाः मृगाः कल्लोलमालाकुलां एतां अम्बुधिकामिनीं (v.l. गामिनीं) सङ्गाहितुं कथं व्यवसिताः। यद् अत्रैव उच्छलदम्बुनिर्भरमहावर्तैः समावर्तितः असौ गजग्रामणीः पुनः ग्रावा इव रसातलं यातः।

व्याख्या:—चाञ्चल्यजुषश्चञ्चलाः। कल्लोला महान्तस्तरङ्गाः। अम्बुधिकामिनीं नदीम्। व्यवसिता उद्युक्ताः। वात्रावधारणे प्रश्नदृढीकरणे वा। उच्छलन्नुद्रच्छन्नम्बुनिर्भरो येषां तथाविधैर्महावर्तैर्महाम्भोभ्रमैः समावर्तित इतस्ततश्चलितः। ग्रावा पाषाणः। गाहमानो गजो यत्र शं नालभत तत्र भवतां का कल्याणकथेति भावः।

Eng.Tr.:-O deer! inhabiting the mountains and taking pleasure in fickleness, how have you prepared (resolved) yourself to bathe in this river which is agitated (boisterous) on account of its surging waves ? Since in this same (river) even that lord of elephants, has (been drownd) gone to the bottom like a stone, being once tossed by the great whirlpools of the surging mass of waters.

पिब स्तन्यं पोत! त्वमिह मददन्तावलधिया
दृगन्तानाधत्से किमिति हरिदन्तेषु परुषान्।

त्रयाणां लोकानामपि हृदयतापं परिहर-
न्नयं धीरं धीरं ध्वनति नवनीलो जलधरः॥६०॥

अन्वयः–(हे) पोत स्तन्यं पिब, इह त्वं मददन्तावलधिया हरिदन्तेषु परुषान् दृगन्तान् किमिति आधत्से ! त्रयाणां लोकानां अपि हृदयतापं परिहरन् अयं नवनीलो जलधरः धीरं धीरं ध्वनति।

व्याख्याः–स्तन्यं पयः। मददन्तावलधिया मत्तवारणभ्रमेण।

Eng.Tr.:-O cub! suck milk, why do you here cast angry side glances at the ends of quarters thinking that (there are) rutting elephants ? This is the new and dark cloud that is sonorously thundering, (the cloud) which removes mental anguish of all three worlds even.

धीरध्वनिभिरलं ते नीरद! मे मासिको गर्भः।
उन्मदवारणबुद्ध्या मध्येजठरं समुच्छलति॥६१॥

अन्वयः–(हे) नीरद, अलं ते धीरध्वनिभिः मे मासिको गर्भः उन्मदवारणबुद्ध्या मध्येजठरं समुच्छलति।

व्याख्याः–नीरद मेघ। उन्मदो मत्तः। मध्येजठरं जठरस्य मध्ये। पारे मध्ये षष्ठ्या वेत्यव्ययीभावः। प्राचीनानां मतेऽसम्बन्धेऽपि सम्बन्धरूपेय-मतिशयोक्तिः। स च सम्बन्धोवर्ण्योत्कर्षार्थः। यथास्मिन् पद्ये सिंहीवचने समुच्छलनासम्बम्धेऽपि समुच्छलनसम्बन्धोक्तिः शौर्यातिशायिका। नव्यास्तु नेमामतिशयोक्तिं मन्यन्ते।

Eng.Tr.:-O cloud! enough of your sonorous rumblings (because) my foetus, one month old, moves about in my abdomen, considering you to be an intoxicated elephant.

वेतण्डगण्ड[१]कण्डूतिपाण्डित्यपरिपन्थिना।
हरिणा हरिणालीषु कथ्यतां कः पराक्रमः?॥६२॥

अन्वयः–वेतण्डगण्डकण्डूतिपाण्डित्यपरिपन्थिना हरिणा हरिणालीषु कः पराक्रमः कथ्यताम्।

१. 'वेतण्ड' इति पाठान्तरम्।

व्याख्या:–वेतण्डो गजः। परिपन्थी विरोधी। अस्य तात्पर्यार्थः (५१) पद्यस्येव।

Eng. Tr.:-What exploit maybe related to the multitudes of the deer by the lion, who is the obstacle in the skill in the rubbing of the temples by the elephants ?

नीरान्निर्मलतो जनिर्मधुरता वामा[१]मुखस्पर्धिनी
वासो यस्य हरेः करे परिमलो गीर्वाणचेतोहरः।
सर्वस्वं तदहो महाकविगिरां कामस्य चाम्भोरुह!
त्वं चेत्प्रीतिमुरीकरोषि मधुपे तत्त्वां किमाचक्ष्महे?॥६३॥

अन्वयः–हे अम्भोरुह यस्य तव जनिः निर्मलताः नीरात्, यस्य (तव) मधुरता वामामुखस्पर्धिनी, यस्य तव हरेः करे वासः, परिमलः (च) गीर्वाणचेतोहरः, (त्वं) अहो महाकविगिरां कामस्य च तत् सर्वस्वं, त्वं मधुपे प्रीतिमुरीकरोषि चेत् त्वां किमाचक्ष्महे।

व्याख्या:–वामा ललना। महाकविगिरां कामस्य च सर्वस्वमित्यन्वयः। कवयस्त्वां वारम्वारमुपमानतयाङ्गीकुर्वन्ति कामस्य च त्वममोघमस्त्रमिति भावः। तदहो इत्युत्तरवाक्येनान्वीयते। यद्वा तत् प्रसिद्धम्। मधुपे भ्रमरे मद्यप इति च ध्वन्यते! आचक्ष्महे वयं तटस्था इति शेषः।

Eng. Tr.:-O lotus! you are born of clear water, your sweetness vies with the face of a beautiful lady, your habitation is the hand of Hari, your fragrance captivates the minds of Gods, you are the whole and sole possession of the words of the great poets and of cupid, yet if you entertain love for a bee, what shall we talk to you ?

लीलामुकुलितनयनं किं सुखशयनं समातनुषे।
परिणामविषमहरिणा करिनायक! वर्धते वैरम्॥६४॥

अन्वयः–हे करिनायक लीलामुकुलितनयनं सुखशयनं कि समातनुषे, परिणामविषमहरिणा (सह तव) वैरं वर्धते।

---

१. 'रामा' इति पाठान्तरम्।

व्याख्या:—लीलामुकुलितनयनमिति क्रियाविशेषणम्। समातनुषे करोषि। परिणामे विषमो दुःसहः।

Eng.Tr.:-O lord of elephants! why do you enjoy sleeping at ease with your eyes half—closed in the amorous sport ? your enmity with the lion the result of which will be grave, is waxing (thereby).

विदुषां वदनाद्वाचः सहसा यान्ति नो बहिः।
याताश्चेन्न पराञ्चन्ति द्विरदानां रदा इव॥६५॥

अन्वयः—विदुषां वदनाद् वाचः सहसा बहिः नो यान्ति। याताः चेत् द्विरदानां रदा इव न पराञ्चन्ति।

व्याख्या:—सहसाऽविमृश्य। पराञ्चन्ति परावर्तन्ते।

Eng.Tr.:-Words do not come out of the mouth of the wise thoughtlessly; but if once they come out they are never withdrawn like the tusks of elephants.

औदार्यं भुवनत्रयेऽपि विदितं संभूतिरम्भोनिधे-
र्वासो नन्दनकानने परिमलो गीर्वाणचेतोहरः।
एवं दातृगुरोर्गुणाः सुरतरोः सर्वेऽपि लोकोत्तराः
स्यादर्थिप्रवरार्थितार्पणविधावेको विवेको यदि॥६६॥

अन्वयः—औदार्यं भुवनत्रयेऽपि विदितं, संभूतिरम्भोनिधेर्वासो नंदनकानने, परिमलो गीर्वाणचेतोहरः एवं दातृगुरोः सुरतरोः सर्वेऽपि गुणाः लोकोत्तराः (अभविष्यन्) यदि (तस्मिन्) अर्थिप्रवरार्थीतार्पणविधौ एकः विवेकः स्यात्।

व्याख्या:—अर्थिप्रवराणां यदर्थितं याचितं तस्यार्पणविधौ। अविवेकेन सर्वेप्यन्ये गुणास्तथा न शोभन्त इति भावः।

Eng.Tr.:-The generosity is well-known even in the three worlds; (its) birth is from the reservoir of water (sea); (its) residence is in the नन्दन garden, (its) fragrance captivates the minds of Gods, thus even all the merits of the celestial tree-the best of donors, would have been extra-ordinary had there been one (merit of) discretion (on his part) in the act of granting the requests of the best of supplicants.

एको विश्वसतां हराम्यपघृणः प्राणानहं प्राणिना-
मित्येवं परिचिन्त्य मास्म[१] मनसि व्याधानुतापं कृथाः।
भूपानां भवनेषु किं च विमलक्षेत्रेषु गूढाशयाः
साधूनामरयो वसन्ति कति न[२] त्वत्तुल्यकक्षाः खलाः॥६७॥

अन्वयः–एकः अहं अपघृणः विश्वसतां प्राणिनां प्राणान् हरामि इति एवं परिचिन्त्य हे व्याध मनसि मास्म अनुतापं (अ) कृथाः। (यतः) भूपानां भवनेषु किं च विमलक्षेत्रेषु साधूनां अरयः गूढाशयाः त्वत्तुल्यकक्षाः खलाः कति न वसन्ति।

व्याख्याः–अपघृणो निर्दयः। गूढाशया गुप्ताभिप्रायाः। त्वत्तुल्यकक्षास्त्वत्समानावस्थाः। अत्रौपम्यप्रदर्शनस्य व्याधानुतापनाशः फलम्।

Eng.Tr.:-O fowler! do not feel remorse at heart after thinking thus, "I alone being relentless, destroy the life of animals confiding (in me,)" (for) there dwell in the palaces of kings and holy places thousands of wicked persons with their motives concealed, that are the enemies of the good and have a state similar to that of yours.

विश्वास्य मधुरवचनैः साधून् ये वञ्चयन्ति नम्रतमाः।
तानपि दधासि मातः काश्यपि यातस्तवापि च विवेकः॥६८॥

अन्वयः–ये नम्रतमाः साधून् मधुरवचनैः विश्वास्य (तान्) वञ्चयन्ति तानपि (हे) मातः काश्यपि, दधासि। (हन्त) तवापि च विवेकः यातः।

व्याख्याः–काश्यपि पृथ्वि। क्षोणिर्ज्या काश्यपी क्षितिरित्यमरः।

Eng.Tr.:-O mother earth! you bear even those who, (pretending to be) the humblest, deceive the good by inspiring them with confidence by palatable words; even you have lost discretion.

---

१. 'माऽऽत्ममनसि' इति पाठान्तरम्।

२. 'नो' इति पाठान्तरम्।

अन्या जगद्धितमयी मनसः प्रवृत्ति-
रन्यैव कापि रचना वचनावलीनाम्।
लोकोत्तरा च कृतिराकृतिरार्यहृद्या
विद्यावतां सकलमेव गिरां दवीयः॥६९॥

अन्वयः—अन्या जगद्धितमयी मनसः प्रवृत्तिः, वचनावलीनां रचना काऽपि अन्या एव, लोकोत्तरा च कृतिराकृतिरार्यहृद्या विद्यावतां सकलमेव गिरां दवीयः।

व्याख्या:—अन्या लोकोत्तरा। गिरां वाचां दवीयो दूरतरम्। अवर्णनीयमित्यर्थः। अतिशयोक्तिरियं प्राचीनानां मते। अतिशयश्चात्राभेदेपि भेदो लोकोत्तरत्वप्रतिपत्त्यर्थः। अस्मिन् पद्ये प्रवृत्त्यादीनामन्यत्वं वर्ण्यमानं लोकोत्तरत्वं प्रतिपादयति।

Eng. Tr.:-Unusual is the inclination of (their) mind, beneficial to the world; extra-ordinary is the composition of the multitude of (their) worlds; uncommon is their action; captivating is their form to the noble; (any) everything belonging to the learned is beyond description.

आपद्गतः किल महाशयचक्रवर्ती
विस्तारयत्यकृतपूर्वमुदारभावम्।
कालागुरुर्दहनमध्यगतः समन्ता-
ल्लोकोत्तरं परिमलं प्रकटीकरोति॥७०॥

अन्वयः—महाशयचक्रवर्ती किल आपद्गतः अकृतपूर्वं उदारभावं विस्तारयति। दहनमस्य गतः कालागुरुः समन्तात् लोकोत्तरं परिमलं प्रकटीकरोति।

व्याख्या:—महाशयानामुदारप्रकृतीनां चक्रवर्ती श्रेष्ठः। कालागुरुः कृष्ण-चन्दनः। इयं प्रतिवस्तूपमा।

Eng. Tr.:-The best of the magnanimous, indeed, when fallen into adversity, extends the unprecedented generosity;

sandal when cast into fire emits (all) around extra-ordinary fragrance.

विश्वाभिरामगुणगौरवगुम्फितानां
रोषोऽपि निर्मलधियां रमणीय एव।
लोकम्पृणैः परिमलैः परिपूरितस्य
काश्मीरजस्य कटुतापि नितान्तरम्या॥७१॥

अन्वयः—विश्वाभिरामगुणगौरवगुंफितानां निर्मलधियां रोषोऽपि रमणीयः एव, लोकंपृणैः परिमलैः परिपूरितस्य काश्मीरजस्य कटुताऽपि नितान्तरम्या।

व्याख्याः—लोकम्पृणैर्लोकतर्पकैः। काश्मीरजस्य कुंकुमस्य। इयमपि प्रतिवस्तूपमा।

Eng.Tr.:-Even the wrath of persons whose minds are pure, and who are filled with abundance of qualities pleasing to the whole world, is pleasing. Even the bitter taste of saffron which is filled with fragrance pleasant to the people, is excessively pleasing.

लीलालुण्ठितशारदापुरमहासम्पद्भराणां[१] पुरो
विद्यासद्मविनिर्गलत्कणमुषो वल्गन्ति चेत्पामराः।
अद्य श्वः फणिनां शकुन्तशिशवो दन्तावलानां शशाः[२]
सिंहानां च सुखेन मूर्धसु पदं धास्यन्ति शालावृकाः॥७२॥

अन्वयः—लीलालुण्ठितशारदाः पुरमहासम्पद्भराणां पुरो विद्यासद्मविनिर्गलत्कणमुषः पामरा वल्गन्ति चेत् अद्यश्वः शकुन्तशिशवः फणिनां (मूर्धसु), शशाः दन्तावलानां मूर्धसु, शालावृकाः सिंहानां (मूर्धसु) च सुखेन पदं धास्यन्ति।

व्याख्याः—लीलया लुण्ठितः शारदापुरमहासम्पद्भरो यैस्तेषाम्। महापण्डितानामित्यर्थः। लीलालुण्ठितशारदापुरधियामस्मादृशानां पुर इति रसगङ्गाधरे पाठः। तेनायं श्लोकः कविनात्मानमुद्दिश्य रचित इति भाति। विद्यासद्मनो विनिर्गलन्तो ये कणास्तान् मुष्णन्त्यपहरन्ति तथाविधाः। अल्पविधा इत्यर्थः।

१. 'नराणां' इति पाठान्तरम्।
२. 'वृकाः' इति पाठान्तरम्।

वल्गान्ति कथ्यते। पामरा मूर्खाः। अद्यश्वोऽद्य वा श्वो वा। सुप्सुपेति समासः। समनन्तरमेवेत्यर्थः। शालावृकाः श्वानः। शालावृकः कपिकोष्टुश्वान इत्यमरः। अर्थापत्यलंकारोऽयम्। अर्थापत्तिश्च केनचिदर्थेन तुल्यन्यायत्वादर्थान्तरस्यापत्तिः। महापण्डितानामग्रेऽल्पविद्या वल्गन्ति चेत् तुल्यन्यायत्वाच्छकुन्तपोताः फणिनां मूर्धसु पदं धास्यन्तीत्यप्यायातमेव।

Eng.Tr.:-If ignorant persons, stealing particles dropping from the house of knowledge, were to prattle before those who in a mere sport plundered the store of great wealth in the town of learning, to-day or tomorrow, (it may happen that) young birds will subdue the (hooded) serpents, the rabbits will overpower the elephants and the foxes (or dogs) will easily defeat the lions.

गीर्भिर्गुरूणां परुषाक्षराभि-
स्तिरस्कृता यान्ति नरा महत्त्वम्।
अलब्धशाणोत्कषणा नृपाणां
न जातु मौलौ मणयो वसन्ति॥७३॥

अन्वयः–गुरूणां परुषाक्षराभिः गीर्भिः तिरस्कृताः नराः महत्वं यान्ति, अलब्धशाणोत्कषणाः मणयः नृपाणां मौलौ न जातु वसन्ति।

व्याख्याः–शाणो रत्नपरिष्करणपाषाणः। जातु कदाचिदपि। वैधर्म्येणेयं प्रतिवस्तूपमा।

Eng.Tr.:- Persons scolded by the utterances of great persons containing harsh words, attain to greatness. Never do the jewels (ornaments) (ascend) live on the heads of the kings, unless they undergo the scratching on the touch-stone.

वहति विषधरान्पटीरजन्मा
शिरसि मसीपटलं दधाति दीपः।
विधुरपि भजतेतरां कलङ्कं
पिशुनजनं खलु बिभ्रति क्षितीन्द्राः॥७४॥

अन्वयः–(यत्) क्षितींद्राः खलु पिशुनजनं विभ्रति (तत्) पटीरजन्मा विषधरान्वहति दीपः शिरसि मसी (षी) पटलं दधाति, विधुरपि कलंकं भजतेतराम्।

व्याख्याः–पटीरजन्मा चन्दनः। इयं मालाप्रतिवस्तूपमा। अत्र वहनाधनभजनभरणानां वस्तुत एकार्थतैव।

Eng.Tr.:-(In as much as) the kings nourish the wicked, the sandle-tree gives resort to the serpents, the lamp bears the coat of soot, (and) even the moon bears the stain.

सत्पूरुषः खलु हिताचरणैरमन्द-
मानन्दयत्यखिललोकमनुक्त एव।
आराधितः कथय केन करैरुदारै-
रिन्दुर्विकासयति कैरविणीकुलानि॥७५॥

अन्वयः–खलु सत्पूरुषः अनुक्तः एव हिताचरणैः अखिललोकं अमन्दं आनन्दयति कथय, केन आराधितः इन्दुः उदारैः करैः कैरविणीकुलानि विकासयति।

व्याख्याः–अनुक्तोऽप्रार्थितः। स्वयमेवेत्यर्थः। उदारैर्महद्भिः। कैरविणी कुमुदिनी। अयं दृष्टान्तालंकारः।

Eng.Tr.:-A good person indeed, though not requested incessantly, gives pleasure to the whole world by his charitable actions, say, at whose request does the moon cause the clusters of moon-lotuses to bloom by his benevolent rays ?

कृतमपि महोपकारं पय इव पीत्वा निरातङ्कः।
प्रत्युत हन्तुं यतते काकोदरसोदरः खलो जगति॥७६॥

अन्वयः–पय इव कृतमपि महोपकारं पीत्वा प्रत्युत निरातङ्कः काकोदरसोदरः खलः जगति (उपकारिणं) हन्तुं यतते।

व्याख्याः–निरातङ्को निःशङ्कः। काकोदरः सर्पः। सोदरः सहोदरः।

सदृश इत्यर्थः। यथा सर्पः पयः पीत्वा दातारमेव दशति तथा खलोऽपि महोपकारं विस्मृत्योपकारिणं हन्तुं यतत इति भावः।

Eng.Tr.:-A wicked man, the brother of a cobra, strives, on the contrary, to kill (his benefactor) without any fear, after swallowing up (i.e. forgetting) the obligation done to him like milk (in the case of the cobra).

पाण्डित्यं परिहृत्य यस्य हि कृते बन्दित्वमालम्बितं
दुष्प्रापं[१] मनसाऽपि यो गुरुतरैः क्लेशैः पदं प्रापितः।
रूढस्तत्र स चेन्निगीर्य सकलां पूर्वोपकारावलिं
दुष्टः प्रत्यवतिष्ठते तदधुना कस्मै किमाचक्ष्महे॥७७॥

अन्वयः—यस्य हि कृते पाण्डित्यं परिहृत्य (अस्माभिः) बंदित्वमालम्बितं, यो (अस्माभिः) गुरुतरैः क्लेशैः मनसा अपि दुष्प्रापं पदं प्रापितः स दुष्टः तत्र (तस्मिन् पदे) रूढः सकलां पूर्वोपकारावलिं निगीर्य प्रत्यवतिष्ठते चेत् तद् अधुना कस्मै किम् आचक्ष्महे।

व्याख्या:—पाण्डित्यं परिहृत्य सदसद्विवेचनशक्तिरूपं विद्वत्वं त्यक्त्वा। बन्दित्वगलम्बितं स्तुतिपाठकत्वं स्वीकृतम्। यस्य हिताय सत्यासत्यमविगणय्य मिथ्यास्तुतिः कृतेति भावः। हि निश्चये विषादे वा। रूढः प्राप्तपदतया बद्धमूलः। प्रत्यवतिष्ठते परिपन्थीभवति। दुष्टेषु कृत उपकारः परिणामे न सुखं जनयतीति तात्पर्यार्थः।

Eng.Tr.:-If that wicked person, for whom we condescended to become bards, setting aside learning; and who was raised to a position, difficult to be attained even by mind, (by us) with prodigious efforts, being established there goes against (us) after forgeting (intentionally) all the series of previous obligations, than now what shall we say to anybody ?

खलः कापट्यदोषेण दूरेणैव विसृज्यते।
अपायशङ्किभिर्लोकैर्विषेणाशीविषो यथा॥७८॥

---

१. 'दुष्प्राप्यम्' इति पाठान्तरम्।

अन्वयः–अपायशङ्किभिर्लोकैः कापट्यदोषेण खलः दूरेणैव विसृज्यते, यथा आशीविषः (अपायशङ्किभिर्लोकैः) विषेण (विषदोषेण) दूरेण विसृज्यते।

व्याख्याः–आश्यां दंष्ट्रायां विषं यस्य स आशीविषः सर्पः। उपमेयम्। दूरतो विसर्जनमत्रानुगामी समानो धर्मः। कापट्यं विषं च दूरतो विसर्जने हेतुः।

Eng.Tr.:-A wicked person is left at a distance by persons who apprehend danger, owing to his deceitful nature like a serpent, owing to his venom.

परार्थव्यासङ्गादुपजहदथ[१] स्वार्थपरता-
मभेदैकत्वं यो वहति गुणभूतेषु[२] सततम्।
स्वभावाद्यस्यान्तः स्फुरति ललितोदात्तमहिमा
समर्थो यो नित्यं स जयतितरां कोऽपि पुरुषः॥७१॥

अन्वयः–परार्थव्यासंगात् स्वार्थपरतां उपजहदपि यः सततं गुणभूतेषु अभेदैकत्वं वहति; यस्य अन्तः ललितोदात्तमहिमा स्वभावात् स्फुरति यः नित्यं समर्थः सः कोऽपि पुरुषः जयतितराम्।

व्याख्याः–इयं समासोक्तिः। अस्यां च लौकिके व्यवहारे वाच्ये शास्त्रीयव्यवहारस्यारोपः कृतः। य एके सत्पुरुषा परार्थघटकाः स्वार्थं परित्यज्य य इति भर्तृहरिप्रोक्तलक्षणोपेतः परोपकारव्यासक्त्या स्वार्थे तात्पर्यं त्यजति यः सदा स्वस्मादवरजनेष्वप्यभेदबुद्ध्यैकत्वं तादात्म्यं धारयति तस्यान्तःकरणे स्वाभाविकमेव शोभनं सर्वोत्कृष्टं महत्वं विराजते यश्च सर्वसाधुकार्यनिर्वाह-शक्तियुक्तः स कोपि सत्पुरुषो नित्यं सर्वोत्कर्षेण वर्तत इति लौकिकोऽर्थः। अस्मिन्नर्थे समर्थः पदविधिरिति पाणिनिसूत्रगतमहाभाष्यप्रतिपाद्यशास्त्रीय-व्यवहारस्यारोपः। तत्र हि राजपुरुषेत्यादिसमासघटकपदानि शुद्धं स्वं स्वमर्थं विहाय राजाद्यर्थविशिष्टं पुरुषाद्यर्थं प्रतिपादयन्त्यतस्तद्घटिततत्पुरुषसमासादिरपि विशिष्टार्थप्रतिपादक एव समासादिवृत्तै! विशिष्टशक्तेरेकार्थीभावरूपाया वैयाकरणैरभ्युपगमात्। तथा राजपुरुष इत्यादौ राज्ञः पुरुषो राज्ञोः पुरुषो राज्ञां पुरुष इत्येवं रूपेण विशेषणीभूतपूर्वपदार्थादौ संख्याविशेषस्य प्रतिपत्त्यभावेऽपि

१. 'उपजहदथ' इति पाठान्तरम्।
२. 'गुरुभूतेषु' इति पाठान्तरम्।

सामान्यरूपेणैकत्वसंख्याप्रतिपत्तिः। अस्याः संख्याया अभेदैकत्वसंख्येति पारिभाषिकं नाम शास्त्रकारैः कल्पितम्। किं चासमासे पदानां भिन्नभिन्न-स्वरकत्वेऽपि समासे कृते समासस्वभावादेव समासस्येति सूत्रेण समासान्त्योजुदात्तो भवति। एवं वस्त्रं राज्ञः पुरुषश्चैत्रस्येत्यादावसमर्था-नामनन्वितानां राजपुरुषादिपदानां समासवारणाय समर्थः पदविधिरिति सूत्रेण समर्थपदानामेव समासादिविधिर्बोधितः। एवं शास्त्रीयव्यवहार- विषयीभूतस्य तत्पुरुषस्य लौकिकव्यवहारविषयीभूते सत्पुरुष आरोपः।

Eng.Tr.:-He, who leaving aside his selfishness through (his) extreme fondness for doing good to others shows (lit. bears) great unity due to identity towards Guṇas and beings, in whose mind the pleasing and generous greatness arises (lit. throbs) by his very nature and who is always capable, such a super-human person is always successful.

वंशभवो गुणवानपि सङ्गविशेषेण पूज्यते पुरुषः।
न हि तुम्बीफलविकलो वीणादण्डः प्रयाति महिमानम्॥८०॥

अन्वयः—वंशभवो गुणवानपि पुरुषः सङ्गविशेषेण पूज्यते। तुम्बीफलविकलो वीणादण्डः महिमानं न हि प्रयाति।

व्याख्याः—वंशभवः सत्कुलप्रसूतो वेणुप्रभवश्च। गुणवान् विद्याविनयादि युक्तस्तन्त्र्यादिगुणवांश्च। तुम्बीफलं भोंपला इति प्रसिद्धम्। वैधर्म्येणेयं प्रतिवस्तूपमा।

Eng.Tr.:-A man though born in a respectable family and possesed of good qualities, becomes an object of adoration by his special companionship (with the noble). A staff of a lute, though made of a good bamboo, and possessed of strings, does not attain greatness (lit. is not praised) (as long as) it is void of the fruit of a gourd (i.e. void of the base made of gourd.)

अमितगुणोऽपि पदार्थो दोषेणैकेन निन्दितो भवति।
निखिलरसायनमहितो गन्धेनोग्रेण लशुन इव॥८१॥

अन्वयः–(यथा) निखिलरसायनमहितः लशुनः उग्रेण गन्धेन (निन्दितो भवति) तथा अमितगुणोऽपि पदार्थः एकेन दोषेण निन्दितो भवति।

व्याख्या:–निखिलेषु रसायनेषु महितो मान्यः। अयमुदाहरणालंकारः। अस्मिन्नलंकारे सामान्येन निरूपितस्यार्थस्य सुखप्रतिपत्तये तदेकदेशं निरूप्य तयोरवयवावयविभावः शब्देनोपादीयते। इवशब्दोऽत्रावयवावयविभावस्य वाचकः।

Eng.Tr.:-A thing possessed of innumerable (good) qualities is condemned for (even) a single defect like garlic (लशुन) because of its violent odour, (although) prominent among all the medicines.

उपकारमेव तनुते[१] विपद्गतः सद्गुणो नितराम्।
मूर्छां गतो मृतो वा निदर्शनं पारदोऽत्र रसः॥८२॥

अन्वयः–सद्गुणः विपद्गतः मुर्छां गतः मृतः वा नितरां उपकारमेव तनुते अत्र निदर्शनं पारदो रसः।

व्याख्या:–मूर्च्छामृतिश्च वैद्यशास्त्रोक्तसंस्कारविशेषौ। निदर्शनमुदाहरणम्। अयमप्युदाहरणालंकारः।

Eng.Tr.:-A meritorious man though in adversity, in swoon, or in death, confers abundant obligations, only the instance here is of the fluid mercury.

वनान्ते खेलन्ती शशकशिशुमालोक्य चकिता
भुजप्रान्तं भर्तुर्भजति भयहर्तुः सपदि या।
अहो सेयं सीता दशवदननीता हलरदैः
परीता रक्षोभिः श्रयति विवशा कामपि दशाम्॥८३॥

अन्वयः–या (सीता) वनान्ते खेलन्ती शशकशिशुमालोक्य चकिता (भूत्वा) सपदि भयहर्तुः भर्तुः भुजप्रान्तं भजति, सा इयं सीता अहो दशवदननीता हलरदैः रक्षोभिः परीता, विवशा, कामपि दशां श्रयति।

---

१. 'कुरुते' इति पाठान्तरम्।

व्याख्या:—वनान्ते वनप्रदेशे। भर्तू राघवस्य। हलरदैर्हलसदृशदन्तैः।। परीता व्याप्ता। विवशा पराधीना। अहो विधेर्बलीयस्त्वमिति भावः

Eng. Tr.:-That Sītā, who while sporting in the skirts of the garden being startled at the sight of the young one of a hare immediately resorts to the bosom of her husband, the remover of her fears, alas ! that सीता (now) when kindnapped by रावण, and surrounded by demons, with plough-like teeth, (resorts to) is reduced to an indescribable (pitiable) condition through helplessness.

पुरो गीर्वाणानां निजभुजबलाहोपुरुषिका-
महो कारं कारं पुरभिदि शरं सम्मुखयतः।
स्मरस्य स्वर्बालानयनसुममालार्चनपदम्
वपुः सद्यो भालानलभसितजालास्पदमभूत्।।८४।।

अन्वयः—अहो ! गीवार्णानां पुरः निजभुजबलाहोपुरुषिकां कारं कारं पुरभिदि शरं संमुखयतः स्मरस्य स्वर्बालानयनसुममालार्चनपदं वपुः वद्यो भालानलभसितजालास्पदमभूत्।

व्याख्या:—गीर्वाणानां पुरो निजभुजबलाहोपुरुषिकां कारं कारं पुरभिदि शरं सम्मुखयतः स्मरस्य वपुर्भालानलभसितजालास्पदमभूदित्यन्वयः।। अहं पुरुष इत्यहंकारवानहोपुरुषस्तद्भाव आहोपुरुषिका। आहोपुरुषिका दर्पाद् या स्यात् संभावनात्मनीत्यमरः। कारं कारमभीक्ष्णं कृत्वा। पुरभिदि शिवे। सम्मुखयतः सम्मुखं कुर्वतः। आभिमुख्येन त्यजत इत्यर्थः। स्वर्बाला देवाङ्गनाः। सुमं पुष्पम्। अर्चनपदं पूजास्थानम्। सद्यस्तत्कालमेव। भालानलस्य यद्भसितजालं भस्मसमूहस्तदास्पदम्। गुरुमहिमभूतेषु प्रयुक्तोऽपकारः स्वापकारायैव भवतीति भावः। अयं विषमालंकारः। परस्य दुःखसाधनानवाप्तिः स्वस्य दुःखान्तरसाधनप्राप्तिश्चेत्युभयमत्रालंकारप्रयोजकम्।

Eng. Tr.:-Alas ! the body of the God of love, who aimed his arrow towards the destroyer of (three) cities (i.e. God Śiva), after showing frequently the self-conceitedness of the strength of his arms, in front of Gods, (the body of मदन) the receptacle of worship by the garlands of flowers in the form of eyes of celestial damsels, at once became the abode of the heat of ashes of the fire (on his forehead).

The poet here refers to the verse in the कुमारसंभव ३/७२ कोधं प्रभो संहर संहरेति यावद्गिरः खे मरुतां चरन्ति। तावत्स वह्निर्भवनेत्रजन्मा भस्मावशेषं मदनं चकार।।

युक्तं सभायां खलु मर्कटानां
शाखास्तरूणां मृदुलासनानि।
सुभाषितं चीत्कृतिरातिथेयी
दन्तैर्नखाग्रैश्च विपाटितानि॥८५॥

अन्वयः–मर्कटानां सभायां खलु (इदं) युक्तम्। तरूणां शाखाः मृदुलासनानि (स्युः), चीत्कृतिः सुभाषितं (स्यात्), दन्तैः नखाग्रैः च विपाटितानि आतिथेयी (स्यात्)।

व्याख्याः–खल्वत्र वाक्यालंकारे। चीत्कृतिः सुभाषितं विपाटितान्यातिथेयीत्यन्वयः। आतिथेय्यतिथिसत्क्रिया। अयं समालंकारः।

Eng.Tr.:-This is indeed proper in the assembly of monkeys: Twigs of trees are soft seats; their चीत्कारs are excellent speeches and their hospitality (consists of) scratches (made) by their teeth and points of their nails.

किं तीर्थं हरिपादपद्मभजनं किं रत्नमच्छा मतिः
किं शास्त्रं श्रवणेन यस्य गलति द्वैतान्धकारोदयः।
किं मित्रं सततोपकाररसिकं तत्त्वावबोधः सखे!
कः शत्रुर्वद खेददानकुशलो दुर्वासनासञ्चय[१]:॥८६॥

अन्वयः–किं तीर्थं? हरिपादपद्मभजनं, किं रत्नम्? अच्छा मतिः, कि शास्त्रं? श्रवणेन यस्य गलति द्वैतान्धकारोत्करः, किं सततोपकाररसिकं मित्रं? सखे तत्त्वाबोधः। वद, कः खेददानकुशलः शत्रुः? दुर्वासनासंचयः।

---

१. 'दुर्वासनानां चयः' इति पाठान्तरम्।

व्याख्याः–अच्छा निर्मला। द्वैतमन्धकार इव तस्योत्करो राशिः। द्वैतं जीवपरमात्मभेदबुद्धिः। एतादृशं वेदान्तदर्शनम्। तत्वावबोधोऽपरोक्षात्मानुभवः। प्रश्नपरिसंख्येयम्! परिसंख्या च सामान्यतः प्राप्तस्यार्थस्य कस्माच्चिदोषाद्वावृत्तिः। अत्र हरिपादभजनादिकमेव तीर्थादिकं नान्यदित्यर्थस्तात्पर्यमर्यादया प्रतीयते।

Eng.Tr.:-What is a holy place (in this worldly existence)? Devotion to the lotus-like feet of Hari. What is a jewel ? The pure intellect. What is a science ? That on hearing which the mass of darkness in the form of dualism vanishes. What is a friend, always fond of obliging ? Knowledge of the truth. What is an enemy clever in giving pain ? The accumulation of evil desires.

निष्णातोऽपि च वेदान्ते साधुत्वं नैति दुर्जनः।
चिरं जलनिधौ मग्नो मैनाक इव मार्दवम्॥८७॥

अन्वयः–चिरं जलनिधौ मग्नः मैनाकः इव मार्दवं (यथा मैनाकः मार्दवं न एति तथा) वेदान्ते (च) निष्णातोऽपि दुर्जनः साधुत्वं न एति।

व्याख्याः–वेदान्ते वेदान्तशास्त्रजनितविचारे। मैनाकः पर्वतविशेषो हिमवतः पुत्रः। अस्य कथा प्रसिद्धैव। अयमवज्ञालंकारः। अन्यस्यान्यदीयगुणदोषप्रयुक्तगुणदोषाधानविरहोऽवज्ञा। यथास्मिन् पद्ये प्रथमार्धेप्रपञ्चानित्यत्वबोधकतारूपवेदान्तशास्त्रगुणप्रयुक्तस्य खले वैराग्यरूपगुणाधानस्योत्तरार्धे च द्रवत्वरूपजलधिगुणप्रयुक्तस्य मैनाके मार्दवरूपगुणाधानस्य विरहो वर्णितः।

Eng.Tr.:-Just as the मैनाक mountain does not become soft, though plunged in ocean for a long time, so also a wicked man though well-versed in Vedānta does not attain to goodness.

नैर्गुण्यमेव साधीयो धिगस्तु गुणगौरवम्।
शाखिनोऽन्ये विराजन्ते खण्ड्यन्ते चन्दनद्रुमाः॥८८॥

अन्वयः–नैर्गुण्यमेव साधीयो धिगस्तु गुणगौरवम्। अन्ये शाखिनः विराजन्ते, चन्दनद्रुमाः (तु) खण्ड्यन्ते।

व्याख्या:–साधीय: साधुतरम् । अन्ये शाखिन: पिचुमन्दादय:। विराजन्तेऽनभिभूता: शोभन्ते । अयं लेशालंकारोऽर्थान्तरन्यासानुविद्ध:। लेशश्च गुणस्यानिष्टसाधनतया दोषत्वेन दोषस्येष्टसाधनतया गुणत्वेन च वर्णनम्।

गुणानामेव दौरात्म्याद् धुरि धुर्यो नियुज्यते।
असंजातकिणस्कन्ध: सुखं स्वपिति गौर्गलि:।।

इति कस्यचित्पद्यमेतत् समानार्थकमेव।

Eng.Tr.:-The absence of virtues (qualities) is better; fie upon the multitude of virtues. Other (ordinary) trees thrive, (while) the sandle trees are cut of.

परोपसर्पणानन्तचिन्तानलशिखाशतै:।
अचुम्बितान्त:करणा: साधु जीवन्ति पादपा:।।८९।।

अन्वय:–परोपसर्पणानन्तचिंतानलशिखाशतै: अचुम्बितान्त:करणा: पादपा: साधु जीवन्ति।

व्याख्या:–अत्र पादपस्तुति: सांसारिकजननिन्दायां पर्यवस्यति।

Eng.Tr.:-Happily do the trees live, whose hearts are not touched by the hundreds of flames arising from fire in the form of endless anxiety which is the result of approaching others (for begging for something).

शून्येऽपि च गुणवत्तामातन्वान: स्वकीयगुणजालै:।
विवराणि मुद्रयन्द्रागूर्णायुरिव सुजनो जयति।।९०।।

अन्वय:–शून्येऽपि स्वकीयगुणजालै: गुणवत्तामातन्वान: द्राक् विवराणि मुद्रयन् च ऊर्णायु: इव सज्जनो जयति।

व्याख्या:–शून्येऽर्थरहिते स्थले शून्यहृदये जने च। गुणवत्तां तन्तुमत्तां विनयादिगुणशालितां च। गुणजालैस्तन्तुसमूहैर्दयादाक्षिण्यादिभिश्च। विवराणि शून्यभागान् पररन्ध्राणि च। मुद्रयन्नाच्छादयन् गोपयंश्च। ऊर्णायु: कोली इति प्रसिद्धो जन्तुभेद:। श्लिष्टोपमेयम्।

Eng.Tr.:-A good man is successful who transforms a

dunce also into a person of qualities, by means of his own stock of qualities by hiding his faults immediately like a spider who builds his web in a place which is empty, by his net of thread, and covers the openings (in the house) immediately.

खलः सज्जनकार्पासरक्षणैकहुताशनः।
परदुःखाग्निशमनो मारुतः केन वर्ण्यताम्॥९१॥

अन्वयः—सज्जनकार्पासरक्षणैकहुताशनः परदुःखाग्निशमनमारुतः खलः केन वर्ण्यताम्।

व्याख्याः—इदं रूपकम्। अत्र रक्षणशमनपदे विरोधिलक्षणया विपरीतार्थ-बोधके।

Eng.Tr.:-Who can describe the wicked man who is an unique fire in burning the cotton in the form of a good man, and kind wind that aggravates the fire in form of miseries of others.

परगुह्यगुप्तिनिपुणं गुणमयमखिलैः समीहितं नितराम्।
ललिताम्बरमिव सज्जनमाखव इव दूषयन्ति खलाः॥९२॥

अन्वयः—परगुह्यगुप्तिनिपुणं गुणमयं अखिलैः नितरां समीहितं ललितांबरमिव सज्जनं खलः आखवः इव दूषयन्ति।

व्याख्याः—परगुह्यगुप्तिः परगुह्याङ्गाच्छादनं पररन्ध्रगोपनं च। गुणमयं तन्तुमयं विनयादिगुणयुक्तं च। समीहितमपेक्ष्यमाणम्। ललिताम्बरं सुन्दरवस्त्रम्। आखुर्मूषकः। श्लेषोत्त्थापितेयमुपमा।

Eng.Tr.:-Wicked men spoil (the reputation of a) good man who is well-versed in protecting the secrets (गुह्य) of others, is possessed of good merits and is much liked by all, like mice which spoil a fine garment which is skilled in protecting the private parts (गुह्य) of others, which is full of threads and is much desired by all.

यशः सौरभ्यलशुनः शान्तिशैत्यहुताशनः।
कारुण्यकुसुमाकाशः खलः सज्जनदुःखदः॥९३॥

अन्वयः–सज्जनकार्पासर क्षणैकहुताशनः परदुःखाग्निशमने मारुतः खलः केन वर्ण्यताम्?

व्याख्याः–कारुण्यमेव कुसुमं तस्याकाशः शून्यभागः। अनाश्रय इति यावत्। अनेन खले कारुण्यस्यात्यन्ताभावः सूच्यते। एवमपरत्रापि। अस्य तात्पर्यं (९१) पद्यस्येव।

Eng.Tr.:-A wicked man giving pain to the good is a garlic to fragrance in the form of fame, a fire to the cold in the form of tranquillity, the sky to the flower in the form of compassion.

धत्ते भरं कुसुमपत्रफलावलीनां
घर्मव्यथां वहति शीतभवां रुजं च।
यो देहमर्पयति चान्यसुखस्य हेतो-
स्तस्मै वदान्यगुरवे तरवे नमोऽस्तु॥९४॥

अन्वयः–यः कुसुमपत्रफलावलीनां भरं धत्ते, घर्मव्यथां शीतभवां रुजं च वहति अन्यसुखस्य च हेतोः देहमर्पयति तस्मै वदान्यगुरवे तरवे नमोऽस्तु।

व्याख्याः–घर्मव्यथां निदाघातपजनितपीडाम्।

Eng.Tr.:-A bow to that tree, the foremost among the liberal, which bears the burden of the clusters of flowers, leaves and fruits, puts up with the afflictions of heat and cold and which sacrifices its own body for the bliss of others.

हालाहलं खलु पिपासति कौतुकेन
कालानलं परिचुचुम्बिषति प्रकामम्।
व्यालाधिपं च यतते परिरब्धुमद्धा
यो दुर्जनं वशयितुं तनुते[१] मनीषाम्॥९५॥

अन्वयः–यः दुर्जनं वशयितुं मनीषा तनुते (सः) खलु कौतुकेन हालाहलं पिपासति, कालानलं प्रकामं परिचुचुम्बिषति अद्धा च व्यालाधिपं परिरब्धुं यतते।

---

१. 'कुरुते' इति पाठान्तरम्।

व्याख्या:—कालानलं प्रलयकालीनमग्निम्। अद्धा तत्त्वतः। वशयितुं वशीकर्तुम्। मनीषामिच्छाम्। मालानिदर्शनेयम्।

Eng.Tr.:-He who cherishes a desire to win over a wicked man, wishes indeed to drink deadly poison with curiosity, to kiss closely the fire of final destruction or to embrace actually the lord of serpents.

दीनानामिह परिहाय शुष्कसस्या-
न्यौदार्यं प्रकटयतो महीधरेषु।
औन्नत्यं परममवाप्य दुर्मदस्य
ज्ञातोऽयं जलधर ते[१] मयाऽविवेकः॥९६॥

अन्वयः—हे जलधर, परममौन्नत्यमवाप्य इह दीनानां शुष्कसस्यानि परिहाय महीधरेषु औदार्यं प्रकटयतः दुर्मदस्य ते मया अयं विवेकः ज्ञातः।

व्याख्या:—दीनानां शुष्कशस्यानि परिहाय महीधरेष्वौदार्यं प्रकटयतः परममौन्नत्यमवाप्य दुर्मदस्य तावको विवेको ज्ञात इत्यन्वयः। दीनानामाय-विहीनाम्। इह योग्यभूमौ। औदार्यं जलवर्षणरूपम्। औन्नत्यमुच्च- देशस्थितिः। उच्चपदप्राप्तिरित्यपि ध्वन्यते। अत्यन्तानुचितमिदमिति भावः।

Eng.Tr.:-This indiscrimination of you, O cloud! is known (to me)-you who being elated with pride on account of your exalted position, display your generosity towards the mountains, leaving aside here dried corn of the poor.

गिरयो गुरवस्तेभ्योऽप्युर्वी गुर्वी ततोऽपि जगदण्डम्।
तस्मादप्यतिगुरवः प्रलयेऽप्यचला महात्मानः॥९७॥

अन्वयः— गिरयः गुरवः तेभ्यः अपि उर्वी गुर्वी ततः अपि जगदण्डम् तस्माद् अपि अतिगुरवः प्रलये अपि अचलाः महात्मानः (सन्ति)।

व्याख्या:—उर्वी पृथ्वी। महापुरुषाणां प्रलयकालेऽपि निर्विकारत्वमिति भावः। अयं सारालंकारः। स चोत्तरोत्तरमुत्कर्षो भवेत् सारः परावधिरिति काव्यप्रकाशे लक्षितः।

Eng.Tr.:-Mountains are great, the earth is greater still

---

१. 'तावको' 'ते यथा' च इति पाठान्तरद्वयम्।

than they, the universe is yet greater than the earth and the high-souled persons who are firm even at the world-deluge are the greatest.

व्योमनि बीजाकुरुते[1] चित्रं निर्माति सुन्दरं पवने।
रचयति रेखाः सलिले यस्तु खले चरति सत्कारम्॥९८॥

अन्वयः—यः तु खले सत्कारं चरति (सः) व्योमनि बीजाकुरुते, पवने सुन्दरं चित्रं निर्माति, सलिले रेखाः रचयति।

व्याख्याः—व्योमन्याकाशे। वीजाकुरुते बीजप्रक्षेपपूर्वकं कर्षणं कुरुते। कृञो द्वितीयतृतीयशंबबीजात्कृषाविति सूत्रेण कृञ्धातोर्योगे द्वितीयादिशब्देभ्यो डाज् भवति। तु निश्चये। निदर्शनेयम्।

Eng.Tr.:-He who treats the wicked with respect, as if sows seeds in the sky, draws a beautiful picture in wind and draws lines in water.

हारं वक्षसि केनापि दत्तमज्ञेन मर्कटः।
लेढि जिघ्रति संक्षिप्य करोत्युन्नतमाननम्॥९९॥

अन्वयः—केनाप्यज्ञेन दत्तं हारं मर्कटः लेढि, जिघ्रति (पश्चात्) संक्षिप्य आननं उन्नतं करोति।

व्याख्याः—दत्तमर्पितम्। अज्ञेनानभिज्ञेन। हारं संक्षिप्यैकीकृत्य तस्येन्नतामासनं करोतीत्यर्थः। अनभिज्ञेषु रमणीयवस्तुसमर्पणं तन्नाशाय भवद्गति भावः।

Eng.Tr.:-An ape, licks and smells a necklace given to him by an ignorant man and (then) raises his face by placing that necklace below (its haunches).

मलिनेऽपि रागपूर्णां विकसितवदनामनल्पजल्पेऽपि।
त्वयि चपलेऽपि च सरसां भ्रमर! कथं वा सरोजिनीं त्यजसि॥१००॥

अन्वयः—हे भ्रमर मलिनेऽपि त्वयि रागपूर्णां, अनल्पजल्पेऽपि (त्वयि) विकसितवदनां, चपलेऽपि (त्वयि) सरसां सरोजिनं त्वं कथं वा त्यजसि।

व्याख्याः—मलिने कृष्णवर्णे कपटवति च। रागस्ताम्रत्वमनुरागश्च।

---
१. 'व्योम्नि स वासं कुरुते' इति पाठान्तरम्।

विकसितवदनां प्रफुल्लसरोजां सहासवदनां च। अनल्पजल्पे सततगुञ्जार-वकारिणि बहु भाषमाणे च चपलेऽस्थिरे चञ्चलचित्ते च। सरसां मधुयुक्तां प्रीतिमतीं च। अत्र भ्रमरवृत्तान्तन वाच्येन श्लिष्टविशेषणमाहात्म्यात् कामुक-वृत्तान्तः प्रतीयते। अलंकारः प्रकरणभेदात् समासोक्तिरप्रस्तुतप्रशंसा वा।

Eng.Tr.:-O bee! the lotus creeper maintains its reddish colour although you are blue (dirty), it blooms its lotuses (lit. face) although you are constantly humming (talkative), it is full of honey (full of love) even though you are volatile (and thus faithless), how do you leave it then ?

स्वार्थं धनानि धनिकात्प्रतिगृह्णतो य-
दास्यं भजेन्मलिनतां किमिदं विचित्रम्।
गृह्णन्परार्थमपि वारिनिधेः पयोऽपि
मेघोऽयमेति सकलोऽपि च कालिमानम्॥१०१॥

अन्वयः–यद् स्वार्थं (स्वार्थाय) धनिकात् धनानि प्रतिगृह्णतः (नरस्य) आस्यं मलिनतां भजेत् इदं किम् विचित्रं? अयं मेघः परार्थं अपि वारिनिधेः पयः अपि गृह्णन् सकलः किल कालिमानम् एति।

व्याख्या:–स्वार्थं स्वप्रयोजनसिद्धये। परार्थमपीत्यत्र न स्वकार्यसाध-नायेत्यप्यर्थः। पयोऽपि न धानानीत्यर्थः कालिमानं मालिन्यम्।

Eng.Tr.:-What wonder is there when the face of a person who takes money from the rich for selfish motives will be blackened ? (why) this cloud taking even water (what to talk of wealth !) from the ocean (the store of water) even for others, indeed becomes dark all over.

जनकः सानुविशेषो जातिः काष्ठं भुजङ्गमैः सङ्गः।
स्वगुणैरेव पटीरज! यातोऽसि तथापि महिमानम्॥१०२॥

अन्वयः–हे पटीरज, (तव) जनकः सानुविशेषः, जातिः काष्ठं, सङ्गः भुजङ्गमैः, तथापि त्वं स्वगुणैरेव महिमानं यातोऽसि।

व्याख्या:–सानुविशेषो मलयः। गुणा एव गुणिषु पूजास्थानमित्यर्थः।

Eng.Tr.:-O sandal! your father is a particular summit, by caste you are wood, your companionship is with the serpents, yet you have reached greatness only by your intrinsic merits.

कस्मै हन्त फलाय सज्जन! गुणग्रामार्जने सज्जसि
स्वात्मोपस्करणाय चेन्मम वचः पथ्यं समाकर्णय।
ये भावा हृदयं हरन्ति नितरां शोभाभरैः संभृता-
स्तैरेवास्य कलेः कलेवरपुषो दैनन्दिनं वर्तनम्॥१०३॥

अन्वयः—हे सज्जन, हन्त कस्मै फलाय गुणग्रामार्जने सज्जसि ? "स्वात्मोपस्करणाय" (इति) चेत्, मम पथ्यं वचः समाकर्णय, ये भावा शोभाभरैः संभृताः नितरां हृदयं हरन्ति तैरेव अस्य कलेवरपुषः कलेः दैनंदिनं वर्तनम्।

व्याख्या:—हन्त खेदे। ग्रामः समूहः। स्वात्मोपस्करणायात्मनमलंकर्तुम्। भावा वस्तूनि। कलेवरपुषः शरीरपोषकस्य। इह रमणीयाः पदार्थाः कलेर्नित्यम-दनीया इति वस्तुना मर्तुं कामयसे चेद् गुणप्राप्तौ यतस्वेति वस्तु व्यज्यते।

Eng.Tr.:-O good man ! alas ! With what aim in view are you prepared to accomplish a multitude of merits ? If you reply 'for decorating myself, listen to my wholesome advice. This Kali who is getting stronger gains his livelihood from those very things which, being full of great beauty, greatly attract the mind.

धूमायिता दशदिशो दलितारविन्दा
देहं दहन्ति दहना इव गन्धवाहाः।
त्वामन्तरेण मृदुताम्रदलाम्रमञ्जु-
गुञ्जन्मधुव्रत! मधो किल कोकिलस्य॥१०४॥

अन्वयः—मृदुताम्रदलाम्रमञ्जन्मधुव्रत! मधो! त्वाम् अन्तरेण किल कोकिलस्य दलितारविन्दाः दश दिशः धूमायिताः गन्धवाहाः दहना इव देहम् दहन्ति।

व्याख्या:—धूमायिता धूमपूर्णाः। त्वामन्तरेण त्वां विना। मृदुताम्रणि दलानि येषां तेष्वाम्रेषु मञ्जु गुञ्जन्तो मधुव्रता यस्मिन्। इदं मधुविशेषणम्।

Eng.Tr.:-O spring ! having bees sweetly humming on mango-trees with tender and reddish foliage, without you, ten quarters having lotuses full-blown are turned smoky and winds (hot) like fire scorch the body of the cuckoo.

भिन्ना महागिरिशिलाः करजाग्रजाग्र-
दुद्दामशौर्यनिकरैः करटिभ्रमेण।
दैवे पराचि करिणामरिणा तथापि
कुत्रापि नापि खलु हा पिशितस्य लेशः॥१०५॥

अन्वयः—करिणामरिणा करटिभ्रमेण करजाग्रजाग्रदुद्दामशौर्यनिकरैः महागिरिशिलाः भिन्नाः तथापि दैवे पराचि (सति) कुत्रापि (करिणां) पिशितस्य लेशः न खलु अपि।

व्याख्याः—करजाग्रेषु नखाग्रेषु जाग्रद् यदुद्यामशौर्यं तस्य निकरैः। पराचि प्रतिकूले। करिणामरिणा हरिणा। नापि न प्राप्तः। पिशितस्य मांसस्य।

Eng.Tr.:-Although rocks of gigantic mountains are not torn asunder by the enemy of elephants (i.e. a lion) with a great deal of valour, active and prominent at the ends of nails, mistaking (the rocks) for elephants yet, fate being adverse, nowhere did he obtain even a bit of flesh (of elephants).

गर्जितमाकर्ण्य मनागङ्के मातुर्निशार्धजातोऽपि।
हरिशिशुरुत्पतितुं द्रागङ्गान्याकुञ्च्य लीयते निभृतम्॥१०६॥

अन्वयः—निशार्धजातोऽपि हरिशिशुः मातुः अङ्के मनाग् गर्जितं आकर्ण्य, द्राग् उत्पतितुं निभृतं अङ्गानि आकुञ्च्य लीयते।

व्याख्याः—गर्जितं मेघस्येति शेषः। आकुञ्च्य संकुच्य। लीयते तिष्ठति। निभृतं निश्चलम्। हरिशिशोः शिशुत्वेऽप्येवंविध एव स्वभाव इति भावः।

Eng.Tr.:-Having slightly listened to the thundering while on the lap of its mother, the cub of a lion though half a night old, lurks secretly after contracting its limbs, in order to quickly pounce upon (mistaking the thunder for the voice of an elephant).

किमहं वदामि खल! दिव्यमते
गुणपक्षपातमभितो भवतः।
गुणशालिनो निखिलसाधुजनान्
यदहर्निशं न खलु विस्मरसि॥१०७॥

अन्वयः—हे दिव्यमते खल अभितः भवतः गुणपक्षपातं अहं किं वदामि, यत् खलु अहर्निशम् गुणशालिनः निखिलसाधुजनान् न विस्मरसि।

व्याख्याः—दिव्यमतेऽलौकिकबुद्धे। खलविशेषणमेतत्। भवतो गुणपक्षपातं किं वदामीत्यन्वयः। अत्र गुणिनां सततस्मरणमापाततो गुणत्वेनोपात्तम्। इयं व्याजस्तुतिः। खलदुश्चरितोत्कीर्तनप्रस्ताव आमुखप्रतीता स्तुतिरत्र निन्दायां पर्यवस्यति। खलः साधुजनान् यत्सततं स्मरति तद्रन्ध्रान्वेषणतत्परतया न हिताकांक्षया।

Eng.Tr.:-O wicked person of celestial intellect ! how can I (adequately) describe your partiality (enmity) for qualities, since you do not forget (i.e. remember) all the good persons possessing qualities, by day and night ?

रे खल! तव खलु चरितं विदुषामग्रे[१] विविच्य वक्ष्यामि।
अथवालं पापात्मन्! कृतया कथयापि ते हतया॥१०८॥

अन्वयः—हे खल! तव चरितम् विदुषाम् अग्रे विविच्य वक्ष्यामि खलु! पापात्मन्! अथवा ते हतया कृतया कथया अपि अलम्।

व्याख्याः—विविच्य निर्णीय। हतया दग्धया। अत्यन्ताप्रिययेत्यर्थः। केषाञ्चिन्मतेऽयमाक्षेपालंकारः। अत्र वक्ष्यमाणस्य खलवृत्तान्तस्य निषेधः कथ्यमानस्तस्याचिन्तितदुःखप्रदतां व्यनक्ति।

Eng.Tr.:-O wicked man! I shall relate your life (behaviour) in detail in front of the learned or O sinner! what

१. 'मध्ये' इति पाठान्तरम्।

is the use of your wretched account, even though related? (So of course I shall abstain from it).

आनन्दमृगदावाग्निः शीलशाखिमदद्विपः।
ज्ञानदीपमहावायुरयं खलसमागमः॥१०९॥

अन्वयः—अयं खलसमागमः आनन्दमृगदावाग्निः, शीलशाखिमदद्विपः, ज्ञानदीपमहावायुः (च अस्ति)।

व्याख्याः—आनन्दरूपमृगस्य दावाग्निः। नाशक इत्यर्थः। एवमपरत्रापि। रूपकमिदम्।

Eng.Tr.:-This companionship with the wicked is (like) a forest conflagration to the deer in the form of joy, a rutting elephant to the tree in the form of character and tempestuous wind to the lamp in the form of knowledge.

खलास्तु कुशलाः साधुहितप्रत्यूहकर्मणि।
निपुणाः फणिनः प्राणानपहर्तुं निरागसाम्॥११०॥

अन्वयः—खलाः तु साधुहितप्रत्यूहकर्मणि कुशलाः, फणिनः निरागसाम् प्राणानपहर्तुं निपुणाः।

व्याख्याः—प्रत्यूहकर्मणि प्रतिरोधक्रियायाम्। इयं प्रतिवस्तूपमा।

Eng.Tr.:-The villains are experts in putting impediments in the welfare of the good. The snakes are experts in taking away the lives of innocent persons.

वदने विनिवेशिता भुजङ्गी
पिशुनानां रसनामिषेण धात्रा।
अनया कथमन्यथावलीढा
न हि जीवन्ति जना मनागमन्त्राः॥१११॥

अन्वयः—धात्रा रसनामिषेण पिशुनानां वदने भुजंगी विनिवेशिता अन्यथा अनया अवलीढाः जनाः अमंत्राः मनाग् (अपि) न हि जीवन्ति (इति) कथम्।

व्याख्याः—रसनामिषेण जिह्वाच्छलेन। अमन्त्रा गारुडादिमन्त्ररहिताः। इयमपन्हुतिः।

Eng.Tr.:-The creator has placed a female serpent in the form of tongue, in the mouths of the wicked, otherwise how is it that persons bit by her do not live even a minute longer without the application of magic charms ?

कृतं त्वयोन्नतं[१] कृत्यमर्जितं चामलं यशः।
यावज्जीवं सखे! तुभ्यं दास्यामो विपुलाशिषः॥११२॥

अन्वयः—हे सखे त्वया उन्नतं कृत्यं कृतम्, अमलं यशः च अर्जितम् यावज्जीवं तुभ्यं विपुलाशिषः दास्यामः।

व्याख्या:—इयं कस्यचिदपकारिणं प्रत्युक्तिः। त्वया कृतेऽप्यपकारे परमखेदहेतौ मधुरमेव यो भाषे न पुरुषं तस्मिन्मयि पापमाचरस्तव पापिष्ठत्वं कथं शक्यते वक्तुमिति व्यंग्यम्।

Eng.Tr.:-O friend! (enemy) you have done an exalted (mean) deed and have gained untarnished fame (notoriety). So long as we live, we shall give you plenty of blessings (curses).

अविरतं परकार्यकृतां सतां
मधुरिमातिशयेन वचोऽमृतम्।
अपि च मानसमम्बुनिधिर्यशो
विमलशारदचन्दिरचन्द्रिका॥११३॥

अन्वयः—अविरतं परकार्यकृतां सतां वचः मधुरिमातिशयेन अमृतम् अप च मानसम् अम्बुनिधिः, यशः विमलशारदपार्वणचन्द्रिका (भवति)।

व्याख्या:—मानसमम्बुनिधिर्गाम्भिर्येण। यशश्चन्द्रिका धवलत्वात्। शारदः शरत्कालीनः। चन्दिरश्चन्द्रः।

Eng.Tr.:-The speech of persons incessantly engaged in obliging others, resembles nectar owing to its excessive sweetness, their mind is (magnanimous) like the sea and their fame resembles the moon-light of the clear autumnal moon. (i.e. gives excessive pleasure). v. i. पार्व्वणचन्द्रिका- moon-light of the full moon, because पर्व means the full moon-day.

---

१. 'महोन्नतं' इति पाठान्तरम्।

एत्य कुसुमाकरो मे सञ्जीवयिता गिरं चिरं मग्नाम्।
इति चिन्तयतो हृदये पिकस्य समधायि शौभिकेन शरः॥११४॥

अन्वयः—'कुसुमाकर एत्य मे चिरं मग्नां गिरं सञ्जीवयिता' इति चिन्तयतः पिकस्य हृदये शौभिकेन शरः समधायि।

व्याख्याः—कुसुमाकरो वसन्तः। सञ्जीवयिता पुनरुज्जीवयिता। शौभिकेन व्याधेन। अस्य तात्पर्यं (५८) श्लोकस्येव।

Eng.Tr.:-The spring having arrived, will restore my voice that has been silent for a long time, while a cuckoo was thus thinking, an arrow was discharged at its heart by a fowler.

निर्गुणः शोभते नैव विपुलाडम्बरोऽपि ना।
आपातरम्यपुष्पश्रीशोभितः शाल्मलिर्यथा॥११५॥

अन्वयः—विपुलाडम्बरः अपि निर्गुणः ना न एव शोभते यथा आपातरम्यपुष्पश्रीशोभिता शाल्मलिः (नैव शोभते)

व्याख्याः—विपुलाडम्बरो विपुलोपकरणः। ना पुरुषः। आपातेनाविचारितबुद्ध्या रम्या या पुष्पश्रीस्तया शोभितः। वस्तुतस्तु न सा रम्येत्यर्थः। शाल्मलिः साम्वरी इति प्रसिद्धो वृक्षः।

Eng.Tr.:-A man devoid of good merits does not appear to advantage, though set off by a fine (outward) display as a शाल्मलि tree though adorned with the beauty of flowers for the present moment.

पङ्कैर्विना सरो भाति सदः खलजनैर्विना।
कटुवर्णैर्विना काव्यं मानसं विषयैर्विना॥११६॥

अन्वयः—सरः पङ्कैः विना, सदः खलजनैः विना, काव्यं कटुवर्णैः विना, मानसं विषयैः विना भाति।

व्याख्याः—विनोक्तिरियं तुल्ययोगितानुकूला।

Eng.Tr.:-A lake without mud, an assembly without

wicked persons, poetry without harsh words and mind void of the sensual objects look beautiful.

तत्त्वं किमपि काव्यानां जानाति विरलो भुवि।
मार्मिकः को मरन्दानामन्तरेण मधुव्रतम्॥११७॥

अन्वयः—काव्यानां किमपि तत्त्वं भुवि विरलो जानाति। मधुव्रतं अन्तरेण मरन्दानां मार्मिकः कः (विद्यते)।

व्याख्या:—किमपि लोकोत्तरं। तत्त्वं मर्म।

Eng.Tr.:-In this world, scarcely anyone knows the extra-ordinary essence of poetry; who but the bee is the appreciator of honey (in flowers)?

सरजस्कां पाण्डुवर्णां कण्टकप्रकराङ्किताम्।
केतकीं सेवसे हन्त कथं रोलम्ब! निस्त्रपः॥११८॥

अन्वयः—हे रोलम्ब हन्त ! सरजस्कां पाण्डुवर्णां कंटकप्रकरांकितां केतकीं निस्त्रपः कथं सेवसे।

व्याख्या:—सरजस्कां पुष्परजोयुक्ताम्। रजस्वलामिति च ध्वन्यते। कण्टकप्रकराङ्कितां कण्टकसमूहचिताम्। पुलकितामिति च ध्वन्यते। रोलम्ब भ्रमर।

Eng.Tr.:-O bee ! How is it, alas ! that you shamelessly enjoy a केतकी which is सरजस्का, पाण्डुवर्णा and कण्टकप्रकराङ्किता?

यथा तानं विना रागो यथा मानं विना नृपः।
यथा दानं विना हस्ती तथा ज्ञानं विना यतिः॥११९॥

अन्वयः—रागः यथा तानं विना, नृपः यथा मानं विना, हस्ती यथा दानं विना, यतिः तथा ज्ञानं विना न शोभते।

व्याख्या:—तान इतरस्वरधारणार्थः स्वरविशेषः। रञ्जकः स्वरसन्दर्भो रागः। इयं विनोक्तिरुपमानुकूला।

Eng.Tr.:-As a राग without तान, a king without respect and an elephant without rut, so is an ascetic (worthless) without knowledge (of ब्रह्मन्).

सन्तः स्वतः प्रकाशन्ते गुणा न परतो नृणाम्।
आमोदो न हि कस्तूर्याः शपथेन विभाव्यते॥१२०॥

अन्वयः–नृणां सन्तः गुणाः स्वतः प्रकाशन्ते न परतः। कस्तूर्याः आमोदः शपथेन न हि विभाव्यते।

व्याख्याः–नानुभाव्यते नानुभवं प्राप्यते। घ्राणेन्द्रियेणैव साक्षाद् गृह्यत इत्यर्थः। प्रतिवस्तूपमेयम्।

यदि सन्ति गुणाः पुंसां विकसन्त्यैव ते स्वयम्।
न हि कस्तूरिकामोदः शपथेन विभाव्यते॥

इति कस्यचित् कवेः पद्यस्य रूपान्तरमेवेदम्।

Eng.Tr.:-The good merits of men shine by themselves and not from (the mouths of) others. The fragrance of musk is, indeed, not known on oath.

अयि बत गुरुगर्वं मास्म कस्तूरि! यासी-
रखिलपरिमलानां मौलिना सौरभेण।
गिरिगहनगुहायां लीनमत्यन्तदीनं
स्वजनकममुनैव प्राणहीनं करोषि॥१२१॥

अन्वयः–अयि कस्तूरि, अखिलपरिमलानां मौलिना सौरभेण गर्वं मास्म बत यासीः अमुनैव सौरभेण गिरिगहनगुहायां लीनम् अत्यन्तदीनं स्वजनकं प्राणहीनं करोषि।

व्याख्याः–मौलिना श्रेष्ठेन। स्वजनकं कस्तूरीमृगम्। अत्र पूर्वोक्तलक्षणो लेशालंकारः।

Eng.Tr.:-O musk! alas ! do not pride yourself upon your fragrance which is the best of all. Owing to that (fragrance) alone you bring death to your father who is very innocent and who hides himself in the dens in the mountain-forests.

दूरीकरोति कुमतिं विमलीकरोति
चेतश्चिरन्तनमघं चुलुकीकरोति।
भूतेषु किं च करुणां बहुलीकरोति
सङ्गः सतां किमु न मंङ्गलमातनोति॥१२२॥

अन्वयः–सतां संगः कुमतिं दूरीकरोति, चेतः विमलीकरोति, चिरन्तनं अघं चुलुकीकरोति, किं च भूतेषु करुणां बहुलीकरोति, किमु मङ्गलं न आतनोति।

व्याख्याः–चुलुकीकरोति पिबति। नाशयतीति यावत्।

Eng. Tr.:-The company of the good removes ill-thoughts, purifies the mind, destroys the sin of long standing, moreover it widens humanity (the love for creatures), what auspicious thing does it not beget ?

अनवरतपरोपकारव्यग्रीभवदमलचेतसां महताम्।
आपातकाटवानि स्फुरन्ति वचनानि भेषजानीव॥१२३॥

अन्वयः–अनवरतपरोपकारव्यग्रीभवदमलचेतसां महतां आपातकाटवानि वचनानि भेषजानीव स्फुरन्ति।

व्याख्याः–कट्व काटवम्। स्वार्थे अण्। आपातेनाविचारितबुद्ध्या काटवानि कटूनि। यद्वा। आपातेन काटवं कटुत्वं येषां तानि। परिणामे परमसुखकराणीत्यर्थः।

Eng. Tr.:-The speech of the great, whose pure mind is always engrossed in the incessant (performance of) philanthropic deeds and which are bitter only at the beginning, shine (i.e. are) like medicines (bringing happiness in the end).

व्यागुञ्जन्मधुकरपुञ्जमञ्जुगीता-
न्याकर्ण्य श्रुतिमुदयन्नयातिरेकात्[१]**।**
आभूमीतलनतकन्धराणि मन्ये-
ऽरण्येऽस्मिन्नवनिरुहां कुटुम्बकानि॥१२४॥

---

१. 'श्रुतिमदजाल्लयातिरेकात्' इति पाठान्तरम्।

अन्वयः–व्यागुंजन्मधुकरपुंजमंजुगीतां स्तुतिं आकर्ण्य उदयन्नयातिरेकात् अस्मिन्नरण्ये अवनिरुहां कुन्धकानि आभूमीतलनतकन्धराणि इति मन्ये।

व्याख्या:–उदयन्नुद्भवन् यो नयः शालीनता तस्यातिरेकादतिशयात्। अवनिरुहां वृक्षाणाम्। कुटुम्बकानि कुलानि। इयं हेतूत्प्रेक्षा। अत्र नतकन्धरत्व उदयन्नयातिरेकादिति हेतुरुत्पेक्षितो न वास्तवः।

Eng.Tr.:-I imagine that the families (clusters) of trees in this forest have bent their necks (branches) down to the surface of the earth because of the excess of modesty (नय) generated in them on hearing their own praise sung by the clusters of beautifully humming bees.

मृतस्य लिप्सा कृपणस्य दित्सा
विमार्गगायाश्च रुचिः स्वकान्ते।
सर्पस्य शान्तिः कुटिलस्य मैत्री
विधातृसृष्टौ न हि दृष्टपूर्वा॥१२५॥

अन्वयः–विधातृसृष्टौ हि मृतस्य कृतस्य लिप्सा, कृपणस्य दित्सा, विमार्गगायाश्च स्वकान्ते रुचिः, सर्पस्य शान्तिः कुटिलस्य मैत्री (च) दृष्टपूर्वा।

व्याख्या:–मृतस्येति कर्मणि षष्ठी। लिप्सा लाभेच्छा। मृतलाभस्येच्छेत्यर्थः। कृपणस्येति कर्तरि षष्ठी। दित्सा दानेच्छा। विमार्गगा जारिणी। अत्र तुल्ययोगितालंकारः। मृतकृपणादीनां कस्यचित् प्रकृतत्वे तु दीपकं स्यात्।

Eng.Tr.:-The desire to obtain, to a dead man; the desire to give in a miserly person; the love for her own husband in a wanton woman; calmness in a serpent; friendship in a crooked man, have never been witnessed before in the creation of God Brahma (i.e. in the world).

उत्तमानामपि स्त्रीणां विश्वासो नैव विद्यते।
राजप्रियाः कैरविण्यो रमन्ते मधुपैः सह॥१२६॥

अन्वयः–उत्तमानामपि स्त्रीणां विश्वासो नैव विद्यते, राजप्रियाः कैरविण्यः मधुपैः सह रमन्ते।

व्याख्याः–राजप्रियाश्चंद्रप्रियाः। भूपप्रिया इत्यपि ध्वन्यते। मधुपैभ्रमरैः। मद्यपायिभिरित्यपि ध्वन्यते।

Eng.Tr.:-There is no faith (i.e we do not confide in) even in the best women; the night lotuses though the favourites of the moon enjoy with मधुपs (bees or drunkards).

अयाचितः सुखं दत्ते याचितश्च न यच्छति।
सर्वस्वं चापि हरते विधिरुच्छृङ्खलो नृणाम्॥१२७॥

अन्वयः–नृणां उच्छृङ्खलः विधिः अयाचितः सुखं दत्ते याचितः च (सुखं) न यच्छति सर्वस्वं च अपि हरते।

व्याख्याः–दैवाधीनं सर्वमिति भावः।

Eng.Tr.:-The unruly fate of men gives happines when unasked and does not give it when asked (for it), (not only this but also) it takes away everything (when it is adverse).

दोर्दण्डद्वयकुण्डलीकृतलसत्कोदण्डचण्डाशुग-
ध्वस्तोद्दण्डविपक्षमण्डलमथ त्वां वीक्ष्य मध्येरणम्।
वल्गद्गाण्डिवमुक्तकाण्डवलयज्वालावलीताण्डव-
भ्रश्यत्खाण्डवरुष्टपाण्डवमहो को न क्षितीशः स्मरेत्॥१२८॥

अन्वयः–दोर्दडद्वयकुण्डलीकृतलसत्कोदण्डचण्डाशुगध्वस्तो द्दण्डविपक्षमण्डलं त्वां मध्येरणं वीक्ष्य वल्गद्गांडिवमुक्तकाण्डवलयज्वालावलीतांडवभ्रश्यत्खांड-वरुष्टपांडवमहो कः क्षितीशः न स्मरेत्।

व्याख्याः–इयं कस्यचिद्राज्ञः स्तुतिः। त्वां मध्येरणं वीक्ष्य कः क्षितीशः पाण्डवं न स्मरेदित्यन्वयः। दोर्दण्डद्वयेन कुण्डलीकृतं यल्लसत् कोदण्डं धनुस्तस्य चण्डाशुगैस्तीक्ष्णबाणैर्ध्वस्तमुदण्डविपक्षमण्डलं प्रचण्डशत्रुमण्डलं येन तथाविधम्। मध्येरणमित्यव्ययीभावः। वल्गाच्छद्धं कुर्वद् यद् गाण्डिवं

तस्मान्मुक्तं यत्काण्डवलयं शरचक्रं तस्य ज्वालाबलीताण्डवेन भ्रश्यन्नयश्द् यत् खाण्डवं नाम वनं तस्मिन् रुष्टं पाण्डवम्। अर्जुनमित्यर्थः। अत्र स्मरणालंकारः। अयं श्लोकः पण्डितराजकृतप्राणाभरणकाव्येऽपि दृश्यते। किं तु तत्र ग्रन्थपरिसमाप्त्यनन्तरं स्थितोऽनुचित इवाभाति।

Eng. Tr.:-Having observed in the battle field you who destroyed the circle of powerful enemies by the terrible darts (discharged) from his brilliant bow bent round by the pair of his (strong) arms, what king will not remember (i.e. every king will remember) that indignat पाण्डव (namely अर्जुन) who was standing in the खाण्डव wilderness which was destroyed by the movement of the series of flames (issuing) from the circle of arrows discharged from his twanging गाण्डिव bow ?

खण्डितानेत्रकञ्जालिमञ्जुरञ्जनपण्डिताः।
मण्डिताखिलदिक्प्रान्ताश्चण्डांशोः पान्तु भानवः॥१२१॥

अन्वयः—चण्डांशोः खण्डितानेत्रकंजालिमंजुरंजनपंडिताः मण्डिताखिल-दिक्प्रान्ताश्च भानवः पान्तु।

व्याख्या:—यस्याः पराङ्गनागेहात् पतिः प्रातर्गृहेऽञ्चति सा खण्डिता। कञ्जालिः कमलपंक्तिः। चण्डाशोः सूर्यस्य। भानवः कराः।

Eng. Tr.:-May the rays of the sun protect you-the rays which are ingenious in giving sweet charm to the lotuses in the form of the eyes of खण्डिता ladies-the rays which brightened all the nooks and corners to the quarters.

(इति भमिनीविलास-व्याख्यायां काव्यमर्मप्रकाशाख्यायां प्रास्ताविकविलासः।)

भामिनीविलासे

(II)

शृङ्गारविलासः

(Śṛṅgāravilāsaḥ)

II

शृङ्गारविलासः

न मनागपि राहुरोष[१]शङ्का
न कलङ्कानुगमो न पाण्डुभावः।
उपचीयत एव कापि शोभा
परितो भामिनि ते! मुखस्य नित्यम्॥१॥

अन्वयः-हे भामिनि! ते मुखस्य परितः नित्यम् काऽपि शोभा उपचीयते एव, (यतः) मनाक् राहुरोधशङ्का न, (यतः) न कलङ्कानुगमः, न पाण्डुभावः (वा अस्ति)।

व्याख्याः-भामिनीवदनवर्णनमिदम्। अत्र व्यतिरेकालङ्कारध्वनिः। उपमानादुपमेयस्य गुणविशेषवत्त्वेनोत्कर्षो व्यतिरेकः। अत्र चोपमानस्य चन्द्रस्य तद्विशेषणानां चोपादानमन्तरेणैवोपमेयस्य मुखस्य चन्द्रापेक्षयोत्कर्ष उपात्तैर्विशेषणै-र्वस्तुस्थितिप्रकाशनेन कृतार्थैरप्याकूतविशेषेण प्राधान्येन व्यज्यत इति व्यतिरेकस्य ध्वनित्वम्। मुखस्य मनागपि न राहुरोषशङ्का चन्द्रस्य तु साऽस्त्येव। एवमपरत्रापि। पाण्डुभावः पाण्डुत्वम्। उपचीयते वर्धते। भामिनि मानिनि। नित्यमित्यनेन चन्द्रस्य शोभा सितपक्ष एव वर्धते न सर्वदेति ध्वनितम्।

Eng. Tr.:-Oh my beloved! your face sheds some indescribable lustre all round, there being no danger of Rāhu's wrath, nor from contamination or fading.

नितरां परुषा सरोजमाला
न मृणालानि विचारपेशलानि।
यदि कोमलता तवाङ्गकाना-
मथ का नाम कथाऽपि पल्लवानाम्॥२॥

---

१. 'राहुरोध०' इति पाठान्तरम्।

अन्वयः–यदि तव अङ्गकानाम् कोमलता (अस्ति) अथ सरोजमाला नितराम् परुषा, मृणालानि विचारपेशलानि न, पल्लवानाम् कथा अपि का नाम?

व्याख्याः–भामिन्यङ्गवर्णनमिदम्। परुषा कठिना। विचारे पेशलानि रुचिराणि। अङ्गवन्मृणालानि न वेति विचारेऽपि समर्थानि नेत्यर्थः। यदि तवाङ्गकानां कोमलता प्रस्तूयत इति शेषः। अङ्गकानामित्यत्र स्वार्थे कन्। अथ तर्हि। अत्र पल्लवादितिरस्कारेण नायिकाङ्गानां सौकुमार्यातिशयो व्यज्यते।

Eng.Tr.:-Lotus-garlands are extremely rough, and lotus stalks are not worth considering. And how should foliage be mentioned when the tenderness of your limbs is our theme.

स्वेदाम्बुसान्द्रकणशालिकपोलपाली-
दोलायितश्रवणकुण्डलवन्दनीया।
आनन्दमङ्कुरयति स्मरणेन काऽपि
रम्या दशा मनसि मे मदिरेक्षणायाः॥३॥

अन्वयः–मदिरेक्षणायाः स्वेदाम्बुसान्द्रकणशालिकपोलपाली-दोलायितश्रवणकुण्डलवन्दनीया काऽपि रम्या दशा स्मरणेन मे मनसि आनन्दम् अङ्कुरयति।

व्याख्याः–इयं नायिकामधिकृत्य नायकस्योक्तिः। स्वेदाम्बूनां ये सान्द्राः कणास्तैः शालेते शोभेते एवंविधे ये कपोलपाली तयोर्दोलायिते चलिते ये श्रवणकुण्डले ताभ्यां वन्दनीया स्तुत्या नम्या च। अङ्कुरयति जनयति। मदिरे मदकारके ईक्षणे नेत्रे यस्यास्तथाविधाया नायिकायाः। प्रथमार्धगतविशेषण-बलादियं सुरतावस्थेति ज्ञायते।

Eng.Tr.:-The charming state of her whose eyes are intoxicated produces some unspeakable delight in my mind by its resemblance to the state that deserves praise owing to her ear-rings dangling on the region of her cheeks having thick drops of perspiration.

कस्तूरिकातिलकमालि! विधाय सायं
स्मेरानना सपदि शीलय सौधमौलिम्।
प्रौढिं भजन्तु कुमुदानि मुदामुदारा-
मुल्लासयन्तु परितो हरितो मुखानि॥४॥

अन्वयः—हे आलि! कस्तूरिकातिलकं विधाय सायं स्मेरानना सपदि सौधमौलिम् शीलय (यतः) कुमुदानि मुदानि मुदाम् उदाराम् प्रौढिम् भजन्तु (तथा) परितः हरितः मुखानि उल्लासयन्तु।

व्याख्याः—नायकस्य नायिकां प्रत्युक्तिः। आलि सखि स्मेरानना सस्मितवदना सती सौधमौलिं शीलय सुधानिर्मितप्रासादोर्ध्वप्रदेशं भज। तेन च कुमुदानि मुदामुदारां प्रौढिं भजन्तु हरितश्च स्वमुखान्युल्लासयन्तु। उदारां महतीम्। मुदां प्रौढिं हर्षाणां वृद्धिम्। उल्लसयन्तु विकासयन्तु। लोकेभ्यो दर्शयन्त्विति यावत्। अयं रूपकध्वनिः। अत्र कस्तूरिकातिलकविशिष्टं सस्मितं त्वदीयाननं कलङ्कचन्द्रिकाविशिष्टचन्द्राभिन्नमिति रूपकं कुमुदविकासादिना चन्द्रोदयकार्येण ध्वन्यते।

Eng. Tr.:-Oh love! now at the evening tide go to the top of the palace with a smiling face and light the quarters around and let the lotuses, thereby, enjoy abundantly the highest delight.

तन्मञ्जु मन्दहसितं श्वसितानि तानि
सा वै कलङ्कविधुरा मधुराननश्रीः।
अद्यापि मे हृदयमुन्मदयन्ति हन्त
सायन्तनाम्बुजसहोदरलोचनायाः॥५॥

अन्वयः—सायन्तनाम्बुजसहोदरलोचनायाः तत् मञ्जु मन्दहसितम् तानि श्वसितानि, कलङ्कविधुरा वै सा मधुराननश्रीः हन्त! अद्य अपि मे हृदयम् उन्मदयन्ति।

व्याख्याः—नायकोक्तिरियम्। तत् पूर्वानुभूतम्। एवमपरत्रापि। वै निश्चयेन। कलङ्कविधुरा निष्कलङ्का। उन्मदयन्त्युत्कटमदयुक्तं कुर्वन्ति। हन्त खेदे। सायन्तनाम्बुजसहोदरलोचनायाः सन्ध्याकालीनकमलतुल्यनयनायाः।

मुकुलितनेत्राया इति यावत्। भावध्वनिरयम्। पूर्वदृष्टाया नायिकायाः स्मृतिरत्र व्यंग्या।

Eng. Tr.:-Alas! that agreeable smile, those breathings, and that chaste and pleasant beauty of the face of her whose eyes are as the evening lotuses, still maddens my heart.

प्रातस्तरां प्रणमने विहिते गुरूणा-
माकर्ण्य वाचममलां भव पुत्रिणीति।
नेदियसि प्रियतमे परमप्रमोद-
पूर्णादरं दयितया दधिरे दृगन्ताः॥६॥

अन्वयः—प्रातस्तरां गुरूणाम् प्रणमने विहिते पुत्रिणी भव इति अमलां वाचम् आकर्ण्य दयितया नेदीयसि प्रियतमे परमप्रमोदपूर्णादरम् दृगन्ताः दधिरे।

व्याख्याः—प्रातस्तरां प्रणमने विहिते पुत्रिणी भवेति गुरुणां वाचमाकर्ण्य दयितया नेदीयसि प्रियतमे दृगन्ता दधिर इत्यन्वयः। गुरूणामिति काकाक्षिगोल-कन्यायेन प्रणमन इत्यनेनाप्यन्वेति। प्रभाते गुरवो वन्दनीया इति कुलवधू-नामाचारः। गुरूणां श्वश्व्रादिजनानाम्। नेदीयस्यातिनिकटवर्तिनि। परमप्रमोदपूर्णा-दरमिति क्रियाविशेषणम्। अत्र द्दगन्ताधानेन पुत्रिणी भवेत्याशिषाक्षिप्ता पुत्रप्राप्त्याशंसा सूचिता।

Eng. Tr.:-While offering her obeisance in the early morning, listening to the fervent blessing-Be thou the mother of a son- of the elders, the dear one cast her glances at her lover very significantly implying thereby, her full faith (in the blessing) and consequent delight.

गुरुजनभयमद्विलोकनान्तः समुदयदाकुलभावमावहन्त्याः।
दरदलदरविन्दसुन्दरे[१] हा हरिणदृशो नयने[२] न विस्मरामि॥७॥

अन्वयः—गुरुजनभयमद्विलोकनान्तः समुदयदाकुलभावम् उद्वहन्त्याः हरिणदृशः दरदलदरविन्दसुन्दरे नयने हा! न विस्मरामि

१. '०सुन्दरं' इति पाठान्तरम्।
२. 'नयनं' इति पाठान्तरम्।

व्याख्याः–नायकोक्तिरियम्। गुरुजनाद् यद् भयं तेन यन्मद्विलोकनं मत्कर्मकमवेक्षणं तस्मिन्नन्तर्मनसि समुदयन्नुत्पद्यमानो य आकुलभावो व्याकुलत्वं तमावहन्त्याः। हा खेदे। अत्र विप्रलम्भशृङ्गारः प्रधानम्। नयनस्यारविन्दोपमा स्मृत्युपस्करणद्वारा तस्योपस्कारिका। गुरुजनभयप्रिय-विलोकनयोर्मध्ये व्याकुलत्वोदयेन नायिकागते त्रासौत्सुक्ये परस्पराभिभवकामे व्यज्येते।

Eng.Tr.:-Alas! I cannot forget the eyes lovely as the slightly opening lotus of the deer-eyed one betraying, while looking at me, extreme embarrasment caused by the fear of the elderly persons.

बदरामलकाम्रदाडिमाना-
मपहृत्य श्रियमुन्नतौ क्रमेण।
अधुना हरणे कुचौ यतेते
दयिते ते करिशावकुम्भलक्ष्म्याः॥८॥

अन्वयः–हे दयिते! ते उन्नतौ कुचौ क्रमेण बदरामलकाम्रदाडिमानाम् श्रियम् अपहृत्य अधुना करिशावकुम्भलक्ष्म्याः हरणे यतेते।

व्याख्याः–नायकस्य नायिकां प्रत्युक्तिः। बदरं बदर्याः फलं बोर इति ख्यातम्। आमलकमामलक्याः फलं आम्वला इति ख्यातम्। उन्नतामुत्कृष्टाम्। क्रमेणाऽनुक्रमतः। अयं सारालंकारः।

Eng.Tr.:-Ah dear! your breasts having in succession surpassed the beauty of bore, myro-bolen, mango, and the pomogranat fruit, are now vieing with temples of the cub of elephant.

जम्बीरश्रियमतिलंघ्य लीलयैव
व्यानम्रीकृतकमनीयहेमकुम्भौ।
नीलाम्भोरुहनयनेऽधुना कुचौ
ते स्पर्धेते किल कनकाचलेन सार्धम्॥९॥

अन्वयः–हे नीलाम्भोरुहनयने। व्यानम्रीकृतकमनीयहेमकुम्भौ ते कुचौ लीलया एव जम्बीरश्रियम्! अतिलङ्घ्य अधुना किल कनकाचलेन सार्द्धं स्पर्द्धेते।

व्याख्याः–जम्बीरं ईडनिबू इति प्रसिद्धम्। व्यानम्रीकृतौ जितौ कमनीयौ

स्पृहणीयौ हेमकुम्भौ याभ्यां तथाविधौ। स्पर्धेते परिभवेच्छां कुर्वाते। अयमपि सारालंकारः।

Eng.Tr.:-Oh thou with eyes like the black lotus! thy breathing having surpassed the beauty of citron fruit and easily pusorn aside the grace of the beautiful golden jar are now viewer with Golden mount.

कपोलपालिं तव तन्वि! मन्ये
लावण्यधन्ये! दिशमुत्तराख्याम्।
विभाति यस्यां ललितालकायां
मनोहरा वैश्रवणस्य लक्ष्मीः॥१०॥

अन्वयः—हे लावण्यधन्ये! तन्वि! तव कपोलपालिम् उत्तराख्याम् दिशम् मन्ये, ललितालकायां यस्यां वैश्रवणस्य मनोहरा लक्ष्मीः विभाति।

व्याख्याः—तव कपोलपालिमुत्तराख्यां दिशं मन्य इत्यन्वयः। श्लेषोत्थापितेयमुत्प्रेक्षा। मन्ये उत्प्रेक्षे। ललितालकायां ललितकेशवत्यां ललितालकावत्यां च। अलका नाम कुबेरपुरी। वैश्रवणस्य निश्चयेन कर्णस्य। (दिक्पक्षे) वैश्रवणस्य कुबेरस्य। लक्ष्मीः शोभा सम्पच्च।

Eng.Tr.:-Oh thou of slender body and blessed with beauty! The region of your cheek appears to be the northern quarter, since therein surely the beauty of thy ear (the riches, of Kubera) shines under the lovely tresses of your hair in the city of Alakā)

नीवीं नियम्य शिथिलामुषसि प्रकाश-
मालोक्य वारिजदृशः शयनं जिहासोः।
नैवावरोहति कदाचन मानसान्मे
नाभेर्निभा सरसिजोदरसोदरायाः॥११॥

अन्वयः—उषसि प्रकाशम् आलोक्य शिथिलाम् नीवीम् नियम्य शयनम् जिहासोः वारिजदृशः सरसिजोदरसोदरायाः नाभेः प्रथा कदाऽपि च मे मानसात् न एव अवरोहति।

व्याख्याः—नायकोक्तिरियम्। उषसि प्रकाशमालोक्य नीवीं नियम्य

शयनं जिहासोर्वारिजदृशः सरसिजोदरसोदराया नाभेर्निभा मे मानसान्नवरोहतीत्यन्वयः। नीवीं वसनग्रन्थिम्। वारिजदृशः कमलनेत्रायाः। जिहासोर्हातुमिच्छोः। सरसिजोदरसोदरायाः कमलोदरसदृशायाः। इदं नाभिविशेषणम्। नैवावरोहति नैवापयाति। तत्रैव व्याप्रियत इत्यर्थः।

Eng.Tr.:-The grace of the navel of that lotus-eyed one resembling in complexion the interior of the (white) lotus, seen at the dawn while being desirous of quiting the bed and trying the loosened knot of her garment, does not vanish from my mind.

आलीषु केलीरभसेन बाला
मुहुर्ममालापमुपालपन्ती।
आरादुपाकर्ण्य गिरं मदीयां
सौदामिनीयां सुषमामयासीत्॥१२॥

अन्वयः–बाला आलीषु केलीरभसेन मुहुः मम आलापम् उपालपन्ती (सती) आरात् मदीयाम् गिरम् उपाकर्ण्य सौदामिनीयां सुषमाम् अयासीत्।

व्याख्याः–नायकोक्तिरियम्। केलीरभसेन क्रीडावेगेन। बाला नवोढा। उपालपन्त्यनुकुर्वाणा। आरद्दूरत एव। सौदामिनीयां सुषमां विद्युतः शोभाम्। पत्या स्ववचनाकर्णनं विशङ्क्य त्रस्ता बाला झटित्यालापं त्यक्त्वाऽन्यत्र गतवतीत्यर्थः।

Eng.Tr.:-In the heat of sport while frequently imitating my speech to friends, the young lady, when she heard my voice from a distance, attained the beauty of a lightening.

मुधैव मन्तुं[१] परिकल्प्य गन्तुं
मृषैव रोषादुपजल्पतो मे।
उदश्रुचञ्चन्नयना नताङ्गी
गिरन्न कां कामुररीचकार[२]॥१३॥

अन्वयः–नक्तम् मुधा एव गन्तुम् परिकल्प्य मृषा एव रोषाद मे उपजल्पतः उदश्रुचञ्चन्नयना नताङ्गी काम् काम् गिरम् न उररीचकार।

---

१. 'नक्तं' इति पाठान्तरम्।
२. 'कामुररीकरोति' इति पाठान्तरम्।

व्याख्या:–गन्तु मुधैव मन्तु परिकल्प्य मृषैव रोषादुपजल्पतो मे नताङ्गी कां कां गिरं नोररीचकारेत्यन्वयः। गन्तुं गमनार्थम् मुधैव मिथ्यैव। गन्तुमपराधम्। उदश्रुचञ्चन्नयनोदिताश्रुपातयुक्तचपलनयना। उररीचकार स्वीचकार। तत्तदुक्त्वा नताङ्गी मामनुनेतुं प्रायततेति भावः।

Eng.Tr.:-Pretending to have received an offence (from her) when I with feigned anger reproached her and pretended to go away, with her body bent and tears rising in her eyes she spared no importunities to detain me.

तदवधि कुशली पुराणशास्त्र–
स्मृतिशतचारुविचारजो विवेकः।
यदवधि न पदं दधाति चित्ते
हरिणकिशोरदृशो दृशोर्विलासः॥१४॥

अन्वयः–यदवधि हरिणकिशोरदृशः दृशोः विलासः चित्ते पदम् न दधाति तदवधि पुराणशास्त्रस्मृतिशतचारुविचारजो विवेकः कुशली।

व्याख्या:–तदवधि तावत्पर्यन्तम्। कुशली चैतसि स्वस्थानापन्नः। विवेकः कर्तव्याकर्तव्यज्ञानम्। दृशोर्नयनयोः। अहो कामिनीशृङ्गारचेष्टितस्य प्रभाव इति भावः। विकसन्मुखी बभूव

Eng.Tr.:-Oh clever mind! the discernment which arises from fitting meditations of hundreds of Purāṇas, Śāstras and Smṛtis, would be able to make a stand only so long as the eyes of the fawn-eyed one has not possessed you.

आगतः पतिरितीरितं जनैः शृण्वती चकितमेत्य देहलीम्।
कौमुदीव शिशिरीकरिष्यते लोचने मम कदा मृगेक्षणा॥१५॥

अन्वयः–मृगेक्षणा कदा जनैः (ते पतिः आगतः इति ईरितं शृण्वती चकितम् देहलीम् एत्य कौमुदीव मम लोचने शिशिरीकरिष्यते।

व्याख्या:–कस्यचित्पथिकस्याशंसावचनमिदम्। ईरितमुक्तम्। जनैः सखीजनैः। चकितं सविस्मयम्। देहलीं द्वारोपान्तभागम्। अत्र शृण्वतीति

शत्रा प्रत्यापितेन श्रवणसमकालमेव देहल्यागमनमित्यर्थेन प्रियायास्त्वरातिशयो गम्यते। स च तद्गतमौत्सुक्यातिशयं पुष्णाति।

Eng.Tr.:-When will the deer-eyed one hearing from her friends that her husband is come, coming in surprise to the threshold refresh my eyes like the moon-light?

अवधौ दिवसावसानकाले
भवनद्वारि विलोचने दधाना।
अवलोक्य समागतं तदा मा-
मथ रामा विकसन्मुखी बभूव॥१६॥

अन्वयः—दिवसावसानकाले अवधौ भवनद्वारि विलोचने दधाना रामा तदा समागतम् माम् अवलोक्य विकसन्मुखी बभूव

व्याख्याः—अवधौ प्रतिश्रुतवेलायाम्। तदाऽवधिकाले। अथावलोकनानन्तरम्। हर्षानन्तरमिति नागेशभट्टः। अत्र मुखविकासेन नायकागमनजन्यो नायिकागतो हर्षो व्यज्यते।

Eng.Tr.:-That lovely lady directing her eyes towards the gate of the house in the evening which was the usual time (of my returning home) had her face brightened up on seeing me come.

वक्षोजाग्रं पाणिनामृश्य दूरं
यातस्य द्रागाननाब्जं प्रियस्य।
शोणाग्राभ्यां भामिनी लोचनाभ्यां
जोषं जोषं जोषमेवावतस्थे॥१७॥

अन्वयः—भामिनी पाणिना वक्षोजाग्रम् आमृश्य द्राक् दूरं यातस्य प्रियस्य आननाब्जं शोणाग्राभ्याम् लोचनाभ्याम् जोषम् जोषम् एव अवतस्थे।

व्याख्याः—दूरे यातस्य प्रियस्याननाब्जं जोषं भामिनी जोषमेवावतस्थ इत्यन्वयः। आस्पृश्यासमन्तादीषद्वा स्पृष्ट्वा। शोणाग्राभ्यामारक्त प्रान्ताभ्याम्। जोषं जोषं संसेव्य संसेव्य। निर्निमेषं दष्ट्वा दृष्ट्वात्यर्थः। जोषमेव तूष्णीमेव।

इहाकस्मिकस्तनाग्रस्पर्शजन्यो प्रियागतोऽमर्षो नयनारुण्येन निर्निमेषनिरीक्षणेन च व्यज्यते।

Eng. Tr.:-When the dear one who was about to start for a istant land touched with his hand the nipples of her breasts, the lovely lady with her eyes red at the corners incessantly oated on his face and remained motionless.

गुरुभिः परिवेल्लिताऽपि गण्डस्थलकण्डूयनचारुकैतवेन।
दरदर्शितहेमबाहुनाला मयि बाला नयनाञ्चलं चकार॥१८॥

अन्वयः–गुरुभिः परिवेल्लिता अपि बाला गण्डस्थलकण्डूयनचारुकैतवेन दरदर्शितहेमबाहुनाला मयि नयनाञ्चलम् चकार।

व्याख्याः–परिवेल्लितापि परिवेष्टितापि। कैतवेन मिषेण। नयनाञ्चलं चकार कटाक्षेण द्दष्टवती। अत्र कटाक्षवीक्षणेन प्रियागतोऽनुरागो व्यज्यते।

Eng. Tr.:-Though surrounded by elderly persons the young lady under the happy pretext of scratching the surface of her neck, cast a glance at me and (thereby) slightly discovered her golden stalk like arm.

गुरुमध्यगता मया नताङ्गी
निहता नीरजकोरकेण मन्दम्।
दरकुण्डलताण्डवं नतभ्रूलतिक-
मामवलोक्य घूर्णिताऽऽसीत्॥१९॥

अन्वयः–गुरुमध्यगता नताङ्गी मया नीरजकोरकेण मन्दम् निहता दरकुण्डलताण्डवम् नतभ्रूलतिकम् माम् अवलोक्य आसीत्।

व्याख्याः–नीरजकोरकेण कमलकलिकया। मन्दमीषत् यदरेषत् कुण्डलताण्डवं यत्र तद्यथा तथा। नता भ्रूलतिका यस्मिन् कर्मणि तद्यथा तथा। घूर्णिता भ्रान्तचित्ता। इह घूर्णितासीदित्यनेनासमीक्ष्यकारिन् किमिदमनुचितं कृतवानसीत्यर्थसम्वलितोऽमर्षो नायिकागतः प्राधान्येन व्यज्यते।

Eng. Tr.:-When that young lady of pliant limbs while in the midst of elderly persons, was gently struck by me with a lotus-bud, she become confused with her ear-ring dangling slightly and her creeper like eye-brows knitted.

विनये नयनारुणप्रसाराः
प्रणतौ हन्त निरन्तराश्रुधाराः।
अयि जीवितसंशयः प्रयाणे
नहि जाने हरिणाक्षि केन तुष्येः॥२०॥

अन्वयः—हे हरिणाक्षि! विनये नयनारुणप्रसारः, प्रणतौ निरन्तराश्रुधाराः, प्रयाणे जीवितसंशयः अपि, हन्त! केन तुष्येः? न हि जाने।

व्याख्या:—मानवतीं प्रति नायकस्यानुनयोक्तिरियम्। विनये नमने। क्रियमाण इति शेषः। नयनारुणप्रसारा नयनयोरारुण्यस्य विस्ताराः कोपसूचकाः। अरुण आरुण्यम्। भावप्रधानो निर्देशः। प्रणतौ क्रियमाणायामिति शेषः। हन्त खेदे। जीवितसंशयो जीविष्यसि न वेत्या कारकः संशयः। प्रयाणे क्रियमाण इति शेषः। तुष्येः सन्तोषं प्राप्नुयाः।

Eng. Tr.:-Your eyes become radiant when I am humble; continuous streams of tears flow from eyes when I fall at your feet; and life is in danger if I depart from thus Hence I am, a loss, oh dear eyed one! to know the means of propitiating you.

अकरुण मृषाभाषासिन्धो विमुञ्च ममाञ्चलं
तव परिचितः स्नेहः सम्यङ् मयेत्यभिधायिनीम्।
अविरलगलद्वाष्पां तन्वीं निरस्तविभूषणां
क इह भवतीं भद्रे निद्रे विना विनिवेदयेत्॥२१॥

अन्वयः—हे भद्रे! निद्रे! इह भवतीं विना कः, अकरुण! मृषाभाषा-सिन्धो!! मम अञ्चलं विमुञ्च, मया तव स्नेहः सम्यक् परिचितः इति अभिधायिनीम् अविरलगलद्वाष्पाम् निरस्तभूषणाम् तन्वीम् विनिवेदयेत्।

व्याख्या:—एषा प्रवासगतस्य स्वप्ने प्रियामेवंभाषिणीं दृष्टवतो निद्रां प्रति कस्यचिदुक्तिः। भद्रे निद्रे भवतीं विना क इहैवंविधां तन्वीं विनिवेद-

येदित्यन्वयः। मृषाभाषासिन्धो मिथ्याभाषिन्। इह प्रवासे। भद्रे कल्याणि। विनिवेदयेन्मदधीनां कुर्यात्। एवंभूतायाः प्रियतमावस्थाया निवेदनेन निद्रे मम भवत्या महानुपकारः कृत इति वस्तु विप्रलंभशृंगारश्चात्र प्रतीयते।

Eng. Tr.:-Oh blessed sleep! who else but you could win over to me that slender-bodied one who is stripped off her ornaments and who having tears continuously flowing from her eyes reproaches me with words like these-Oh you hard hearted, ocean of flase words! leave the hem of my garments your love is thoroughly made out.

तीरे तरुण्या वदनं सहासं
नीरे सरोजं च मिलद्विकासम्।
आलोक्य धावत्युभयत्र मुग्धा
मरन्दलुब्धाऽलिकिशोरमाला॥२२॥

अन्वयः—तीरे तरुण्याः सहासं वदनम् च नीरे मिलद्विकासाम् सरोजम् आलोक्य मुग्धा मरन्दलुब्धा अलिकिशोरमाला उभयत्र धावति।

व्याख्या:—तीरे सरस्या इति शेषः। मिलद्विकासं प्रकाशमानम्। मुग्धा मूढा। इदं सरोजमिदं वा सरोजमिति निश्चयशून्येत्यर्थः। अलिकिशोरमाला भ्रमरबालपंक्तिः। अयं ससंदेहालंकारः। अत्र पुरोवर्तिव्यक्तिद्वये कमलमिदमिदं वेति भ्रमरगतः संशयो व्यंग्यः। स च वदनकमलयोः सादृश्यातिशयं पुष्णाति।

Eng. Tr.:-Seeing the smiling face of the young lady on the bank and an expanding lotus in the waters (of the lake) the swarm of the silly young bees fly both ways.

वीक्ष्य वक्षसि विपक्षकामिनी-
हारलक्ष्म दयितस्य भामिनी।
अंसदेशविनिवेशितां क्षणा-
दाचकर्ष निजबाहुवल्लरीम्॥२३॥

अन्वयः—कामिनी दयितस्य वक्षसि विपक्षकामिनीहारलक्ष्म वीक्ष्य क्षणात् अंसदेशविनिवेशिताम् निजबाहुवल्लरीम् आचकर्ष।

व्याख्या:—विपक्षकामिन्याः सपत्न्या हारलक्ष्म हारचिह्नम्। क्षणाद् वीक्षणसमकालमेव। बाहुवल्लरीं बाहुलताम्। अत्र सपत्नीहारलक्ष्मदर्शनेने भामिन्या मनसि झटिति रोषः प्रादुर्भूत इति बाहुलताकर्षणेन ध्वन्यते।

Eng.Tr.:-On the bosom of her lover having observed the impression (made by) the necklace of a rival woman, the lovely lady at once withdrew her creeper-like arm from his shoulder.

दरानमत्कन्धरबंधमीषन्निमीलितस्निग्धविलोचनाब्जम्।
अनल्पनिःश्वासभरालसाङ्गं स्मरामि सङ्गं चिरमङ्गनायाः॥२४॥

अन्वयः—दशनमत्कन्धरबन्धम् ईषन्निमीलितस्निग्धविलोचनाब्जम् अनल्पनिःश्वासभरालसाङ्गं अङ्गनायाः सङ्गम् चिरं स्मरामि।

व्याख्या:—कस्यचित्कामिन उक्तिरियम्। सङ्गं रतिसङ्गम्।

Eng.Tr.:-I remember for a long time the sexual intercourse with the woman in the course of which her neck was slightly bent, her lotus-like loving eyes partially closed, and her limbs had grown lanquid owing to heavy breathings.

रोषवेशान्निर्गतं यामयुग्मादेत्य द्वारं कांचिदाख्यां गृणन्तम्।
मामाज्ञायैवाययौ कातराक्षी मन्दं मन्दं मन्दिरादिंदिरेव॥२५॥

अन्वयः—रोषवेशात् निर्गतं यामयुग्माद् द्वारम् एष्य कचित् आख्यां गृणन्तम् माम् अज्ञा कातराक्षी मन्दिरात् इन्दिरेव मन्दम् आययौ।

व्याख्या:—रोषेण केलिमन्दिरान्निर्गतस्य रोषनिर्वाहाक्षमतया च भूयोपि निवृत्तस्य कस्यचिदुक्तिरियम्। निर्गतं केलिगृहादिति शेषः। यामयुग्मात् प्रहरद्वयात्। प्रहरद्वये व्यतिक्रान्त इत्यर्थः। द्वारमर्थात् केलिगृहस्य। काञ्चिदाख्यां किञ्चिदलीकं नाम। गृणते कथयन्तम्। मामाज्ञायैव मां ज्ञात्वैव। कथितेप्यलीके नामन्ययं प्रिय एव आगत इति निश्चित्यैवेत्यर्थः। इन्दिरेव लक्ष्मीरिव।

Eng.Tr.:-When I in the heat of anger went out, but after the lapse of two *yamas* returned and announced false name at the door, she like the goddess Lakṣmī, recognising me for certain came slowly out of the pleasure-house with eyes betraying fear.

हृदये कृतशैवलानुषङ्गा
मुहुरङ्गानि यतस्ततः क्षिपन्ती।
प्रियनामपरे मुखे सखीना-
मतिदीनामियमादधाति दृष्टिम्॥२६॥

अन्वयः—हृदये कृतशैवलानुषङ्गा मुहुः यतः ततः अङ्गानि क्षिपन्ती इयम् प्रियनामपरे सखीनाम् मुखे अतिदीनाम् दृष्टिम् आदधाति।

व्याख्याः—विरहिणीदशावर्णनमिदम्। कृतशैवलानुषङ्गा स्थापितशैवला। अनुषङ्गः संपर्कः। अत्र नायिकाया मनस्तापो व्यंग्यः।

Eng. Tr.:-Placing moss on her bosom and frequently tossing her limbs here and there, the lady fixes her extremely forlorn looks on the face of her companions whispering the name of her lover.

इत एव निजालयं गताया
वनिताया गुरुभिः समावृतायाः।
परिवर्तितकन्धरं नतभ्रु
स्मयमानं वदनाम्बुजं स्मरामि॥२७॥

अन्वयः—गुरुभिः समावृतायाः इतः एव निजालयम् गतायाः वनितायाः परिवर्तितकन्धरम् नतभ्रु स्मयमानं वदनाम्बुजं स्मरामि।

व्याख्याः—इत एवास्मादेव प्रदेशात्। स्मयमानं सस्मितम्।

Eng. Tr.:-I remember the lotus like face-which was slightly smiling, in which the eye-brows were knitted and the neck was slightly bent of that lady while surrounded by elderly persons when she went away from this very place to her own appartment.

कथय कथमिवाशा जायतां जिविते मे
मलयभुजगवान्ता वान्ति वाताः कृतान्ताः।
अयमपि खलु गुञ्जन्मञ्जु माकन्दमौलौ
चुलुकयति मदीयां चेतनां चञ्चरीकः॥२८॥

अन्वयः—यदा मलयभुजगवान्ता कृतान्ताः वाताः वान्ति, माकन्दमौलौ मञ्जु गुञ्जन् अयम् यञ्चरीकः अपि मदीयाम् चेतनाम् चुलुकयति कथय जीविते मे आशा कथमिव जायताम्।

व्याख्याः—कस्याश्चिद्विरहिण्या उक्तिरियम्। वान्ता उद्गीर्णाः। मलय-भुजगवान्ता इत्यनेन वातानां विषसंपर्कः सूचितः। कृतान्ता यमाः। विरहिना-शकत्वाद् यमसदृशा इत्यर्थः। चुलुकयति पिबति। हरतीति यावत्। चञ्चरीको भ्रमरः।

Eng.Tr.:-Oh speak, how I may hope to live (any more) since the winds set in motion by the snakes on the Malaya mount blow like the God of death and even this bee buzzing sweetly on the top of the mango deprives me of consciousness.

प्राणापहरणेनासि तुल्यो हालाहलेन मे।
शशाङ्क केन मुग्धेन सुधांशुरिति भाषितः॥२९॥

अन्वयः—हे शशाङ्क! मे प्राणापहरणेन (त्वम्) हालाहलेन तुल्यः असि। केन मुग्धेन सुधांशुः इति भाषितः।

व्याख्याः—कस्यचिद् विरहिणश्चन्द्रं प्रत्युक्तिः। भाषितोसीति शेषः।

Eng.Tr.:-What follish person denominated you as one possessing nectariferous rays; since to me oh moon! you are like a deadly poison in taking life.

निरुध्य यान्तीं तरसा कपोतीं कूजत्कपोतस्य पुरो दधाने।
मयि स्मितार्द्रं वदनारविन्दं सा मन्दमन्दं नमयाम्बभूव॥३०॥

अन्वयः—मयि तरसा यान्तीम् कपोतीम् निरूध्य कूजत्कपोतस्य पुरः दधाने सा स्मिताद्रं वदनारविन्दम् मन्दमन्दम् नमयाम्बभूव।

व्याख्या:–नायकोक्तिः। तरसा बलात्कारेण शीघ्रं वा। कूजत्कपोतस्य शब्दं कुर्वाणस्य पारावतस्य। स्मितार्द्रं सस्मितम्। सा नायिका। प्रियकर्तृकं कपोतस्याग्रे कपोत्याः समर्पणं दृष्ट्वा प्रिया व्रीडया वदनं नमयाञ्चकारेति भावः।

Eng. Tr.:-When I stopping perforce the mate that was going away placed here before the cooing pigeon she geatly bent down here lotus-like face smiling at me.

तिमिरं हरन्ति हरितां पुरःस्थितं
तिरयन्ति तापमथ तापशालिनाम्।
वदनत्विषस्तव चकोरलोचने
परिमुद्रयन्ति सरसीरुहश्रियः॥३१॥

अन्वयः–हे चकोरलोचने! तव निरयन्ति वदनत्विषः हरिताम् तिमिरं हरन्ति अथ पुरः स्थिताः तापशालिनाम् तापं। सरसारुहश्रियाः परिमुद्रयन्ति।

व्याख्या:–तिमिरमन्धकारम्। पुरःस्थितमग्रे वर्तमानम्। तिरयन्ति दूरीकूर्वन्ति वदनत्विषो मुखकान्तयः। परिमुद्रयन्त्याच्छादयन्ति। अयं रूपकध्वनिः। इह चन्द्रोदयकार्याणि मुखकान्तिभिरेव सम्पाद्यत इत्यनेन मुखं चन्द्र इति गम्यते।

Eng. Tr.:-Oh cakora-eyed one, though the luster of your face dispels darkness lying in front of the quarters, and removes the affliction of those who suffer from it, it impairs the beauty of lotus (sun-lotus).

कुचकलशयुगान्तर्मामकीनं नखाङ्कं
सपुलकतनु मन्दं मन्दमालोकमाना[१]।
विनिहितवदनं मां वीक्ष्य बाला गवाक्षे
चकितनतनताङ्गी सद्म सद्यो विवेश॥३२॥

अन्वयः–कुचकलशयुगान्ताः मामकीनम् नखाङ्कं सपुलकतनु मन्दम् मन्दम् आलोकमाना बाला गवाक्षे विनिहतवदनम् मां वीक्ष्य चकितनतनताङ्गी सद्यः सद्म विवेश।

१. 'मन्दमालोकयन्ती' इति पाठान्तरम्।

व्याख्या:–कुचकलशयुगान्तः। स्तनघटद्वन्द्वमध्ये सपुलकतन्विति क्रियाविशेषणम्। गवाक्षे विनिहितवदनं मां वीक्ष्येत्वन्वयः। विनिहितवदनं स्थापितमुखम्। चकितेत्यत्र द्वौ कर्मधारयौ। सद्म गृहम्। प्रियस्य नखक्षत-मालोकमाना बाला तं गवाक्षे दृष्ट्वा ब्रीडाकुला सद्यः सदनं प्रविवेशेति भावः।

Eng.Tr.:-That young lady with her body horripulated when while stealthily observing the nail-mark on the interval between the two jar-like breasts, saw me peeping through the window, at once withdrew into the house with her limbs startled and bent.

विधाय सा मद्वदनानुकूलं कपोलमूलं हृदये शयाना।
तन्वी तदानीमतुलां बलारेः साम्राज्यलक्ष्मीमधरीचकार॥३३॥

अन्वयः–मद्वदनानुकूलाम् कपोलमूलं विधाय हृदये शयाना सा तन्वी तदानीत् बलारेः अतुलां साम्राज्यलक्ष्मीम् अधरीचकार।

व्याख्या:–कपोलमूलं चिबुकम्। हृदयं उरसि। तदानीं तस्मिन् काले। स्मृतिविषयभूते प्रसङ्ग इति यावत्। बलारेरिन्द्रस्य। अधरीचकार निकृष्टां चकार। तया हृदये शयनयाऽहमिन्द्रादप्यधिकं सुखमन्वभवमिति भावः।

Eng.Tr.:-When the slender-bodied one placing her cheek conveniently near my mouth was lying on my bosom, she surpassed the incomparable beauty of Indra's sovereignty.

मुहुरर्थितयाद्य निद्रया मे
बत! यामे चरमे निवेदितायाः।
चिबुकं सुदृशः स्पृशामि[१] याव-
न्मयि तावन्मिहिरोऽपि[२] निर्दयोऽभूत्॥३४॥

अन्वयः–अद्य मुहुः अर्थितिया मे निद्रया चरमे यामे निवेदितायाः सुदृशः यावत् चिबुकं स्पृशामि, बत! तावत् मिहिरः अपि मयि निर्दयः अभूत।

व्याख्या:–कस्यचित् प्रवासगतस्य स्वप्नेऽपि प्रियां द्रष्टुकामस्येयमुक्तिः।

---

१. 'मृशामि' इति पाठान्तरम्।

२. 'मदिरोऽपि' इति पाठान्तरम्।

अर्थितया प्रर्थितया। बत खेदे। चरमे यामे चतुर्थप्रहरे। निवेदिताया: स्वप्नावस्थामुत्पाद्य दर्शिताया:। मिहिर: सूर्य: स्वोदयेन मां विबोध्य प्रियावचनश्रवणोल्लासनाशं कृत्वा सूर्योपि निर्दयदैवकृतविरहभाजो मे निर्दय: सम्पन्न इति भाव:।

Eng.Tr.:-Alas! at the close of the last quarter of night while I was on the point of kissing the chin of my beloved presented to me (in dream) by sleep so frequently courted, even the sun became ruthless towards me.

श्रुतिशतमपि भूय: शीलितं भारतं वा
विरचयति तथा नो हन्त सन्तापशान्तिम्।
अयि[१] सपदि यथायं केलिविश्रान्तकान्ता-
वदनकमलवल्गत्कान्तिसान्द्रो नकार:॥३५॥

अन्वय:–अपि! (सखे) भूय: शीलिनं श्रुतिशतम् वा भारतम् अपि हन्त! तथा सन्तापशान्तिम् नो विरचयति यथा सपदि केलिविश्रान्तकान्तावदनकमलवल्गकान्तिसान्द्र: अयम् नकार:

व्याख्या:–भूयो वारंवारम्। शीलितं सम्यग्विचारितम्। हन्त खेदे। केलिविश्रान्ताया: सुरतक्रीडाजनितायासाया: कान्ताया वदनकमलाद् वल्गन्त्या निर्यान्त्या कान्त्या सान्द्र: पूरित:। नकारोऽपीत्यन्वय:। विधिप्रत्यायको हीकार: संतापशान्तिं रचयेदिति किं वक्तव्यमित्यप्यर्थ:।

Eng.Tr.:-Frequent pounderings over hundreds of smṛtis and over Bhāratas too, do not produce as much satisfaction as suddenly does the word "enough" full of luster coming from the lotus-like mouth of a young lady overwhelmed with embraces.

लवलीं तव लीलया कपोले कवलीकुर्वति कोमलत्विषा।
परिपाण्डुरपुण्डरीकखण्डे परिपेतु: परितो महाधय:॥३६॥

अन्वय:–तव कपोले कोमलत्विषा लीलया लवलीम् कवलीकुर्वति परिपाण्डुरपुण्डरीकखण्डे परित: महाधय: परिपेतु:।

१. 'अपि' इति पाठान्तरम्।

व्याख्या:–तव कपोले लवलीं कवलीकुर्वति सतीत्यन्वय:। लवलीं लताविशेषम्। कवलीकुर्वति ग्रसमाने। अधरयतीति यावत्। त्विषा कान्त्या। पुण्डरीकखण्डे कमलसमूहे। परित: सर्वत:। महाधयो महांति भयानि। अस्मानप्यवश्यमास्या: कपोल: कवलीकरिष्यतीति कमलानां भयम्।

Eng.Tr.:-While your cheek by its tender lustre was easily excelling (lit, devouring) the lavalī creeper, unusually great anxiety was felt all round by groups of white lotuses.

यौवनोद्गमनितान्तङ्किता: शीलशौर्यबलकान्तिलोभिता:।
सङ्कुचन्ति विकसन्ति राघवे जानकीनयननीरजश्रिय:॥३७॥

अन्वय:–जानकीनयननीरजश्रिय: राघवे यौवनोद्गमनितान्तशङ्किता: संकुचन्ति (च) शीलशौर्य्यबलकान्तिलोभित: विकसन्ति।

व्याख्या:–यौवनोद्गमस्तारुण्योपगम:। अर्थाद्दाशरथिगत:। शीलशौर्यबल-कान्तिभिर्लोभिता: संजातलोभा:। जानकीनयननीरजश्रिय: सीतानेत्रकमल-कान्तय:। अत्र नेत्रयो: संकोचविकासाभ्यां जानकीगते व्रीडौत्सुक्ये परस्पराभि-भवकामे व्यज्येते।

Eng.Tr.:-The beauty of the lotus-like eye of Jānakī, constrained by the advent of youth (in Rāma) and attracted by effulgence, strength, and prowess of Rāma, closed and expanded alternately.

अधिरोप्य हरस्य हन्त चापं
परितापं प्रशमय्य बान्धवानाम्।
परिणेष्यति वा न वा युवायं
निरपायं मिथिलाधिनाथपुत्रीम्॥३८॥

अन्वय:–अयं युवा हरस्य चापम् अधिरोप्य बान्धवानाम् परितापम् प्रशमय्य, हन्त! मिथिलाधिनाथपुत्रीम् निरपायम् वा परिणेष्यति वा न।

व्याख्या:–भगवान् दाशरथिर्जानकीं परिणेष्यति वा न वेति सन्दिहानस्य मिथिलास्थजनस्योक्तिरियम्। अधिरोप्य सज्जीकृय। युवा तरुण:। अयं पुरोवर्ती। निरपायं निर्विघ्नम्। मिथिलाधिनाथपुत्रीं जनककन्याम्।

Eng.Tr.:-Ye! whether this youth stringing the bow of Śiva and thereby removing the anxieties of the relations (of the bride) will without any obstruction marry the daughter of the lord of Mithilā?

भुजपञ्जरे गृहीता नवपरिणीता वरेण रहसि वधूः।
तत्कालजालपतिता बालकुरङ्गीव वेपते नितराम्॥३९॥

अन्वयः—नवपरिणीता वधूः रहसि वरेण भुजपञ्जरे गृहीता, तत्काल-जालपतिता बालकुरङ्गीव नितरां वेपते।

व्याख्याः—नवपरिणीता नवोढा। जालमानाय। अत्र नववध्वा रतेर्मनागप्यस्पर्शादनुभयनिष्ठत्वेनाभासत्वं शृङ्गारस्य।

Eng.Tr.:-A newly wedded bride while caught in privacy into the embraces of her bridegroom awfully, trembles like a female deer cought all of a sudden into a trap.

उपनिषदः परिपीता गीतापि च हन्त मतिपथं नीता।
तदपि न हा विधुवदना मानससदनाद्बहिर्याति॥४०॥

अन्वयः—उपनिषदः परिपीताः, च हन्त! गीता अपि मतिपथम् नीता, तद् अपि हा! विधुवदना मानससदनात् बहिः न याति।

व्याख्याः—उपनिषदो वेदशिरोभागाः। परिपीताः सादरमाकर्णिताः। गीता भववद्गीता। हन्त खेदे। इयं विशेषोक्तिः। प्रसिद्धकारणकलापसामानाधिकरण्येन वर्ण्यमाना कार्यानुत्पत्तिर्विशेषोक्तिः। अत्रोपनिषदर्थविमर्शेन सकललोका-नित्यत्वज्ञाने प्रसिद्धे विरतिहेतौ सत्यपि विरत्यनुत्पत्तिर्वर्णिता। विरत्यनुत्पत्त्या च रागाधिक्यं प्रतीयते।

Eng.Tr.:-The philosophical lore has been completely digested; Gītā, too, was made the object of meditation. But alas! the moon-faced one does not leave my mental abode.

अकरुणहृदय प्रियतम मुञ्चामि त्वामितः परं नाहम्।
इत्यालपति कराम्बुजमादायालीजनस्य विकला सा॥४१॥

अन्वयः–विकला सा आलीजनस्य कराम्बुजम् आदाय, हे अकरुण-हृदय! प्रियतम! इतः परम् त्वाम् अहम् न मुञ्चामि इति आलपति।

व्याख्याः–एषा प्रवासगतं स्वनायिकावृत्तान्तं पृच्छन्तं नायकं प्रति कस्याश्चित्सन्देशहारिण्या उक्तिः। अत्रासम्बद्धोक्त्या नायिकागतः प्रियविरह-जन्मोन्मादः प्रतीयते।

Eng.Tr.:-The distracted one, holding the hand of her female companion speaks thus to her—"Oh you hard-hearted lover, henceforth I shall never let you go."

लोभाद्वराटिकानां विक्रेतुं तक्रमनिशमटन्त्या।
लब्धो गोपकिशोर्या मध्येरथ्यं महेन्द्रनीलमणिः॥४२॥

अन्वयः–वराटिकानाम् लोभात् तक्रं विक्रेतुम् अविरतम् अटन्त्या गोपकिशोर्या मध्येरथ्यम् महेन्द्रनीलमणिः लब्धः।

व्याख्याः–वराटिकानां लोभात् कपर्दिका लप्स्यन्त इत्याशया। आनिशं निशाबधि। अटन्त्येतस्ततो गच्छन्त्या। गोपकिशोर्या गोपालकन्यया। मध्येरथ्यं रथ्याया मध्ये। महेन्द्रनीलमणिर्महार्घरत्नविशेषः। अत्र निगीर्याध्यवसानाति-शयोक्त्या श्रीकृष्णोऽपि गृह्यते। बराटिकालाभार्थमटन्त्या गोपकिशोर्या महेन्द्र-नीलमणिर्लब्ध इति वाञ्छितार्थसिद्ध्यर्थं यत्ने क्रियमाणे ततोप्यधिकार्थ-लाभादयं प्रहर्षणालंकारः।

Eng.Tr.:-A cowherd girl being desirous of *cowries* while wandering till nightfall to sell butter-milk found a costly saphire stone in the midst of street.

रूपारुचिं निरसितुं रसयन्त्या
हरिमुखस्य लावण्यम्।
सुदृशः शिव शिव सकले
जाता सकलेवरे जगत्यरुचिः॥४३॥

अन्वयः—रूपारुचिं निरसितुं हरिमुखस्य लावण्यं रसयन्त्याः सुदृशः शिव! शिव!! जगति सकले सकलेवरे अरुचिः जाता।

व्याख्याः—रूपारुचिं रूपस्याप्रीतिम्। निरसितुं दूरीकर्तुम्। रसयन्त्या आस्वादयन्त्याः। हरिमुखस्य ब्रह्माभिन्नश्रीकृष्णमुखस्य। सुदृशो नायिकायाः। सकलेवरे स्वशरीरसहिते। अरुचिर्वैराग्यरूपा। अयं स्वस्य दुःखसाधनानिवृत्त्या दुखान्तरसाधनावाप्त्या च विषमालंकारः। अत्र नायिकाया रूपारुचिं निरसितुमिच्छन्त्या न केवलं रूपारुचिर्न दूरीभूता किं तु जगत्यपि वैराग्यलक्षणाऽरुचिरुत्पन्ना।

Eng.Tr.:-Alas! the fine-eyed one conceived a dislike for the whole world including her own body, while she was contemplating (lit-relishing) the beauty of the face of Hari to remove her apathy for beauty.

किं जल्पसि मुग्धतया हन्त ममाङ्गं सुवर्णवर्णमिति।
तद्यदि पतति हुताशे तदा हताशे तुलां तवारोहेत्॥४४।

अन्वयः—हन्तः! मम अङ्गं सुवर्णवर्णम् इति मुग्धतया किम् जल्पसि? अरे हताशे! तद् यदि हुताशे पतति तदा तव तुलाम् आरोहेत्।

व्याख्याः—नायिकां प्रति नायकोक्तिः। हन्त हर्षे। तत् सुवर्णम्। हुताशे वह्नौ। हताशे स्वल्पा अयं प्रतीपालंकारः। अत्र सुवर्णरूपस्य प्रसिद्धोपमानस्योपमेयीकरणादुपमेयस्योपमानीकृतस्य नायिकाङ्गस्योत्कर्षो गम्यते। हुताशपातं विना प्रतीपमपि दुर्लभमुपमा तु स्वप्नेऽपि न संभवतीति मुग्धत्वहताशत्वाभ्यां गम्यते।

Eng.Tr.:-Ah! cursed one, how do you foolishly say that your body has the colour of gold; for it would stand comparison with your body only when it is put into fire.

औत्सुक्यात्परिमिलतां त्रपया संकोचमञ्चतां च मुहुः।
नवसंगमयोर्यूनोर्नयनानामुत्सवो जयति॥४५॥

अन्वयः—नवसङ्गमयोः यूनोः औत्सुक्यात् परिमिलताम् च त्रपया मुहुः सङ्कोचम् अञ्चताम् नयनानाम् उत्सवः जयति।

व्याख्याः–संकोचमञ्चतामप्रसरणभावं प्राप्तवताम्। यूनोर्युवतिश्च युवा च तयोः।

Eng.Tr.:-All blessed is the delight of the eyes of the new wedded couple of the young,—the eyes that frequently met together through eagerness and closed through bashfulness.

गरिमाणमर्पयित्वा लघिमानं कुचतटात्सरोजदृशाम्।
स्वीकुर्वते नमस्ते यूनां धैर्याय निर्विवेकाय॥४६॥

अन्वयः–गरिमाणम् अर्पयित्वा कुरङ्गदृशाम् कुचतटात् लघिमानं स्वीकुर्वते यूनां निर्विवेकाय धैर्याय ते नमः।

व्याख्याः–गरिमाणं गुरुत्वम्। श्रेष्ठत्वमित्यपि गम्यते। लघिमानं लघुत्वम्। नीचत्वमिति श्लिष्टोऽर्थः। सरोजदृशां कमलाक्षीणाम्। स्वीकुर्वते युनां धैर्याय ते नम इत्यन्वयः। धैर्यस्य लघुगुरुविनिमयेन निर्विवेकत्वम् अयं परिवृत्त्यलंकारः।

Eng.Tr.:-A bow to the indescriminate fortitude of youths who bestowing gravity to the breasts of the lotus-eyed women, receive levity therefrom.

न्यञ्चति वयसि प्रथमे
समुदञ्चति किञ्च तरुणिमनि सुदृशः।
दधति स्म मधुरिमाणं वाचो
गतयश्च विभ्रमाश्च भृशम्॥४७॥

अन्वयः–सुदृशः प्रथमे वयसि अञ्चति तदा तरुणिमनि समुदञ्चति वाचः च गतयः च विभ्रमाः च भृशम् मधुरिमाणम् दधति स्म।

व्याख्याः–न्यञ्चति निःशेषेण गच्छति सति। प्रथमे वयसि बाल्ये। समुदञ्चत्याविर्भवति सति। तरुणिमनि तारुण्ये। मधुरिमाणं माधुर्यम्।

Eng.Tr.:-When the first part of the life (child-hood) had passed away and youth set in, the mode of speech, the gait of walking, and the gestures of the fair-eyed one became extremely charming.

निस्सीमशोभासौभाग्यं नताङ्ग्या नयनद्वयम्।
अन्योन्यालोकनानन्दविरहादिव चञ्चलम्॥४८॥

अन्वयः—नताङ्ग्याः निःसीमशोभासौभाग्यम् नयनद्वयम् अन्योऽन्यालोक-नांनन्दविरहादिव चञ्चलम् (भवति)।

व्याख्याः—अन्योन्यालोकने य आनन्दस्तस्य विरहादिव। इयं कामिनी-नयनद्वन्द्वविषया हेतूत्प्रेक्षा। कामिनीनयनद्वन्द्वं स्वभावत एव चञ्चलम्। हेतुस्त्वत्रोत्प्रेक्षितः।

Eng.Tr.:-The pair of the eyes of her whose body is pliant, possessing the bliss of measureless beauty are tremulous, as if through a lack of delight of beholding each other.

गुरुमध्ये हरिणाक्षी[१] मार्तिकशकलैर्निहन्तुकामं माम्।
रदयन्त्रितरसनाग्रं तरलितनयनं निवारयाञ्चक्रे॥४९॥

अन्वयः—हरिणाक्षी गुरुमध्ये मार्तिकशकलैः निहन्तुकामम् माम् रदयन्त्रितरसनाग्रम् तरलितनयनम् निवारयाञ्चक्रे।

व्याख्याः—गुरुमध्ये वृद्धस्त्रीजनानां मध्ये। मार्तिकशकलैर्मृत्पिण्डखण्डैः। रदैर्यन्त्रितं पीडितं रसनाग्रं यस्मिन् कर्मणि तथा। इयं स्वभावोक्तिः। अस्य पद्यस्य भावार्थो (१९) पद्यस्येव।

Eng.Tr.:-When I was desirous of hitting a piece of clod at the deer-eyed one witting amidst the elderly persons, she prevented me from doing so by a wink of her eye and by pressing the tip of her tongue between her teeth.

नयनाञ्चलावमर्शं न या कदाचित्पुरा सेहे।
आलिङ्गितापि जोषं तस्थौ सा गन्तुकेन दयितेन॥५०॥

---

१. 'कमलाक्षी कमलाक्षेण प्रहर्तुंकामं' इति पाठान्तरम्।

अन्वयः—या पुरा कदाचित् नयनाञ्चलावमर्शम् न सेहे सा गन्तुकेन दयितेन आलिङ्गिता अपि जोषम् तस्थौ।

व्याख्याः—नयनाञ्चलावमर्शं कटाक्षविक्षेपम्। पुरा पूर्वम्। गन्तुकेन देशान्तरं जिगमिषुणा। या वधूः पूर्वं कटाक्षविक्षेपमपि न सेहे सा प्रवस्यत्पतिका प्रस्थानपूर्वरजन्यां दयितेनालिङ्गितापि तूष्णीं तस्थाविति भावः।

Eng. Tr.:-She who formerly could not bear the casting of a glance of her lover remained motionless though embraced by him when he was about to depart.

मानपराग्वदनापि प्रिया शयानेव दयितकरकमले।
उद्वेल्लद्भुजमलसग्रीवाबन्धं कपोलमाधत्ते॥५१॥

अन्वयः—मानपराग्वदना अपि सा प्रिया शयानेव करकमले उद्वेल्लद्भुजम् अलसग्रीवाबन्धम् कपोलम् आधत्ते।

व्याख्याः—मानपराग्वदना मानेन परांमुखी। शयानेव निद्रां प्राप्तेव। निद्राव्याजेनेति यावत्। उद्वेल्लद्भुमूर्ध्वीकृतबाहु यथा तथा।

Eng. Tr.:-The beloved though she turned away her face through anger, still feigning sleep, placed her cheek on the lotus-like palm of her lover in such a position in which her neck was hanging languidly and her arm was raised up.

लोचनफुल्लाम्भोजद्वयलोभान्दोलितैकमनाः शुभे!
कस्तूरीतिलकमिषादयमलिकेऽलिस्तवोल्लसति॥५२॥

अन्वयः-हे शुभे! लोचनफुल्लाम्भोजद्वयलोभान्दोलितैकमनाः अयम् अलिः तव अलिके कस्तूरीतिलकमिषात् उल्लसति।

व्याख्याः—नायकस्य नायिकां प्रत्युक्तिः। लोचनरूपफुल्लाम्भोजद्वयेनां दोलितं तरलितमेकं मनो यस्य सः। अलिके ललाटे। अलिर्भ्रमरः। इयमपन्हुतिः। अत्र कस्तूरीतिलकस्य कस्तूरीतिलकत्वं निषिध्य तस्मिन् भ्रमरत्वमारोपितम्।

Eng. Tr.:-The bee whose mind is wavering through the desire (of sucking) the honey from the two full-blown your lotuses in the shape of your eyes, glistens on your forehead under the guise of the musk *tilaka* mark.

अधिरजनि प्रियसविधे कथमपि संवेशिता गुरुभिः।
किं भवितेति सशङ्कं पङ्कजनयना परामृशति॥५३॥

अन्वयः–अधिरजनि गुरुभिः कथमपि बलात् प्रियसविधे संवेशिता पङ्कजनयना किम् भविता? इति सशङ्कम् परामृशति।

व्याख्याः–अधिरजनि रात्रौ। कथमपि महता प्रयासेन। संवेशिता शयनं प्रापिता। गुरुभिर्वृद्धस्त्रीजनैः। परामृशति चिन्तयति। इयं मुग्धावस्था।

Eng.Tr.:-At night the lotus-eyed one made to lie down by the side of her lover with great difficulty by elderly persons, revolves in her mind with apprehension what would follow.

चिन्तामीलितमानसो मनसिजः सख्यो विहीनप्रभाः
प्राणेशः प्रणयाकुलः पुनरसावास्तां समस्ता कथा।
एतत्त्वां विनिवेदयामि मम चेदुक्तिं हितां मन्यसे
मुग्धे! मा कुरु मानमाननमिदं राकापतिर्जेष्यति॥५४॥

अन्वयः–हे मुग्धे! मनसिजः चिन्तामीलितमानसः, सख्यः विहीनप्रभाः, प्राणेशः प्रणयाकुलः, पुनः असौ समस्ता कथा आस्ताम्, चेत् मम उक्तिं हिताम् मन्यसे त्वाम् एतत् प्रतिबोधयामि (यत्) मानम् मा कुरु अन्यथा राकापतिः इदम् आननम् जेष्यति।

व्याख्याः–मानिनीं प्रति कस्यचिदुक्तिः। चिन्तामीलितमानसो चिन्तया शून्यीकृतचेताः। विरतव्यापार इति यावत्। मनसिजो मदनः। त्वां जेतुमशक्नुवानः स चिन्ता भजत इति भावः। विहीनप्रभाः स्वोक्त्यनाकर्णनेन हीनतेजस्काः। प्रणयाकुलः प्रेमव्याकुलः। प्रणतिपर इति यावत्। विनिवेदयामि कथयामि। हितां सुखदाम्। मानं न त्यजसि चेदिदमाननं राकापतिर्जेष्यति। पीडादानं मानमलीमसनायिकामुखसादृश्यस्य स्वस्मिन्। संपादनं वा जयकारणम्।

Eng.Tr.:-The god of Love has become vacant-minded through anxiety; your companions have lost their liveliness; and the lord of your life (lover) is distracted with love. These circumstances apart, oh silly one! if you think my advice a salutary one, I worn you not to hold back, or else the moon (the husband of *Rākā*) will surpass your face.

अलङ्कर्तुं कर्णौ भृशमनुभवन्त्या नवरुजं
ससीत्कारं तिर्यग्वलितवदनाया मृगदृशः।
कराब्जव्यापारानतिसुकृतसारान् रसयतो
जनुः सर्वश्लाघ्यं जयति ललितोत्तंस! भवतः॥५५॥

अन्वयः—हे ललितोत्तंस! कर्णौ अलंकर्तुम् भृशम् नवरुजम् अनुभवन्त्या सशीत्कारम् तिर्यग्वलितवदनायाः मृगदृशः अतिसुकृतसारान् कराब्जव्यापारान् रसयतः (ते) सर्वश्लाघ्यम् जनुः जयति।

व्याख्या:—इयं कस्यचित्कामिनीकर्णभूषणं प्रत्युक्तिः। भृशमत्यन्तम्। ससीत्कारमिति क्रियाविशेषणम्। अतिसुकृतसारान् महतः पुण्यस्य फलभूतान्। रसयतः आस्वादयतः। जनुजर्न्म। सर्वश्लाघ्यं सकलैस्तुत्यम्। ललितोत्तंस रम्यकर्णभूषण। अयं कामिन्या प्रथममेव क्लेशेन कर्णे क्रियमाणस्योत्तंसस्य वृत्तान्तः प्रत्यग्रखण्डिताधरकामुकवृत्तान्ताभेदेन स्थितः। सा ह्यधरखण्डनसमये नवरुजमनुभवति ससीत्कारं वदनं परावर्तयति कामुके च कराब्जं व्यापारयति। अत एवेयं समासोक्तिः। यत्र प्रस्तुतधर्मिको व्यवहारः साधारणविशेषणमात्रो-पस्थापिताप्रस्तुतधर्मिकव्यवहाराभेदेन भासते सा समासोक्तिः।

Eng.Tr.:-Oh, lovely ear-ring! Blessed is birth deserving universal praise, which enjoys (the pleasure of) the touches, the fruit of your virtuous deeds (in past life), of the deer-eyed one who to decorate her ears experiences (at every moment) fresh and great pain, and who turns her head aside with a heavy sigh.

आयातैव निशा निशापतिकरैः कीर्णं[१] दिशामन्तरं
भामिन्यो भवनेषु भूषणगणैरङ्गान्यलङ्कुर्वते।
मुग्धे मानमपाकरोषि न मनागद्यापि रोषेण ते
हा हा बालमृणालतोऽप्यतितरां तन्वी तनुस्ताम्यति[२]॥५६॥

---

१. 'पूर्णं' इति पाठान्तरम्।
२. 'तनुः क्षाम्यति' इति पाठान्तरम्।

अन्वयः–हे मुग्धे! निशा आयाता एव, निशापतिकरैः दिशाम् अन्तरम् कीर्णम्, भामिन्यः भवनेषु भूषणगणैः अङ्गानि अलङ्कुर्वते, अद्य अपि मानम् मनाक् न अपाकरोषि, हा! हा!! रोषेण ते बालमृणालतः अपि अतितराम् तन्वी तनुः ताम्यति।

व्याख्या:–मानिनीं प्रति सखीजनस्योक्तिः। निशाऽऽयातैव प्राप्तैव। मानापनोदे प्रतीक्ष्यमाण इयान् कालो व्यतीत इत्यर्थः। कीर्णं व्याप्तम्। अन्तरमन्तरालम्। भामिन्य इतरकामिन्यः। भवनेषु स्वस्वगृहेषु। अपाकरोषि त्यजसि। तन्वी कृशा।

Eng.Tr.:-The night has already set in, the rays of the lord of the night has pervaded the whole space between the quaters, lovely women in their houses adorn their bodies with ornaments. Yet oh, silly girl! you do not let your haughtiness abate even in the least. your lissom body much more tender even than the young lotus flower, is alas! afflicted with anger.

वाचो माङ्गलिकीः प्रयाणसमये जल्पत्यनल्पं जने
केलीमन्दिरमारुतायनमुखे विन्यस्तवक्त्राम्बुजा।
निःश्वासग्लपिताधरं परिपतद्बाष्पार्द्रवक्षोरुहा
बाला लोलविलोचना शिव शिव प्राणेशमालोकते॥५७॥

अन्वयः–प्रयाणसमये जने माङ्गलिकीः वाचः अनल्पम् जल्पति केलीमन्दिरमारुतायनमुखे विन्यस्तवक्त्राम्बुजम् परिपतद्बाष्पार्द्रवक्षोरुहा लोलविलोचना बाला, शिव! शिव! निःश्वासग्लपिताधरम् प्राणेशम् आलोकते।

व्याख्या:–प्रवस्यत्पतिकावर्णनमिदम्। विप्रलम्भशृङ्गारश्चात्र प्राधान्येन व्यंग्यः। माङ्गलिकीर्मङ्गलफलकाः। प्रयाणसमये पत्युरिति शेषः। जने भवनस्थे सुहृज्जने। मारुतायनमुखे गवाक्षविवरे। निःश्वासैर्ग्लपितो ग्लापितोऽधरो यस्मिन् कर्मणि तथा। शिव शिवेति खेदातिशये।

Eng.Tr.:-Alas! while other persons (of the house) are uttering plenty of auspicious words on the eve of his departure, the young lady placing her lotus-like face in the window of her private apartment beholds her lord, with tears falling from her eyes and her lower lip parched with heavy breathing.

यदवधि दयितो विलोचनाभ्यां
सहचरि दैववशेन दूरतोऽभूत्।
तदवधि शिथिलीकृतो मदीयै-
रथकरणैः प्रणयो निजक्रियासु॥५८॥

अन्वयः—हे सहचरि! दैववशेन यदवधि दयितः विलोचनाभ्याम् दूरतः अभूत् अथ तदवधि मदीयैः करणैः निजक्रियासु प्रणयः शिथिलीकृतः।

व्याख्या:—कस्याश्चिद्विरहिण्याः सखीं प्रत्युक्तिरियम्। सहचरि सखि दूरतो दूरे। शिथिलीकृतो मन्दीकृतः। अर्थशब्दोऽत्र साकल्ये। करणैरिन्द्रियैः। प्रणयः स्नेहः। निजक्रियासु स्वकर्तव्येषु। अत्र नायिकागता जडता व्यंग्या। जडता च विरहादिजन्याऽवश्यकर्तव्यार्थप्रतिसन्धानविकला चित्तवृत्तिः।

Eng.Tr.:-Oh, friend! since the day my husband through the influence of fate, went away from my sight my limbs have their regard slackened for their respective duties.

निखिलां रजनीं प्रियेण दूरा-
दुपयातेन विबोधिता कथाभिः।
अधिकं न हि पारयामि वक्तुं
सखि मा जल्प तवायसी रसज्ञा॥५९॥

अन्वयः—दूरात् उपयातेन प्रियेण कथाभिः निखिलां रजनीं विबोधिता अधिकं वक्तुम् न हि पारयामि (अतः) ~~हे~~ सखि! मा जल्प, तव रसज्ञा आयसी (अस्ति)।

व्याख्या:—एषा प्रियागमनद्वितीयदिवसे मुहुर्निशावृत्तान्तं पृच्छन्तीं सखीं प्रति रजनिजागरणजनितालस्यायाः कस्याश्चिदुक्तिः। निखिलां रजनीं विबोधिताऽहं वक्तुं न पारयामीत्यन्वयः। रजनीमित्यत्र कालाध्वनोरत्यन्तसंयोग

इति द्वितीया। न हि नैव। पारयामि शक्नोमि। आयसी लोहमयी। रसज्ञा जिह्वा।

Eng.Tr.:-I was kept awake the whole night with talk by my lover who had come from a distant place. I cannot be more plain. Do not talk, oh friend! your tnugue is made of bronze (iron).

निपतद्बाष्पसंरोधमुक्तचाञ्चल्यतारकम्।
कदा नयननीलाब्जमालोकेय मृगीदृशः॥६०॥

अन्वयः—मृगीदृशः निपतद्बाष्पसंरोधमुक्तचाञ्चल्यतारकम् नयननीलाब्जम् कदा आलोकेय?

व्याख्या:—कस्यचित् पूर्वदृष्टकामिनीदर्शनोत्सुकस्योक्तिरियम्। निपतद्बाष्पसंरोधेन गलदश्रुजलावरोधेन मुक्तचाञ्चल्या तारका यस्य तत्। आलोकेय पश्येयम्।

Eng.Tr.:-When shall I see the lotus-like eye of the deer-eyed one whose pupils have become steady owing to the stifling of the rising tears?

यदि लक्ष्मण सा मृगेक्षणा
न मदीक्षासरणिं समेष्यति।
अमुना जडजीवितेन मे
जगता वा विफलेन किं फलम्॥६१॥

अन्वयः—हे लक्ष्मण! यदि सा मृगेक्षणा मदीक्षासरणिम् न समेष्यति अमुना जडजीवितेन वा विफलेन जगता मे किम् फलम् (भविष्यति।)।

व्याख्या:—दण्डकायां वैदेहीविरहव्यथाविकलितस्य भगवतो रामस्योक्तिरियम्। सा सीता। मदीक्षासरणिं मन्नेत्रपथम्। जडजीवितेनाचेतनजीवितेन। विफलेन विरुद्धफलेन। अत्र रामगतो निराशाजन्यो निर्वेदो व्यंग्य:।

Eng.Tr.:-Oh Lakṣmaṇa! if that deer-eyed one will not come within the range of my sight what is the use of this burdensome life or this fruitless world.

भवनं करुणावती विशन्ती
गमनाज्ञालवलाभलालसेषु।
तरुणेषु विलोचनालमाला-
मथ बाला पथि पातयाम्बभूव॥६२॥

अन्वयः–भवनं विशन्ती करुणावती बाला पथि गमनाज्ञालवलाभ-लालसेषु तरुणेषु अथ विलोचनाब्जमालाम् पातयाम्बभूव।

व्याख्याः–भवनं स्वगृहम्। करुणावती परिश्रमस्मरणेन तरुणेषु सञ्ञातकरुणा। कुतश्चिदागच्छन्त्या पथि तदीयरूपयौवनगृहीतमानसैर्युवभिरनुगम्यमानया कयाचिद्भवनप्रवेशसमये निजसेवासार्थक्याङ्गीकाराय गमनाज्ञापनरूपलाभलालसेषु तरुणेषु गमनाज्ञादानसूचिका नयनकमलमाला परिचिक्षिप इत्यर्थः। अत्र बहुवचनेन बालागताऽनेकतरुणविषया रतिर्गम्यते। अत एवायं शृङ्गाराभासः।

Eng.Tr:.-The sympathetic young lady while entering the house cast wreaths of lotus-like glances towards youths on the way who coveted from her at least a signal to depart.

पापं हन्त मया हतेन विहितं सीताऽपि यद्यापिता
सा मामिन्दुमुखी विना बत वने किं जीवितं धास्यति।
आलोकेय कथं मुखं सुकृतिनां किं ते वदिष्यन्ति मां
राज्यं यातु रसातलं पुनरिदं न प्राणितुं कामये॥६३॥

अन्वयः–हन्त! मया हतेन पापं विहितं यत् सीता अपि यापिता। बत! सा इन्दुमुखी किम् माम् विना वने जीवितम् धास्यति? (अहम्) सुकृतिनाम् मुखम् कथम् आलेकेय? ते माम् किं वदिष्यन्ति? इदं राज्यम् पुनः रसातलं यातु (अहम्) प्राणितुम् न कामये।

व्याख्याः–इयं कठोरगर्भां जानकीं वने त्यक्तवतो भगवतो रामस्योक्तिः। अत्र भावानां मत्यसूयाविषादस्मृतिवितर्कव्रीडाशङ्कानिर्वेदानां व्यामिश्रणं चमत्कारकारि। तत्र पापमित्येनेन मतिर्हन्तेत्यादिनाऽसूया सीता पीत्यादिना विषादः सेत्यनेन स्मृतिर्मामित्यादिना वितर्क आलोकेयेत्यादिना व्रीडा किं त इत्यादिना शङ्का राज्यमित्यादिना च निर्वेदो व्यज्यते। हन्त खेदे। यापिता निर्वासिता। मां विनेत्यन्वयः। इदं राज्यमित्यन्वयः।

Eng. Tr.:-Sin has alas! been committed by my cursed self since Sītā has been turned away by me. Alas! how will that moon-faced one in the forest hold her life without me? How shall I look into the face of the virtuous? What will they say to me? let my kingdom go to the lowest depths of this earth. I have no more desire to live.

उषसि प्रतिपक्षकामि[१]नीसदनादन्तिकमञ्चति प्रिये।
सुदृशो नयनाब्जकोणयोरुदियाय त्वरयाऽरुणद्युतिः॥६४॥

अन्वयः—उषसि प्रिये प्रतिपक्षकामिनीसदनात् अन्तिकम् अञ्चति सुदृशः नयनाब्जकोणयोः त्वरया अरुणद्युतिः उदियाय।

व्याख्याः—प्रतिपक्षकामिनी सपत्नी। अचन्ति गच्छति। अरुणद्युतिरारुण्यम्। अत्र नेत्रयोरारुण्योदयेन नायिकायां रोषोदयो व्यज्यते।

Eng. Tr.:-Red effulgence appeared in the corner of the lotus-like eyes of the fair-eyed one when her lover went to her in the morning from the abode of her rival woman.

क्षमापणैकपदयोः पदयोः पतति प्रिये।
शेमुः सरोजवदनानयनारुणकान्तयः॥६५॥

अन्वयः—प्रिये क्षमापणैकपदयोः पदयोः पतति सरोजवदनानयनारुणकान्तयः शेमुः।

व्याख्याः—क्षमापणस्यैकपदयोर्मुख्यस्थानभूतयोः। पततीति सप्तम्यन्तम्। अत्र नायिकायां रोषशान्तिर्व्यङ्ग्या।

Eng. Tr.:-The red lustre of the eyes of the lotus-eyed one abated when her lover prostrated to her feet the chief abode of forgiveness.

निर्वासयन्तीं धृतिमङ्गनानां
शोभां हरेरेणदृशो धयन्त्याः।
चिरापराधस्मृतिमांसलोऽपि
रोषः क्षणप्राघुणिको बभूव॥६६॥

---

१. 'नायिका' इति पाठान्तरम्।

अन्वयः—अङ्गनानाम् धृतिम् निर्वासयन्ती हरेः शोभाम् धयन्त्याः एणदृशः चिरापराधस्मृतिमांसलः अपि रोषः क्षणप्राघुणिकः बभूव।

व्याख्या:—निर्वासयन्तीं दूरीकुर्वंतीम्। धृतिं धैर्यम्। माननिर्वहणक्षमत्व-मिति यावत्। एणदृशो हरिणनयनायाः। धयन्त्या आस्वादयन्त्याः। मांसलः पुष्टः। क्षणप्राघुणिकोऽचिरस्थाय्यभ्यागतः। गमनोन्मुख इति यावत्।

Eng.Tr.:-The anger which had increased on account of the remembrance of a fault (against her) committed long ago, of the fawneyed one enjoying Hari's beauty capable of depriving the self-control of women, became a temporary visitor.

राज्ञो मत्प्रतिकूलान्मे महद्भयमुपस्थितम्।
बाले वारय पान्थस्य वासदानविधानतः॥६७॥

अन्वयः—हे बाले! मत्प्रतिकूलात् राज्ञः उपस्थितम् महत् भयम् मे पान्थस्य वासदानविधानतः वारय।

व्याख्या:—कस्यचित्पान्थस्य काञ्चित्तरुणीं प्रत्युक्तिः। बाले मत्प्रतिकूला-द्राज्ञ उपस्थितं पान्थस्य मे महद्भयं वासदानविधानतो वारयेत्यन्वयः। राज्ञो नृपाच्चन्द्राच्च। वासस्य यद्दानं तस्य विधानतः। वसत्यर्थं स्थलदानेनेत्यर्थः। अत्रोपभोगं देहीति वस्तु राजपदात्प्रतीयते। राजपदाद् व्यञ्जनावृत्त्या चन्द्रोपस्थितौ हि चन्द्रजनितभयवारणकारणत्वेनोपभोगस्याभिव्यक्तिः।

Eng.Tr.:-Oh young lady! the king being adverse to me a great danger has befallen me. Give me shelter and shield me therefrom.

मलयानिलमनलीयति मणिभवने काननीयति क्षणतः।
विरहेण विकलहृदया निर्जलमीनायते महिला॥६८॥

अन्वयः—विरहेण विकलहृदया महिला क्षणतः मलयानिलम् अनलीयति मणिभवनम् काननीयति, निर्जलमीनायते।

व्याख्या:—विरहिण्यवस्थावर्णनम्। अनलीयत्यनलमिवाचरति। उपमानादाचार इति सुत्रेणानलशब्दात् क्यच्। मणिभवने रत्ननिर्मितप्रासादे।

काननीयतीत्यत्राधिकरणाच्चेति वार्तिकेन काननशब्दात् क्यच्। निर्जलमीनायते निर्जलस्थलस्थमीन इव व्याकुला भवति। निर्जलमीनशब्दात्कर्तुः क्यङ् सलोपश्चेति क्यङ्। महिला कामिनी।

Eng.Tr.:-When the heart of a young woman is distracted with the pangs of separation, in a single moment she feels the Malaya-breezes to be fires, regards the crystal palace to be forest, and is reduced to the condition of a fish out of water.

कालागुरुद्रवं सा हालाहलवद्विजानती नितराम्।
अपि नीलोत्पलमालां बाला व्यालावलिं किलामनुते॥६९॥

अन्वयः—कालागुरुद्रवम् नितरां हालाहलवद् विजानती सा बाला नीलोत्पलमालामपि व्यालावलिम् किल आमनुते।

व्याख्याः—विरहिणीमधिकृत्य कस्यचिदुक्तिः। कालागुरुद्रवं कृष्ण-चन्दनरसम्। विजानती मन्यमाना। व्यालावलिं सर्पश्रेणीम्। अमनुतामन्यत।

Eng.Tr.:-Verily, that young lady regards the black agaru-gum to be a deadly poison; while even wreaths of blue lotuses she takes for series of serpents.

विधिवञ्चितया मया न यातं
सखि संकेतनिकेतनं प्रियस्य।
अधुना बत किं विधातुकामो
मयि कामो नृपतिः पुनर्न जाने॥७०॥

अन्वयः—हे सखि! विधिवञ्चितया मया प्रियस्य संकेतनिकेतनम् न यातम्, अधुना पुनः बत नृपतिः कामः मयि किं विधातुकामः न जाने।

व्याख्याः—संकेतस्थानाऽगमनेन शङ्किताया नायिकायाः सखीं प्रत्युक्तिः। विधिर्दैवम्। निकेतनं स्थानम्। कामो नृपतिः कामरूपो राजा। शासनलङ्घनेन कृतापराधायां मयि कामनृपतिः किमाचरिष्यतीति न जान इति भावः।

Eng.Tr.:-Friend! beguiled by fate I did not call upon

my lover at the appointed place. Now alas! I know not what does the cupid, the lord of men, intends doing with me?

विरहेण विकलहृदया विलपन्ती दयित दयितेति।
आगतमपि तं सविधे परिचयहीनेव वीक्षते बाला॥७१॥

अन्वयः—विरहेण विकलहृदया बाला दयित! दयित! इति विलपन्ती सविधे आगतम् अपि प्रियम् परिचयहीनेव वीक्षते।

व्याख्या:—तं दयितम्। अत्र नायिकागतो मोहो व्यंग्यः।

Eng.Tr.:-Although her lover had come near her, the young lady with her heart distracted with the pangs of separation, crying out—Oh love, oh love,—gazes at him as though unacquainted with him.

दारद्र्यं भजते कलानिधिरयं राकाऽधुना म्लायति
स्वैरं कैरवकाननेषु परितो मालिन्यमुन्मीलति।
द्योतन्ते हरिदन्तराणि सुहृदां वृन्दं समानन्दति
त्वं चेदञ्चसि काञ्चनाङ्गि वदनाम्भोजे विकासश्रियम्॥७२॥

अन्वयः—हे काञ्चनाङ्गि! चेत् त्वम् वदनाम्भोजे विकासश्रियम् अञ्चसि अधुना अयम् कलानिधिः दारिद्र्यम् भजते, राका म्लायति कैरवकाननेषु परितः स्वैरम् मालिन्यम् उन्मीलति, हरिदन्तराणि द्योतन्ते, सुहृदां वृन्दं समानन्दति।

व्याख्या:—मानिनीं प्रति सखीजनस्योक्तिः। भजते भजिष्यते। वर्तमान-सामीप्ये वर्तमानवद्वेति लट्। एवमपरत्रापि। कलानिधिश्चन्द्रः। अयं पुरोवर्ती। राका पौर्णमासी। स्वैरं परप्रयत्नमन्तरेणैव। परितः समन्तात्। मालिन्यं संकोचरूपम्। उन्मीलत्युदयते। वृन्दं समूहः। अञ्चस्यङ्गीकरोषि। काञ्चनाङ्गि सुवर्णगौराङ्गि। विकासश्रियं प्रकाशलक्ष्मीम्। मानत्यागः सर्वथैव श्रेयानिति भावः।

Eng.Tr.:-Oh you of gold colour! if you do assume the splendour of blooming lotus on your lotus-like face, this store of digits will appear impoverished, the full-moon night will fade away (in lustre), and a dirth of beauty will pervade all over the forest of white lotuses, the place between the quarters will be lighted, and the host of your friends will be delighted.

पाटीरद्रुभुजङ्गपुङ्गवमुखायाता इवातापिनो
वाता वान्ति दहन्ति लोचनममी ताम्रा रसालद्रुमाः।
एते हन्त किरन्ति कूजितमयं हालाहलं कोकिला
बाला बालमृणालकोमलतनुः प्राणान् कथं रक्षतु॥७३॥

अन्वयः—पाटीरद्रुभुजङ्गपुङ्गवमुखात् याता इव आतापिनः वाता वान्ति, अमी ताम्रा रसालद्रुमाः लोचनम् दहन्ति, एते कोकिलाः कूजितमयं हालाहलम् किरन्ति, हन्त! बालमृणालकोमलतनुः बाला प्राणान् कथं रक्षतु।

व्याख्याः—वसन्ते विरहिणीदशावर्णनमिदम्। पाटीरद्रुषु चन्दनवृक्षेषु स्थिता ये भुजङ्गपुङ्गवास्तेषां मुखेभ्य आयाता इवातापिनः सन्तापकारकाः। ताम्रास्ताम्रपर्णाः। रसालद्रुमा आम्रवृक्षाः। वसन्ते चूतः पल्लवं प्रसूत इति प्रसिद्धमेव। अत्र वाता रसालद्रुमाः कोकिलाश्चेति त्रयोऽपि बालायाः प्राणनाशार्थं युगपदहमहमिकया सम्पतन्तीतिसमुच्चयालंकारोऽयम्।

Eng.Tr.:-Here blow the winds afflicting the body as thoughtheyemanatedfrom

the mouths of serpents on sandal trees; there the mang trees afflict the sight; the cuckcos, too, rain deadly p ison in the form of cooing notes. This being the case, how will the young lady having limbs tender like the young lotus fibre, hold her life?

आयातैव निशा मनो मृगदृशामुन्निद्रमातन्वती
मानो मे कथमेष संप्रति निरातङ्कं हृदि स्थास्यति।
ऊहापोहमिमं सरोजनयना यावद् विधत्तेतरां
तावत् कामनृपातपत्रसुषमं बिम्बं बभासे विधोः॥७४॥

अन्वयः–मृगदृशाम् मनः उन्निद्रम् आतन्वती निशा आयाता एव, सम्प्रति एषः मानः मे हृदि कथम् निरातङ्कं स्थास्यति? इमम् ऊहम् उन्नीय सरोजनयना यावत् त्वरां विधत्ते तावद् विधोः कामनृपातपत्रसुषमम् बिम्बम् बभासे।

व्याख्या:–उन्निद्रं विगतनिद्रम्। जाताभिलाषमिति यावत्। निरातङ्कं निःशङ्कम्। ऊहापोहं तर्करूपां चिन्ताम्। सरोजनयना काचिन्मानिनी। विधत्तेतरामतिशयेन करोति। बभासे भासमानं बभूव उदियायेत्यर्थः। कामनृपात-पत्रसुषमं मदननृपतिच्छत्रशोभम्। अत्र रात्रिसन्निधानादपि सिध्यतो मानिनीमानविनाशस्य चन्द्रोदयादनायासेन सिद्धिर्वर्णितेति समाध्यलंकारोऽयम्।

Eng.Tr.:-The disc of the moon beautiful like umbrella of the king cupid, shone in the sky just at the moment when the lotus-eyed one was revolving in her mind that the night that dispels the sleep of the dear-eyed ones has already set in and that now how will her pride hold its own undaunted.

प्रभातसमयप्रभां प्रणयिनि ह्नुवाना रसा-
दमुष्य निजपाणिना दृशममीलयत् लीलया।
अयं तु खलु पद्मिनीपरिमलालिपाटच्चरै-
रवेरुदयमध्यगादधिकचारु तैर्मारुतैः॥७५॥

अन्वयः–रसात् प्रणयिनि प्रथातसमयप्रभां ह्नुवाना, लीलया अमुष्य दृशं निजपाणिना अमीलयत्। तु अयं खलु पद्मिनीपरिमलालिपाटच्चरैः तैः मारुतैः खेः उदयम् अधिक चारु अध्यगात्।

व्याख्या:–उषसि प्रियतमस्य प्रभातकालप्रभादर्शनं वारयितुमिच्छन्त्याः कस्याश्चित् सखीं प्रत्युक्तिः। प्राणयिनि प्रियतमे। ह्नुवाना गोपयन्ती। रसाद्रागद्धेतोः। अमुष्य प्रणयिनः। अयं प्रणयी। पद्मिनीनां ये परिमला विम-र्दोत्त्थगन्धास्तेषामालीनां पंक्तीनां पाटच्चरास्तस्कराः। पद्मिनीगन्धापहारिण इति यावत्। अध्यगादज्ञासीत्। अधिकचार्वतिसम्यक्। तैः पुर्वपरिचितैः। प्रभात-कालीनत्वेन पूर्वं ज्ञातैरित्यर्थः। अत्र कामिन्या प्रियतमकर्तृकप्रभातविषय-कज्ञानाभावः साध्यमानोऽपि न सिद्ध इतीष्टाप्राप्त्या विषमालंकारोऽयम्।

Eng.Tr.:-Friend, through love intending to conceal from

my lover the light of dawn, I in sport covered his eyes with my hands; but he, verily, became conscious of the sun-rise still better (that by witnessing it with his eyes) by means of those breezes, the thieves of lotus-perfume streams.

विदूरादाश्चर्यस्तिमितमथ किञ्चित् परिचया-
दुदञ्चच्चाञ्चल्यं तदनु परितः स्फारितरुचि।
गुरूणां सङ्घाते सपदि मयि याते समजनि
त्रपाघूर्णत्तारं नयनमिह सारङ्गजदृशः॥७६॥

अन्वयः–इह गुरूणां सङ्घाते मयि सपदि याते सारङ्गजदृशः नयनं विदूरात् आश्चर्यस्तिमितम् अथ परिचयात् किञ्चित् उदञ्चच्चाञ्चल्यम् तदनु परितः स्फारितरुचि (ततः) त्रपाघूर्णत्तारं समजनि।

व्याख्याः–अत्र कश्चित् सखायं प्रत्यनपावृते स्थलविशेषे गुरून् शुश्रूषमाणायाश्चिरप्रोषितमसंभावितागमनमात्मानमालोकितवत्याः प्रियाया नयनव्यापारान् वर्णयति। स्तिमितं निश्चलम्। उदञ्चच्चाञ्चल्यं प्राप्तचाञ्चल्यम्। स्फारिता वृद्धिं प्रापिता रुचिः कान्तिर्यस्य तथाविधम्। मयि गुरूणां संघातं याते सतीत्यन्वयः। संघातं समूहम्। त्रपया घूर्णन्ती भ्रमन्तीं तारा कनीनिका यस्य तथाविधम् सारङ्गजदृशो मृगशावाक्ष्याः।

Eng.Tr.:-The eyes of fawn-eyed one became motionless with amazement after patial recognition of me while I was at a distance; later on their brightness increased all round; and when I got into the assembly of elderly persons, they had their pupils rolling through bashfulness.

कपोलावुन्मीलन्नवपुलकपाली मयि मनाङ्
मृशत्यन्तःस्मेरस्तवकितमुखाम्भोरुहरुचः।
कथङ्कारं शक्याः परिगदितुमिन्दीवरदृशो
दलद्राक्षानिर्यद्रसभरसपक्षा भणितयः॥७७॥

अन्वयः–मयि उन्मीलत्पुलकनिकुरम्बौ कपोलौ मनाक् मृशति

अन्तःस्मेरस्तबकितमुखाम्भोरुहरुचेः इन्दीवरदृशः दलद्द्राक्षानिर्य्यद्रसभरसपक्षाः भणितयः कथङ्कारम् परिगदितुं शक्याः?

व्याख्याः—नायकोक्तिरियम्। मय्युन्मीलन्नवपुलकपाली कपोलौ मनाङ् मृशति सतीन्दीवरदृशो भणितयः कथङ्कारं परिगदितुं शक्या इत्यन्वयः। उन्मीलन्तो नवपुलका ययोस्तथाविधे पाली ययोस्तौ। मृशति स्पृशति। अन्तःस्मेरान्तर्विकसिता स्तवकितमुखाम्भोरुहस्य गुच्छायितमुखकमलस्य रुग् यस्यास्तथाविधायाः। कथङ्कारं कथम्। दलन्ती या द्राक्षा तस्याः सकाशन्निर्यन् यो रसभरस्तस्य सपक्षास्तुल्याः।

Eng. Tr.:-How is it possible to describe the speech sweet like the juice oozing out of the bursting grapes, of the lotus-eyed one whose lotus-like mouth was streeked with rays of gentle smile when I touched the region of here cheek on which the hair were beginning to stand on their ends.

राजानं जनायाम्बभूव सहसा जैवातृक त्वां तु यः
सोऽयं कुण्ठितसर्वशक्तिनिकरो जातो जरातो विधिः।
सम्प्रत्युन्मदखञ्जरीटनयनाक्त्राय नित्यश्रिये
दाता राज्यमखण्डमस्य जगतो धाता नवो मन्मथः॥७८॥

अन्वयः—हे जैवातृक! यः विधिः त्वाम् राजानम् जनयाम्बभूव सः तु अयम् जरार्तः सहसा कुण्ठितसर्वशक्तिनिकरः जातः। सम्प्रति अस्य जगतः नवः धाता मन्मथः नित्यश्रिये उन्मदखञ्जरीटनयनावक्त्राय अखण्डं राज्यं दाता।

व्याख्याः—कस्यचिच्चन्द्रं प्रत्युक्तिः। राजानं सौंदर्यातिशयात्सर्वश्रेष्ठम्। जैवातृक चन्द्र। जरातो वृद्धावस्थातः। मन्मथो नवो धातोन्मदखञ्जरीटनयनावक्त्रायास्य जगतोऽखण्डं राज्यं दातेत्यन्वयः। उन्मदखञ्जरीटनयनावक्त्रायोन्मत्त-खञ्जनाक्षीमुखाय। नित्यश्रिये सततश्रीकाय। अनिशं नयनाभिरामायेत्यर्थः। दाता दास्यति अखण्डं निष्कण्टकम्। त्वत्तोप्यधिकरमणीयं नित्यशोभं कामिनीवदनं सर्वमिदं जगज्जेष्यतीति भावः।

Eng. Tr.:-Oh moon! the creator who made you king had all his powers impaired on account of old age; and there fore now the cupid, the juvenile creator, intends to give unqualified sovereignty of this world to the ever beautiful face of her possessing eyes like those of an intoxicated Khañjarīṭa bird.

आविर्भूता यदवधि मधुस्यन्दिनी नन्दसूनोः
कान्तिः काचिन्निखिलनयनाकर्षणे कार्मणज्ञा।
श्वासो दीर्घस्तदवधि मुखे पाण्डिमा गण्डमूले[१]
शून्या वृत्तिः कुलमृगदृशां चेतसि प्रादुरासीत्॥७९॥

अन्वयः–यदवधि नन्दसूनोः निखिलनयनाकर्षणे कार्मणज्ञा मधुस्यन्दिनी काचित् कान्तिः अविर्भूता तदवधि कुलमृगदृशाम् मुखे दीर्घः श्वासः गण्डमूले पाण्डिमा चेतसि शून्या वृत्तिः प्रादुरासीत्।

व्याख्याः–यदवधि यद्दिनादारभ्य। मधुस्यन्दिनी मधुस्त्रविणी। अतीवमधुरेति यावत्। नन्दसूनोः कृष्णस्य। कान्तिः शरीरशोभा। काचिद् निर्वचनीया। कार्मणज्ञा मन्त्रतन्त्रादिकुशला। कुलमृगदृशां कुलस्त्रीणाम् विप्रलम्भशृङ्गारोऽत्र व्यंग्यः।

Eng.Tr.:-Since the day on which the beauty of Nanda's son was seen-beauty which distils honey and which is adept in the art of attracting the eyes of the whole bevy of deer-eyed ladies—deep sighs began to issue from their mouth, pallor showed itself on their cheeks, and a feeling of restlessness filled their mind.

प्रसङ्गे गोपानां गुरुषु महिमानं यदुपते–
रुपाकर्ण्य स्विद्यत्पुलकितकपोला कुलवधूः।
विषज्वालाजालं झटिति वमतः पन्नगपतेः
फणायां साश्चर्यं कथयतितरां ताण्डवविधिम्॥८०॥

अन्वयः–गुरुषु गोपानाम् प्रसङ्गे यदुपतेः महिमानम् उपाकर्ण्य स्विद्यत्पुलकितकपोला कुलवधूःधिगिति विषज्वालाजालं वमतः पन्नगपतेः फणायां साश्चर्यम् ताण्डवविधिम् कथयतितराम्।

---

१. 'गण्डयुग्मे' इति पाठान्तरम्।

व्याख्या:–प्रसङ्गे गोपानां गुरुषु यदुपतेर्महिमानमुपाकर्ण्य स्विद्यत्पुलकित-कपोला कुलवधूर्झटिति विषज्वालाजालं वमतः पन्नगपतेः फणायां ताण्डवविधिं साश्चर्यं कथयतितरामित्यन्वयः। प्रसङ्गे कालियकथाप्रसङ्गे। गोपानां गुरुषु वृद्धगोपसमीपे। यदुपतेः कालियमर्दनस्य कृष्णस्य। स्विद्यन्तौ पुलकितौ च कपोलौ यस्यास्तथाविधा। झटिति सपद्येव। अस्य कथयतितरामित्यनेन सम्बन्धः। पन्नगपतेः कालियस्य। साश्चर्यमाश्चर्येण सहितम्। ताण्डवविधिं यदुपतेरिति भावः। श्रीकृष्णमहिमाश्रवणेन जनिताभिलाषा वधूर्लज्जावती तद्विषयकरतिजन्यं स्वेदादिकं वृद्धगोपेष्वन्यथयितुं साश्चर्यं तादृशताण्डवविधिं कथयतीति भावः। अत्रावहित्थं नाम व्यभिचारी व्यंग्यः। व्रीडादिना निमित्तेन हर्षाद्यनुभावानां गोपनाय जनितो भावविशेषोऽवहित्थम्।

Eng.Tr.:-While in the midst of elderly cowherd persons, a high-born girl, when she heard the greatness of Kṛṣṇa recounted to her and at which perspiration having began to appear on her cheeks and her hair began to stand erect, at once commenced to describe with admiration the mode of his dance on the hood of the serpent-king (Kāliā) vomitting wreaths of flames of deadly poison.

कैशोरे वयसि क्रमेण तनुतामायाति तन्व्यास्तना-
वागामिन्यखिलेश्वरे रतिपतौ तत्कालमस्याज्ञया।
आस्ये पूर्णशशाङ्कता नयनयोस्तादात्म्यमम्भोरुहां
किं चासीदमृतस्य भेदविगमः साचिस्मिते तात्त्विकः॥८१॥

अन्वयः–क्रमशः कैशोरे वयसि तनुताम् आयाति तन्वाः तनौ अखिलेश्वरे रतिपतौ आगामिनि (सति) अस्य आज्ञया तत्कालम् आस्ये पूर्णशशाङ्कता नयनयोः अम्भोरुहाम् तादात्म्यम् किञ्च साचिस्मिते अमृतस्य तात्त्विकः भेदविगमः आसीत्।

व्याख्या:–कैशोरे वयसि बाल्ये। तनुतामायाति गच्छति सति। तनौ मूर्तौ। आगामिन्यागमिष्यति सति। अस्य रतिपतेः। आस्ये मुखे। पूर्णशशाङ्कता पूर्णचन्दत्वम् अम्भोरुहां कमलानां तादात्म्यमभेदः। भेदविगमो भेदराहित्यम्। साचिस्मित ईषद्धसिते। तात्त्विको यथार्थः।

Eng.Tr.:-When the child-hood of the slender-bodied one, was gradually declining from her body and the lord of Rati, the supreme ruler, was about to make his entry, there appeared at once at this instance a complete indentity of her face with the full-moon, of her eyes with lotuses, and besides a complete absence of difference between the nectar and her gentle smile.

शयिता शैवलशयने सुषमाशेषा नवेन्दुलेखेव।
प्रियमागतमपि सविधे सत्कुरुते मधुरवीक्षणैरेव॥८२॥

अन्वयः–सुषमाशेषा नवेन्दुलेखेव शैवलशयने शयिता सविधे आगतम् अपि प्रियतममधुरवीक्षणैः एव सत्कुरुते।

व्याख्याः–सुषमाशेषा शोभामात्रशेषा। अतिकृशेत्यर्थः। मधुरवीक्षणैरेवेत्यत्र न प्रत्युद्गमचरणनिपतनादिभिरित्येवकारार्थः। अत्र नायिकागता प्रियाविरहजन्या ग्लानिर्व्यंग्या।

Eng.Tr.:-Her beauty alone remaining to her, and (thereby) appearing like a digit of the new-moon, she reclining on bed of moss receives only with loving glances her lover though he has come close to her.

अधरद्युतिरस्तपल्लवा मुखशोभा शशिकान्तिलङ्घिनी।
तनुरप्रतिमा च सुभ्रुवो न विधेरस्य कृतिं विवक्षति॥८३॥

अन्वयः–सुभ्रुवः अस्तपल्लवा अधरद्युतिः शशिकान्तिलङ्घिनी मुखशोभा च अप्रतिमा तनुः अस्य विधेः कृतिम् न विवक्षति।

व्याख्याः–अस्तपल्लवा निरस्तकिसलया। पल्लवपदेनात्र पल्लवशोभा ग्राह्या। अस्य विधेः कृतिं न विक्षतीत्यन्वयः। अस्य प्रसिद्धस्य। अस्या निर्माता कोप्यन्यो विधाता स्यादिति भावः।

Eng.Tr.:-The beautiful eye-browed one does not appear to be the creation of Vidhi; since her lowerlip surpasses the beauty of the foliage leaf, the beauty of her face that of the moon, and because her body is matchless.

---

१. 'अकृतप्रतिमा तनुः कृता विधिना कस्य कृते मृगीदृशः' इति पाठान्तरम्।

व्यत्यस्तं लपति क्षणं क्षणमहो मौनं समालम्बते
सर्वस्मिन्विदधाति किं च विषये दृष्टिं निरालम्बनाम्।
श्वासं दीर्घमुरीकरोति न मनागङ्गेषु धत्ते धृतिं
वैदेहीविरहव्यथाविकलितो[१] हा हन्त लङ्केश्वरः॥८४॥

अन्वयः–हा! हन्त!! वैदेहीविरहव्यथाविकलितः लङ्केश्वरः क्षणं व्यत्यस्तम् लपति, अहो! क्षणम् मौनं समालम्बते किञ्चित् सर्वस्मिन् विषये निरालम्बनाम् दृष्टिं विदधाति, दीर्घं श्वासम् उरीकरोति, अङ्गेषु मनाक् धृतिम् न धत्ते।

व्याख्याः–व्यत्यस्तं विपरीतमसम्बद्धं वा। लपति वदति। एकं क्षणमितिपूर्वान्वयि। अपरमुत्तरान्वयि। निरालम्बनां शून्याम्। अङ्गेषु शरीरावयवेषु। धृतिमनवसादम्। वैदेही सीता। विकलितो व्याकुलः। हा हन्तेति खेदातिशये। लङ्केश्वरो रावणः। अत्र रतेरनुभयनिष्ठतया जगद्गुरुपत्नीविषयकतया चाभासत्वं विप्रलम्भस्य।

Eng. Tr.:-Alas! the lord of Laṅkā overpowered with the pangs of separation from Vaidehī, at one moment speaks incoherently, and other moment gazes vacantly all round, and next moment assumes silence and fetches a deep sigh and has no strength remaining in his limbs.

उदितं मण्डलमिन्दो रुदितं सद्यो वियोगिवर्गेण।
मुदितं च सकलललनाचूडामणिशासनेन मदनेन॥८५॥

अन्वयः-इन्दोः मण्डलम् उदितम् सद्यः वियोगिवर्गेण रुदितम्, च सकलललनाचूडामणिशासनेन मदनेन मुदितम्।

व्याख्याः–चन्द्रोदयसमयवर्णनम्। उदितमुदयं प्राप्तम्। मुदितमित्यत्र भावे क्तः। सकलललनानां चूडामणिभूतं शासनं यस्य तेन। अत्र तिस्रः क्रिया युगपत् प्रवृत्ता इति वर्णनात् समुच्चयालंकारोऽयम्। तेन चातिशयोक्तिः कार्यकारणयौगपद्यात्मिका व्यज्यते।

Eng. Tr.:-There the orb of the moon is risen and lo!

१. 'वैदेहीकमनीयताकवलितो' इति पाठान्तरम्।

simultaneously with it rise the wail of separated lovers and the joy of the god of love.

प्रादुर्भवति पयोदे कज्जलमलिनं बभूव नभः।
रक्तं च पथिकहृदयं कपोलपाली मृगीदृशः पाण्डुः॥८६॥

अन्वयः—पयोदे प्रादुर्भवति नभः कज्जलमलिनम् पथिकहृदयम् च रक्तं मृगीदृशः कपोलपाली पाण्डुः बभूव।

व्याख्याः—कज्जलमिव मलिनम्। रक्तं रागयुक्तम्। पाण्डुर्विरहदुःखादिति भावः। अयं समुच्चयालंकारः।

Eng. Tr.:-At the appearance of cloud, the sky becomes dark as pitch, the traveller's heart radiant with passion, and pale the region of the cheek of the deer-eyed one.

इदमप्रतिमं पश्य सरः सरसिजैर्वृतम्।
सखे! मा जल्प नारीणां नयनानि दहन्ति माम्॥८७॥

अन्वयः—हे सखे! सरसिजैः वृतम् इदम् अप्रतिमं सरः पश्य, मा जल्प, माम् नारीणाम् नयनानि दहन्ति।

व्याख्याः—सरस्तटगतयोः कयोश्चित् सम्वादोऽयम् एकेन प्रथमार्धमुक्तं द्वितीयार्धं चापरेण। वृतं चितम्। मा जल्पेदमप्रतिममित्यादि मा भण यतः सरसिजसादृश्यद्वारा स्मृतानि नारीनयनानि मां सन्तापयन्ति। अयं स्मरणालंकारध्वनिः।

Eng. Tr.:-Behold this matchless lake full of lotuses "Friend" (says the other)! do not say so; the eyes of women afflict me

मुञ्चसि नाद्यापि रुषं भामिनि मुदिरालिरुदियाय।
इति सुदृशः[१] प्रियवचनैरपायि नयनाब्जकोणशोणरुचिः॥८८॥

अन्वयः—हे भामिनि! मुदिरालिः उदियाय (किन्तु) अद्य अपि रुषम् न मुञ्चसि इति प्रियवचनैः सुदृशः नयनाब्जकोणशोणरुचिः अपायि।

१. 'तन्व्याः' इति पाठान्तरम्।

व्याख्या:–रुष्टां नायिकां प्रति नायकस्योक्तिः। मुदिरालिर्मेघपंक्तिः। अपायि पीता। निःशेषं यापितेत्यर्थः। नयनाब्जकोणस्य नयनकमलप्रांतस्य शोणरुची रक्तकांतिः। अत्र नायिकाया रोषनाशो व्यंग्यः।

Eng. Tr.:-"O haughty one, (behold) the line of clouds has appeared in the sky, but still you do not quit your anger." These words uttered by the lover of the fair-eyed one removed the radiant colour from the corner of her lotus-eye.

आलोक्य सुन्दरि मुखं तव मन्दहासं
नन्दन्त्यमन्दमरविन्दधिया मिलिन्दाः।
किं चासिताक्षि[1] मृगलाञ्छनसंभ्रमेण
चञ्चूपुटं चटुलयन्ति चिरं चकोराः॥८९॥

अन्वयः–हे सुन्दरि! मिलिन्दाः तव मन्दहासम् मुखम् आलोक्य अरविन्दधिया अमन्दम् नन्दन्ति, किञ्च हे असिताक्षि! चकोराः मृगलाञ्छन-सम्भ्रमेण चञ्चूपुटम् चिरम् चटुलयन्ति।

व्याख्या:–नन्दन्ति हृष्यन्ति। अमन्दमत्यन्तम्। अरविन्दधिया कमल-मिदमिति मत्वा। मिलिन्दा भ्रमराः। असिताक्षि कृष्णनयने। मृगलाञ्छनसंभ्रमेण चन्द्रभ्रान्त्या। चटुलयन्ति चपलयन्ति। अत्रोल्लेखालंकारो भ्रान्तिमता संकीर्णः। उल्लेखश्चैकस्य वस्तुनो निमित्तवशादनेकैर्ग्रहीतृभिरनेकप्रकारकं ग्रहणम्।

Eng. Tr.:-O beautiful one! seeing your slightly smiling face, the bees mistaking it for a lotus, become filled with great delight. Moreover, o raven-eyed one! the Cakora birds thinking it to be the moon (one having black spots) move about their beaks.

स्मितं नैतत् किन्तु प्रकृतिरमणीयं विकसितं
मुखं ब्रूते को वा[2] कुसुम[3]मिदमुद्यत्परिमलम्।

---

१. 'किञ्चालि पूर्ण' इति पाठान्तरम्।
२. 'मूढः' इति पाठान्तरम्।
३. 'कुमुद' इति पाठान्तरम्।

स्तनद्वन्द्वं मिथ्या कनकनिभमेतत् फलयुगं
लता रम्या सेयं भ्रमरकुलनम्या न रमणी॥९०॥

अन्वयः—एतत् स्मितम् न किन्तु प्रकृतिरमणीयं विकसितम् वा कः उदम् उद्यत्परिमलम् कुसुमम् मुखम्, एतत् कनकनिभम् फलयुगम्, स्तनद्वन्द्वं मिथ्या ब्रूते? इयम् भ्रमरकुलनम्या रम्या लता, सा रमणी न।

व्याख्याः—एतत् पुरो भासमानम्। प्रकृत्या स्वभावेनैव रमणीयम्। उद्यत्परिमलं प्राप्तामोदम्। भ्रमरकुलनम्या भ्रमरसंघभजनीया। सावयवेयमपह्नुतिः।

Eng.Tr.:-Ah! this is not a woman, but a beautiful creeper pressed down by swarms of bees; for this is not a smile but a naturally charming blooming (of a lotus) ; and that which is talked of as mouth, is surely a flower whence fragrance is issuing; and to say that these are breasts is utter falsehood, since they are a pair of gold coloured fruits.

संग्रामाङ्गणसम्मुखाहतकियाद्विश्वम्भराधीश्वर-
व्यादीर्णीकृतमध्यभागविवरोन्मीलन्नभोनीलिमा।
अङ्गारप्रखरैः करैः कवलयन्नेत[१]न्महीमण्डलं
मार्तण्डोऽयमुदेति केन पशुना लोके शशाङ्कीकृतः॥९१॥

अन्वयः—संग्रामाङ्गणसम्मुखाहतकियद्विश्वम्भराधीश्वरव्यादीर्णकृतमध्यभागविवरोन्मीलन्नभोनीलिमा, अङ्गारप्रखरैः करैः एतत् महीमण्डलम् कवलयन् अयम् मार्तण्डः उदेति, लोके केन पशुना शशाङ्कीकृतः?

व्याख्याः—उदयन्तं चन्द्रं दृष्ट्वा कस्यचिद्विरहिण उक्तिरियम्। संग्रामाङ्गणे संमुखमाहता ये कियन्तः कतिपये विश्वंभराधीश्वरा राजानस्तैर्व्यादीर्णीकृतो विदारितो यो मध्यभागस्तस्य विवरेणोन्मीलन् प्रकाशमानो नभोनीलिमाऽऽकाशकालिमा यस्मिन् सः। कवलयन् कवलीकुर्वन् शशचिह्नवत्त्वेन चन्द्रत्वेन कल्पितः। अत्र विरहि भ्रान्तत्वाच्चन्द्रं सच्छिद्रं मार्तंडं मन्यते। रणे संमुखं हतानां वीराणां सूर्यमण्डलभेदेन ब्रह्मलोकगमनं शास्त्रसिद्धम्। उक्तं च महाभारते।

---

१. 'सद्यो जगन्मण्डलं' इति पाठान्तरम्।

द्वाविमौ पुरुषौ लोके सूर्यमण्डलभेदिनौ।
परिव्राड् योगयुक्तश्च रणे चाभिमुखो हतः।।

Eng.Tr.:-W hat foolish person in this world supposed this to be the moon (one having hare-like mark); for it is the sun that rises encircling the expanse of the earth by its rays terrible like living fire, and the azure hue of the sky peeps through its central hole bored by countless lords of the earth slain on the field of battle.

श्यामं सितं च सुदृशो न दृशोः स्वरूपं
किन्तु स्फुटं गरलमेतदथामृतं च।
नो चेत् कथं निपतनादनयोस्तदैव
मोहं मुदं च नितरां दधते युवानः।।९२।।

अन्वयः–एतत् श्यामम् च सितम् सुदृशः दृशोः स्वरूपम् न किन्तु स्फुटम् गरलम् अथ च अमृतम् (अस्ति) नो चेत् युवानः अनयोः निपतनात् तदा एव मोहम् च मुदम् कथम् दधते?

व्याख्याः–सितं श्वेतम्। दृशोर्नयनयोः। गरलामृतयोर्मोहमुदोश्च यथा संख्येन संबंधः। नो चेदन्यथा। श्यामसितस्वरूपयोर्गरलत्वामृतत्वाभाव इत्यर्थः। अनयोर्दृशोः। तदैव तस्मिन्नेवक्षणे। निपतनसमकालमेवेत्यर्थः। इयमपह्नुतिः।

Eng.Tr.:-The black and the white that appears in the eyes of the fair-eyed one is not the colour of the respective parts; for surely it is due to the existence of deadly poison and nectar in them; or else, how could the falling (of their glances) on youths bring on deadly stupour and create great delight in them simultaneously?

अलिर्मृगो वा नेत्रं वा यत्र किञ्चिद्विभासते।
अरविन्दं मृगाङ्को वा मुखं वेदं मृगीदृशः।।९३।।

अन्वयः–इदम् मृगीदृशः मुखम्, वा मृगाङ्कः, वा अरविन्दम्, यत्र नेत्रं वा मृगः वा अलिः किञ्चित् न भाषते।

व्याख्याः–ससन्देहालंकारोऽयम्। संशयश्चात्राहार्यस्तत्त्वज्ञकविगतत्वात्। यत्र यस्मिन् मुखरूपे. वस्तुनि। विभासते शोभते। इदं पुरोवर्ति।

Eng.Tr.:-Is it a lotus, or the moon, or the face of the deer-eyed one on which something like a bee, or a deer or an eye is appearing?

सुविरल[१]मोक्तिकतारे धवलांशुकचन्द्रिकाचमत्कारे।
वदनपरिपूर्णचन्द्रे सुन्दरि राकाऽसि नात्र सन्देहः॥९४॥

अन्वयः–हे सुन्दरि! सुविमलमौक्तिकतारे धवलांशुकचन्दिकाचमत्कारे वदनपरिपूर्णचन्द्रे (सति त्वम्) राका असि, अत्र सन्देहः न (अस्ति)।

व्याख्याः–इदं सुन्दर्युपमेयकं राकोपमानकं समस्तवस्तुविषयं सावयवं रूपकम्। सुविरलमोक्तिकान्येव तारा यस्यां तथाविधे। धवलांशुकमेव चन्द्रिका तस्याश्चमत्कारो यस्यां तथाविधे। वदनमेव परिपूर्णचन्द्रो यस्यां तथाविधे राका पौर्णमासी।

Eng.Tr.:-Ah, beautiful one! you are no doubt the full-moon lit night having shining pearls for its stars, white garment of its brilliant moon-light and face for the full moon.

रूपजला चलनयना नाभ्यावर्ता कचावलिभुजङ्गा।
मज्जन्ति यत्र सन्तः सेयं तरुणी तरङ्गिणी विषमा॥९५॥

अन्वयः- इयम् तरुणी रूपजला चलनयना नाभ्यावर्ता कचावलीभुजंगा सा विषमा तरङ्गिणी (अस्ति) यत्र सन्तः मज्जन्ति।

व्याख्याः–इदं तरुण्यां तरङ्गिणीरूपकमेकदेशविवर्ति सावयवम्। रूपमेवजलं यस्याः सा। आवर्तोऽभोभ्रमः। तरङ्गिणी सरित्। विषमा दुस्तरा। अत्र जलावर्तादिरूपकैर्नयनयोर्मीनरूपकं कवेरभिप्रेततयाऽक्षिप्यते। अत एव चलनयनेति विशेषणं चलनयनमीनेत्यर्थे ग्राह्यम्।

Eng.Tr.:-Here in the shape of this young lady is an unfordable river wherein the righteous take their baths—the river having the complexion for its water, the eye for its fish, the navel of its whirlpool, and the tresses for its billows.

शोणाधरांशुसंभिन्नास्तन्वि ते वदनाम्बुजे।
केसरा इव काशन्ते कान्तदन्तालिकान्तयः॥९६॥

---

१. 'सुविमल०' इति पाठान्तरम्।

अन्वयः–हे तन्वि! ते वदनाम्बुजे शोणाधरांशुसम्भिन्नाः कान्तदन्तालिकान्तयः केशरा इव काशन्ते।

व्याख्याः–शोणाधरस्य रक्ताधरस्यांशुभिः प्रभाभिःसंभिन्ना मिश्रीभूताः। वदनाम्बुजमित्युपमितसमासः। काशन्ते शोभन्ते। कान्तदन्तालिकान्तयः सुन्दरदन्तपंक्तिप्रभाः।

Eng.Tr.:-Oh you of slender frame! in your lotus-like mouth the luster of the rows of thy beautiful teeth, blended with that of the red lower lip, shines forth like filaments of flower.

दयिते रदनत्विषां मिषादयि तेऽमी विलसन्ति केसराः।
अपि चालकवेषधारिणो मकरन्दस्पृहयालवोऽलयः॥९७॥

अन्वयः–अयि दयिते! अमी ते रदनत्विषाम् मिषात् केसराः अपि च मकरन्दस्पृहयालवः अलकवेषधारिणः अलयः विलसन्ति।

व्याख्याः–नायकस्य नायिकां प्रत्युक्तिः। रदनत्विषां दन्तकान्तिनाम्। अलकवेषधारिणो केशरूपेण वर्तमानाः। मकरन्दस्पृहयालवो मकरन्दस्पृहां कुर्वाणाः। अत्र वाच्याभ्यां द्वाभ्यामपह्नुतिभ्यां न त्वं नारी किं तु नलिनीति तृतीयापह्नुतिर्व्यज्यते।

Eng.Tr.:-Ah love, these are indeed, the filaments that sparkle under the guise of the streeks of the lustre of your teeth, and these are indeed the bees desirous of flower-juice, which have assumed the form of your hair.

तया तिलोत्तमीयन्त्या मृगशावकचक्षुषा।
ममाऽयं मानुषो लोको नाकलोक इवाभवत्॥९८॥

अन्वयः–तिलोत्तमीयन्त्या मृगशावकचक्षुषा तया मम अयम् मानुषः लोकः नाकलोक इव अभवत्।

व्याख्याः–तया कयाचिद्वक्तृबुद्धिस्थया कामिन्या। तिलोत्तमीयन्त्या तिलोत्तमामिवात्मानमाचरन्त्या। तिलोत्तमा नाम काचिदप्सराः। नाकलोकः स्वर्गः।

Eng.Tr.:-While that fawn-eyed one was conducting herself likeTilottamā, this mortal world was heaven to me.

अङ्कायमानमलिके मृगनाभिपङ्कं
पङ्केरुहाक्षि वदनं तव वीक्ष्य बिभ्रत्।
उल्लासपल्लवितकोमलपक्षमूला-
श्चञ्चूपुटं चटुलयन्ति[१] चिरं चकोरा[२]:॥९९॥

अन्वय:–हे पंकेरुहाक्षि! अलिके अङ्कायमानम् मृगनाभिपङ्कम् बिभ्रत् तव वदनं वीक्ष्य उल्लासपल्लवितकोमलपक्षमूला: चकोरा: चिरम् चञ्चूपुटम् चटुलयन्ति।

व्याख्या:–काञ्चित् कामिनीं प्रति कस्यचिदुक्ति:। अङ्कायमानमंकीभूतम् चन्द्रगताङ्कमिव दृश्यमानमित्यर्थ:। अलिके भाले। मृगनाभिपङ्क कस्तूरिका-तिलकम्। मृगनाभिपङ्क बिभ्रत्तव वदनं वीक्ष्येत्यन्वय:। उल्लासेनानन्देन पल्लवितं प्रसारितं कोमलपक्षमूलं येषां ते। अत्र सकस्तूरीतिलके कान्तावदने सकलंकचन्द्रभ्रम एव चञ्चूचापल्ये हेतुरिति भ्रान्तिमानलंकार: प्राधान्येन व्यंग्य:।

Eng.Tr.:-Ah! lotus-eyed one! seeing your face with its forehead bearing the tilaka mark of musk, the Cakora birds spreading through joy the tender pinion-roots, alternately open and close the hollow of their beaks for a long time.

शिशिरेण यथा सरोरुहं दिवसेनामृतरश्मिमण्डलम्।
न मनागपि तन्वि शोभते तव रोषेण तथेदमाननम्॥१००॥

अन्वय:–हे तन्वि! यथा शिशिरेण सरोरुहम्, दिवसेन अमृतरश्मि-मण्डलम् तथा (एव) रोषेण तव इदम् आननम् मनाक् अपि न शोभते।

व्याख्या:–अमृतरश्मि: सूर्य:।

Eng.Tr.:-Just as a frost beaten lotus wears no charm, nor does the lunar disc in the broad day-light, so also, oh slender bodied one! your face loses its beauty by anger.

चलद्भृङ्गमिवाम्भोजमधीरनयनं मुखम्।
तदीयं यदि दृश्येत काम: क्रुद्धोऽस्तु किं तत:॥१०१॥

---

१. 'चपलयन्ति' इति पाठान्तरम्।

२. 'चकोरपोता:' इति पाठान्तरम्।

अन्वयः–यदि तदीयम् चलद्भृङ्गम् अम्भोजम् इव अधीरनयनम् मुखम् दृश्येत, कामः क्रुद्धः अस्तु, ततः किम्?

व्याख्याः–नायकोक्तिः। अधीरनयनं चञ्चलनयनम्। तदीयं पूर्वदृष्ट-कामिनीसंबंधि।

Eng.Tr.:-If your face with eyes tremulous like a lotus with bees moving in their interior, were seen, what wonder then that the god of love becomes excited.

शतकोटिकठिनचित्तः सोऽहं तस्याः सुधैकमयमूर्तेः।
येनाकारिषि मित्रं स विकलहृदयो विधिर्वाच्यः॥१०२॥

अन्वयः–येन सुधैकमयमूर्तेः तस्याः मित्रम् शतकोटिकठिनचित्तः सः अहम् अकारिषि सः विधिः विकलहृदयः वाच्यः।

व्याख्याः–एषा सीतां विवासितवतो रामस्य स्वात्मगतोक्तिः। शतकोटिर्वज्रम्। येन सोऽहं तस्या मित्रमकारिषीत्यन्वयः। तस्याः सीतायाः। अकारिषि कृतः। कर्मणि लुक्। विकलहृदयोऽरसिकचित्तः। सदृशसं-योगपराङ्मुख इति यावत्।

Eng.Tr.:-The Creator by whom I of an adamantine heart was made a companion of her, the embodiment of nectar, must be censured for his silly taste.

श्यामलेनाङ्कितं बाले भाले केनापि लक्ष्मणा।
मुखं तवान्तरासुप्तभृङ्गफुल्लाम्बुजायते॥१०३॥

अन्वयः–हे बाले! भाले केन अपि श्यामलेन लक्ष्मणा अङ्कितम् तव मुखम् अन्तरासुप्तभृङ्गफुल्लाम्बुजायते।

व्याख्याः–श्यामलेन लक्ष्मणेत्यन्वयः। श्यामलेन श्यामेन। लक्ष्मणा चिह्नेन। अन्तरासुप्तभृङ्गफुल्लाम्बुजायन्तेऽतः सुप्तभ्रमरं विकसितकमलमिवा-भाति।

Eng.Tr.:-Ah girl! your face with an indescribable black mark tilaka on the fore-head, appears like a full blown lotus with a bee reposing in it.

अद्वितीयं रुचात्मानं मत्वा किं चन्द्र हृष्यसि।
भूमण्डलमिदं मूढ केन वा विनिभालितम्॥१०४॥

अन्वयः—अयि चन्द्र! रुचा आत्मानम् अद्वितीयम् मत्वा किम् हृष्यसि? अरे मूढ? इदम् भूमण्डलम् वा केन विनिभालितम्।

व्याख्या:—कस्यचिद्विदेशस्थितस्य किरणैरात्मानं सन्तापयन्तं चन्द्रं प्रत्येषोक्तिः। रुचा कान्त्या। विनिभालितं दृष्टम्। अत्रास्ति मम प्रियायाः कदापि बहिरनिर्गताया अत एव त्वयाप्यदृष्टाया आननं त्वत्सदृशमिति प्रतीयमानोपमा मूढपदेन ध्वन्यमानायां चन्द्रविषयायां वक्तृगतायामसूयायामलंकारः।

Eng.Tr.:-Ah moon! why do you exalt at thinking your luster complexion to be matchless. Ah silly one! who has explored the whole expanse of this world?

नीलाञ्चलेन संवृतमाननमाभाति हरिणनयनायाः।
प्रतिबिम्बित इव यमुनागभीरनीरान्तरेणाङ्कः॥१०५॥

अन्वयः—हरिणनयनायाः नीलाञ्चलेन संवृतम् आननं यमुनागभीरनीरान्तः प्रतिबिम्बितः एणाङ्कः इव आभाति।

व्याख्या:—नीलाञ्चलेन नीलपटान्तेन। एणाङ्कश्चद्रः।

Eng.Tr.:-The face of the deer-eyed one being covered with the hem of her blue garment, appears like the moon reflected in the waters of the Yamunā.

स्तनाभोगे पतन् भाति कपोलात्कुटिलोऽलकः।
शशाङ्कविम्बतो मेरौ लम्बमान इवोरगः॥१०६॥

अन्वयः—कपोलात् स्तनाभोगे पतन् कुटिलः अलकः मेरौ शशाङ्कबिम्बतः लम्बमानः उरगः इव भाति।

व्याख्या:—आभोगो विस्तारः। उरगः सर्पः।

Eng.Tr.:-The curling tresses hunging from her temples

down to the region of her breast, appear like serpents hanging from the disc of the moon on the mountain Meru.

यथा लतायाः स्तबकानतायाः
स्तनावनम्रे नितरां समाऽसि।
तथा लता पल्लविनी सगर्वे
शोणाधरायाः सदृशी तवाऽपि॥१०७॥

अन्वयः–हे स्तनावनम्रे! यथा (त्वम्) स्तबकानतायाः लतायाः नितरां समा असि, तथा हे सगर्वे! पल्लविनी लता अपि शोणाधरायाः तव सदृशी (अस्ति)।

व्याख्याः–कस्यचित् काञ्चित्कामिनीं प्रत्युक्तिः। स्तबकानतायाः पुष्पगुच्छैरवनम्रायाः। स्तनावनम्राऽहं स्तबकानताया लताया उपमानमस्मीति गर्वं मा विदध्या यतः शोणाधराया उपमेयायास्तवापि पल्लविनी लतोपमानं भवतीति भावः।

Eng.Tr.:-Oh you! bent down by the weight of your breast just as thou dost resemble creepers pressed down by flower bunches, so do, Oh proud one! the sprouted creeper resemble you having red lower lip.

इदं लताभिः स्तबकानताभिर्मनोहरं हन्त वनान्तरालम्।
सदैव सेव्यं स्तनभारवत्यो न चेद्युवत्यो हृदयं हरेयुः॥१०८॥

अन्वयः–हन्त! चेत! स्तनभारवत्यः युवत्यः हृदयम् न हरेयुः (तदा) स्तबकानताभिः लताभिः मनोहरम् इदं बनान्तरालं सदा एव सेव्यम् (स्यात्)।

व्याख्याः–इदं पुरोवर्ति। सेव्यं भवेदित शेषः। अत्र वनान्तरालगताभिः स्तबकानताभिर्लताभिः स्तनभारवतीनां युवतीनां स्मरणं प्रधान्येन व्यज्यते। अत एवायं स्मरणालंकारध्वनिः।

Eng.Tr.:-Ah! this interior of the forest charming on account of the creepers laden with bunches of flowers deserves to be resorted to always, if the young ladies bent with the weight of their breasts did not attract the heart.

सा मदागमनबृंहिततोषा जागरेण गमिताखिलदोषा।
बोधिताऽपि बुबुधे मधुपैर्न प्रातराननजसौरभलुब्धैः॥१०९॥

अन्वयः—मदागमनबृंहिततोषा जागरेण गमिताखिलदोषा सा प्रातः आननजसौरभलुब्धैः मधुपैः बोधिता अपि न बुबुधे।

व्याख्याः—नायकोक्तिः। सा नायिका। मदागमनेन बृंहितो वृद्धिं गतो तोषो यस्याः सा दोषा रात्रिः। मधुपैर्भ्रमरैः। अत्र नायिकाया रात्रिजागरणप्रयोज्यं चेतःसंमीलनं व्यंग्यम्। एतादृशं चेतःसंमीलनमालंकारिकैर्निद्रापदेन व्यवह्रियते।

Eng.Tr.:-She whose delight was greatly increased by my coming back, passed the whole night quite sleepless, and in the morning though the bees attracted by the fragrance issuing from her mouth, tried to awake her, she did not.

अविचिन्त्यशक्तिविभवेन सुन्दरि
प्रथितस्य शम्बररिपोः प्रभावतः।
विधुभावमञ्चतितमां तवाननं
नयने सरोजदलनिर्विशेषताम्॥११०॥

अन्वयः—हे सुन्दरि! अविचिन्त्यशक्तिविभवेन प्रथितस्य शम्बररिपोः प्रभावतः तव आननं विधुभावम् अञ्चतितमाम्, नयने सरोजदलनिर्विशेषताम् (अञ्चतस्तमाम्)।

व्याख्याः—नायकोक्तिः। अविचिन्त्यशक्तिविभवेन प्रथितस्येत्यन्वयः। प्रथितस्य प्रसिद्धस्य। शंबररिपोर्मदनस्य। अञ्चतितमां गच्छतितमाम्। निर्विशेषतां तुल्यताम्। नयने अञ्चतस्तमामिति शेषः।

Eng.Tr.:-Oh fair one! through the influence of the enemy of Sambara renowned for the unbounded greatness of his prowess, your face truly attains the beauty of the moon and your eyes does not differ from the lotus.

मीनवती नयनाभ्यां करचरणाभ्यां प्रफुल्लकमलवती।
शैवालिनी च केशैः सुरसेयं सुन्दरी सरसी॥१११॥

अन्वयः–सुरसा इयं सुन्दरी सरसी नयनाभ्याम् मीनवती करचरणाभ्याम् प्रफुल्लकमलवती च केशैः शैवालिनी अस्ति।

व्याख्या:–सुन्दर्यां सरसीरूपकमिदम्। नयनाभ्यामित्यादाव-भेदस्तृतीयार्थः। शैवालिनी सशैवाला।

Eng.Tr.:-This fair one having eyes for the fish, hands for the blooming lotuses and hair for the moss, is a lake full of water (love).

पान्थ मन्दमते किं वा सन्तापमनुविन्दसि।
पयोधरं समाशास्व येन शान्तिमवाप्नुयाः॥११२॥

अन्वयः–हे मन्दमते पान्थ! किं वा सन्तापम् अनुविन्दसि? पयोधरं समाशास्व येन शान्तिम् अवाप्नुयाः।

व्याख्या:–कस्यचित्पान्थं प्रत्युक्तिः। किं वा किमिति। वात्र प्रश्नदृढी-करणे। सन्तापं दाहं स्मरतापं च। अनुविन्दसि प्राप्नोषि। पयोधरं मेघं कामिनीस्तनं च। अत्र सहृदयस्य स्मरतापवत्तावैशिष्ट्यबुद्धौ सत्यां तादृशतापशामकरमणी-स्तनरूपविषयस्य मेघरूपविषयिणि तादूप्यबुद्धिर्भवति।

Eng.Tr.:-Ah! dull witted traveller why are you afflicted? Have recourse to *Payodhara* (water-cloud, breasts) whereby you will obtain ease.

संपश्यतां तामतिमात्रतन्वीं
शोभाभिराभासितसर्वलोकाम्।
सौदामिनी वा सितयामिनी वे-
त्येवं जनानां हृदि संशयोऽभूत्॥११३॥

अन्वयः–शोभाभिराभासितसर्वलोकाम् अतिमात्रतन्वीम् ताम् सम्पश्यताम् जनानां हृदि वा सौदामिनी वा सितयामिनी? इति एवम् अभूत्।

व्याख्या:–संपश्यतां जनानां हृदीत्यन्वयः। तां काञ्चित्कामिनीम्।

आभासितसर्वलोकां धवलितसमस्तजगतीतलाम्। सौदामिनी विद्युत्। सितयामिनी धवलरात्रिः। ज्योत्स्नीति यावत्। ससन्देहालंकारोऽयम्।

Eng.Tr.:-The minds of the people beholding the slender-bodied one who illumined the whole world by her beauty were at a loss to know whether she was the lightening or the fullmoon lit night.

सपल्लवा किं नु विभाति वल्लरी
सफुल्लपद्मा किमियं नु पद्मिनी।
समुल्लसत्पाणिपदां स्मितानना-
मितीक्षमाणैः समलम्भि संशयः॥११४॥

अन्वयः—समुल्लसत्पाणिपदां स्मिताननाम् ताम् ईक्षमाणैः किम् नु इयम् सपल्लवा वल्लरी नु किम् सफुल्लपद्मा पद्मिनी विभाति इति संशयः समलम्भि।

व्याख्या:—वल्लरी वल्लिः। स्मिताननामीक्षमाणैरिति संशयः समलम्भीत्यन्वयः। ईक्षमाणैः पार्श्ववर्तिभिर्जनैरिति शेषः। अयमपि ससन्देहालंकारः।

Eng.Tr.:-People gazing at her who had a smiling face and nimble limbs (hands and feet) entertained a doubt as to whether it was a lotus-creeper with full-blown lotuses or a creeper adorned with foliage leaves.

नेत्राभिरामं रामाया वदनं वीक्ष्य तत्क्षणम्।
सरोज चन्द्रबिम्बं वेत्यखिलाः समशेरत॥११५॥

अन्वयः—तत्क्षणम् अखिलाः रामायाः नेत्राभिरामं वदनं वीक्ष्य सरोजम् वा चन्द्रबिम्बम् इति समशेरत।

व्याख्या:—रामायाः कान्तायाः। समशेरत संशयं प्रापुः। सन्देहालंकारः।

Eng.Tr.:-Beholding the face, pleasing to the sight (eyes) of the lovely lady, all suddenly and unanimously were puzzled as to whether it was a lotus, or the fullmoon disc.

कनकद्रवकान्तिकान्तया मिलितं राममुदीक्ष्य कान्तया।
चपलायुतवारिदभ्रमान्ननृते चातकपोतकैर्वने॥११६॥

अन्वयः–वने चातकपोतकैः कनकद्रवकान्तिकान्तया कान्तया मिलितं रामम् उदीक्ष्य चपलयुतवारिदभ्रमात् ननृते।

व्याख्याः–कनकद्रवकान्तिकान्तया सुवर्णरसकान्तिमनोज्ञया। कान्तया सीतया। चपलायुतवारिदभ्रमात् सतडिन्मेघभ्रान्त्या। अत्र भगवति रामचन्द्रे श्यामवर्णत्वाच्चातकपोतकगता मेघभ्रान्तिरुपनिबद्धा। जानक्यां च कनकद्रवकान्तिकान्तत्त्वात्तडिद्भ्रान्तिः। अत एवायं भ्रान्तिमानलंकारः। चातको मेघं दृष्ट्वा मोदत इति प्रसिद्धमेव।

Eng.Tr.:-In the forest the young cakora birds seeing Rāma united with his beloved fascinating as the luster of the molten gold, danced under impression of his being a water-cloud united with lightening.

वनितेति वदन्त्येतां लोकाः सर्वे वदन्तु ते।
यूनां परिणता सेयं तपस्येति मतं मम॥११७॥

अन्वयः–सर्वे लोकाः एतां वनिता इति वदन्ति, ते वदन्तु (किन्तु) इयं यूनाम् परिणता सा तपस्या इति मम मतम्।

व्याख्याः–एतां काञ्चित् पुरोवर्तिनीम्। परिणता फलरूपेणावतीर्णा। अयमुल्लेखोऽपह्नुत्या संकीर्णः।

Eng.Tr.:-People take her for a woman; let them. To me it appears that she is the consumation of the penance performed by youths.

स्मयमानाननां तत्र तां विलोक्य विलासिनीम्।
चकोराश्चञ्चरीकाश्च मुदं परतरां ययुः॥११८॥

अन्वयः—तत्र स्मयमानाननाम् तां विलासिनीं विलोक्य चकोराः च चञ्चरीकाः च परतराम् मुदं ययुः।

व्याख्या:—स्मयमानाननां सस्मितवदनाम्। तां पूर्वदृष्टाम्। अत्र मुखे चन्द्रभ्रमश्चकोराणां कमलभ्रमश्च चञ्चरीकाणामानन्दे हेतुः। अयमुल्लेखध्वनि-र्ध्वन्यमानया भ्रान्त्या संकीर्णः।

Eng. Tr.:-There the cakora birds and the bees seeing the amorous lady with smilling face, were extremely delighted.

वदनकमलेन बाले स्मितसुषमालेशमादधासि[१] यदा।
जगदिह तदैव जाने दशार्धबाणेन विजितमिति॥११९॥

अन्वयः—हे बाले! यदा वदनकमलेन स्मितसुषमालेशम् आदधासि तदा एव इह जगत् दशार्द्धबाणेन विजितम् (भवति) इति जाने।

व्याख्या:—नायकोक्तिः। दशार्धबाणेन पञ्चबाणेन मदनेन।

Eng. Tr.:-Oh girl! the moment you do put on your face the slightest grace of smile, I feel sure that the whole world will be conquered by the five arrowed god.

कलिन्दजानीरभरेऽर्धमग्ना
वकाः प्रकामं कृतभूरिशब्दाः।
ध्वान्तेन वैराद्विनिगीर्यमाणाः
क्रोशन्ति मन्ये शशिनः किशोराः॥१२०॥

अन्वयः—कलिन्दजानीरभरे अर्द्धमग्नाःप्रकामम् कृतभूरिशब्दाः बकाः वैराद् ध्वान्तेन विनिगीर्य्यमाणाः शशिनः किशोराः क्रोशन्ति (इति) मन्ये।

व्याख्या:—अत्र बकेषु शशिकिशोरत्वं तत्कृतशब्दे च क्रोशनत्व-मुत्प्रेक्ष्यते। कलिन्दजानीरभरे यमुनाजलपूरे। ध्वान्तेनान्धकारेण। इदं पद्यं शृङ्गारविलासे कथं संनिवेशमर्हतीति न ज्ञायते।

Eng. Tr.:-Cranes half drowned in the depth of the waters of the Yamunā (the daughter of Kalinda) and screaming aloud

१. 'आवहसि (आवहसे)' इति पाठान्तरम्।

to their utmost, appear like the young ones of the moon, crying aloud on account of their being swallowed up by darkness through hostility (to moon).

परस्परासङ्गसुखान्नतभ्रुवः पयोधरौ पीनतरौ बभूवतुः।
तयोरमृष्यन्नयमुन्नतिं परामवैमि मध्यस्तनिमामञ्चति॥१२१॥

अन्वयः—परस्परासङ्गसुखात् नतभ्रुवः पयोधरौ पीनतरौ बभूवतुः। तयोः पराम् उन्नतिम् अमृष्यन् अयम् मध्यः तनिमानम् अञ्चति (इति) अवैमि।

व्याख्याः—परस्परासङ्गसुखादन्योन्यासङ्गसुखप्राप्त्यै। अमृष्यन्नसहमानः। अयमग्रे दृश्यमानः। तनिमानं तनुत्वम्। उत्प्रेक्षेयम्।

Eng. Tr.:-The breasts of her whose eye-brows are curved, have grown plump (are elevated) by the enjoyment of the happiness of reciprocal union; whereas her waist not bearing (to behold) their elevation is reduced to thinness.

जनमोहकरं तवालि मन्ये
चिकुराकारमिदं घनान्धकारम्।
वदनेन्दुरुचामिहाप्रचारादिव
तन्वङ्गि नितान्तकान्तिकान्तम्॥१२२॥

अन्वयः—हे तन्वङ्गि! आलि! जनमोहकरम् नितान्तकान्तिकान्तम् तव इदम् चिकुराकारम् इह वदनेन्दुरुचाम् अप्रचारादिव घनान्धकारं मन्ये।

व्याख्याः—मोहकरं मोहोत्पादकम्। आलि सखि। चिकुराकारं केश-रूपेण स्थितम्। अप्रचारादसञ्चारत्। उत्प्रेक्षालंकारः।

Eng. Tr.:-Oh slender-bodied friend, it seems to me that under the disguise of your hair, this is a thick darkness of an extremely pleasing hue which by reason of the light of the moon in shape of your face, not reaching it, is capable of fascinating the whole world.

दिवानिशं वारिणि कण्ठदघ्ने
दिवाकराराधनमाचरन्ती।
वक्षोजतायै किमु पक्ष्मलाक्ष्या-
स्तपश्चरत्यम्बुजपंक्तिरेषा॥१२३॥

अन्वयः—दिवानिशम् कण्ठदघ्ने वारिणि दिवाकराराधनम् आचारन्ती एषा अम्बुजपंक्तिः किमु पक्ष्मलाक्ष्याः वक्षोजतायै तपः चरति।

व्याख्याः—कण्ठदघ्ने कण्ठप्रमाणे। प्रमाणेद्वयसज्दघ्नञ्मात्रच इति दघ्नच्प्रत्ययः। इयं फलोत्प्रेक्षा। वक्षोजतालाभरूपं फलमत्रोत्प्रेक्षितम्।

Eng. Tr.:-This row of lotuses placing themselves day and night in water as far as their neck, is, as it were, propitiating the sun that they might attain the grace of the breasts of her who has long eyelashes.

वियोगवह्निकुण्डेऽस्मिन् हृदये ते वियोगिनि।
प्रियसङ्गसुखायेव मुक्ताहारस्तपस्यति॥१२४॥

अन्वयः—हे वियोगिनि! (अयम्) मुक्ताहारः वियोगवह्निकुण्डे ते अस्मिन् हृदये प्रियसङ्गसुखाय इव तपस्यति।

व्याख्याः—कस्यचिद् विरहिणीं प्रत्युक्तिः। तपस्यति तपश्चरति। इयमपि फलोत्प्रेक्षा।

Eng. Tr.:-Oh love-lorn lady, for the attainment of the pleasure of union with your beloved this pearl necklace as it were practises penance on your bosom, the sacrificial hearth with separation for its fire.

निधिं लावण्यानां तव खलु मुखं निर्मितवतो
महामोहं मन्ये सरसिरुहसूनोरुपचितम्।
उपेक्ष्य त्वां यस्माद्विधुमयमकस्मादिह कृती
कलाहीनं दीनं विकल इव राजानमकरोत्॥१२५॥

अन्वयः–लावण्यानाम् निधिम् तव मुखम् निर्मितवता सरसिरुहसूनोः उपचितम् महामोहम् मन्ये यस्मात् अयम् कृती त्वाम् उपेक्ष्य इह विकल इव कलाहीनम् दीनम् विधुम् राजानम् अकरोत्।

व्याख्या:–नायकस्य नायिकां प्रत्युक्तिः। लावण्यानां निधिं मुखमित्यन्वयः। सरसिरुहसूनोः प्रजापतेः। उपचितं प्राप्तम्। अयं सरसिरुहसूनु विकल इव भ्रांतचित्त इव। राजानमकरोत् सकलरम्यवस्तूनामग्रे स्थापयामास। यस्मात् त्वन्मुखादधरं कलाहीनं दीनं विधुं प्रजापतिः सकलरम्यविषयाणामग्रेसरं कृत्वा स्वाविचार्यकारित्वं ख्यापयत्यतः स तवाननं निर्माय महामोहोपहतोऽभूदिति मन्य इति भावः।

Eng. Tr.:-I think that while creating your face, the store house of beauty, an utter delusion took possession of the lotus-born God; for, thereby, he, the adept, heedlessly leaving your aside made the poor moon which is wanting in lustre, the king (i.e. the foremost among the beautiful).

स्तनान्तर्गतमाणिक्यवपुर्बहिरुपागतम्।
मनोऽनुरागि ते तन्वि मन्ये वल्लभमीक्षितुम्॥१२६॥

अन्वयः–हे तन्वि! स्तनान्तर्गतमाणिक्यवपुः ते अनुरागि मनः वल्लभम् ईक्षितुम् बहिः उपागतम् मन्ये।

व्याख्या:–नायिकां प्रत्युक्तिः। स्तनान्तर्गतमाणिक्यवपुः स्तनवद्वयमध्यगतमाणिक्याकारम्। तद्व्याजादित्यर्थः। अनुरागि रागयुक्तम्। अत्र वल्लभेक्षणरूपफलस्य मनस्युत्प्रेक्षा। तन्निमित्तं चान्तःप्रदेशाद्बहिरागमनं यदप्रेक्ष्यते तद्बहिः प्रदेशस्थितमाणिक्यमात्रवृत्ति मनसो न संभवतीत्यपह्नुत्या मनोगतं क्रियते।

Eng. Tr.:-Oh you of slender frame, I think that under the disguise of a jewel intervening your breasts, your passionate heart has come out of your body to behold lover.

जगदन्तरममृतमयैरंशुभिरापूरयन्नितराम्।
उदयति वदनव्याजात् किमु राजा हरिणशावनयनायाः॥१२७॥

अन्वयः—हरिणशावनयनायाः वदनव्याजात् जगदन्तरम् अमृतमयैः अंशुभिः नितराम् आपूरयन् किम् राजा उदयति।

व्याख्याः—जगदंतरं जगतीतलम्। राजा चन्द्रः। इयमप्युत्प्रेक्षा।

Eng.Tr.:-Is it the moon which completely filling the whole world with its nectarious rays, is rising under the disguise of the face of the fawn-eyed one?

तिमिरशारदचन्दिरचन्द्रिकाः कमलविद्रुमचम्पककोरकाः।
यदि मिलन्ति कदापि तदाननं खलु तदा कलया तुलयामहे॥१२८॥

अन्वयः—यदि कदापि तिमिरशारदचन्दिरचन्द्रिकाः कमलविद्रुमचम्पक कोरकाः मिलन्ति तदा खलु तदाननम् कलया तुलयामहे।

व्याख्याः—केषाञ्चिन्मत इयमतिशयोक्तिरसम्बन्धेऽपि सन्बन्धरूपा। सम्बन्धश्चात्र वर्ण्योत्कर्षार्थः। अत्र तिमिरादीनां मुखावयवसदृशानां मुखेना-सम्बन्धेऽपि सम्बन्धवर्णनामुखस्योत्कर्षः प्रतीयते। शारदचन्दिरः शरच्चन्द्रमा। तस्याः पूर्वावलोकितायाः कामिन्या आननं मुखम्।

Eng.Tr.:-If darkness, the antumnal moonlight, lotus flower, the coral, and the campaka bud were all to unite together then only we might slightly comapre them with that face (of her).

प्रिये विषादं जहिहीति वाचं
प्रिये सरागं वदति प्रियायाः।
वारामुदारा विजगाल धारा
विलोचनाभ्यां मनसश्च मानः॥१२९॥

अन्वयः—प्रिये सरागम् प्रिये! विषादम् हति हि इति वाचं वदति प्रियायाः विलोचनाभ्याम् वाराम् उदारा धारा, च मनसः मानः विजगाल।

व्याख्याः—मानिनीं प्रति नायकोक्तिः। प्रथमं प्रिये इति सम्बोधनविभक्त्यन्तं द्वितीयं सप्तम्यन्तम्। प्रियाया विलोचनाभ्यां वारां धारा विजगाल मनसश्च

मानो विजगालेत्यन्वयः। वारामश्रुजलानाम्। उदारा महती। तुल्ययोगितालंकारोऽयम्। प्रकृतानामेवाप्रकृतानामेव वा गम्यौपम्य एकधर्मान्वयस्तुल्ययोगिता।

Eng.Tr.:-When the lover lovingly said to her beloved—Oh love, give up dejection—profuse streams of tear ran down her eyes, and pride (withholding) vanished from her mind.

राज्याभिषेकमाज्ञाय शम्बरासुरवैरिणः।
सुधाभिर्जगतीमध्यं लिम्पतीव सुधाकरः॥१३०॥

अन्वयः—शम्बरासुरवैरिणः राज्याभिषेकम् आज्ञाय सुधाकरः जगतीमध्यम्, सुधाभिः लिम्पति इव।

व्याख्याः—शम्बरासुरवैरिणे मदनस्य। इयं समासोक्तिमूलोत्प्रेक्षा। अत्र हि स्वामिसेवकव्यवहारो व्यंग्यः। तन्मूला च किरणव्यापने विषये सुधालेपनोत्प्रेक्षा।

Eng.Tr.:-Having heard of the coronation ceremony of the enemy of the demon Śambara, the moon as it were besmears the whole world with nectar.

आननं मृगशावाक्ष्या वीक्ष्य लोलालकावृतम्।
भ्रमद्भ्रमरसम्भारं स्मरामि सरसीरुहम्॥१३१॥

अन्वयः—मृगशावाक्ष्याः लोलालकावृतम् आननं वीक्ष्य भ्रमद् भ्रमरसम्भारं सरसीरुहं स्मरामि।

व्याख्याः—लोलालकावृतं चलत्केशावृतम्। अयं स्मरणालंकारः।

Eng.Tr.:-On seeing the face of the fawn-eyed one, covered (topped) over with hair playing over it, I am put in mind of the lotus covered with swarms of bees.

यान्ती गुरुजनैः साकं स्मयमानाननाम्बुजा।
तिर्यग्ग्रीवं यदद्राक्षीत् तन्निष्पत्राकरोज्जगत्॥१३२॥

अन्वयः—गुरुजनैः सांक यान्ती स्मयमानाननाम्बुजा यत् तिर्य्यग्ग्रीवम् अद्राक्षत् तत् जगत् निष्पत्राकरोत्।

व्याख्या:–साकं सह। तिरश्ची ग्रीवा यस्मिन् कर्मणि तद्यथा तथा। निष्पत्राकरोत् सपुंखशरस्यापरपार्श्वे निर्गमनात्पत्ररहितमकरोत्। गतप्राणामिवाकरोदिति यावत्। सपत्रनिष्पत्रादतिव्यथन इति डाच्। अत्र क्रियाविशेष्यकबोधवादिनां मते रूपकं प्रथमान्तविशेष्यकबोधवादिनां मते च निदर्शनालंकारः।

Eng.Tr.:-While going with elderly persons, when the beloved with her smiling lotus like face, looked with her neck turned sideway, the whole world was, as it were, struck dead.

[१]नयनानि वहन्तु खञ्जनानामिह नानाविधमङ्गभङ्गभाग्यम्।
सदृशं कथमाननं[२] सुशोभं सुदृशो भङ्गुरसम्पदाम्बुजेन॥१३३॥

अन्वयः–हे अङ्गने! इह ते नयने खञ्जनानाम् नानाविधं भयं वहतः नु। सुदृशः सुशोभम् मुखम् भङ्गुरसम्पदः अम्बुजस्य तुलाम् कथम् एतु?

व्याख्या:–खञ्जनानां नयनानीह भङ्गभाग्यं वहंत्वित्यन्वयः। खञ्जनानां खञ्जरीटानाम्। इहास्मिन् सुदृशो नयने वर्तमानम्। अङ्गेत्यव्ययं खल्वर्थे। भङ्गभाग्यं तरङ्गसौभाग्यम्। भङ्गुरसम्पदाऽस्थिरशोभेन। अयं व्यतिरेकालंकारः।

Eng.Tr.:-The grace of the varied play of the eyes of the fair-eyed one, may possibly be found in those of the wagtail bird; but how could her face of exquisite beauty be likened to lotus possessing a transitory beauty!

मृणालमन्दानिलचन्दनानामुशीरशैवालकुशेशयानाम्।
वियोगदूरीकृतचेतनानां विनैव शैत्यं भवति प्रतीतिः॥१३४॥

अन्वयः–वियोगदूरीकृतचेतनानाम् मृणालमन्दानिलचन्दनानाम् उशीरशैवालकुशेशयानां शैत्यं विना एव प्रतीतिः भवति।

व्याख्या:–वियोगदूरीकृतचेतनानां जनानामिति शेषः। शैत्यं विनैव प्रतीतिरुष्णत्वेन प्रतीतिः। विनोक्तिरियमलंकारभाष्यकारमते।

---

१. 'नयने वहता नु' इति पाठान्तरम्।

२. 'मुखमेतु तुलां कथं' इति पाठान्तरम्।

Eng.Tr.:-On those whose vitality is impaired or nullified through the pangs of separation, the lotus stalk, the gentle breeze, the sandal ointment, and ropagan muricatus, the moss, and the lotus, produce effects other than those of cooling.

विबोधयन् करस्पर्शैः पद्मिनीं मुद्रितानननाम्।
परिपूर्णोऽनुरागेण प्रातर्जयति भास्करः॥१३५॥

अन्वयः—प्रातः मुद्रितानननाम् पद्मिनीं करस्पर्शैः विबोधयन् अनुरागेण परिपूर्णः भास्करः जयति।

व्याख्या:—विबोधयन् विकासयंश्चालयंश्च। करस्पर्शैः किरणस्पर्शैर्हस्तस्पर्शैश्च। पद्मिनीं कमलिनीं नायिकाविशेषं च। मुद्रिताननां मुकुलितां म्लानवदनां च। अनुरागेण ताम्रत्वेन स्नेहेन च अत्र किरणस्पर्शैः कमलिनीं विकासयतो भास्करस्य वृत्तांतो वाच्यो हस्तस्पर्शैर्नायिकामनुनयतो नायकस्य वृत्तांतेनाभिन्नतया स्थितः। इयं समासोक्तिः।

Eng.Tr.:-In morning-tide all glorious is the sun full of rediance (passion) awakening with the touch of its rays (hands) the lotus creeper that have their flowers (mouths) closed (shut).

आनम्य वल्गुवचनैर्विनिवारितेऽपि
रोषात् प्रयातुमुदिते मयि दूरदेशम्।
बाला कराङ्गुलिनिदेशवशंवदेन
क्रीडाबिडालशिशुनाऽऽशु रुरोध मार्गम्॥१३६॥

अन्वयः—आनम्य वल्गुवचनैः विनिवारिते अपि रोषात् मयि दूरदेशम् प्रयातुम् उदिते बाला आशु कराङ्गुलिदेशवशंवदेन क्रीडाविडालशिशुना मार्गं रुरोध।

व्याख्या:—कस्यचिद्विदेशगमनोद्यतस्य निमित्तवशात्प्रतिनिवृत्तस्य सखायं प्रत्युक्तिः। वल्गुवचनैर्मधुरवचनैः। कराङ्गुल्या यो निदेशस्तस्य वशं वदेनाधीनेन।

बिडालशिशुना मार्जारपोतेन। प्रस्थानकाले मार्जारेण मार्गरोधो महदनिमित्तमिति शकुनज्ञाः। अत्राहं प्रवासान्निवृतोऽस्मीति प्रस्तुतं कार्यमप्रस्तुतेन कारणेन गम्यत इत्यप्रस्तुतप्रशंसेयम्।

Eng.Tr.:-Although my young love bowed down and with flattering words tried to disuade me, yet in spite of that, when through anger I was on the point of starting for a distant land, she suddenly barred my way by means of a playing-kitten all-obedient to the movement of the finger of her hand.

अभूदप्रत्यूहः कुसुमशरकोदण्डमहिमा
विलीनो लोकानां सह नयनतापोऽपि तिमिरैः।
तवास्मिन् पीयूषं किरति परितस्तन्वि वदने
कुतो हेतोः श्वेतो विधुरयमुदेति प्रतिदिनम्॥१३७॥

अन्वयः—हे तन्वि! यदा तव अस्मिन् वदने परितः पीयूषम् किरति कुसुमशरकोदण्डमहिमा अप्रत्यूह अभूत्, तिमिरेः सह लोकानाम् नयनतापः अपि विलीनः (अभूत्) (तर्हि) अयम् श्वेतः विधुः कुतः हेतोः प्रतिदिनम् उदेति।

व्याख्याः—अप्रत्यूहो निर्विघ्नः। कुसुमशरकोदंडमहिमा मदनचापप्रतापः। अस्मिंस्तव वदने पीयूषं किरति सतीत्यन्वयः। अत्र कामिनीवदनस्य विधुसं-बंधिसकलप्रयोजननिष्पादनक्षमत्वान्निष्प्रयोजनत्वेन विधुरधिक्षिप्यते। आक्षेपालंकारोऽयमित्येके। प्रतीपप्रभेद इत्यपरे। द्वितीयपादे सहोक्तिः स्पष्टैव। इदं पद्यम्-अभूदप्रत्यूहः सकलहरिदुल्लासनविधि-र्विलीनो लोकानां स हि नयनतापोऽपि कमले। तवास्मिन् पीयूषं किरति वदने रम्यवदने कुतो हेतोश्चेतो विधुरयमुदेति स्म जलधेः॥

इति रूपेण पंडितराजकृतलक्ष्मीलहर्यामपि दृश्यते।

Eng.Tr.:-Oh slender bodied one! to what purpose does this moon rise? Since, while your face scatters nectar all around, the glory (effect) of the bow of the flower arrowed god became unobstructed and the afflictions of people vanished with darkness.

विनैव शस्त्रं हृदयानि यूनां
विवेकभाजामपि दारयन्त्यः।
अनल्पमायामयवल्गुलीला
जयन्ति नीलाब्जदलायताक्ष्यः॥१३८॥

अन्वयः—शास्त्रं विना एव विवेकभाजाम् अपि यूनां हृदयम् दारयन्त्यः नीलाब्जदलायताक्ष्याः अनल्पमायामयवल्गुलीलाः जयन्ति।

व्याख्याः—अनल्पमायामय्यो वल्गवश्च लीला यासां ताः। बल्गवो मनोज्ञाः। अत्र शस्त्ररूपकारणाभावसामानाधिकरण्येनकारणरूपकार्योत्पत्ति- र्निबद्धेति विभावनालंकारोऽयम्।

Eng.Tr.:-Victorious are the sports of her whose eyes are pleasing and fascinating like petal of a blue lotus, and who without weapon of any sort breaks the hearts even of those youths who passessed discernment.

यदवधि विलासभवनं यौवनमुदियाय चन्द्रवदनायाः।
दहनं विनैव तदवधि यूनां हृदयानि दह्यन्ते॥१३९॥

अन्वयः—यदवधि चन्द्रवदनायाः विलासभवनं यौवनम् उदियाय तदवधि यूनां हृदयानि दहनं विना एव दह्यन्ते।

व्याख्याः—अयं विभावनालंकारः प्रसिद्धकारणस्य दहनस्याभावेऽपि दाहरूपकार्योत्पत्तिवर्णनात्।

Eng.Tr.:-As soon as youth, the pleasure-house, of the moon faced one set in, the hearts of the young were inflamed even (without the aid) of fire.

न मिश्रयति लोचने सहसितं न सम्भाषते
कथासु तव किं च सा विरचयत्यरालां भ्रुवम्।
विपक्षसुदृशः कथामिति निवेदयन्त्या पुरः
प्रियस्य शिथिलीकृतः स्वविषयेऽनुरागग्रहः॥१४०॥

अन्वयः–सा लोचने न मिश्रयति, सहसितम् न सम्भाषते किञ्च तव कथासु भ्रुवम् अरालाम् विरचयति इति प्रियस्य पुरः विपक्षसुदृशः कथां निवेदयन्त्या स्वविषये अनुरागग्रहः शिथिलीकृतः।

व्याख्याः–सपत्न्यां प्रियेणाज्ञातयौवनात्वेनैव विदितायां तदनुराग-प्रतिबन्धार्थं प्रियस्य पुरस्तदीयदुर्गुणानावेदयन्त्याः कस्याश्चित् प्रौढनायिकाया उक्तिरियम्। तव कथासु त्वद्विषयककथासु। अरालां वक्राम्। अप्रियसूचिकामिति भावः। विपक्षसुदृशः सपत्न्याः। पुरोऽर्थात् प्रियस्य। स्वविषय आत्मनि। अत्र प्रौढनायिकया चिकीर्षितोऽर्थो न सम्पादितः स्वस्मिन्ननुरागक्षतिश्च सम्पादितेति विषमालंकारोऽयम्।

Eng.Tr.:-"While something pertaining to you is being talked of, she does neither look into the face, nor does she join in the conversation, but on the contrary knits her eye-brows"—while the co-wife was thus talking to her lover his love was stackened for her ownself.

वडवानलकालकूटवन्मकरव्यालगणैः सहैधितः।
रजनीरमणो भवेन्नृणां न किं प्राणवियोगकारणम्॥१४१॥

अन्वयः–वडवानलकालकूटवन्मकरव्यालगणैः सह एधितः रजनीरमणः नृणाम् प्राणवियोगकारणम् किम् न भवेत्।

व्याख्याः–कस्यचिद्विरहिण उक्तिरियम्। एधितो वृद्धिं गतः। रजनी-रमणश्चन्द्रः। अयं समालंकारः।

Eng.Tr.:-How the lord of the night brought up as he is, like the forest conflagration and the deadly poison, with hosts of serpents and aligators, will not become the cause of taking away the life of men?

लभ्येत पुण्यैर्गृहिणी मनोज्ञा
तया सुपुत्राः परितः पवित्राः।
स्फीतं यशस्तैः समुदेति नित्यं
तेनास्य नित्यः खलु नाकलोकः॥१४२॥

अन्वयः—पुण्यैः मनोज्ञा गृहिणी लभ्येत तया पवित्राः सुपुत्राः तैः नित्यम् परितः स्फीतं यशः समुदेति तेन खलु अस्य नित्यः नाकलोकः।

व्याख्याः—स्फीतं विमलम्। अस्य प्रस्तुतस्य कस्यचित् पुरुषस्य। इयं कारणमाला। यथोत्तरं चेत् पूर्वस्य पूर्वस्यार्थस्य हेतुता। तदा कारणमालेति सा काव्यप्रकाशे लक्षिता। इदं पद्यं शृङ्गारविलासे नान्तर्भावमर्हतीति भाति।

Eng.Tr.:-By merits (in past birth) a charming wife is obtained; through her virtuous and well-conducted sons; by their means ever arises great fame; and by that one gets the eternal dwelling place.

प्रभुरपि याचितुकामो भजते वामोरु लाघवं सहसा।
यदहं त्वयाऽधरार्थी सपदि विमुख्या निराशतां नीतः॥१४३॥

अन्वयः—हे वामोरु! प्रभुः अपि याचितुकामः (सन्) सहसा लाघवम् भजते, यत् सपदि विमुख्या त्वया अधरार्थी अहम् निराशताम् नीतः।

व्याख्याः—नायकस्य नायिकां प्रत्युक्तिः। विमुख्या मुखं परावर्तयन्त्या। अयमर्थान्तरन्यासः। अत्र कामुकयोर्वृत्तान्तेन विशेषेण दातृयाचकवृत्तान्तः सामान्यात्मा समर्थ्यते।

Eng.Tr.:-Oh beautiful thighed one when one though a lord stoops to beg, incures lowliness; (notwithstanding truth) I, a beggar of your lower lip, am at once disappointed by you with your face turned away (from me).

जलकुम्भमुम्भितरसं सपदि सरस्याः समानयन्त्यास्ते।
तटकुञ्जगूढसुरतं भगवानेको मानोभवो वेद॥१४४॥

अन्वयः—सपदि सरस्याः उम्भितरसम् जलकुम्भं समानयन्त्याः ते तटकुञ्जगूढसुरतम् एको भगवान् भनोभवः वेदः।

व्याख्याः—गूढसुरतरतां काञ्चित् कामिनीं प्रति सख्या उक्तिः। उम्भितरसं पूरितजलम्। सपदि झटिति। त्वरयेति यावत्। सरस्याः सरोवरात्। तटकुञ्जगूढसुरतमिति सप्तमीतत्पुरुषः। मनोभवो मदनः। वेद जानाति। अत्र सुरतगमकानां स्वेदकम्पनिःश्वासानां जलकुम्भानयनत्वराजनितैस्तै–

भेंदस्याग्रहणात् सुरतस्य प्रकाशो न भवति। अयं मीलितालंकारः। स्फुटमुपलभ्यमानस्य कस्यचिद्वस्तुनो लिङ्गैरतिसाम्याद्भिन्नत्वेनागृह्यमाणानां वस्त्वन्तरलिङ्गानां स्वकारणाननुमापकत्वं च तल्लक्षणम्।

Eng.Tr.:-The divine mind-born alone knows the clandestine sexual enjoyments in the bowers on the bank indulged by you who was returning in haste from the lake carrying a jar full of water (on your head).

त्वमिव पथिकः प्रियो मे विटपिस्तोमेषु गमयति क्लेशान्।
किमितोऽन्यत् कुशलं मे सम्प्रति यत्पान्थ जीवामि॥१४५॥

अन्वयः–हे पान्थ! त्वमिव मे पथिक प्रियः विटपिस्तोमेषु क्लेशान् गमयति, सम्प्रति यत् (अहम्) जीवामि इतः अन्यत् मे किम् कुशलम् (अस्ति)?

व्याख्याः–इयं कस्याश्चित् प्रोषितभर्तृकायाः कञ्चित् पथिकं प्रत्युक्तिः। विटपिस्तोमेषु वृक्षखण्डेषु। इदमुन्नीतप्रश्नमुत्तरम्। अत्र प्रोषितभर्तृकाया उत्तरेण पथिकर्तृकः कुशलप्रश्नोऽनुमीयते कुशलमपृष्टायाः कुशलोक्तेरयोगात्।

Eng.Tr.:-Oh traveller my husband, a traveller like you beguiles his afflictions under groups of trees. That I am still alive is the only bliss that I have (at present).

किमिति कृशाऽसि कृशोदरि किं तव परकीयवृत्तान्तैः।
कथय तथापि मुदे मम कथयिष्यप्ति पान्थ[१] तव जाया॥१४६॥

अन्वयः–हे कृशोदरि! किम् इति कृशा असि? हे पथिक! परकीयवृत्तान्तैः तव किम्? तथाऽपि मम मुदे कथय! तव जाया कथयिष्यति।

व्याख्याः–कस्याश्चित् पथिककामिन्याः पथिकान्तरेण सम्वादोऽयम्। इदं निबद्धप्रश्नमुत्तरम्। अत्र हेतुं चेद्वदसि तदा प्रतिकरिष्यामीत्याद्यप्रश्नस्य व्यंग्यम्। उत्तरस्य तु न मया पतिव्रतया हेतुर्वक्तुं परपुरुषं प्रति योग्यो न च त्वया प्रतिकर्तुं शक्य इति। द्वितीयप्रश्नस्य व्यंग्यमलं पातिव्रत्येनाविदग्धजनहठ–

---

१. 'पथिक' इति पाठान्तरम्।

मात्रविलसितेन स्वपरसन्तोष एव संसारसार इति। द्वितीयोत्तरस्य तु या मम दशा सैव तव जायाया अपि दशास्ति सैव प्रतिक्रियताम्। न हि स्वकीयं सदनं दह्यमानमुपेक्ष्य कश्चित् परसदनाग्निं प्रतिकरोतीत्यादि व्यंग्यम्।

Eng.Tr.:-Ah thin bellied one, why are you reduced? What have you to do with others concern? For my pleasure, tell me. Your own wife will do it better.

तुलामनालोक्य निजामखर्वं गौराङ्गि गर्वं न कदापि कुर्याः।
लसन्ति नानाफलभारवत्यो लताः कियत्यो गहनान्तरेषु॥१४७॥

अन्वयः–हे गौराङ्गि! निजाम् तुलाम् अनालोक्य कदापि अखर्वम् गर्वम् न कुर्याः (यतः) गहनान्तरेषु नानाफलभारवत्यः कियत्यः लताः लसन्ति।

व्याख्या:–कस्यचित्काञ्चित् कामिनीं प्रत्युक्तिः। अखर्वं महान्तम्। गहनान्तरेषु काननप्रदेशेषु। केषाञ्चिन्मतेऽयं प्रतीप्रभेदः।

Eng.Tr.:-Oh you of sallow frame! not seeing similarity in anything you do not entertain so much pride; for in the midst of forest there do bloom some creepers bearing a variety of fruits.

इयमुल्लसिता मुखस्य शोभा
परिफुल्लं नयनाम्बुजद्वयं ते।
जलदालिमयं जगद्वितन्वन्
कलितः क्वापि किमालि नीलमेघः॥१४८॥

अन्वयः–हे अलि इयम् ते मुखस्य शोभा उल्लसिता, नयनाम्बुजद्वयम् परिफुल्लम्, क्व अपि जगत् जलदालिमयं वितन्वन् नीलमेघः कलितः?

व्याख्या:–श्रीकृष्णं दृष्टवतीं काञ्चित् गोपिकां प्रति सख्या उक्तिः कलितो दृष्टः। नीलमेघो नीलमेघत्वेनाध्यवसितः कृष्णः। इदं पद्यमस्पष्टार्थम्।

Eng.Tr.:-Here shines the beauty of the face, and the pair of lotuses in the shape of your eyes blooms (thereby) Oh friend! have you ever known a blue cloud filling the whole world with rows of cloud.

आसायं सलिलान्त[१]: सवितारमुपास्य सादरं तपसा।
अधुनाब्जेन मनाक् तव मानिनि तुलना मुखस्याप्ता[२]॥१४९॥

अन्वयः—हे मानिनि! आसायं सलिलान्तः सादरम् तपसा सवितारम् उपास्य अधुना अब्जेन तव मुखस्य मनाक् तुलना आप्ता।

व्याख्याः—नायकस्य नायिकां प्रत्युक्तिः। आसायं पश्चिमसन्ध्या-समयादारभ्य। अधुना द्वितीयेऽह्नि। आपि प्राप्ता। कर्मणि लुङ्। कमलादपि तव मुखमधिकशोभमिति भावः।

Eng.Tr.:-Oh haughty lady! the lotus having till evening respectfully propitiated the sun with penance has now attained only a slight likeness of your face.

अयि मन्दस्मितमधुरं वदनं तन्वङ्गि यदि मनाक् कुरुषे।
अधुनैव कलय शमितं राकारमणस्य हन्त साम्राज्यम्॥१५०॥

अन्वयः—अयि तन्वङ्गि! यदि वदनम् मनाक् मन्दस्मित मधुरम् कुरुषे (तदा) हन्त! अधुना एव राकारमणस्य साम्राज्यं शमितम् कलय।

व्याख्याः—नायिकां प्रत्युक्तिः। अधुनैव न तु कालान्तरे। कलय जानीहि। हन्त हर्षे। मन्दस्मितमधुरं तव मुखं निःसंशयं चन्द्रं जेष्यतीति भावः।

Eng.Tr.:-Oh slender bodied one! the moment you do make your face pleasing by gentle smile even to the slightest degree be sure that the sole-sovereignty of the moon, the lover of the full-moon night is brought to an end.

मधुरतरं स्मयमानः स्वस्मिन्नेवालपञ्च्छनैः किमपि।
कोकनदयंस्त्रिलोकीमालम्बनशून्यमीक्षते क्षीबः॥१५१॥

अन्वयः—मधुरतरं स्मयमानः क्षीबः स्वस्मिन् एव शनैः किमपि आलपन् त्रिलोकीम् कोकनदयन् आलम्बनशून्यम् ईक्षते।

व्याख्याः—मत्तस्वभाववर्णनमिदम्। शनैरित्यनेनाव्यक्तत्वं किमपीत्यनेन

---

१. 'सलिलभरे' इति पाठान्तरम्।

२. 'मुखस्यापि' इति पाठान्तरम्।

चासङ्गतत्वं गम्यते। कोकनदयन् कोकनदं कुर्वन् त्रिलोकीं कोकनदमिव रक्तवर्णां पश्यन्नित्यर्थः। आलम्बनशून्यमलक्षितविषयविशेषम्। क्षीबो मत्तः। अत्र सुरापानमत्तपुरुषगतो मदो प्राधान्येन व्यंग्यः। स्वभावोक्तिश्च तदुपस्कारिका।

Eng.Tr.:-An intoxicated person smiling sweetly and muttering to himself, seeing the three worlds red as red-lotus, stares vacantly all round.

मधुरसान्मधुरं हि तवाधरं
तरुणि मद्वदने विनिवेशय।
मम गृहाण करेण कराम्बुजं
प प पतामि ह हा भु भु भूतले॥१५२॥

अन्वयः—हे तरुणि! मधुरसात् हि मधुरम् तव अधरम् मद्वदने विनिवेशय, करेण मम कराम्बुजम् गृहाण, हा हा! (अहम्) भु भु भूतले प, प पतामि।

व्याख्याः—सुराक्षीवस्य कस्यचिदुक्तिरियम्। अत्रापि मद एव व्यंग्यः। चतुर्थपादेऽधिकवर्णोच्चारणं मदकार्यम्। पूर्वार्धगता भ्राम्योक्तिरुत्तरार्धे तरुणीकरेऽम्बुजोपमेयतया निरूपणीये स्वकरस्य तदुपमेयतया निरूपणं च मदमेव पोषयतः।

Eng.Tr.:-Oh young lady! Put your lower lip sweeter than even wine into my mouth; take hold of my lotus like hand with thine; lo! I am falling on the ground.

शतेनोपायानां कथमपि गतः सौधशिखरं
सुधाफेनस्वच्छे रहसि शयितां पुष्पशयने।
विबोध्य क्षामङ्गी चकितनयनां स्मेरवदनां
सनिःश्वासं श्लिष्यत्यहह सुकृती राजरमणीम्॥१५३॥

अन्वयः—अहह! उपायानां शतेन कथमपि शौधशिखरम् गतः सुकृती रहसि सुधाफेनस्वच्छे पुष्पशयने शयिताम् क्षामाङ्गीम् चकितनयनां स्मेरवदनां राजरमणीं विबोध्य सनिःश्वासं श्लिष्यति।

व्याख्याः— राजरमणीमुपभुक्तवतः कस्यचिद्वर्णनमिदम्। सुधाफेन

इवामृतफेन इव स्वच्छे। चकितनयनामित्यनेनान्तःपुरे परपुरुषागमनस्यात्यन्ता-सम्भावनयाऽऽकस्मिकबोधजनितस्त्रासो व्यज्यते। स्मेरवदनामित्यनेन च मत्प्रियो मदर्थं प्राणानपि तृणीकृत्यागत इति ज्ञानजन्यो हर्षः। अयं शृङ्गाराभासोऽ-नुचितप्रणयाया राजरमण्या आलम्बनत्वात्।

Eng.Tr.:-Ah, the fortunate one! (for) with great difficulty and (resorting to) innumerable expedients having reached the top of the palace and having awakened the royal mistress sleeping in seclusion on a flower-bed white as nectar, he breathing heavily embraces her who has slender body, bewildered eyes, and smiling face.

गुञ्जन्ति मञ्जु परितो गत्वा धावन्ति सम्मुखम्।
आवर्तन्ते विवर्तन्ते सरसीषु मधुव्रताः॥१५४॥

अन्वयः—सरसीषु मधुव्रताः परितः गत्वा मञ्जु गुञ्जन्ति, सम्मुखम् धावन्ति आवर्तन्ते विवर्तन्ते।

व्याख्याः—अयं वस्तुध्वनिः। अत्र मधुव्रतकर्तृकमञ्जुगुञ्जनादिभिर्वस्तु भिरासन्नसरसिजोत्पत्तिध्वननद्वारा शरदागमनैकट्यरूपं वस्तु व्यज्यते।

Eng.Tr.:-(Some) swarms of bees going round the lake buzz sweetly; some proceed towards it; while others wheel round and back again.

यथा यथा तामरसेक्षणा मया
पुनः सरागं नितरां निषेविता।
तथा तथा तत्त्वकथेव सर्वतो
विकृष्य मामेकरसं चकार सा॥१५५॥

अन्वयः—यथा यथा मया पुनः तामरसेक्षणा सरागम् नितराम् निषेवित तथा तथा सा तत्त्वकथेव माम् सर्वतः विकृष्य एकरसम् चकार।

व्याख्याः—नायकोक्तिः। तामरसेक्षणा कमलनयना। एकरसं तदेकरतचित्तम्।

Eng.Tr.:-The more I passionately contemplated the

lotus-eyed one the more she like a philosophical discourse abstracting my attention from every thing around filled me with one sentiment alone.

हरिणीप्रेक्षणा यत्र गृहिणी न विलोक्यते।
सेवितं सर्वसम्पद्भिरपि तद्भवनं वनम्॥१५६॥

अन्वयः—यत्र हरिणीप्रेक्षणा गृहिणी न विलोक्यते, तद् भवनं सर्वसम्पद्भिः सेवितम् अपि वनम् (अस्ति)।

व्याख्याः— सर्वसम्पद्भिः सेवितं सकलसम्पत्तिपरिपूर्णम्।

Eng.Tr.:-The house in which a deer-eyed hostess is not seen even though resorted to by all sorts of reaches, is like a (dreary) forest.

लोलालकावलिचल[१]न्नयनारविन्द-
लीलावशंवदितलोकविलोचनायाः।
सायाहनि प्रणयिनो भवनं व्रजन्त्या-
श्चेतो न कस्य हरते गतिरङ्गनायाः॥१५७॥

अन्वयः—सायाहनि प्रणयिनः भवनं व्रजन्त्याः लोलालकावलि-चलन्नयनारविन्दलीला वंशवदितलोकविलोचनायाः अङ्गनायाः गतिः कस्य चेतः न हरते।

व्याख्याः—लोलालकावल्याश्चलन्नयनारविन्दस्य च लीलया वशंवदिता-नि स्वाधिनीकृतानि लोकविलोचनानि यया तस्याः। सायंकाले।

Eng.Tr.:-Whose mind is not rivetted by the women's gait of walking while they proceed in the evening tide to the abode of their lovers-women, whose hair are playing about (in the air), whose lotus-like eyes are tremulous, and who have enchanted the people with ease?

दन्तांशुकान्तमरविन्दरमापहारि[२]
सान्द्रामृतं वदनमेणविलोचनायाः।

१. 'वलन्' इति पाठान्तरम्।
२. 'हीरस्फुरद्रदनशुभ्रिमशोभि किं च' इति पाठान्तरम्।

वेधा विधाय पुनरुक्तमिवेन्दुबिम्बं
दूरीकरोति न कथं विदुषां वरेण्यः॥१५८॥

अन्वयः—विदुषां वरेण्यः वेधाः एणविलोचनायाः दन्तांशुकान्तम् अरविन्दरमापहारि सान्द्रामृतं वदनं विधाय पुनरुक्तमिव इन्दुबिम्बम् कथं न दूरीकरोति।

व्याख्या:—दन्तांशुभी रदनप्रभाभिः कान्तं मनोज्ञम्। रमा शोभा। सान्द्रं घनममृतं यस्मिंस्तत्। एणविलोचनाया हरिणनयनायाः। वेधा विधिः। पुनरुक्तमिव व्यर्थमिव। वरेण्यः श्रेष्ठः। चन्द्रप्रयोजनं सकलमेव मुखेनैव साध्यतेऽतो विधिरिन्दुबिम्बं किमर्थं न दूरीकरोतीति न ज्ञायत इति भावः।

Eng.Tr.:-Why does not the creator, the foremost amongst the wise, having created the face of the deer-eyed one remove the disc of the moon it being only a repetition of it (face) which is pleasing by reason of the rays of teeth, which outshines the beauty of lotus, and which has viscid nectar in the shape of her mouth?

सानुकम्पाः सानुरागाश्चतुराः शीलशीतलाः।
हरन्ति हृदयं हन्त कान्तायाः स्वान्तवृत्तयः॥१५९॥

अन्वयः—हन्त! कान्तायाः सानुकम्पाः सानुरागाः चतुराः शीलशीतलाः स्वान्तवृत्तयः हृदयं हरन्ति।

व्याख्या:—नायकोक्तिरियम्। शीलं पातिव्रत्यम्। हृदयं ममेति शेषः।

Eng.Tr.:-The sympathetic, loving, and skilful propensities of the beloved, which are refreshing by reason of their natural purity, fascinate the heart.

अलकाः फणिशावतुल्यशीला
नयनान्ताः परिपुङ्खितेषुलीलाः।
चपलोपमिता खलु स्वयं या
बत लोके सुखसाधनं कथं सा॥१६०॥

अन्वयः–(यस्याः) अलकाः फणिशावतुल्यशीलाः नयनान्ताः परिपुङ्खितेषु लीलाः, या स्वयम् खलु चपलोपमिता, बत, सा लोके सुख-साधनम् कथम् (भवितुमर्हति)।

व्याख्याः–फणिशावतुल्यशीलाः सर्पशिशुसदृशस्वभावाः। नयनान्ता नेत्रप्रान्ताः। परिपुंखितेषुलीलाः। सपुंखबाणसदृशलीलाः। चपलया विद्युतोपमिता। या कामिनी। यासामेतादृशः परिवारो याश्च स्वयं विद्युच्चञ्चलास्ताः कामिन्यो लोके कथं सुखसाधनत्वेन ग्राह्या इति भावः।

Eng. Tr.:-How has she been counted amongst the means of happiness, when her hair are like the young ones of serpents, the corners of her eyes have the play of a feathered arrow and who is herself verily compared to a lightening.

वदने[१] तव यत्र माधुरी सा
हृदि पूर्णा करुणा च कोमलेऽभूत्।
अधुना हरिणाक्षि हा कथं वा[२]
गतिरन्यैव विलोक्यते गुणानाम्॥१६१॥

अन्वयः–हे हरिणाक्षि! यत्र तव वदने सा माधुरी च कोमले हृदि पूर्णा करुणा अभूत्, अधुना हा (तत्रैव) गुणानाम् अन्या एव गतिः कथं वा विलोक्यते।

व्याख्याः–नायिकां प्रत्युक्तिः। सा पूर्वानुभूता। कोमले हृदीत्यन्वयः। वाऽत्र वाक्यालंकारे। गुणानामन्यैव गतिर्विलोक्यते माधुर्यकरुणयोः स्थाने यथाक्रमं कटुता कठोरता चाविर्भूता दृश्यते।

Eng. Tr.:-Ah, when formerly there was sweetness in your face and full compassion in your tender heart, alas! oh deer-eyed one, how is it that these qualities have now taken quite a different turn!

अनिशं नयनाभिरामया
रमया संमदिनो मुखस्य ते।

---

१. 'वचन' इति पाठान्तरम्।
२. 'कटुता तत्र कठोरताविरासीत्' इति पाठान्तरम्।

निशि निःसरदिन्दिरं कथं
तुलयामः कलयापि पङ्कजम्॥१६२॥

अन्वयः–अनिशम् नयनाभिरामया रमया सम्मदिनः ते मुखस्य कलया अपि निशि निःसरदिन्दिरम् पङ्कजम् कथम् तुलयामः?

व्याख्याः–नायकस्य नायिकां प्रत्युक्तिः। अनिशं सर्वदा। नयनाभिरामया नेत्रयोः प्रीतिजनकया। रमया शोभया। संमदिनो गर्वभाजः। निशि रात्रौ। निःसरदिन्दिरं विगतशोभम्। कलयाप्येकांशेनापि। अयं व्यतिरेकालंकारः।

Eng.Tr.:-How shall we compare even to a slight degree, the lotus whose beauty fades by evening with your face which prides itself upon possessing beauty which is ever pleasing to the eye?

अङ्गैः सुकुमारतरैः सा कुसुमानां श्रियं हरति।
विकलयति कुसुमबाणो बाणालीभिर्मम प्राणान्॥१६३॥

अन्वयः–सा सुकुमारतरैः अङ्गैः कुसुमानां श्रियं हरति, कुसुमबाणः बाणालीभिः मम प्राणान् विकलयति।

व्याख्याः–नायकोक्तिः। अङ्गैरवयवैः। सुकुमारतरैरत्यन्तकोमलैः। सा कामिनी। कुसुमबाणः पुष्पशरो मदनः। अयमसंगत्यलंकारः। विरुद्धत्वेनापाततो भासमानं हेतुकार्ययोर्वैयधिकरण्यमसंगतिः। अस्मिन् पद्ये कामिन्या स्वास्त्रभूत-कुसुमश्रीहरणात्तस्यामेव युक्तो दण्डो मदनेन नायके नियुक्त इति हेतुकार्य-योर्वैयधिकरण्यम्। एतादृशं वैयधिकरण्यं न वस्तुतः संभवतीति स्पष्टमेव।

Eng.Tr.:-She with her limbs extremely tender casts into shade the beauty of flowers; and (in revenge of which) the flower-arrowed God overpowers my soul with a series of arrows.

खिद्यति सा पथि यान्ती कोमलचरणा नितम्बभारेण।
खिद्यामि हन्त परितस्तद्रूपविलोकनेन विकलोऽहम्॥१६४॥

अन्वयः–कोमलचरणा सा पथि यान्ती नितम्बभारेण खिद्यति, हन्त! अहम् परितः तद्रूपविलोकनेन विकलः (सन्) खिद्यामि।

व्याख्याः–नायकोक्तिः। सा नायिका। हन्त खेदे। परितः समन्ततः। विकलो निश्चेष्टः।

Eng. Tr.:-She, the tender-footed, while going by the way is oppressed by the weight of her buttocks; whereas, alas! being completely over powered I am distracted at seeing her beauty everywhere.

मथुरागमनोनोन्मुखे मुरारा-
वसुभारार्तिभृतां व्रजाङ्गनानाम्।
प्रलयज्वलनायते स्म राका
भवनाकाशमजायताम्बुराशिः॥१६५॥

अन्वयः–मुरारौ मथुरागमनोन्मुखे असुभारातिभृतां व्रजाङ्गनानां राका प्रलयज्वलनायते स्म, भवनाकाशत् अम्बुराशिः अजायत्।

व्याख्याः–मुरारौ श्रीकृणे। असुभारार्तिभृतां प्राणभारपीडामावहन्तीनाम्। व्रजाङ्गनानां गोकुलकामिनीनाम्। प्रलयज्वलनायते स्म प्रलयकालीनदहन इवाभवत्। भवनाकाशं भवनप्रदेशः। दुःखार्तः पूर्णिमां प्रलयज्वलनं भवनप्रदेशं च समुद्रममन्यन्तेत्यर्थः।

Eng. Tr.:-When the enemy of Māra was about to start for Mathurā, the women fo Vraja tortured with the pain of having to bear the burden of life, felt the full-moon-lit-night to be schorching like the doom's day fire and the interior of their own houses like ocean.

केलीमन्दिरमागतस्य शनकैरालीरपास्येंगितैः
सुप्तायाः सरुषः सरोरुहदृशः संवीजनं कुर्वतः।
जानंत्याप्यनभिज्ञयेव कपटव्यामीलिताक्ष्या सखि
श्रांतासीत्यभिधाय वक्षसि तया पाणिर्ममासञ्जितः॥१६६॥

अन्वयः–केलीमन्दिरमागतस्य शनकैः इङ्गितैः आलीः अपास्य सरुषः

सुप्तायाः सरोरुहदृशः संवीजनम् कुर्वतः मम पाणिः जानन्त्याः अपि अनभिज्ञयेव कपटव्यामीलिताक्ष्या तया सखि? श्रान्ता असि इति अभिधाय वक्षसि आसञ्जितः।

व्याख्या:—नायकस्य सखायं प्रत्युक्तिः। केलीमन्दिरमागतस्येङ्गितैरालीरपास्य सरोरुहदृशः संवीजनं कुर्वतो मम पाणिस्तया सखि श्रान्तासीत्यभिधाय वक्षस्यासंजित इत्यन्वयः। अपास्य दूरीकृत्य। इङ्गितैर्हृद्गतभावद्योतकैश्चेष्टितैः। सुप्ताया व्याजनिद्रितायाः। सरुषो रुष्टायाः। संजीवनं कुर्वतो व्यजनादिना वायुसञ्चारणं कुर्वतः। जानन्त्याप्ययं प्रिय आगत्य संवीजनं करोति नेयं सखीत्यभिज्ञयापि। अनभिज्ञयेवाज्ञानमिषं कुर्वत्या। वक्षस्यात्मन इति शेषः। तया भामिन्या। आसंजितः स्थापितः। अत्र भामिन्या रोषनिवारणाय यत्ने क्रियमाणे रोषनिवारणादप्यधिकतरसुखप्रदः कामुकेन तत्कुचाधिकरणकः स्वकरासंगो लब्ध इति प्रहर्षणालंकारोऽयम्। अस्मदवलोकितेषु सर्वेष्वे पुस्तकेषु जानन्त्येति पाठो वर्तते। जानत्येति शुद्धं रूपमिति भाति।

Eng.Tr.:-Going into the pleasure house and gradually dismissing the female companions by signs while I was fanning the lotus-eyed one who had become angry and had feighned asleep and who though recognised me, still pretending to keep her eyes closed, saying friend, you are fatigued placed my hand on her own bosom.

मान्थर्यमाप गमनं सह शैशवेन
रक्तं सहैव मनसाऽधरबिम्बमासीत्।
किं चाभवन्मृगकिशोरदृशो नितम्बः
सर्वाधिको गुरुरयं सह मन्मथेन॥१६७॥

अन्वयः—मृगकिशोश्दृशः गमनं शैशवेन सह मान्थर्यम् आप अधरबिम्बम् मनसा सह एव रक्तम् आसीत् किञ्च अयम् नितम्बः मन्मथेन सह सर्वाधिकः गुरु अभवत्।

व्याख्या:—मान्थर्यं मन्दत्वम्। शैशवेन बाल्येन। रक्तं ताम्रवर्णमनुरागयुक्तं च। मृगकिशोरदृशो हरिणशावाक्ष्याः। गुरुर्विस्तृतो महांश्च। इयं सहोक्तिः।

Eng.Tr.:-At the close of girlhood of the fawn-eyed one, her gait of walking attained slowness; her hart became full of love as her lips grew red; and above all, her buttocks swelled in dimensions as the Cupid advanced in power.

श्वासोऽनुमानवेद्यः शीतान्यङ्गानि निश्चला दृष्टिः।
[१]तस्याः सुभग कथेयं तिष्ठतु तावत्कथान्तरं कथय॥१६८॥

अन्वयः–हे सुभग! तस्याः श्वासः अनुमानवेद्यः, अङ्गानि शीतानि, दृष्टिः निश्चला। इयम् कथा तिष्ठतु, तावत् कथान्तरम् कथय।

व्याख्याः–नायकं प्रति विरहपीडितां नायिकामधिकृत्य कस्यचिदुक्तिः। अनुमानवेद्योऽनुमानेनैव ज्ञेयः। अतितनुरित्यर्थः। तस्य नायिकायाः। कथान्तरं कथयान्यत् किञ्चित्कथय। अत्र नायिकासंबंधिन्या वार्ताया अंशं कथयित्वा क्रियमाणो निषेधो वक्ष्यमाणमरणवार्ताया दुःसहत्वं व्यनक्ति। अयमाक्षेपः केषाञ्चिन्मते।

Eng.Tr.:-Her breathing could only be inferred; her limbs were cool, and her sight steady. Oh blessed one! a truce to the description of her. Tell me something else.

पाणौ कृतः पाणिरिलासुतायाः
सस्वेदकम्पो रघुनन्दनेन।
हिमाम्बुसङ्गानिलविह्वलस्य
प्रभातपद्मस्य बभार शोभाम्॥१६९॥

अन्वयः–रघुनन्दनेन पाणौ कृतः इलासुतायाः सस्वेदकम्पः पाणिः हिमाम्बुसङ्गानिलविह्वलस्य प्रभातपद्मस्य शोभाम् बभार।

व्याख्याः–पाणौ कृतः पाणिना गृहीतः। इलासुतायाः सीतायाः। सस्वेद-कम्पस्तत्कालजनितस्वेदकम्पवान्। हिमाम्बुना झंझानिलेन च विह्वलस्य। झंझानिलो महान् वायुः। इयं पदार्थनिदर्शना।

Eng.Tr.:-Sītā's hand trembling and sweaty while taken hold of by Rāma's hand, assumed the beauty of morning lotus beaten by a snow-storm.

---

१. 'न स्यात्' इति पाठान्तरम्।

अरुणमपि विद्रुमद्रुं मृदुलतरं चापि किसलयं बाले।
अधरीकरोति नितरां तवाधरो मधुरिमातिशयात्॥१७०॥

अन्वयः—हे बाले! तव अधरः मधुरिमातिशयात् अरुणम् अपि विद्रमद्रुम् च मृदुलतरम् अपि किसलयम् नितराम् अधरीकरोति।

व्याख्याः—नायकोक्तिः। विद्रुमद्रुं प्रवालदण्डम्। अधरीकरोति नीचीकरोति। अयं व्यतिरेकालंकारः।

Eng.Tr.:-Oh girl, your lower lip owing to its extreme sweatness surpasses a coral piece though red, and a fresh foliage leaf though very tender.

सुदृशो जितरत्नजालया
सुरतान्तश्रमबिन्दुमालया।
अलिकेन च हेमकान्तिना
विदधे काऽपि रुचिः परस्परम्॥१७१।

अन्वयः—सुदृशः जितरत्नमालया सुरतान्तश्रमबिन्दुमालया च हेमकान्तिना अलिकेन परस्परम् काऽपि रुचिः विदधे।

व्याख्याः-सुरतश्रान्तायाः कान्ताया वर्णनम्। जितरत्नजालया पराभूतरत्नसमूहया। अलिकेन ललाटेन। हेमकान्तिना सुवर्णरुचिरेण। काप्यनिर्वचनीया। रुचिः शोभा। अयमन्योन्यालंकारः। द्वयोरन्योन्येनान्योन्यस्य विशेषाधानमन्योन्यम्।

Eng.Tr.:-Some indescribable beauty was reciprocated by her gold complexioned forehead and by lines of the drops of perspiration which were brought by exertion at the conclusion of sexual intercourse and which (thereby) surpassed (the beauty of) the collection of jewels (worne on the body).

परपूरुषदृष्टिपातवज्रा-
हतिभीता हृदयं प्रियस्य सीता।
अविशत् परकामिनीभुजङ्गी-
भयतः सत्वरमेव सोऽपि तस्याः॥१७२॥

अन्वयः–परपूरुषदृष्टिपातवज्राहतिभीता सीता सत्वरम् एव प्रियस्य सः अपि परकामिनीभुजङ्गीभयतः तस्याः हृदयम् अविशत्।

व्याख्याः–हृदयं वक्षःस्थलम्। प्रियस्य रामस्य। सोऽपि रामोऽपि। तस्याः सीताया हृदयमविशदित्यनुषङ्गः। इदमप्यन्योन्यम्।

Eng.Tr.:-Sītā afraid of being struck by the fall of thunderbolt in the shape of glances of person other than her own husband, entered the heart of her husband; while he, too, on his part, afraid of serpents in the shape of other women entered her heart all at once.

अङ्गानि दत्वा हेमाङ्गि प्राणान् क्रीणासि चेन्नृणाम्
युक्तमेतन्न तु पुनः कोणं नयनपद्मयोः॥१७३॥

अन्वयः–हे हेमाङ्गि! चेत् अङ्गानि दत्वा नृणाम् प्राणान् क्रीणासि एतद् युक्तम्, तु पुनः नयनपद्मयोः कोणम् न युक्तम्।

व्याख्याः–कस्यचित्काञ्चित्कामिनीं प्रत्युक्तिः। हेमाङ्गि सुवर्णगौराङ्गि। अङ्गानि दत्वा प्राणन् क्रीणासि चेदेतद्युक्तं नयनपद्मयोः कोणं दत्वा तु प्राणन् क्रीणासि चेदेतत्पुनर्न युक्तमित्यर्थः। अयं परिवृत्त्यलंकारः।

Eng.Tr.:-Oh gold complexioned lady! it would have been proper if you were to buy the lives of men by giving them your limbs; but not so if you were to do giving them (only) a glance (corner) of thy lotus-like eye.

जितमौक्तिकसम्पदां रदानां
सहवासेन परां मुदं दधानाम्।
विरसादधरीकरोति नासा-
मधुना साहसशालि मौक्तिकं ते॥१७४॥

अन्वयः–सदा जितमौक्तिकसम्पदां रदानां सहवासेन पराम् मुदम् दधानम् ते नासाम् अधुना विरसाद् साहसशालिमौक्तिकम् अधरीकरोति।

व्याख्याः–नायिकां प्रत्युक्तिः। रदानां सहवासेन परां मुदं दधानां

नासां मौक्तिकमधरीकरोतीत्यन्वयः। विरसाद्वैरस्यात्। भावप्रधानो निर्देशः। अधरीकरोति नीचीकरोति। शिरसि पदं धत्त इति भावः। साहसशालि विषमाध्यवसायमग्नम्। मोक्तिकमर्थान्नासामौक्तिकम्। अत्र स्वजातीयपराभवं कुर्वतां दन्तानां विक्रियामुत्पादयितुमसमर्थं नासामौक्तिकं दन्तसंबंधिन्या नासाया विक्रियां जनयतिति वर्णनात्प्रत्यनीकालंकारोऽयम्। प्रतिपक्षसंबंधिन-स्तिरस्कृतिः प्रत्यनीकम्।

Eng.Tr.:-Now that your audacious pearl through hostility with your teeth bends down your nose which entertains extreme delight by its association with your teeth which have surpassed the beauty of pearls.

विलसत्याननं तस्या नासाग्रस्थितमौक्तिकम्।
आलक्षितबुधाश्लेषं राकेन्दोरिव मण्डलम्॥१७५॥

अन्वयः—तस्या नासाग्रस्थितमौक्तिकम् आननं राकेन्दोः आलक्षित-बुधाश्लेषम् मण्डलम् इव विलसति।

व्याख्याः—तस्या नायिकायाः। आलक्षितबुधाश्लेषं दुष्टबुधग्रहासङ्गम्। राकेन्दोः पूर्णिमाचन्द्रस्य।

Eng.Tr.:-Her face with a pearl at the tip of her nose, shines just as the full moon-disc in conjunction with the planet mercury dimly seen.

निभाल्य भूयो निजगौरिमाणं मा नाम मानं सहसैव यासीः।
गृहे गृहे पश्य तवाङ्गवर्णा मुग्धे सुवर्णावलयो लुठन्ति॥१७६॥

अन्वयः—हे मुग्धे! निजगौरिमाणम् भूयः निभालय सहसा एव मानम् नाम मा यासीः (यतः) पश्य। गृहे गृहे तव अङ्गवर्णाः सुवर्णावलयः लुठन्ति।

व्याख्याः—निभाल्य सादरं दृष्ट्वा। गौरिमाणं गौरत्वम्। लुठन्त्यनादृता एव पतन्ति। प्रतीपालंकारः।

Eng.Tr.:-Ah! silly girl, frequently looking at your

yellowish complexion do not be filled with pride; look in every house there are lying about heaps of gold of your colour.

करिकुम्भतुलामुरोजयोः
क्रियमाणां कविभिर्विशृङ्खलैः।
कथमालि शृणोषि सादरं
विपरीतार्थविदो हि योषितः॥१७७॥

अन्वयः—हे आलि! विश्रृङ्खलैः कविभिः क्रियमाणम् उरोजयोः करिकुम्भतुलाम् कथं सादरं शृणोषि, हि योषितः विपरीतार्थविदः भवन्ति।

व्याख्याः—नायिकां प्रत्युक्तिः। करिकुम्भतुलां गजगण्डोपमाम्। उरोजयोः स्तनयोः। विशृङ्खलैर्निरङ्कुशैः। सादरश्रवणमनुचितं यतो द्वयोस्तुल्यतैव न संभवतीति भावः। चतुर्थपादोऽमुमेवार्थं पुष्णाति। विपरीतार्थविदोऽयथार्थज्ञानवत्यः। योषितः स्त्रियः। स्त्रीस्वभावसुलभया भ्रान्त्यैव त्वमिदं सादरं शृणोषीति तात्पर्यम् इदमर्थान्तरन्यासानुविद्धं प्रतीपम्।

Eng.Tr.:-Ah, friend! how do you listen with respect to the comparison of your breasts with temples of elephant made by extravagant poets? Surely women take it differently.

परिष्वजन् रोषवशात् तिरस्कृतः
प्रियो मृगाक्ष्या शयितः पराङ्मुखः।
किं दुःखितोऽसाविति कान्दिशीकया
कयाचिदाचुंब्यचिराय सस्वजे॥१७८॥

अन्वयः—रोषवशात् परिष्वजन् तिरस्कृतः पराङ्मुखः शयितः प्रियः किम् असौ दुःखितः इति कदाचिद् कान्दिशीकया आचुम्ब्य चिराय सस्वजे।

व्याख्याः—परिष्वजन्नालिङ्गन्। मृगाक्ष्या तिरस्कृत इत्यन्वयः। असौ प्रियः। कान्दिशीकया भयावृतचित्तया। सस्वज आलिङ्गितः। अत्र नायकस्य यत्नं विनैवेष्टार्थलाभात्प्रहर्षणालंकारः।

Eng. Tr.:-While embracing the deer-eyed one, the lover being treated with contempt by her in a fit of anger, when lying with his face turned away from her, was with kisses embraced by her for a long time afraid as she become of his being afflicted.

चेलाञ्चलेनाननशीतरश्मिं संवृण्वतीनां हरिदृश्वरीणाम्।
व्रजाङ्गनानां स्मरजातकंपादकांडसंपातमियाय नीवी॥१७९॥

अन्वयः—चेलाञ्चलेन आननशीतरश्मिं संवृण्वतीनां हरिदृश्वरीणां व्रजाङ्गनानां नीवी स्मरजातकम्पात् अकाण्डसम्पातम् इयाय।

व्याख्याः—चेलाञ्चलेन वस्त्रप्रान्तेन। आननशीतरश्मिं मुखचन्द्रम्। संवृण्वतीनामाच्छादयंतीनाम्। हरिदृश्वरीणां कृष्णं दृष्टवतीनाम्। स्मरजात-कम्पान्मदनजनितकम्पात्। अकाण्डसंपातमाकस्मिकविस्त्रंसम्। नीवी वसनग्रंथिः। श्रीकृष्णं विलोक्य लज्जावशान्मुखमावृण्वतीनां गोपीनां नीवी सात्विक-कम्पादकस्मादेव स्त्रस्तेत्यर्थः। अयमिष्टार्थविरुद्धलाभाद्विषादनालंकारः।

Eng. Tr.:-The knot of garment (round their waist) of the women of Vraja who, at the sight of Kṛṣṇa, had covered their moon-like face with the end of their garment, was suddenly loosened by tremour brought about by the feeling of passion.

अधरेण समागमाद्रदाना-
मरुणिम्ना पिहितोऽपि शुक्लभावः।
हसितेन सितेन पक्ष्मलाक्ष्याः
पुनरुल्लासमवाप जातपक्षः॥१८०॥

अन्वयः—रदानां शुक्लभावः अधरेण समागमाद् अरुणिम्ना पिहितः अपि पक्ष्मलाक्ष्याः सितेन हसितेन जातपक्षः (सन्) पुनः उल्लासम् अवाप।

व्याख्याः—समागमात्सहवासात्। रदानां शुक्लभाव इत्यन्वयः। अरुणिम्नाऽरुणवर्णेन पिहितोप्याच्छादितोऽपि। शुक्लभावः श्वेतवर्णः। सितेन

शुभ्रेण। उल्लासमवाप पुनः प्रादुरभूत्। जातपक्षः संजातसहायः। हसितं शुभ्रमिति कविसमयः। अयं तद्गुणः। स्वगुणत्यागपूर्वकं संनिहितवस्त्वन्तरगुणग्रहणं तल्लक्षणम्।

Eng. Tr.:-The white colour of her teeth which owing to their contact with the lower lip was for a while shrouded by its red colour, manifested itself by the white smile of her who has long eye-lashes.

सरसिरुहोदरसुरभावधरितबिम्बाधरे मृगाक्षि तव।
वद वदने मणिरदने ताम्बूलं केन लक्षयेम वयम्॥१८१॥

अन्वयः—हे मृगाक्षि! सरसिरुहोदरसुरभौ, अवधरितबिम्बाधरे शुचिमणिरदने तव वदने ताम्बूलम् केन लक्षयेम।

व्याख्याः—प्रियेण ताम्बूलं कुतो न गृह्णासीत्युक्त एतावन्तं समयं ताम्बुलानि भुक्त्वैव समागतास्मीत्युक्तवतीं प्रति तस्येयमुक्तिः। अधिरितबिम्ब-स्तिरस्कृतबिम्बफलोऽधरो यस्य तस्मिन्। इदं वदनविशेषणम्। मणिरदने मणिसदृशदन्ते। तांबूलभुक्तिलिंगसदृशानि लिंगानि सहजान्येव तव वदने वर्ततेऽतः कथमस्मा- भिस्ताम्बूलभुक्तिरनुमेयेति भावः। अत्र पूर्वोक्तलक्षणो मीलितालंकारः।

Eng. Tr.:-Ah! dear-eyed one! say, how are we to detect *Tāmbūla* in your mouth which has fragrance akin to that of the interior of lotus, which subdues the *Bimba* fruit in redness, and which bears jewel like teeth.

शयिता सविधेऽप्यनीश्वरा सफलीकर्तुमहो मनोरथान्।
दयिता दयिताननाम्बुजं दरमीलन्नयना निरीक्षते॥१८२॥

अन्वयः—सविधे शयिता अपि दयिता मनोरथान् सफली कर्तुम् अनीश्वरा (सती) अहो दरमीलन्नयना दयिताननाम्बुजम् निरीक्षते।

व्याख्याः—शृङ्गारध्वनिरयम्। सविधेऽपि पतिसमीपेऽपि। अनिश्वरा-राऽसमर्था। लज्जावशादिति बोध्यम्। सफलीकर्तुं सफलान् कर्तुम्।

मनोरथानालिङ्गनचुम्बनाद्यभिलाषान्। दरमीलन्नयनेषत्संकुचितनेत्रा। अत्र नेत्रयोर्दरमीलनेन नायिकागता त्रपाऽभिव्यज्यते निरीक्षणेन च रतिः।

Eng. Tr.:-Oh! the beloved though lying close beside her husband, being unable to fulfill her own desire, views with semi-closed eyes his lotus-like face.

वदनारविन्दसौरभलोभादिन्दिन्दिरेषु निपतत्सु।
मय्यधरार्थिनि सुदृशोदृशे जयन्त्यतिरुषा परुषाः॥१८३॥

अन्वयः—वदनारविन्दसौरभलोभात् इन्दिन्दिरेषु निपतत्सु अधरार्थिनि मयि अतिरुषा परुषाः सुदृशः दृशः जयन्ति।

व्याख्याः—इन्दिन्दिरेषु भ्रमरेषु। अधरार्थिन्यधरपानं प्रार्थितवति। सुदृशो भामिन्याः। दृशो दृक्पाताः। अतिरुषाऽतिक्रोधेन। पुरुषाः कर्कशाः। भ्रमरपीडावत्यां नायिकायामधरपानार्थनाऽधिकपीडादानेन रोषोत्पादिका।

Eng. Tr.:-Victorious are the glances of the fair-eyed one, which are stern through extreme wrath towards me who asked for (a kiss of) her lower lip, while bees greedy of fragrance of her lotus-like face were falling over it.

इति भामिनीविलासव्याख्यायां काव्यमर्मप्रकाशाख्यायां
शृङ्गारविलासः।

भामिनीविलासे
(III)
करुणविलासः
(Karuṇavilāsaḥ)

III

करुणविलासः

दैवे पराग्वदनशालिनि हन्त जाते
याते च सम्प्रति दिवं प्रति बन्धुरत्ने।
कस्मै मनः! कथयितासि निजामवस्थां
कः शीतलैः शमयिता वचनैस्तवाधिम्॥१॥

अन्वयः—हन्त! मनः! सम्प्रति दैवे पराग्वदनशालिनि जाते बन्धुरत्ने दिवम् प्रति याते च निजाम् अवस्थाम् कस्मै कथयितासि। कः शीतलैः वचनैः तव आधिं शमयिता।

व्याख्याः—प्रमीतां स्वप्रियामुद्दिश्य कस्यचिच्छोकोक्तिरस्मिन् विलास उपनिबद्धा। पराग्वदनशालिनि परङ्मुखे। प्रतिकूल इति यावत्। बन्धुरत्ने कलत्ररूपे। मन इति संबोधनम्। कथयितासि कथयिष्यसि शमयिता शमयिष्यति।

Eng.Tr.:-Alas! when the fate has turned its face against me and when the best of my relations has now gone to heaven, oh! mind! to whom will you disclose your own condition and who will assuage your agonies by soothing words.

प्रत्युद्गता सविनयं सहसा पुरेव[१]
स्मेरैः स्मरस्य सचिवैः सरसाऽवलोकैः।
मामद्य मञ्जुरचनैर्वचनैश्च बाले
हा! लेशतोऽपि न कथं वद सत्करोषि[२]॥२॥

---

१. 'सखीभिः' इति पाठान्तरम्।
२. 'शिशिरीकरोषि' इति पाठन्तरम्।

अन्वयः—हा! बाले!! पुरेव सहसा अद्य कथम् माम् सविनयम् प्रत्युद्गता स्मरस्य सचिवैः स्मेरेः, सरसावलोकैः च मञ्जुरचनैः वचनैः लेशतः अपि न शिशिरीकरोषि।

व्याख्या:—प्रत्युद्गताऽभिमुखमागता। सहसाऽकस्मात्। पुरेव प्रागिव। स्मेरैःस्मितयुक्तैः। स्मरस्य सचिवैर्मदनस्य सहायैः। कामोद्दीपकैरिति यावत्। सरसावलोकैः सप्रणयवीक्षणैः। हा खेदे। शिशिरीकरोषि शीतलयसि।

Eng.Tr.:-Alas! O lady, why do you not as before, coming forward to receive me with smiles and loving glances, the ministers of love, sooth me in the least today with pleasing words?

सर्वेऽपि विस्मृतिपथं विषयाः प्रयाता
विद्याऽपि खेदकलिता[१] विमुखीबभूव।
सा केवलं हरिणशावकलोचना मे
नैवापयाति हृदयादधिदेवतेव॥३॥

अन्वयः—सर्वे अपि विषयाः विस्मृतिपथम् प्रयाताः, खेदकलिता विद्या अपि विमूखीबभूव, केवलं हरिणशावकलोचना सा अधिदेवतेव मे हृदयात् न एव अपयाति।

व्याख्या:—विषया इन्द्रियार्थाः। खेदकलिता खेदव्याप्ता।

Eng.Tr.:-All objects have been completely forgotten. Even learning overpowered with grief has turned away its face. But that fawn-eyed one alone like presiding deity does not leave my heart.

निर्वाणमङ्गलपदं त्वरया विशन्त्या
मुक्ता दयावति! दयाऽपि किल त्वयाऽसौ।
यन्मां न भामिनि निभालयसि प्रभात-
नीलारविन्दमदभङ्गमदैः कटाक्षैः॥४॥

---

१. 'खेदगलिता' इति पाठान्तरम्।

अन्वयः—हे दयावति! भामिनि! त्वरया निर्वाणमङ्गलपदं विशन्त्या त्वया किल असौ दया अपि मुक्ता? यत् माम् प्रभातनीलारविन्दमदभङ्गकरैः कटाक्षैः न निभालयसि।

व्याख्या:—निर्वाणमङ्गलपदं मोक्षरूपानपायस्थानम्। निमालयसि पश्यसि। प्रभातनीलारविन्दमदभङ्गी प्रातःस्फुरदिन्दीवरभञ्जको मदो येषां तैः।

Eng.Tr.:-O compationate one! you have indeed, given up that compassion while entering all in haste the auspicious regions of final beatitude, O Bhāmini! since you do not look at me with glances whose dignity has brought low the pride of the morning blue lotuses.

धृत्वा पदस्खलनभीतिवशत् करं मे
या रूढवत्यसि शिलाशकलं विवाहे।
सा मां विहाय कथमद्य विलासिनि द्या-
मारोहसीति हृदयं शतधा प्रयाति॥५॥

अन्वयः—हे विलासिनि! या (त्वम्) विवाहे पदस्खलनभीतिवशात् मे करम् धृत्वा शिलाशकलं रूढवती असि, सा (त्वम्) अद्य मां विहाय द्याम् कथम् आरोहसि इति (विचिन्त्य) हृदयं शतधा प्रयाति।

व्याख्या:—आतिष्ठेममश्मानमश्मेव त्वं स्थिरा भव॥

Eng.Tr.:-O gallant lady! my heart splinters into hundreds at the thought that how do you today ascend the heaven leaving me behind-you, who at our nuptial ceremony through the fear of slipping of your foot, catching hold of my hand mounted upon a slab of stone.

निर्दूषणा गुणवती रसभावपूर्णा
सालङ्कृतिः श्रवणकोमलवर्णराजि[१]ः।
सा मामकीनकवितेव मनोऽभिरामा
रामा कदापि हृदयान्मम नापयाति॥६॥

---

१. 'श्रवणमङ्गलवर्णराजिः' इति पाठान्तरम्।

अन्वयः–निर्दूषणा गुणवती रसभावपूर्णा सालङ्कृतिः श्रवणमङ्गलवर्णराजिः मनोऽभिरामा सा रामा मामकीनकवितेव कदापि मम हृदयात् न अपयाति।

व्याख्याः–अत्र श्लिष्टविशेषणद्वारा प्रिया स्वकवितयोपमीयते। निर्दूषणा दौःशील्यादिदोषरहिता श्रुतिकटुत्वादिकाव्यदोषरहिता च। गुणवती दयादाक्षिण्यादिगुणयुता माधुर्यादिकाव्यगुणयुता च।रसभावपूर्णा शृङ्गारेण प्रीत्या च पूर्णा शृङ्गारादिरसैः। श्चिन्तामोहादिव्यभिचारिभिश्च पूर्णा। सालंकृतिः कटककुण्डलादियुतोपमादियुता च श्रवणयोः कर्णयोः कोमला वर्णराजिः शब्दपंक्तिः काव्यघटकवर्णपंक्तिश्च यस्याः सा।

Eng.Tr.:-Never does that beloved of mine vanish from my heart-my beloved who was faultless, possessed of good qualities, full of sentiments and emotions, who was highly decorated, and the flow of whose speech was charming to the mind like my poem which is also faultless, possesses excellences and is full of *Rasas* and *Bhāvas*, which is richly embellished and in which the arrangement of letters are pleasing to the ear.

चिन्ता शशाम सकलाऽपि सरोरुहाणा-
मिन्दोश्च बिम्बमसमां सुषमामयासीत्।
अभ्युद्गतः कलकलः किल कोकिलानां
प्राणप्रिये! यदवधि त्वमितो गताऽसि॥७॥

अन्वयः–हे प्राणप्रिये! त्वम् यदवधि इतः गता असि (तदवधि) सरोरुहाणां सकला अपि चिन्ता शशाम, च इन्दोः बिम्बम् असमां सुषमाम् अयासीत् च कोकिलानाम् कलकलः अपि उद्गतः किल।

व्याख्याः–चिन्ता पराभवभीतिः। असमामतुलाम्। अभ्युद्गतोऽभ्युदयं प्राप्तः।

Eng.Tr.:-O beloved! ever since your departure from this place, the anxiety of lotuses has absolutely subsided, and the disc of the moon has attained the beauty! and the melodious notes of cuckoos have arisen.

सौदामिनीविलसितप्रतिमानकाण्डे
दत्वा कियन्त्यपि दिनानि महेन्द्रभोगान्।
मन्त्रोज्झितस्य नृपतेरिव राज्यलक्ष्मी-
र्भाग्यच्युतस्य करतो मम निर्गताऽसि॥८॥

अन्वयः—कियन्ति अपि दिनानि सौदामिनीविलसितप्रतिमान् महेन्द्र-भोगान् दत्वा मन्त्रोज्झितस्य नृपतेः राज्यलक्ष्मीः इव अकाण्डे भाग्यच्युतस्य मम करतः निर्गता असि।

व्याख्याः—सौदामिनीविलसितप्रतिमान् महेन्द्रभोगान् कियन्त्यपि दिनानि दत्वाऽकाण्डे भाग्यच्युतस्य मम करतो निर्गतासीत्यन्वयः। सौदामिनीविलसित-प्रतिमान् विद्युद्विलाससदृशान्। अतीवास्थिरानिति यावत्। महेन्द्रभोगान् महेन्द्रयोग्योपभोगान्। कियन्त्यपि दिनान्यल्पकालम्। कालाध्वनोरत्यन्तसंयोग इति द्वितीया। मन्त्रोज्झितस्य राजमन्त्रेण त्यक्तस्य। भाग्यच्युतस्य दैवहीनस्य।

Eng.Tr.:-Having for some time given me pleasures befitting the lord of heaven and resembling with the flashes of lightening (in their transitory nature), you like the regal deity of a king forsaken by policy did suddenly escape from my grasp, who I am forsaken by fortune.

केनापि मे विलसितेन समुद्गतस्य
कोपस्य किं नु करभोरु वशंवदाऽभूः।
यन्मां विहाय सहसैव पतिव्रताऽपि
याताऽसि मुक्तिरमणीसदनं विदूरम्॥९॥

अन्वयः—हे करभोरु! किम् नु (त्वम्) मे केन अपि विलसितेन समुद्गतस्य कोपस्य वशंवदा अभू यत् सहसा एव मां विहाय पतिव्रता अपि विदूरम् मुक्तरमणीसदनं याता असि।

व्याख्याः—केनाप्यनुचितेन। विलसितेन चेष्टितेन। समुद्गतस्य समुत्थि-तस्य। करभोरु करभसदृशोरु। करस्य मांसलो बहिर्भागः करभः। वशंवदाऽ-धीना। सहसैवाकस्मादेव। पतिव्रताऽपीत्यत्रापिना पतिव्रतया पतित्यागोऽनुचित एवेति सूचितम्। मुक्तिरमणीसदनं मुक्तिसखीगेहम्। मोक्षपदमित्यर्थः।

Eng.Tr.:-O lady having thighs like the inner edge of the palm of the hand! can it be that you were overpowered by anger consequent upon some unpardonable action on my part since though a devoted wife you abruptly deserting me have gone to the far off abode of your friend, the final beattitude.

काव्यात्मना मनसि पर्यणमन् पुरा मे
पीयूषसारसरसास्तव ये विलासाः।
तानन्तरेण रमणी रमणीयशीले
चेतोहरा सुकविता भविता कथं नः॥१०॥

अन्वयः—पुरा तव पीयूषसारसरसाः ये विलासाः मे मनसि काव्यात्मना पर्यणमन्, तान् अन्तरेण नः रमणी रमणीयशीला चेतोहरा सुकविता कथं भविता?

व्याख्याः—काव्यात्मना काव्यरूपेण। पर्यणमन् परिणता अभूवन्। तानन्तरेण तैर्विना। चेतोहरा मनोहरा।

Eng.Tr.:-O you of an amiable disposition! how will my good poetry become charming in the absence of those amourous sports of thine, which were sweet as the essence of nectar and which formerly developed into poetic composition in my mind?

या तावकीनमधुरस्मितकान्तिकान्ते
भूमण्डले विफलतां कविषु व्यतानीत्।
सा कातराक्षि! विलयं त्वयि यातवत्यां
राकाऽधुना वहति वैभवमिन्दिरायाः॥११॥

अन्वयः—हे कातराक्षि! तावकीनमधुरस्मितकान्तिकान्ते भूमण्डले या कविषु विफलतां व्यतानीत् सा राका अधुना सहसा त्वयि यातवत्याम् इन्दिरायाः वैभवं वहति।

व्याख्याः—तावकीनस्य मधुरस्मितस्य कान्त्या कान्ते कमनीये। कविषु विफलतां व्यतानीत्कविभिर्निष्फलत्वेनागृह्यत। शुभ्रत्ववर्णनप्रस्तावे तव

स्मितमुत्कृष्टमुपमानमुपलभ्य कवयो राकां निष्प्रयोजनाममन्यंतेति भावः। कातराक्ष्यधीरनयने। राका पूर्णिमारात्रिः। इंदिराया वैभवं वहति साक्षाल्लक्ष्म्या एव समृद्धिसौभाग्यं प्राप्नोति।

Eng.Tr.:-O tremulus eyed one! now that you are dead and gone, the full moon-night which was rendered useless to the poets when the whole expanse of the earth was illumined by the lustre of your sweet smiles, attains grandeur of beauty.

मन्दस्मितेन सुधया परिषिच्य या मां
नेत्रोत्पलैर्विकसितैरनिशं समीजे।
सा नित्यमङ्गलमयी गृहदेवता मे
कामेश्वरी हृदयतो दयिता न याति॥१२॥

अन्वयः–या मन्दस्मितेन सुधया परिषिच्च विकसितैः नेत्रोत्पलैः अनिशम् माम् समीजे सा नित्यमङ्गलमयी कामेश्वरी गृहदेवता मे दयिता हृदयतः न याति।

व्याख्या:–मन्दस्मितेन सुधयेत्यत्राभेदेनान्वयः। तेन मन्दस्मिताभिन्नया सुधयेत्यर्थः। परिषिच्य स्नपयित्वा। नेत्रोत्पलैर्नेत्ररूपकमलैः। समीजेऽर्चितवती। नित्यमंगलमयी सततमंगलरूपा। अत्र स्मितसुधया सेचनं नेत्रकमलैः पूजनं च मंगलत्वेनाभिप्रेतम्। गृहदेवता गृहाधिष्ठात्री देवता। कामेश्वरी कामपूरणे समर्था।

Eng.Tr.:-That beloved of mine! the ever auspicious household deity, the desire fulfilling goddess, who having sprinkled me with nectar in the shape of her smiles, propitiated me night and day with blooming lotuses in the shape of her eyes, does not vanish from my heart.

भूमौ स्थिता रमण! नाथ! मनोहरेति
सम्बोधनैर्यमधिरोपितवत्यसि द्याम्।
स्वर्गं गता कथमिव क्षिपसि त्वमेण-
शावाक्षि तं धरणिधूलिषु मामिदानीम्॥१३॥

अन्वयः—हे एणशावाक्षि! भूमौ स्थित (तव) यम् रमण! नाथ! मनोहर! इति सम्बोधनैः द्याम् अधिरोपितवती असि, इदानीं स्वर्गम् गता त्वम् तम् माम् धरणिधूलिषु कथमिव क्षिपसि?

व्याख्या:—भूमिस्थाऽपि त्वं यं रमणेत्यादिभिः संबोधनैर्द्यामधिरोपितवत्यसि तं मामधुना स्वयं स्वर्गं गतापि धरणिधूलिषु क्षिपसीत्यत्यंतानुचितमिदमिति तात्पर्यार्थः। संबोधनैरामंत्रणैः। द्यामधिरोपितवत्यसि स्वर्गं प्रापितवत्यसि। स्वर्गारोहणसुखमनुभावितवत्यसीति यावत्। तं मामित्यन्वयः। धरणिधूलिषु क्षिपसि निजगमनेन शोकदानादिति शेषः। त्वां विनाऽहं धूलिषु पतित्वा रोदिमीति भावः।

Eng.Tr.:-While on this earth thou waft me to heaven by addressing me as my love! "my love"! my lord" "the enchanter of my heart. But O Swan-eyed one! how is it that thou having gone to heaven throw me off into the dust of the earth?

लावण्यमुज्ज्वलमपास्ततुलं च शीलं
लोकोत्तरं विनयमर्थमयं नयञ्च।
एतान् गुणानशरणानथ मां च हित्वा
हा हन्त! सुन्दरि! कथं त्रिदिवं गताऽसि॥१४॥

अन्वयः—हे सुन्दरि! उज्ज्वलम् लावण्यम्, च अपास्ततुलं शीलं, लोकोत्तरं विनयम्, च अर्थमयम् नयम्, एतान् अशरणान् गुणान् अथ च मां हित्वा हा! हन्त! त्रिदिवम् कथम् गता असि?

व्याख्या:—अपास्ततुलमनुपमम्। शीलं वृत्तम्। विनयं नम्रभावम्। अर्थमयं नयं प्रचुरार्थां नीतिम्। एतान् गुणानशरणान् हित्वा मां चाशरणं हित्वेत्यन्वयः। एतान् लावण्यादीन्।

Eng.Tr.:-Having left me and your qualities the resplendent beauty, peerless character, uncommon modesty, and sound morality perfectly helpless, alas! O beautiful one, how have you gone to heaven?

कान्त्या सुवर्णवरया परया च शुद्ध्या
नित्यं स्विकाः खलु शिखाः परितः क्षिपन्तीम्।

चेतोहरामपि कुशेशयलोचने! त्वां
जानामि कोपकलुषो दहनो ददाह॥१५॥

अन्वयः—हे कुशेशयलोचने! सुवर्णवरया कान्त्या च परया शुद्धया नित्यम् खलु परितः स्विकाः क्षिपन्तीम्, चेतोहराम् अपि त्वाम् कोपकलुषः दहनः ददाह इति जानामि।

व्याख्याः—सुवर्णवरया सुवर्णादप्युत्कृष्टया। परया श्रेष्ठया। स्विकाः स्वकीयाः। अर्थादहनस्य। शिखा ज्वालाः। क्षिपन्तीमभिभवन्तीम्। कुशेशयलोचने कमलनेत्रोकोपकलुषस्त्वया कांतिशुद्धिभ्यां जितत्वात्प्राप्तरोषः।

Eng.Tr.:-I believe, O louts eyed one! that though attractive to the heart, you have been consumed by the funeral fire excited with anger caused by having put down its flames all round by your lustre superior to that of gold and by your passing purity.

कर्पूरवर्तिरिव लोचनतापहन्त्री
फुल्लाम्बुजस्रगिव कण्ठसुखैकहेतुः।
चेतश्चमत्कृतिपदं कवितेव रम्या
नम्या नरीभिरमरीव हि सा विरेजे॥१६॥

अन्वयः—कर्पूरवर्तिरिव लोचनतापहन्त्री, फुल्लाम्बुजस्रगिव कण्ठसुखैकहेतुः, रम्या कवितेव चेतश्चमत्कृतिपदं नरीभिः नम्या अमरीव सा विरेजे हि।

व्याख्याः—कर्पूरवर्तिरिव घनसारचूर्णमिव। फुल्लाम्बुजस्रक् प्रफुल्लकमलमाला। चेतश्चमत्कृतिपदं चित्तचमत्कारहेतुः। नरीभिर्नारीभिः। अमरीवाप्सरा इव। विरेजे रराज।

Eng.Tr.:-She, like a camphor-pencil, was (lit-shone) the remover of the burning sensation of the eye; like a garland of full-blown lotuses, the sole producer of pleasure; like a beautiful poem, the object of admiration to the mind; and like a goddess the object of worship to women.

स्वप्नान्तरेऽपि खलु भामिनि! पत्युरन्यं
या दृष्टवत्यसि न कञ्चन साभिलाषम्।
सा सम्प्रति प्रचलिताऽसि गुणैर्विहीनं
प्राप्तुं कथं कथय हन्त परं पुमांसम्॥१७॥

अन्वयः—हे भामिनि! कथय, या (त्वम्) स्वप्नान्तरे अपि पत्युः अन्यम् कञ्चन खलु साभिलाषम् न दृष्टवती असि, हन्त! सा (त्वम्) सम्प्रति गुणैः विहीनम् परम् पुमांसम् प्राप्तुम् कथं प्रचलिता असि।

व्याख्याः—स्वप्नान्तरेऽपि स्वप्नावस्थायामपि। कञ्चन पुरुषमिति शेषः। साभिलाषमिति क्रियाविशेषणम्। गुणैर्विहीनं विनयादिगुणशून्यं। सत्वर-जस्तमोगुणरहितं च। हन्तेति खेदे। परं पुमांसं परपुरुषं परमात्मानं च। अयं श्लेषमूलको विरोधाभासः। अत्र स्वप्नेऽपि परपुरुषदृष्टवती त्वं गुणैर्विहीनं परं पुमांसं प्राप्तुं प्रचलितासीति भासमानस्य विरोधस्य श्लिष्टार्थवशात्परिहारो भवति।

Eng.Tr.:-Alas! tell me, how is, it that you who did not even in a dream longingly looked at any man other than your beloved, have now set out to obtain another man devoid of merits?

दयितस्य गुणाननुस्मरन्ती
शयने सम्प्रति या विलोकिताऽऽसीत्।
अधुना किल हन्त सा कृशाङ्गी
गिरमङ्गीकुरुते न भाषिताऽपि॥१८॥

अन्वयः—सम्प्रति शयने दयितस्य गुणान् अनुस्मरन्ती विलोकिता आसीत् हन्त? अधुना सा खलु कृशाङ्गी भाषिता अपि गिरम् न अङ्गीकुरुते।

व्याख्याः—दयितस्य मम। संप्रति मरणसमयेऽपि। अनेन पदेन चरमा-वस्थायामपि तस्या दयितगुणविस्मरणं नाभूदिति वस्तु व्यज्यते। हंत खेदे। गिरं नांगीकुरुते न प्रतिवदति। भाषिताऽप्युक्ताऽपि।

Eng.Tr.:-That slender-bodied one! who was only just

seen on the bed recalling the virtues of (me) her dear, does not, alas! utter a word though spoken to.

रीतिं गिराममृतवृष्टिकरीं तदीयां
तां चाकृतिं कविवरै[१]रभिनन्दनीयाम्।
लोकोत्तरामथ कृतिं करुणारसार्द्रां
स्तोतुं न कस्य समुदेति मनः प्रसादः॥१९॥

अन्वयः—अमृतवृष्टिकरीम् त्वदीयाम् गिरां रीतिम्, च कविवरैः अभिनन्दनीयाम् ताम् आकृतिम्, अथ करुणारसार्द्रां लोकोत्तराम् कृतिं स्तोतुम् कस्य मनः प्रसादः न समुदेति।

व्याख्या:—गिरां रीतिं भाषणपरिपाटीम्। अमृतवृष्टिकरीं सुधाप्लावनकरीम्। अथ च। करुणारसार्द्रां कृतिं करुणापरिपूर्णां कृत्यपरिपाटीम्। अत्र कविना स्वकृतिरपि कटाक्षितेति भाति।

Eng.Tr.:-Who will not be inspired to extole that manner of her speech producing showers of nectar, that make of her body so fit to be admired by the best of poets, and the uncommon deeds of her so full of sympathy?

इति भामिनीविलासव्याख्यायां काव्यमर्मप्रकाशाख्यायां करुणविलासः।

---

१. 'कृतिवरै०' इति पाठान्तरम्।

भामिनीविलासे

(IV)

शान्तविलासः

(Śāntavilāsaḥ)

IV

शान्तविलासः

विशालविषयाटवीवलयलग्नदावानल-
प्रसृत्वरशिखावलीविकलितं मदीयं मनः।
अमन्दमिलदिन्दिरे निखिलमाधुरीमन्दिरे
मुकुन्दमुखचन्दिरे चिरमिदं चकोरायताम्॥१॥

अन्वयः-अमन्द.......चन्दिरे इदं विशाल.......मदीयं मनः चकोरायताम्।

व्याख्या:-विशालं यद्विषयाटवीवलयं तत्र लग्नस्य दावानलस्य या प्रसृत्वराः प्रसरणशीलाः शिखास्तासामावलीभिर्विकलितं वैकल्यं प्राप्तम्। अमंदं मिलंतींदिरा शोभा यस्मिंस्तस्मिन्। मुकुंदमुखचन्दिरे श्रीकृष्णवदनचंद्रे। चकोरायतां चकोर इवाचरतु। इदं पद्यं पंडितराजकृतकरुणालहर्याः केषुचित्पुस्तकेषु दृश्यते।

Eng.Tr.:-May my mind, which is distressed by the rows of flames, spreading around, of the forest conflagration which is burning the circle of the extensive forest in the form of the objects of senses (that surround me) act like the चकोर bird towards the moon in the form of the face of मुकुन्द, which is the receptacle of all sweetness and whose splendour is rapidly increasing.

अये! जलधिनन्दिनीनयननीरजालम्बन!
ज्वलज्ज्वलनजित्वरज्वरभरत्वराभङ्गुरम्।
प्रभातजलजोन्नमद्गरिमगर्वसर्वङ्कषै-
र्जगत्रीतयरोचनैः शिशिरयाशु मां लोचनैः॥२॥

अन्वयः-अये जलधिनन्दिनीनयननीजालम्बन (विष्णो) ज्वलज्ज्वलन-जित्वरज्वर-भरत्वराभङ्गुरं मां प्रभातजलजोन्नमद्गरिमगर्वसर्वकषैः जगत्रितयरोचनैः लोचनैः आशु शिशिरय।

व्याख्या:-जलधिनन्दिनीनयननीरजालम्बन लक्ष्मीनेत्रकमलाश्रय भगवन् विष्णे। ज्वलन् यो ज्वलनो वह्निस्तस्य जित्वरो जेता त्समादषधिकसन्तापकरो यो ज्वरभरस्तस्य त्वरया वेगेन भङ्गुर भज्यमानम्। प्रभातजलजस्य य उन्नमन्नुद्यन् गरिमा तस्य गर्वस्य सर्वकषैर्नाशकैः। जगत्त्रितयस्य रोचनैः प्रीतिजनकैः। शिशिरस्य शीतलं कुरु। अत्र लोचनपदं कटाक्षपरं ग्राह्यमन्यथा बहुवचनस्य निरर्थकत्वात्।

Eng.Tr.:-O (God Viṣṇu), the support of the lotuses in the form of the eyes of Laxmi, speedily cool me, who am breaking under the force (त्वरा) of the excess of pain that conquers the burning fire, by your glances, liked by the three worlds, and the destroyers of the pride of greatness arising in a morning lotus.

स्मृतापि तरुणातपं करुणया हरन्ती नृणा-
मभङ्गुरतनुत्विषां वलयिता शतैर्विद्युताम्।
कलिन्दनग[1]नन्दिनीतटसुरद्रुमालम्बिनी
मदीयमतिचुम्बिनी भवतु कापि कादम्बिनी॥३॥

अन्वयः-स्मृता अपि (केवलं) करुणया नृणां तरुणातपं हरन्ती, अभङ्गुरतनुत्विषां विद्युतां शतैः वलयिता, कलिन्दनगनन्दिनीतटसुरदुमालम्बिनी, का अपि कादम्बिनी मदीयमतिचुम्बिनी भवतु।

व्याख्या:-व्यतिरेकातिशयोकत्त्योरङ्गागिभावसंकरोऽयम्। अत्र कादंबिनीत्वेनाध्यवसितायाः कृष्णमूर्तेरितरमेघमालात आधिक्यं वर्णितम्। तरुणातपं चण्डातपम्। इतरमेघमाला दृष्टा वर्षणद्वारा स्पृष्टा वा तापं हरतीयं तु स्मृताऽपि। इतरमेघमाला भङ्गशीलतनुकांतिविद्युता वेष्टिते यं तु चिरकालस्थायिशरीरकान्तीनां विद्युतां शतैरावृता। अत्र सुरद्रुमशब्दो नीपवाचको यमुनातीरे कल्पवृक्षाणामभावात्। यद्वा नीपानां सुरद्रुमत्वेनाध्यवसायः। इतरमेघमाला वियदालंबिनीयं तु सुरद्रुमालम्बिनी। मतिचुम्बिनी मतिविषयः। कापीतरमेघमाला विलक्षणा।

Eng.Tr.:-Let the indescribable row of clouds (श्रीकृष्ण) be the object of my contemplation, which when merely remembered removes the terrible anguish through kindness,

---

१. 'गिरि' इति पाठान्तरम्।

which is encircled by hundred of lightnings of everlasting glow, which rests (is seated) on the celestial tree, (growing) on the bank of the daughter of the mountain कलिन्द.

कलिन्दगिरिनन्दिनीतटवनान्तरं भासय[१]न्
सदा पथि गतागतश्रम[२]भरं हरन्प्राणिनाम्।
लतावलिशतावृतो मधुरया रुचा संभृतो
ममाशु हरतु श्रमानतितरां तमालद्रुमः॥४॥

अन्वयः–कलिन्दनगनन्दिनीतटवनान्तरं भासयन् सदा प्राणिनां पथि गतागतश्रमभरं हरन्, लतावलिशतावृतः, मधुरया रुचा संभृतः, तमालद्रुमः आशु मम श्रमान् अतितरां हरतु।

व्याख्या:–इयं सावयवातिशयोक्तिः। अत्र भगवतो कृष्णस्य तमालद्रुमत्वेनाध्यवसायः। तदनुग्रहार्थं चोच्चावचयोनिसंचरणस्य पथित्वेन गोपीनां च लतात्वेनाध्यवसितिः। वनान्तरं वनमध्यम्। भासयन् दीपयन्। पथि मार्ग उच्चावचयोनिसञ्चरणे च। गतागतश्रमभरं गमनागमनश्रमभरमेकयोनित्यागपूर्वकापरयोनिप्रवेशश्रमभरं च। रुचा कांत्या। संभृतो युक्तः।

Eng.Tr.:-May the तमाल tree (श्रीकृष्ण) remove completely and instantly my fatigue the tree which brightens the interior of the wilderness (वृन्दावन) on the banks of the (Jumna) daughter of the कलिन्द mountain, the tree which always removes the burden of the fatigue of going and coming in the journey (of travellers) (journey of births and death), the tree encircled by hundreds of rows of creepers (गोपीs) and adorned by the pleasant splendour.

जगज्जालं ज्योत्स्नामयनवसुधाभिर्जटिलय-
ञ्जनानां सन्तापं त्रिविधमपि सद्यः प्रशमयन्।
श्रितो वृन्दारण्यं नतनिखिलवृन्दारकवृतो
मम स्वान्तध्वान्तं तिरयतु नवीनो जलधरः॥५॥

अन्वयः–ज्योत्स्नामयनवसुधाभिः जगज्जालम् जटिलयन् जनानाम्

१. 'भावयन्' इति पाठान्तरम्।
२. 'क्लम०' इति पाठान्तरम्।

त्रिविधम् अपि सन्तापं सद्यः प्रशमयन् वृन्दारण्यं श्रितः नतनिटिवलवृन्दापरक-वृतः नवीनः जलधरः मम स्वान्तध्वान्तम् तिरयतु।

व्याख्या:-इयमप्यतिशयोक्तिः। अत्र लोकोत्तरजलधरत्वेन भगवतः प्रतिपादनम्। लोकोत्तरत्वपोषकाणि च कल्पितानि त्रिविधतापशामकत्वादीनि विशेषणानि। ज्योत्स्नामयनवसुधाभिः कान्तिरूपनूतनामृतैः। नटिलयन् व्याप्नुवन्। त्रिविधमाध्यात्मिकमाधिदैविकमाधिभौतिकं च। सद्यस्तत्कालमेव। वृन्दारका देवाः। स्वान्तध्वान्तं चित्तांधकारम्। तिरयतु नाशयतु। नवीनो लोकोत्तरः।

Eng.Tr.:-May the new cloud (श्रीकृष्ण) destory the darkness of my heart, the cloud which pervades the surface of the world with the new nectar full of splendour, the cloud which instantaneously removes even the three-fold troubles of the people, the cloud which inhabited the वृन्दावन forest and which was surrounded by all the Gods bowing down (to him)!

ग्रीष्मचण्डकरमण्डलभीष्मज्वालसंसरणतापितमूर्तेः।
प्रावृषेण्य इव वारिधरो मे वेदनां हरतु वृष्णिवरेण्यः॥६॥

अन्वयः:-वृष्णिवरेण्यः प्रावृषेण्यः इव वारिधरः ग्रीष्म...........मूर्तेः मे वेदनां हरतु।

व्याख्या:-ग्रीष्मचण्डकरमण्डलस्येव ग्रीष्मकालसूर्यबिम्वस्येव भीष्मो ज्वालो यस्य तादृशेन संसरणेन संसारेण तापितमूतेर्मे। प्रावृषेण्यः प्रावृड्भवः। वेदनां पीडाम्। वृष्णिवरेण्यो वृष्णिकुलश्रेष्ठः कृष्णः।

Eng.Tr.:-May (श्रीकृष्ण) the best of (वृष्णिs) like the cloud in the rainy season, remove the agony of mine, (I) whose body is distressed by in the form of the worldly existence?!

अपारे संसारे विषमविषयारण्यसरणौ
मम भ्रामं भ्रामं विगलितविरामं जडमतेः।
परिश्रान्तस्यायं तरणितनयातीरनिलयः
समन्तात्सन्तापं हरिनवतमालस्तिरयतु॥७॥

अन्वयः:-अपारे ....सरणौ विगलितविरामं भ्रामं भ्रामं जडमतेः परिश्रान्तस्य मम समन्तात्सन्तापं अयं ....तिरयतु।

व्याख्या:-अयं परिणामालंकारः। विषयी यत्र विषयात्मतयैव प्रकृतोपयोगी न स्वांतत्र्येण तत्रायमलंकारो भवति। अस्मिन् पद्ये भगवदात्मतयैव तमालस्य संसारतापनिवर्तनक्षमत्वम्। विषमा दुःसंचार। विषयारण्यस्य सरणिर्मार्गो यत्र तस्मिन्। भ्रामं भ्रामं परिश्रांतस्य जडमतेर्ममेत्यन्वयः। विगलितो विरामो यस्मिम् कर्मणि तद् यथा तथा। तरणितनया यमुना।

Eng. Tr.:-May this श्रीकृष्ण the new तमाल tree, whose home is on the bank of the daughter of the sun, remove the encircling vexations of mine who am dull-minded, exhausted, and restlessly wandering often and often in this impassable worldly existence, which is a road to the uneven forest in the form of worldly pleasures !

आलिङ्गितो जलधिकन्यकया सलीलं
लग्नः प्रियङ्गुलतयेव तरुस्तमालः।
देहावसानसमये हृदये मदीये
देवश्चकास्तु भगवानरविन्दनाभः॥८॥

अन्वयः-प्रियङ्गुलतया लग्नः तरुः तमालः इव सलीलं जलधिकन्यकया आलिङ्गितः देवः भगवान्, अरविन्दनाभः देहावसानसमये मदीये हृदये चकास्तु।

व्याख्या:-जलधिकन्यकया लक्ष्म्या। देहावसानसमये मरणसमये। अरविन्दनाभो विष्णुः।

Eng. Tr.:-May the divine God विष्णु (with a lotus at his naval) sportively embraced by the (delicate) daughter of the ocean, like the तमाल tree by the प्रियंगु creeper, shine in my heart at the time of the termination of (my) body !

नयनानन्दसन्दोहतुन्दिलीकरणक्षमा।
तिरयत्वाशु सन्तापं कापि कादम्बिनी मम॥९॥

अन्वयः-नयना ....क्षमा कापि कादम्बिनी आशु मम सन्तापं तिरयतु।

व्याख्या:-नयनानंदस्य यः संदोहो भरस्तस्य तुन्दिलीकरणे वर्धने

क्षमा समर्था। कादम्बिनीत्वेनाध्यवसिता भगवतः कृष्णस्य मूर्तिः। इयमप्यतिशयोक्तिः।

Eng. Tr:-May that indescribable row of clouds (श्रीकृष्ण) which is able to enhance the mass of joy to the eyes, immediately remove my mental agony !

वाचा निर्मलया सुधामधुरया यां नाथ शिक्षामदा-
स्तां स्वप्नेऽपि न संस्पृशाम्यहमहं[१] भावावृतो निस्त्रपः।
इत्यागःशतशालिनं पुनरपि स्वीयेषु मां बिभ्रत-
स्त्वत्तो नास्ति दयानिधिर्यदुपते! मत्तो न मत्तोऽपरः॥१०॥

अन्वयः-हे यदुपते, नाथ सुधामधुरया निर्मलया वाचा यां शिक्षां (त्वं) अदाः तां अहं अहंभावावृतः निस्त्रपः च स्वप्नेऽपि न संस्पृशामि, इति आगःशतशलिनं मां पुनरपि स्वीयेषु विभ्रतः त्वत्तः (अन्यः) दयानिधिः नास्ति, मत्तः अपरः मत्तः नास्ति।

व्याख्या:-ईश्वरं प्रति कवेरुक्तिः। शिक्षां वेदरूपाम्। अहंभावावृतोऽहंकारेण व्याप्तः। निस्त्रपो निर्लज्जः। आगःशतशालिनमपराधशतकारिणम्। स्वीयेषु बिभ्रतः स्वकीयजनेषु गणयतः। मत्तो मदपेक्षया। इदं पद्यं पण्डितराजकृत-करुणालहर्याः केषुचित् पुस्तकेषु दृश्यते।

Eng.Tr.:-O Lord the best of यदुs! I, shameless and overwhelmed by ego, do not remember even in dream the advice you gave me by speech which was pure and as sweet as ambrosia. Thus although I have committed hundreds of faults, you consider me among your beloved creatures, there is no ocean of mercy other than you and no arrogant person other than myself.

पातालं व्रज याहि वा सुरपुरीमारोह मेरोः शिरः
पारावारपरम्परां तर तथाप्याशा न शान्तास्तव।

१. 'संस्मराम्यहमहंभावावृतो' इति पाठान्तरम्।

[1]आधिव्याधिपराहतो यदि सदा क्षेमं निजं वाञ्छसि
श्रीकृष्णेति रसायनं रसय रे! शून्यैः किमन्यैः श्रमैः॥११॥

अन्वयः-पातालं व्रज, वा सुरपुरीं याहि, मेरोः शिरः आरोह, पारावार-पम्पराम् तर, तथापि तव आशाः न शान्ताः (अतः) रे (प्राणिन्) आधिव्याधिपराहतः यदि सदा निजम् क्षेमं वाञ्छसि (तर्हि) श्रीकृष्ण इति रसायनं रसय, अन्यैः शून्यैः श्रमैः किम्।

व्याख्याः-आशाग्रस्तं नरं प्रति कवेरुक्तिः सुरपुरीमिन्द्रराजधानीममरावतीम्। परावारपरंपरां सागरश्रेणीम्। न शान्ता भविष्यन्तीति शेषः। पराहत आक्रान्तः। रसायनमौषधम्। रसय सेवस्व। शून्यैर्विफलैः। इदमपि पद्यं पण्डितराज-कृतकरुणालहर्याः केषुचित् पुस्तकेषु दृश्यते।

Eng.Tr.:-Go to Pātāla, or to the city of Gods or ascend the top of the Meru, cross the line of oceans, yet your desires will not cease. Overpowered by mental and physical pains, if you desire eternal bliss (क्षेम), taste the elixir "श्रीकृष्ण"; why resort to other efforts which are fruitless !

गणिकाऽजामिलमुख्यानवता भवता बताहमपि।
सीदन् भवमरुगर्ते करुणामूर्ते न सर्वथोपेक्ष्यः॥१२॥

अन्वयः-गणिकाजामिलमुख्यानवता भवता, भवमरुगर्ते सीदन् अहमपि हे करुणामूर्ते बत न सर्वथा उपेक्ष्यः।

व्याख्याः-नारायणं प्रति कवेर्वाक्यम्। गणिकाजामिलमुख्यान् गणिकाजामिलप्रभृतीन्। गणिका पिङ्गला नाम काचिद्वारवनिता। अजामिलो नाम कश्चिद्राजा। पिङ्गलाजामिलयोरुद्धारवृतं भागवते प्रसिद्धम्। अवता रक्षता। बतेति खेदे। सीदन् दुःखी। भवमरुगर्ते संसाररूपमरुस्थल्याम्। अत्रोपेक्षा-भावे हरेः करुणामृर्तित्वं पोषकम्। कवेः पापिष्ठत्वात्करुणया अभावे प्राप्ते तत्सम्पादकं गणिकेत्यादि सीदन्निति च विशेषणम्।

Eng.Tr.:-O mercy incarnate, Alas! you should not altogether neglect me, who am desponding in the desert of worldly existence, You-who protected sinners of whom गणिका and अजामिल are the chief.

---

१. 'आधिव्याधिजरापराहत' इति पाठान्तरम्।

मृद्वीका रसिता सिता समशिता स्फीतं निपीतं पयः
स्वर्यातेन सुधाऽप्यधायि कतिधा रम्भाधरः खण्डितः।
[१]सत्यं ब्रूहि मदीय जीव भवता भूयो भवे भ्राम्यता
कृष्णेत्यक्षरयोरयं मधुरिमोद्गारः क्वचिल्लक्षितः॥१३॥

अन्वयः-मृद्वीका...खण्डितः (तथापि) हे मदीय जीव त्वया भूयो भवे भ्राम्यता भवता कृष्णेत्यक्षरयोः अयं मधुरिमोद्गारः क्वचिल्लक्षितः (किम्), सत्यं ब्रूहि।

व्याख्या:-मृद्वीका द्राक्षा। रसिता सेविता। सिता खण्डशर्करा! समशिता भक्षिता। स्फीतं स्वच्छम्। स्वर्यातेन स्वर्गं गतवता। अधायि पीता। अयं संप्रत्यनुभूयमानः। लक्षितोऽनुभूतः। अत्र जीवे भगवन्नाममाहात्म्यादनेकजन्म-वृत्तान्ताध्यक्षीकरणशक्तिर्बोध्या।

Eng. Tr.-O my Soul, you have tasted the grapes, enjoyed sugar to your heart's desire, drunk ample milk, when you went to heaven, (how) many times did you drink (suck) nectar and bite the lower lip of रम्भा, yet, tell me the truth, did you anywhere in your wandering in the transmigratory existence witness that stream of sweetness (which oozes) from the two letters of which the word कृष्ण consists ?

वज्रपापमहीभृतां भवगदोद्रेकस्य सिद्धौषधं
मिथ्याज्ञाननिशाविशालतमसस्तिग्मांशुबिम्बोदयः।
क्रूरक्लेशमहीरुहामुरुतरज्वालाजटालः[२] शिखी
द्वारं निर्वृतिसद्मनो विजयते कृष्णेति वर्णद्वयम्॥१४॥

अन्वयः-पापमहीभृतां वज्रम भवगदोद्रेकस्य सिद्धौषधम्, मिथ्या-ज्ञाननिशाविशालतमसः तिग्मांशुबिम्बोदयः स्फूर्जत्क्लेशमहीरुहाम् उरुतज्वाला जटालः शिखी, निर्वृति सद्मनः द्वारम्, कृष्ण इति वर्णद्वयम् विजयते।

व्याख्या:-पापमहीभृतां पापपर्वतानाम्। भवगदोद्रकस्य संसारदीर्घरोगस्य। मिथ्याज्ञानमविद्याजन्यज्ञानमेव निशा तत्वसंबंधि यद्विशालं तमस्तस्या। तिग्मांशुः

---

१. 'तत्त्वं' इति पाठान्तरम्।

२. 'क्रूरक्लेश महीरुहा मुरुभरे ज्वाला जटालः' इति पाठान्तरम्।

सूर्यः। क्रूरंक्लेशमहीरुहामसह्यक्लेशरूपवृक्षाणाम्। उरुतरज्वालाजटालो दीर्घ-ज्वालाभिर्व्याप्तः। शिखी वह्निः। निर्वृतिसद्मनो मोक्षमन्दिरस्य। मालारूपं शुद्धपरं-परितरूपकमिदम्। इदं पद्यं पण्डितराजकृतकरुणालहर्याः केषुचित्पुस्तकेषु-दृश्यते।

Eng.Tr.:-Victorious indeed is the pair of letters "कृष्ण" which is a thunderbolt to the mountains in the form of sins, which is the specific medicine to the prolonged illness in the form of the worldly existence, which is the rise of the disc of the sun to the vast darkness of night in the form of erroneous knowledge, which is fire encircled by gigantic flames to the trees in the form of ruthless affections, which is the entrance to the place of final beatitude.

रे चेतः! कथयामि ते हितमिदं वृन्दावने चारय-
न्वृन्दं कोऽपि गवां नवाम्बुदनिभो बन्धुर्न कार्यस्त्वया।
सौन्दर्यामृतमुद्गिरद्भिरभितः संमोह्य मन्दस्मितै-
रेष त्वां तव वल्लभांश्च विषयानाशु क्षयं नेष्यति॥१५॥

अन्वयः:-रे चेतः इदं हितं ते कथयामि, वृन्दावने गवां वृन्दं चारयन् कोऽपि नवाम्बुदनिभः बन्धुः त्वया न कार्यः। (यतः) एषः अभितः सौन्दर्या-मृतमुद्गिरद्भिः मन्दस्मितैः संमोह्य, त्वां तव वल्लभान् च विषयान् आशु क्षयं नेष्यति॥

व्याख्या:-कवेः स्वमानसं प्रति वाक्यम्। इदं वक्ष्यमाणम्। वृन्दावने गवां वृन्दं चारयन्नित्यन्वयः। कोऽप्यर्थाच्छ्रीकृष्णः। नवाम्बुदनिभो नूतनमेघश्यामः। बन्धुः स्नेही। संमोह्य मोहयित्वा। वल्लभान् प्रियान्। विषयान् शब्दादीन्। श्रीकृष्ण-भक्त्या ज्ञानजननेनाज्ञाननिवर्तनात्तन्मूलको विषयरागो नष्टो भवेदिति भावः।

Eng.Tr.:-O mind, I tell you this for your benefit-you should not form friendship with a certain person (कृष्ण) resembling a new cloud (in complexion) and feeding a herd of cows in the वृन्दावन forest. (For) He will entice you by his charming smiles emitting all around the nectar of his beauty and will quickly lead you and your fond objects to extinction (i.e. will liberate you from this transmigratory existence.)

अव्याख्येयां वितरति परां प्रीतिमन्तर्निमग्ना
कण्ठे लग्ना हरति नितरां यान्तरध्वान्तजालम्।
तां द्राक्षाद्यैरपि बहुमतां माधुरीमुद्गिरन्तीं
कृष्णेत्याख्यां कथय रसने! यद्यसि त्वं रसज्ञा॥१६॥

अन्वयः-(हे) रसने यदि त्वं रसज्ञा असि (तर्हि) या ('कृष्ण' इति आख्या) अन्तनिर्मग्नं अव्याख्येयां परां प्रीतिं वितरति या कण्ठे लग्ना नितरां आन्तरध्वान्तजालं हरति, तां द्राक्षाद्यैरपि बहुमतां माधुरीं उद्गिरन्तीं "कृष्ण" इत्याख्यां कथय।

व्याख्याः-अव्याख्येयामनिर्वचनीयाम्। आन्तरमन्तःस्थितं ध्वान्तजालं गाढान्धकारम्। अज्ञानमित्यर्थः। रसने जिह्वे।

Eng.Tr.:-O tongue, if your are an appreciator of sweetness, repeat that name "कृष्ण" giving out sweetness superior even to the grapes, which when it occupies the interior of the heart, gives inexplicable removes the mass of internal darkness.

सन्त्येवास्मिञ्जगति बहवः पक्षिणो रम्यरूपा-
स्तेषां मध्ये मम तु महती वासना चातकेषु।
यैरध्यक्षैरथ निजसखं नीरदं स्मारयद्भि-
श्चित्तारू[१]ढं भवति किमपि ब्रह्म कृष्णाभिधानम्॥१७॥

अन्वयः-अस्मिन् जगति बहवः रम्यरूपाः पक्षिणः सन्ति एव तेषां मध्ये चातकेषु मम तु महती वासना। यैः अध्यक्षैः अथ निजसखं नीरदं स्मारयद्भिः कृष्णाभिधानं किमपि ब्रह्म चित्तारूढं भवति।

व्याख्याः-तेषां पक्षिणाम्। वासनाऽऽदरबुद्धिः। यैश्चातकैः। अध्यक्षैः प्रत्यक्षैः। अथ प्रत्यक्षानन्तरम्। निजसखं प्रीतिकारित्वात्स्वमित्रम्। चित्तारूढं स्मृतिविषयम्। अत्र चातकदर्शनेन तन्मित्रभूतस्य मेघस्य मेघस्मरणेन च सादृश्य-सम्बन्धात्कृष्णस्य स्मरणं वर्णितम्। स्मरणालंकारोऽयम्।

Eng.Tr.:-There are many beautiful birds in this world; but among them all, I have a great fondness for चातक birds.

---

१. 'स्मृत्यारूढं' इति पाठान्तरम्।

(For) it is on account of them when they fall within the range of (my) sight and (consequently) remind (me) of their friend, cloud, that the indescribable ब्रह्म, named कृष्ण rises (i.e. flashes) in my mind.

विष्वद्रीच्या भुवनमखिलं भासते यस्य भासा
सर्वासामप्यहमिति विदां गूढमालम्बनं यः।
तं पृच्छन्ति स्वहृदयमनावेदिनो[1] विष्णुमन्या-
नन्यायोऽयं शिव! शिव!! नृणां केन वा वर्णनीयः॥१८॥

अन्वयः-यस्य विष्वद्रीच्या भासा अखिलं भुवनं भासते, यः सर्वासां 'अहं' इति विदां गूढमालम्बनम्। तं विष्णुं स्वहृदयं अनावेदिनः अन्यान् पृच्छन्ति। शिव शिव अयं नृणां अन्यायः केन वा वर्णनीयः।

व्याख्याः-विष्वगञ्चतीति विश्वद्रीची सर्वव्यापिनी तया। यस्य विष्णोः। भासा प्रकाशेन। तस्य भासा सर्वमिदं विभातीति श्रुतिः। अहमिति विदामहमित्याकारकज्ञानानाम्। अहंकारप्रत्ययानामिति यावत्। विदित्यत्र सम्पदादित्वाद् भावे क्विप्। गूढं विवेकेनापि निर्णेतुमशक्यम्।आलम्बनमाश्रयः। तत्त्वतो जीवब्रह्मणोरैक्याद्रजतज्ञानाधिष्ठानशुक्तिकावत् सकलाहंकारज्ञानाद्यधिष्ठानं ब्रह्मैवेति भावः। तं विष्णुमन्यान् पृच्छन्तीत्यन्वयः। स्वहृदयमनावेदिनः स्वहृदयमजानानाः। स्वहृदय एव विष्णुर्वर्तत इत्यजानाना इत्यर्थः। अयं विचित्रालंकारः। इष्टसिद्ध्यर्थमिष्टैषिणा क्रियमाणमिष्टाननुकूलाचरणं विचित्रम्। अस्मिन् पद्ये जीवरूपेण सकललोकप्रत्यक्षसिद्धस्य परमेश्वरस्य प्रतिपत्यर्थं मुख्यानुकूले स्वहृदये प्रष्टव्ये परान् प्रति प्रश्नोऽनुकूलाभासः।

Eng.Tr.:-Alas ! who can describe the injustice of those men, who, not knowing their own hearts, inquire of others about विष्णु, by whose brilliance pervading the universe, the whole world shines and who is the incomprehensible basis of all knowledge of the consciousness of "अहं" (one's self).

सेवायां यदि साभिलाषमसि रे! लक्ष्मीपतिः सेव्यतां
चिन्तायामसि सस्पृहं यदि तदा चक्रायुधश्चिन्त्यताम्।

---

१. 'स्वहृदयतलावेदिनो' इति पाठान्तरम्।

आलापं यदि काङ्क्षसि स्मररिपोर्गाथा तदालाप्यतां
स्वापं वाञ्छसि चेन्निरर्गलसुखे चेतः सुखं सुप्यताम्॥१९॥

अन्वयः-हे सखे चेतः यदि त्वं सेवायां साभिलाषं असि (तर्हि) लक्ष्मीपतिः सेव्यताम्। चिन्तायां यदि सस्पृहं असि तदा चक्रायुधः चिन्त्यताम्। आलापं यदि कांक्षसि, सदा स्मररिपोः गाथा (त्वया) आलप्यताम्। स्वापं वांछसि चेत्, निरर्गलसुखे सुप्यताम्।

व्याख्या:-कवेः स्वचित्तं प्रत्युक्तिः। गाथा भगवद्गीतादिरूपा। निरर्गलसुखे निष्प्रतिबन्धसुखे। ब्रह्मानन्द इत्यर्थः। सुप्यतां विषयान्तराद्विरम्य तत्रैव स्थीयताम्।

Eng.Tr.:-O friend mind, if you desire to serve, serve the consort of लक्ष्मी; if you desire to contemplate, contemplate over विष्णु, (whose weapon is the disc). If you want to converse, sing the verses of शिव; if you want to sleep, sleep in unlimited joy (i.e. the joy of Brahma

भवग्रीष्मप्रौढातपनिवहसन्तप्तवपुषो
बलादुन्मूल्य द्राङ्निगडमविवेकव्यतिकरम्।
विशुद्धेऽस्मिन्नात्मामृतसरसि नैराश्यशिशिरे
विगाहन्ते दूरीकृतकलुषजालाः सुकृतिनः॥२०॥

अन्वयः-दूरीकृतकलुषजालाः सुकृतिनः भवग्रीष्म...वपुषः द्राग् निगडं अविवेकव्यतिकरं बलात् उन्मूल्य अस्मिन् विशुद्धे नैराश्यशिशिरे आत्मामृत-सरसि विगाहन्ते।

व्याख्या:-एकदेशविवर्ति सावयवं रूपकमिदम्। अत्रसहचरैन्नि-गडादिरूपकैः कृतिषु गजरूपकमाक्षिप्यते। भवः संसार एव प्रौढातपनिवहस्तेन सन्तप्तं वपुर्येषां ते। निगडं बन्धम्। अविवेकव्यतिकरमज्ञानसमूहम्। आत्मैवा-मृतसरस्तस्मिन्। नैराश्येनाशाराहित्येन शिशिरे शीतले। दूरीकृतं कलुषजालं पापसमूहो यैस्ते।

Eng.Tr.:-Blessed persons, removing the net of the sin, with their bodies scorched by the excessive heat of the summer in the form of this world breaking immediately the chain of contact with ignorance, bathe in this excessively pure pond of the bliss of *Ātmā*, cool on account of hopelessness.

बन्धोन्मुक्त्ये खलु मखमुखान्कुर्वते कर्मपाशा
नन्तःशान्त्यै मुनिशतमतानल्पचिन्तां भजन्ते।
तीर्थे मज्जन्त्यशुभजलधेः पारमारोढुकामाः
सर्वं प्रामादिकमिह भवभ्रान्तिभाजां नराणाम्॥२१॥

अन्वयः:-बन्धोन्मुक्त्यै खलु मखमुखान् कर्मपाशान् कुर्वते, अन्तःशान्त्यै मुनिशतमतानल्पचिन्तां भजन्ते, अशुभजलधेः पारमारोढुकामाः तीर्थे मज्जन्ति। भवभ्रान्तिभाजां नशणां इह सर्वं प्रामादिकं (विद्यते)।

व्याख्या:-अयं विचित्रालंकारः। अत्र भवभ्रान्तैर्नरैरिष्टसिद्ध्यर्थं क्रियमाणमिष्टविपरीताचरणं वर्णितम्। अत्र प्रथमतृतीयचरणगतं विचित्रं रूपकानुप्राणितम्। बन्धोन्मुक्त्यै संसाररूपबन्धमोचनाय। मखमुखान् यज्ञादीन्। अन्तःशांत्यै चित्तशांत्यै। मुनिशतमतानामनल्पचिन्तामधिकचिन्तनम्। अशुभजलधेरमङ्गलरूपसमुद्रस्य। प्रामादिकं विवेकशून्यम्। इहास्मिन्न् जगति। भवभ्रान्तिभाजां संसारभ्रान्तचित्तानाम्।

Eng.Tr.:-Everything done by persons, who are perplexed in this world, is erroneous. They perform a number of कर्मन्s (rites) of which the sacrifices are chief, for getting freedom from bondage, contemplate much over the opinions of hundreds of मुनिs (Sages) and bathe in holy places with a desire of crossing the sea of sins.

प्रथमं चुम्बितचरणा जङ्घजानूरुनाभिहृदयानि।
आश्लिष्य भावना मे खेलतु विष्णोर्मुखाब्जशोभायाम्॥२२॥

अन्वयः:-मे भावना प्रथमं चुम्बितचरणा (पश्चात्) जंघाजानूरुनाभिहृदयानि आश्लिष्य विष्णोर्मुखाब्जशोभायां खेलतु।

व्याख्या:-चुम्बितचरणा ध्यातविष्णुपदा। भावना ध्यानवृत्तिविशेषः। खेलतु रमताम्।

Eng.Tr.:-May my imagination sport on the splendour of the lotus-like face of विष्णु, after first kissing (contemplating over) the feet and then embracing (contemplating) the legs, the knees, the thighs, the naval and the chest !

मलयानिलकालकूटयो रमणीकुन्तलभोगिभोगयोः।
श्वपचात्मभुवोर्निरन्तरा मम भू[१]यात्परमात्मनि स्थितिः॥२३॥

अन्वयः-मलयानिलकालकूटयोः (निरन्तरा) रमणीकुन्तलभोगिभोगयोः (निरन्तरा) श्वपचात्मभुवोः (निरन्तरा) (ईदृशी) परमात्मनि स्थितिः मे भूयात्।

व्याख्या:-शान्तरसध्वनिरयम्। प्रथमार्ध उत्तमाधमयोरुपक्रमं कृत्वा द्वितीयार्धेऽधमोत्तमवचनं वक्तुर्ब्रह्मात्मकतयोत्तमाधमज्ञानवैकल्यद्योतनाय। कुन्तलाः केशाः। भोगिभोगः सर्पशरीरम्। श्वपचात्मभुवोश्चण्डालज्ञानिनोः। निरन्तरा तारतम्यशून्या। इदं स्थितेर्विशेषणम्।

Eng.Tr.:-May I experience the residence in the great soul (unity with it), where one sees non-difference between the breeze coming from the मलय mountain and the body of a serpent and between Chandal and Cupid.

निखिलं जगदेव नश्वरं पुनरस्मिन्नितरां कलेवरम्।
अथ तस्य कृते कियानयं क्रियते हन्त! जनैः[२] परिश्रमः॥२४॥

अन्वयः-निखिलं जगदेव नश्वरं, पुनः अस्मिन् (जगति) कलेवरं नितरां (नश्वरं), हन्त। अथ तस्य (कलेवरस्य) कृते कियानयं परिश्रमः जनैः क्रियते।

व्याख्या:-नश्वरं नाशशीलम्। अस्मिन् जगति। कलेवरं पुनर्नितरां श्वरमित्यन्वयः। कलेवरं शरीरम्। तस्य कलेवरस्य। हन्तेति खेदे।

Eng.Tr.:-The very whole universe is transitory and in it much more so is our body; alas ! What great troubles are undergone by men for its sake?

प्रतिपलमखिलाँल्लोकान्मृत्युमुखं प्रविशतो निरीक्ष्यापि।
हा! हन्त! किमिति चित्तं विरमति नाद्यापि विषयेभ्यः॥२५॥

अन्वयः-प्रतिपल...चित्तं किमिति अद्यापि विषयेभ्यः न विरमति।

व्याख्या:-प्रतिपलं प्रतिक्षणम्। प्रसिद्धकारणसत्वेऽपि कार्याभाववर्णनाद्विशेषोक्तिरियम्।

---

१. 'जाता' इति पाठान्तरम्।
२. 'मया' इति पाठान्तरम्।

Eng. Tr.:-Even after marking every moment all people entering the jaws of Death yet alas! why does not mind desist from the worldly objects?

सपदि विलयमेतु राज्यलक्ष्मी-
रुपरि पतन्त्वथवा कृपाणधाराः।
अपहरतुतरां शिरः कृतान्तो
मम तु मतिर्न मनागपैतु[१] धर्मात्॥२६॥

अन्वयः-राज्यलक्ष्मीः सपदि विलयम् एतु, अथवा उपरि कृपाण धाराः पतन्तु (वा) कृतान्तः शिरः अपहरतुतराम् तु मम मतिः धर्मात् मनाक् न अपैतु।

व्याख्या:-एषाऽधर्मेणापि रिपुर्जेतव्य इति वदन्तं प्रति कस्यचिद्राज्ञ उक्तिः। कृपाणः खड्गः। कृतान्तो यमः। नापैतु न चलतु। धर्मवीरध्वनिरयम्।

Eng. Tr.:-Let royal splendour vanish all at once, or let sword-edges fall over (my body). The God of Death may better take away my head but let not my mind (i.e. thought) budge an inch (lit.a little) from duty.

अपि बहलदहनजालं मूर्ध्नि रिपुर्मे निरन्तरं धमतु।
पातयतु वासिधारामहमणुमात्रं न किञ्चिदपि[२] भाषे॥२७॥

अन्वयः-मे रिपुः (मे) मूर्ध्नि निरन्तरं बहलदहनजालमपि धमतु, वा असिधारां पातयतु, अहमणुमात्रं न किञ्चिद् अपि भाषेपि।

व्याख्या:-दुर्भाषणं परिहरतः कस्यचिदुक्तिरियम्। बहलदहनजालं प्रचण्डवह्निसमूहम्। धमतु प्रदीपयतु।

Eng. Tr.:-Let my enemy incessantly blow excessive fire on my head or fall the edge of the sword (on it), I shall not talk even one offensive word.

तरणोपायमपश्यन्नपि मामक जीव! ताम्यसि कुतस्त्वम्।
चेतःसरणावस्यां किं नागन्ता कदापि नन्दसुतः॥२८॥

---

१. 'मनागपैति' इति पाठान्तरम्।

२. किञ्चिदाभाषे, किञ्चिदपभोषे' इति पाठान्तरद्वयम्।

अन्वयः-हे मामक जीव तरणोपायं अपश्यन्नपि त्वं कुतः ताम्यसि, अस्यां चेतःसरणौ नन्दसुतः कदापि न आगन्ता किम्।

व्याख्याः-तरणोपायं भवसागरतरणोपायम्। चेतःसरणौ चित्तवृत्तौ। किं नागन्ता किं नागमिष्यति। नन्दसुतस्मरणमेव तरणोपाय इति त्वं चिन्तां माकार्षीरिति भावः।

Eng.Tr.:-O my soul, though not conversant with any means to save (yourself) why do you pine ? Will the son of Nanda (Krishna) never (come into the way of your mind) be remembered by you?

श्रियो मे मा सन्तु क्षणमपि च माद्यद्गजघटा-
मदभ्राम्यद्भृङ्गावलिमधुरझङ्कारसुभगाः।
निमग्नानां यासु द्रविणमदिरा[1]घूर्णितदृशां
सपर्यासौकर्यं हरिचरणयोरस्तमयते॥२९॥

अन्वयः-क्षणमपि च माद्यद्गजघटामदभ्राम्यद्भृङ्गावलिमधुरझंकारसुभगाः श्रियः मे मा सन्तु, यासु निमग्नानां द्रविणमदिराघूर्णितदृशां (नराणां) हरिचरणयोः सपर्यासौकर्यं अस्तम् अयते।

व्याख्याः-श्रियः संपदः। माद्यन्ती या गजघटा करिब्रजस्तस्या मदेन भ्राम्यन्ती या भृङ्गावलिस्तस्या मधुरझंकारैः सुभगाः। यासु श्रीषु। द्रविणमदिराघूर्णितदृशां संपत्तिमद्यसेवनेन भ्रान्तदृशाम्। सपर्यासौकर्यमाराधनासुलभत्वम्। अस्तमयते नष्टं भवति। अयं तिरस्कारालंकारः। तिरस्कारश्च दोषविशेषानुबन्धाद् गुणत्वेन प्रसिद्धस्यापि द्वेषः।

Eng.Tr.:-May I not even for a moment possess the wealth which is attractive owing to the humming of the row of bees, hovering over the rut of the crowds of (rutting) elephants; because in the case of the people merged in लक्ष्मी the ease of worship of the feet of Hari disappears owing to their eyesight rolling (frenzied) through the wine in the form of wealth.

किं निःशङ्कं शेषे शेषे वयसः समागतो मृत्युः।
अथवा सुखं शयसीथा निकटे जागर्ति जाह्नवी जननी॥३०॥

---

१. 'द्रविणरसपर्याकुलदृशां' इति पाठान्तरम्।

अन्वयः-वयसः शेषे किं निःशङ्क शेषे (यतः) मृत्युः समागतः। अथवा, सुखं शयीथाः (यतः) निकटे जननी जाह्नवी जागर्ति।

व्याख्या:-स्वजीवं प्रति कवेरुक्तिः। निःशंकं निर्भयम्। शेषे स्वपिषि। वयसः शेषे वार्धके। केषाञ्चिन्मतेऽयमाक्षेपालंकारः। अप्पदीक्षितस्य पण्डितराजं प्रत्युक्तिरियमिति लोकप्रवादः।

Eng.Tr.:-Why do you sleep fearlessly in the remaining part of (your) life as death has arrived ? Or sleep happily as the mother Ganges is awake near (you).

सन्तापयामि किमहं धावं धावं धरातले हृदयम्।
अस्ति मम शिरसि सततं नन्दकुमारः प्रभुः परमः॥३१॥

अन्वयः-धरातले धावं धावं किमहं हृदयं सन्तापयामि। (यतः) मम शिरसि सततं परमः प्रभुः नन्दकुमारः अस्ति।

व्याख्या:-धावं धावं धावित्वा धावित्वा। अत्र वक्तृगता धृतिर्व्यज्यते।

Eng.Tr.:-Why do I torment my heart by running frequently. (after everything) on the surface of the earth ? The Supreme Lord, the son of नन्द, is there always over my head (i.e.to rescue me).

रे रे मनो मम मनोभवशासनस्य[१]
पादाम्बुजद्वयमनारतमानमन्तम्।
किं मां निपातयसि संसृतिगर्तमध्ये
नैतावता तव गमिष्यति पुत्रशोकः॥३२॥

अन्वयः-रे रे मम मनः मनोभवशासनस्य पादाम्बुजद्वयं अनारतं आनमन्तं मां संसृतिगर्तमध्ये किं निपातयसि। एतावता तव पुत्रशोकः न गमिष्यति।

व्याख्या:-कवेः स्वमनः प्रत्युक्तिः मनोभवशासनस्य पादाम्बुजद्वयमानमन्तं मां संसृतिगर्तमध्ये किं निपातयसीत्यन्वयः। मनोभवशासनस्य मदनशत्रोः शिवस्य मनोभवपदप्रयोगेणात्र मदनस्य मनस उत्पत्तिः सूच्यते। अनारतम-विरतम्। संसृतिगर्तमध्ये संसारश्वभ्रमध्ये। एतावताऽनेनोपायेन। तव मनसः।

---

१. 'मनोभवशातनस्य' इति पाठान्तरम्।

पुत्रशोकः स्वपुत्रमदननाशजन्यशोकः। अत्र मदनस्य मनःपुत्रत्वेन कल्पनं तस्य मनः प्रभवत्वात्। अत्र प्रागुक्तः प्रत्यनीकालंकारः।

Eng.Tr.:-O my mind, why do you hurt me into the pit of the transmigratory existence-me who am incessantly bowing down at the lotus like feet of the slayer of the mind-born (your son-Cupid)? By doing this much your grief for the loss of your son will not cease.

मरकतमणिमेदिनीधरो वा
तरुणतरस्तरुरेष वा तमालः।
रघुपतिमवलोक्य तत्र दूरा-
दृषिनिकरैरिति संशयः प्रपेदे।।३३।।

अन्वयः-तत्र दूराद् रघुपतिं अवलोक्य एषः मरकतमणिमेदिनीधरः वा तरुणतरः तमालः तरुः इति ऋषिनिकरैः संशयः प्रपेदे।

व्याख्याः-मरकतमणीनां मेदिनीधरो वृक्षः। मरकतो हरिन्मणिः। तत्र दण्डकारण्ये। दूरादवलोक्येत्यन्वयः। अयं ससंदेहालंकारः।

Eng.Tr.:-There (in the Daṇḍakāraṇya) at the sight of the lord of Raghus from a distance, a doubt was entertained by the groups of sages as to whether it was a mountain of emeralds or a young Tamāla tree.

तरणितनया किं स्यादेषा? न तोयमयी हि सा
मरकतमणिज्योत्स्ना वा स्यान्न सा मधुरा कुतः।
इति रघुपतेः कायच्छायाविलोकनतत्परै-
रुदितकुतुकैः कैः कैरादौ न संदिदिहे जनैः।।३४।।

अन्वयः-एषा तरणितनया स्यात् किम्? न, सा कुतः (ईदृशी) मधुरा? इति विलोकनतत्परैः उदितकुतुकैः कैः कैः जनैः आदौ रघुपतेः कायच्छाया न सन्दिदिहे? (सवैरेव सन्दिदिहे इति अर्थः।)

व्याख्याः-रघुपतिं पश्यतां दण्डकारण्यवासिनां संदेहा अत्र निबद्धाः। अयं निश्चयगर्भः ससंदेहः। तरणितनया यमुना। एषा पुरो दृश्यमाना। रघुपतेः कायक्छाया देहकान्तिः। उदितकुतुकैः प्राप्तकुतूहलैः।

Eng.Tr.:-Is this possibly the daughter of the Sun? No. She, indeed, is full of water; or is this the lustre of emerald? No. How can it be so pleasant? What persons were there, who, being curiously absorbed in observation, did not mistake the complexion of the body of the lord of रघुs (for यमुना etc.) thus?

चपला जलदाच्च्युता लता वा
तरुमुख्यादिति संशये निमग्नः।
गुरुनिःश्वसितैः कपिर्मनीषी
निरणैसीदथ तां वियोगिनीति॥३५॥

अन्वयः:-जलदात् च्युता चपला (इयं) वा तरुमुख्यात् च्युता लता (इयं) इति संशये निमग्नेः मनीषी कपिः अथ गुरुनिश्वसितैः तां (सीतां) वियोगिनी इति निरणैषीत्।

व्याख्या:-अयं निश्चयान्तः ससंदेहः। चपला विद्युत्। तरुमुख्याच्च्युता लता वेत्यन्वयः। गुरुनिश्वसितैर्दीर्घनिःश्वासैः। कपिर्हनूमान्। मनीषी चतुरः। निरणैन्निश्चिकाय। तां सीताम्। वियोगिनी विरहिणी।

Eng.Tr.:-The wise monkey (हनुमान्) entertained doubts like "Is this the lightning dropped down from a cloud? or a creeper dropped from a celestial tree? Afterwards, he ascertained that she was a वियोगिनी lady (i.e. सीता) from her deep long sighs.

भूतिर्नीचगृहेषु विप्रसदने दारिद्र्यकोलाहलो
नाशो हन्त! सतामसत्पथजुषामायुः समानां शतम्।
दुर्नीतिं तव वीक्ष्य कोपदहनज्वालाजटालोऽपि सन्
किं कुर्वे जगदीश! यत्पुनरहं दीनो भवानीश्वरः[१]॥३६॥

अन्वयः:-First two lines, the same. हे जगदीश, तव दुर्नीतिं वीक्ष्य कोपदहनज्वालाजटालोऽपि सन् अहं कि कुर्वे? यद् अहं दीनः भवान् पुनः ईश्वरः।

---

१. 'भवानीपतिः' इति पाठान्तरम्।

२ **व्याख्या**:-भूतिः सम्पत्तिः। सतां साधूनाम्। असत्पथजुषां दुर्मार्गवर्तिनां खलानाम्। समानां संवत्सराणाम्। कोपदहनज्वालाजटालोऽपि क्रोधाग्निज्वालाव्याप्तोऽपि। अनेनास्मिल्लोके साधूनां सुखं खलानां च दुःखमिति न नियम इति दर्शितम्।

Eng.Tr.:-There is prosperity (reigning) in the houses of the wicked, (while) in the house of a Brahmin there is the uproar of poverty, also! the good are ruined (while) followers of an evil path have a life of a hundred years (in store for them). O Lord of this world, although I am filled with the flames of the fire in the form of anger, at the sight of this injustice of yours, what shall I do since I am a pauper, whereas you are the lord ?

आमुलाद्रत्नसानोर्मलयवलयितादा च कूलात्पयोधे-
र्यावन्तः सन्ति काव्यप्रणयनपटवस्ते विशङ्कं वदन्तु।
मृद्वीकामध्यनिर्यन्मसृणरसझरीमाधुरीभाग्यभाजां
वाचामाचार्यतायाः पदमनुभवितुं कोऽस्ति धन्यो मदन्यः॥३७॥

अन्वय:-रत्नसानोः मूलात् आ मलयवलयितात् पयोधेः च कूलात् आ यावन्तः काव्यप्रणयनपटवः सन्ति ते विशङ्कं वदन्तु। मृद्वीका...भाजां वाचां आचार्यतायाः पदं अनुभवितुं मदन्यः कः धन्यः अस्ति।

व्याख्या:-अतः परं पण्डितराजो ग्रन्थमुपसंहरन्नात्मानमुद्दिश्य ब्रवीति रत्नसानोः सुमेरोरामूलान्मूलमभिव्याप्य। मलयवलयितान्मलयपर्वतवेष्ठितात्। कूलात्तीरात्। पयोधेर्दक्षिणं तीरं मलयवलयितमिति प्रसिद्धमेव। कूलादा कूलमभिव्याप्य। अखिले भारतवर्ष इति चरणतात्पर्यम्। काव्यप्रणयनपटवः काव्यनिर्माणकुशलाः। विशङ्कं निर्भयम्। न तान् वारयाम इति भावः। मृद्वीकाया द्राक्षाया मध्यान्निर्यती निःसरन्ती या रसझरी रसप्रवाहस्तस्या मधुर्या भाग्यं भजन्ति तासाम्। आचार्यता दीक्षाकर्तुता। अत्र स्वकवित्वप्रयुक्तात्मोत्कर्षज्ञानजन्यः पण्डितराजगतो गर्वो व्यंग्यः।

Eng.Tr.:-Let all those declare undoubtedly those who

are wellversed in composing poems, (those living) from the foot of the Meru mountain down to the shores of the Ocean, encircled by the Malaya Mountain, if there is any blessed person other than myself (blessed enough) to experience the position (or dignity) of being the master of words, possessed of the fortune of having the sweetness of the flow of the sweet juice, issuing out of the interior of grapes.

गिरां देवी वीणागुणरणनहीनादरकरा
यदीयानां वाचाममृतमयमाचामति रसम्।
वचस्तस्याकर्ण्य श्रवणसुभगं पण्डितपते-
रधुन्वन्मूर्धानं नृपशुरथवायं पशुपतिः॥३८॥

अन्वयः-वीणागुणरणनहीनादरकरा गिरा देवी यदीयानां वाचां अमृतमयं रसं आचामति तस्य पण्डितपतेः श्रवणसुभगं वचः आकर्ण्य मूर्धानं अधुन्वन् अयं नृपशुः अथवा पशुपतिः (विद्यते)।

व्याख्याः-गिरां देवी सरस्वती। वीणाया गुणरणने तन्त्रीशब्दकर्मणि हीनादरः करो हस्तो यस्याः सा। आचामति पिबति। आस्वादयतीति यावत्। श्रवणसुभगं कर्णमधुरम्। पण्डितपतेः पण्डितराजजगन्नाथस्य। अध ुन्वन्नचालयन्। नृपशुर्नरो भूत्वा पशुतुल्यः। पशुपतिः शिवः। तद्व्द्रिरक्त इति भावः। पण्डितपतेर्वचांस्याकर्ण्य यस्य चित्तं न द्रवते स मुक्तोऽथ वा पशुरिति तात्पर्यार्थः।

Eng.Tr.:-He must be either शिव or a beast in the form of a man who does not nod his head on hearing the poems (lit. speech) of the lord of poets (i.e. जगन्नाथपण्डित himself) charming to the ears-(the lord of poets) the sentiment of whose poetical composition, full of nectar, the goddess of speech sips, suffering her hand to disregard the playing upon the chords of her lute.

मधु द्राक्षा साक्षादमृतमथ वामाधरसुधा
कदाचित्केषांचिन्न खलु विदधीरन्नपि मुदम्।

ध्रुवं ते जीवन्तोऽप्यहह मृतका मन्दमतयो
न येषामानन्दं जनयति जगन्नाथभणितिः॥३९॥

अन्वयः-मधु, द्राक्षा, साक्षात अमृतम्, अथ वामाधरसुधा कदाचित् केषाञ्चित् खलु मुदम् न अपि विदधीरन् (किन्तु) जगन्नाथभणितिः येषां आनन्दं न जनयति अहह ! ते मन्दमतयः जीवन्तः अपि ध्रुवं मृतकाः (सन्ति)।

व्याख्या:-अथ च वामाधरसुधा कान्ताधरामृतम्। न विदधीरन्न कुर्युः। मुदमानन्दम्। ध्रुवं निश्चयेन। अहहेत्यनुकम्पायाम्। मृतका मृततुल्या इत्यर्थः।

Eng.Tr.:-Honey, grapes, nectar itself and also the nectar on the lower lips of lovely ladies may not give delight even to some on some occasions (कदाचित्). But alas ! those dull persons in whom the poems of Jagannāth do not produce delight, are really dead, though (they are) living.

निर्माणे यदि मार्मिकोऽसि नितरामत्यन्तपाकद्रवन्-
मृद्वीकामधुमाधुरीमदपरीहारोद्धुराणां गिराम्।
काव्यं तर्हि सखे सुखेन कथय त्वं सम्मुखे मादृशां
नो चेद् दुष्कृतमात्मना कृतमिव स्वान्ताद्बहिर्मा कृथाः॥४०॥

अन्वयः-हे सखे! यदि त्वम् अत्यन्तपाकद्रवन्मृद्वीकामधुमारीमदपरीहारोद् धुराणाम् गिरम् निर्माणे नितराम् मार्मिकः असि, तर्हि मादृशां सम्मुखे सुखने काव्यम् कथय, चेत् नो आत्मना कृतम् दुष्कृतम् इव स्वान्ताद् बहिः मा कृथाः।

व्याख्या:-पण्डितराजस्यान्यं कञ्चित् कविं प्रत्युक्तिः। अत्यन्तपाकेन द्रवद् यन्मृद्वीकामधु तस्य माधुरीमदस्य परीहार उद्धुराणां समर्थानाम्। दुष्कृतं पापम्। मत्कृतकाव्यतुल्यमन्यत् काव्यं नास्तीति कवेराशयः।

Eng.Tr.:-If you are exceedingly capable of composing (words) poems which are successful in removing the pride of the sweetness of juice dropping from the grapes which are fully ripe, then, friend, you may, with pleasure, sing your poem before me; if not, do not show it outside your own heart, like a sinful act committed by you.

मद्वाणि मा कुरु विषादमनादरेण
मात्सर्य्यमग्नमनसां सहसा खलानाम्।
काव्यारविन्दमकरन्दमधुव्रताना-
मास्येषु धास्यसितमां कियतो[१] विलासान्॥४१॥

अन्वयः-हे मद्वाणि! मात्सर्यमग्नमनसाम् खलानाम् सहसा अनादरेण विषादम् मा कुरु (यतः) काव्यारविन्दमकन्दमधुव्रतानाम् आस्येषु कति विलासान् नो धास्यतितमाम्।

व्याख्याः-खलानामनादरेण विषादं मा कुर्वित्यन्वयः। काव्यारविन्दमकरन्दमधुव्रतानां काव्यकमलमकरन्दस्य सेवने भ्रमरभूतानां सहृदयानाम्। आस्येषु मुखेषु। धास्यसि धारयिष्यसि। रसिकास्त्वामासाद्य धन्यवादात् करिष्यन्त्येवेति भावः।

Eng.Tr.:-O my speech, do not be desponding because of the disrespect shown towards you by the wicked whose minds are full of jealousy because you will create immense pleasure on the faces of those, who are like bees to the honey in the lotus in the form of poetry.

विद्वांसो वसुधातले परवचःश्लाघासु वाचंयमा
भूपालाः कमलाविलासमदिरोन्मीलन्मदाघूर्णिताः।
आस्ये धास्यति कस्य लास्यमधुना धन्यस्य कामालस-
स्वर्वामाधरमाधुरीमधरयन् वाचां विपाको मम॥४२॥

अन्वयः-वसुधातले विद्वांसः परवचः श्लाघासु वाचंयमाः (सन्ति) भूपालाः कमलाविलासमदिरोन्मीलन्मदाघूर्णिताः (सन्ति), अधुना कामालसस्वर्वामा...धरयन् मम वाचां विपाकः कस्य धन्यस्य आस्ये लास्यं धास्यति।

व्याख्याः-वाचंयमा मूकाः। कमलाविलासरूपा या मदिरा तयोन्मीलन्नुत्पद्यमानो यो मदस्तेनाघूर्णिता भ्रान्ताः। कस्य धनस्यास्य इत्यन्वयः। लास्यं नृत्यम्। कामालसानां स्वर्वामानामप्सरसामधरमाधुरीम्। अधरयंस्तिरस्कुर्वन्।

---

१. 'कति नो' इति पाठान्तरम्।

वाचां विपाको वाक्प्रौढिः। इदं पद्यं पण्डितराजकृतप्राणाभरणकाव्यस्यारम्भेऽपि दृश्यते। तत्र स्वव्याख्यायां पण्डितराजेनैवोक्तम्। विद्वांस इत्यादि प्रायदर्शनाभिप्रायमेतत्। तेन सहृदयैर्न मनागपि विमनायितव्यमिति।

Eng. Tr.:-On the surface of the Earth (in this world) the learned people are very sparing in praising the poems of others; the kings are staggering with the intoxication arising from the wine in the form of the pleasures of wealth. Now, on whose face, will the best poetry of mine, which surpasses the sweetness of the lowerlip of the impassioned heavenly damsels, dance? (i.e. those who will enjoy my poetry will be really blessed.)

धुर्यैरपि माधुर्यैर्द्राक्षाक्षीरेक्षुमाक्षिकसुधानाम्[१]।
वन्द्यैव माधुरीयं पण्डितराजस्य कवितायाः॥४३॥

अन्वयः:-द्राक्षाक्षीरेक्षु...सुधानाम् धुर्यैः माधुर्यैः अपि पण्डितराजस्य कवितायाः इयं माधुरी वन्द्या एव।

व्याख्या:-धुर्यैः श्रेष्ठैः। माक्षिकं मधु।

Eng. Tr.:-The sweetness of the verses of the prince of poets (जगन्नाथ himself) is really praiseworthy even to the best sweetness of grapes, milk, sugarcane, honey and nectar.

शास्त्रण्याकलितानि नित्यविधयः सर्वेऽपि सम्भाविता
दिल्लीवल्लभपाणिपल्लवतले नीतं नवीनं वयः।
सम्प्रत्युज्झितवासनं मधुपुरीमध्ये हरिः सेव्यते
सर्वं पण्डितराजराजितिलकेनाकारि लोकाधिकम्॥४४॥

अन्वयः:-शास्त्राणि आकलितानि, सर्वेऽपि नित्यविधयः संभाविताः, दिल्लीवल्लभपाणिपल्लवतले नवीनं वयः नीतम्। मधुपुरीमध्ये हरिः उज्झितवासनं सेव्यते। (एवं) पण्डितराजराजितिलकेन सर्वं लोकाधिकं अकारि।

व्याख्या:-आकलितानि सम्यगधितानि। नित्यविधयः संध्यावन्दनादयः।

---

१. 'माक्षिकादीनाम्' इति पाठान्तरम्।

सम्भाविताः कृताः। दिल्लीवल्लभपाणिपल्लवतले शहाजहाननामकदिल्लीपतिकरतले। तदाश्रयेण तत्प्रसादेन चेत्यर्थः। नवीनं वयस्तारुण्यम्। उज्झितवासनं त्यक्तविषयाभिलाषम्। मधुपुरी मथुरा इति ख्याता नगरी। पण्डितराजराजितिलकेन पण्डितराजश्रेणीमुख्येन। अत्र ई संज्ञितपुस्तके तृतीयचरणे संप्रत्यन्धकशासनस्य नगरे तत्त्वं परं चिन्त्यते इति पाठान्तरं दृश्यते। तत्रान्धकशासनस्य शिवस्य नगरं काशी इति प्रसिद्धमिति बोद्धव्यम्।

Eng. Tr.:-The śāstras were mastered; all the usual duties also were attended to; the prime of life was led under the blossom like hands of the king of Delhi. Now, Viṣṇu is being worshipped (by me) in the city of Muttra in a manner in which all the desires are given up. (Thus) everything extraordinary has been done by (me), the foremost of the lines of the princes of poets.

दुर्वृत्ता जारजन्मानो हरिष्यन्तीति शङ्कया।
मदीयपद्यरत्नानां मञ्जूषैषा कृता मया॥४५॥

अन्वयः-"जारजन्मानः दुर्वृत्ताः हरिष्यन्ति" इति शङ्कया मया एषा मदीयपद्यरत्नानां मञ्जूषा कृता।

व्याख्याः-दुर्वृत्ता दुराचाराः। जारजन्मानोऽन्यस्त्रियामन्यजाताः। हरिष्यन्ति स्वकृतत्वेन ख्यापयिष्यन्ति। मञ्जूषा पेटिका। एषा भामिनीविलासरूपा।

Eng. Tr.:-I have made this box (a safe, as it were) of the precious stones in the form of my verses, through the fear of their being plagiarised (i.e. stolen away) by the people of bad conduct and born of paramours.

इति भामिनीविलासव्याख्यायां काव्यमर्मप्रकाशाख्यायां
शान्तविलासः।

NOTES

I

PRĀSTĀVIKAVILĀSA

1. माधुर्यस्य परमा सीमा-माधुर्यपरमसीमा, the highest limit of sweetness. सारस्वतं एव जलधि-कर्म तस्य मथनं-तस्मात् संभूता, न अल्पं अनल्पम्-अनल्पं सुख ददाति इति-उ त. । सुधा इव कविता-सुधाकविता-कर्म. This way of opening a book will indeed seem unusual, but it is not strange in the case of जगन्नाथपण्डित who indulged rather too much in self-praise as we shall see later on. It should also be noted in connection with this verse that it is not found in any other edition except that of Mr. Vaidya, which we are following and may probably be an interpolation.

2. करटिन्-formed by the affix इन् showing possession करटः अस्ति अस्य. Here करट is used in the sense of a temple of an elephant. "काकेभगण्डौ करटौ" मदेन मलिनाः गण्डाः येषां ते (बहु). The elephant's rutting in the prime of youth is proverbial and has been referred to several times by the Sanskrit poets. दिशां अन्ताः-दिगन्ताः। करिणी menas a female elephant. They are by very nature objects of pity. कारुण्यस्य आस्पदं, by rule पात्र आस्पद स्थान etc. (vide Apet's guide sec 11-b) which requires these words to be used always in the neu. gender Sing. number. मृग्यन्ते (व्याधैः) इति मृगा। Beasts of prey. Ordinary beasts of prey are not worthy of even being attacked by the lion because they are insignificant. नखानां पाण्डित्यं the prowess of his nails which are extra-ordinarily sharp. नास्त्युपमा येषां ते अनुपमा-अनुपमाः शिखाः येषां-तेषाम्-of unparalleled sharpness.

The lion here complains that throughout the length and breadth of the world there is no animal that can match him in valour.

This type of verses is technically called an अन्योक्ति or अपस्तुतप्रशंसा. अप्रस्तुतप्रशंसा या सा सैव प्रस्तुताश्रया (K.Pr. 10-15) i. e. description of what is not the matter in hand, leading to the implication of the matter in hand. For example, in the present verse the poet expresses the invincibility of the lion, implying thereby his (the poet's) unique accomplishments in the sphere of poetry, polemics (science of discussion) and his versatility in all śāstras. मम्मट further sub-divides this अप्रस्तुत-प्रशंसा in five sections, which does not form the province of the present course of studies. Some think-and that very correctly perhaps that herein जगन्नाथ paṇḍita gives free vent to his egoistic nature, which is amply corroborated when we refer to many of his other verses (see introduction.) Leaving aside modesty, which a learned man must avoid, he waxes eloquent in praising his own unique accomplishments and vast erudition.

Idea:—The elephant is sorry because he has no match.

Application:—Extra-ordinary persons feel uneasy when they do not find a competitor to fight with them.

3. मानस is the conventional abode of राजहस (vide मेघदूत पूर्वमेघ latter half of v.11 आकैलासाद् etc.) विकचानि च तानि सारसानि तेषामालयः ताभ्यः स्खलन्तः ये परागाः तैः सुरभीकृतं, adj. of पयः अभूततद्भावे च्विः (by Pan. 5-4-50), मिलतां अनेकेषां भेकानां कुलैः आकुलम्-तस्मिन्-adj. of मरालानां कुलानां नायकः 'परागः कौसुमे रेणौ" "पल्वलं चाल्पसरः" Herein the contrast is very effectively brought out by placing the crystalline and highly scented waters enjoyed in the मानस, side by side with the filthy water of a puddle, repulsive owing to the shrill croaking of frogs.

Idea:—How is it possible for a person once rolling in luxuries to live in adversity?

Appli:—This is applicable to a person who was once affluent (rich) but now indigent (poor).

Cf. सुखात्तु यो याति नरो दरिद्रतां धृतः शरीरेण मृतः स जीवति (M. K. 1-10).

4. तृष्णया लोले विलोचने यस्य सः adj. to चकोरीगणे। प्रस्थातुं कामः यस्य सः adj. to माने. For the compound see Apte's guide Sec. 181. धारणां धराः तेषां आडम्बरः। 'आडम्बरः समारम्भे' इति विश्वः। Here are four locative absolute constructions. It is a convention of Sanskrit poets that the चकोरी birds long for drinking the rays of the moon. कैरव is a night-lotus which blooms at the appearance of the moon. The bud of a lotus resembles a closed mouth and hence the poet naturally likens this opening of the bud to that of the mouth.

The rise of the moon causes the disappearance of the anger of proud ladies, provoked by the jealousy in love as the moon infuses love in the heart of ladies so effectively that they are compelled to forget their anger.

Cf. for the conventions about चकोर and कैरव and the **Idea** in the third line.

शृङ्गारदीक्षामणिः ... ...
... चकोरपरिषच्चिन्तामणिश्चन्द्रमाः।। प्रसन्न ७-६०
स्वैरं कैरवकोरकान् विदलयन् यूनां मनः खेदय-
न्नम्भोजानि निमीलयन् मृगदृशां मानं समुन्मूलयन्।
... ... इन्दुः समुज्जृम्भते।। प्रसन्न ७-५९

धाराधराडम्बरः विधातुमुचितः Here the infinitive is used in the passive sense cf. उचितः प्रणयो वरं विहन्तुं M 3-3.

Idea:—It does not become the creator to cover up the moon when so many are longing for its appearance.

Appli:—It is not proper for a prosperous man to nip in the bud, for nothing, the hopes of future prospects of the humble.

5. निरपेक्ष: (विद्यते) v. l. स्पन्दमानं. meaning throbbing is not so appealing.

दलच्च तदरविन्दं च तस्य संबोधनम्। गन्धं वहति. the conveyer of fragrance i.e. wind. निर्गता अपेक्षा यस्मात् सः-निरपेक्षः मञ्जु is used here adverbially. अन्य the other or here it may mean extra-ordinary cf. अन्या जगद्धितमयी मनसः प्रवृत्तिः etc, तावकीन- is an adjective from युष्मद् formed according to तवकामेव कविकवचने (Pan 4-3-3). "विमर्दोत्थे परिमलो गन्धो जनमनोहरे" मलते धारयति जनमनांसीति परिमला परिमलः is so called because it attracts the minds of the people. "अनुनये तु अयि" The particle अयि is used for gentle address. Also see. Bh. V-1-10.

Idea:—The wind, unlike the bee, is the disinterested friend of the lotus.

Appli:—It is necessary to learn to understand the real worth of persons who hover around us, humming our panegyrics, with a view to the achievement of their selfish ends, and those noble minded, selfless souls who utilize their life for the good of others. Here bees represent selfish persons and wind the selfless one.

6. कुटज is a kind of flower growing on the summits of mountains (Meghadūta 1-4) मा गाः-मा अगाः मा or मा स्म in the prohibitive sense, is used with the aorist in the imperative sense the augment अ being dropped. cf. क्लैव्यं मास्म गमः पार्थ। (B. G. 2-3) मधु करोति तच्छीलः इति मधुकरः मकरन्देन तुन्दिलाः (corpulent) "मास्म माऽलं च वारणे". The कुटज is an insignificant

flower and it is consequently a great honour done to it if a bee, greatly respected by the lotuses, sanctifies it by its visit.

Idea:—O Kuṭaja! do not disrespect the bee.

Appli:—It is an excellent piece of advice to an ordinary man wherein he is asked not to lose the splendid opportunity of treating a dignified guest who was once extremely honoured by the great persons although he has come to him at that time as a mendicant.

7. वनस्य अन्तरम्-in the heart of the forest and not अन्यद् वनं as usual. मिलन्त्यः अलिमालाः यस्मिन् सः adj. to रसालाः"आम्रश्चूतो रसाल;" Hence विरसान्-विगुणान्-Dull, without any interest. According to convention of poets, the कोकिल and the आम्रवृक्ष are closely connected for which cf. चूताङ्कुरास्वादकषायकण्ठः पुंस्कोकिलो यन्मधुरं चुकूज। मनस्विनीमानविघातदक्षं तदेव जातं वचनं स्मरस्य ।। (K. S. 3-32). The cuckoo when alone is prohibited from cooing by the Sanskrit poets in general lest it be harassed by the crows through natural antipathy. When a mango tree blossoms generally all cuckoos flock there and enjoy by cooing. At that time they unitedly will be antipathy of the cuckoos and crows cf. Bh. V 1-25. The crows are so dull that they cannot recognise the cuckoos unless they coo. If the second interpretation i.e. अन्यत् वनम् is followed the danger of the cuckoos being harassed by crows remains as it is. Here यावत् means Untill" cf. स्तन्यत्यागं यावत् पुत्रयोरवेक्षस्व। U. 7.

Idea:—O cuckoo! pass your days quietly until a mango blossoms.

Appli:—One should bear with the apathetic circumstances until fortune favours him.

8. कमलिनी-कमलानि सन्ति अस्याः a lotus plant, मलिनीकरोषि

soil, a verb formed by च्वि formation (न मलिनं अमलिनं, अमलिनं संपद्यमानं करोषि) "मकरन्दः पुष्परसः" न अभिजानन्ति इति अनभिज्ञाः- non-conversant, ignorant. परिणतः च असौ मकरन्दः च तस्य मार्मिकाः appreciators of developed honey. चिरं आयुः येषां ते long lived.

Idea:—The कमलिनी should not repent because it is disrespected by herons.

Appli:—Meritorious man! why are you sorry if you are disrespected by fools ? As long as the learneds who appreciate your merit are alive, you have gained everything.

9. The beauty of this verse depends upon the natural puns on the words नीच, रस, etc., and the consequent implied senses to which it leads, अत्यन्तं, सरसं हृदयं यस्य सः- अत्यन्तसरसहृदयः। बहु-परेषां गुणग्रहीता. This is the example of a सापेक्षसमास, सापेक्षत्वेऽपि गमकत्वात्समासः। Although there is an अपेक्षा (need) of a compound yet the compound is not formed. Here गुण ought to have been connected with परेषां as परगुणग्रहीता. But even though it is not connected this सापेक्षसमास indicates that while interpreting the words we cannot but understand it as one समास though according to actual words परेषां is away from गुणग्रहीता. गुणानां ग्रहीता-गुणग्रहीता ष. त. मा कृथाः for this construction see मा गाः (Bh. V. I-6).

The following are the principal puns नीच (1) low (2) poor. हृदय (1) bottom (2) Heart. रस (1) water (2) love. ग्रहीता (1) acceptor (2) appreciator. गुण (1) Rope to draw water (2) merit.

Idea:—O well! do not be disheartened because you are deep, the people are bound to come to you as they want fresh water which you possess in abundance. The Idea with reference to the person, "Do not get dejected because you are poor, other people are bound to seek you as you have sincerity of love and appreciation for their merits".

Appli :—O man! never be sorry with the thought 'I am exceedingly poor (नीच); because your heart is full of love (रस) and you are the appreciator (ग्रहीता) of merits (गुण) of others.

अमन्दः मरन्दः यस्मिन् तत्-बहु. adj. to अरविन्दम्, दलत्च तदरविन्दं च कर्म. " हा विषादशुगार्तिषु" The tragic element is obvious since the bee, who passed his days once in a paradise as it were, in the form of the lotus incessantly dripping with honey, is now pursuing the mean desire of resorting to a कुटज.

Idea :—How does a bee long for a कुटज flower ?

Appli :—The poet is annoyed at the sight of a man who once passed his days rolling in luxuries, now stooping before his perverse fortune and yielding to degenerating conduct. He expects him to break, never to bend before misfortunes.

The Idea is parallel to

वरं विभवहीनेन प्राणैः सन्तर्पितोऽनलः।

नोपचारपरिभ्रष्टः कृपणः प्रार्थितो जनः। सुभाषितम्.

11. गिरां विषयः अस्तु maybe the subject of speech i. e. who will describe your greatness. फणिन्- a serpent. पुष्टि पुष् to nourish. उद्+गृ to vomit. उद्गिरतः genitive sing. of the present participle of the above root. परिमलस्य उद्गारः- outpourings of fragrance.

Idea :—O Sandal! none is able to describe your greatness.

Appli :—This refers to persons mad with an inordinate

desire for charity, even towards those who deserve immediate annihilation, being a bane to society.

12. उरीकृ- to imitate-to accept "ऊरर्यूरी चोररी च विस्तारेऽङ्गीकृतौ त्रयम्" पटीयस् expert. पुष्टिं तनोषि bring fragrance to पिषन् reducing to atoms, grinding

Idea :—O Sandal! none can imitate your generosity.

Appli :—This refers to too good people of the type of शंकर, who do not refuse to give even a self-destructive boon to their enemies. They cannot overcome their nature which is goodness unalloyed.

13. नीरं च क्षीरं च (द्वंद्व) तयोः विवेकः-तस्मिन् in separating milk from water, which is the peculiar characteristic of the swans. cf. हंसः श्वेतो बकः श्वेतः को भेदो बकहंसयोः। नीरक्षीरविभागे तु हंसो हंसः बको बकः।। आलस्यं तनुषे become lazy. कुलव्रतम् a vow handed down from one generation to another. cf. गलितवयसामिक्ष्वाकूणामिदं हि कुलव्रतम्। R. V. 3-70. विष्ठव is treated as a pronoun and hence the loc. is विष्ठवस्मिन् and not विष्ठवे.

Idea :—O swan! don't leave your hereditary characteristics.

Appli :—If the leaders of society themselves set at naught their own hereditary duties none of the followers also will abide by his duty.

14. करवालस्य धारायाः इव आकारः येषां ते (बहु.)-similar in form to the blade of a sword. 'कौक्षेयको मण्डलाग्रः करवालः" कराः=क्रूतराः here. पुमान् गौः पुंगवः the best of cows. भुजंगमेषु पुंगवा (स. त.) "स्युरुत्तरपदे व्याघ्रपुङ्गवर्षभकुञ्जराः। सिंहशार्दूलनागाद्याः पुंसि श्रेष्टार्थगोचराः" द्राक्षाणां दीक्षायां गुरवः who are fit to become preceptors to teach sweetness to grapes. केऽपि indescribable. See Bh. V. I. 5.

Appli :—This refers to persons who are outwardly quite apathetic but inwardly very sympathetic.

15. स्वस्य छन्द: यथा स्यात्तथा स्वच्छन्दम् (अव्य) अन्या: हरित: हरिदन्तराणि other quarters. 'दिशश्च ककुभ: काष्ठा आशाश्च हरितश्च ता: 'दलत्-blooming अथ but. if. for the use, vide यदि यथा वदति क्षितिपस्तथा त्वमसि किं पितुरुत्कुलया त्वया। अथ तु वेत्सि शुचिव्रतमात्मन: पतिकुले तव दास्यमपि क्षमम्।। शाकुं. ५-२७.

Idea : Wind is not a selfish parasite like bees.

16. निदाघे (in summer) मिहिरस्य (sun) ज्वालानां शतै:-निदाघा मिहिरज्वालाशतै:। नितरां दह्यन्तेऽत्र इति निदाघ:। "निदाघ उष्णोपगम उष्ण ऊष्मागमस्तप:" पान्थानां सन्तति: a line of travellers. सन्तापस्य मालाभि: आकुला perturbed by continuous heat. निर्गतं अन्तरं यस्य स: adj. to आधि: -तस्य पटलै: (by constant mental anguish). धिक् sometimes takes the nom. मयि याते loc. absolute construction गन्ता 3rd pers. sing. of the first future of गम्.

Idea :—Even though oceans have a tremendously great stock of water, yet it is of no use to people in general.

Appli :—Even the life of the poor who get emaciated by the sincere thought of sympathy for others in their miseries is far better than that of the rich who do not give vent to such feelings.

17. पतङ्ग: birds. "पतङ्गो पक्षिसूर्यौ च" संकोचम् अञ्चति literally means getting contracted. अम्बरस्य पन्था: अम्बरपथ: formed irregularly by ऋक्पूरब्धू: पथामानक्षे (Pan. 5-4-74) दीनदीन: utterly miserable. The repetition here shows the intensity of meaning. कतमां गतिं अभ्युपैतु is a question for which no other adequate answer can be found out except that he should fall a victim to death. रसाल means a mango tree. "आम्रश्चूतो रसालोऽसौ" हन्त Alas ! "हन्त हर्षेऽनुकम्पायाम्"

Idea :—What should a fish do, when the pond is dried up?

Appli :—Here is described the utter helplessness of a miserable servant, in contrast with those fortunate ones who have shelter elsewhere, when their master is in adversity.

18. अम्बुजिनि O lotus-plant. मा अमंस्था: don't consider, don't show. अस्मिन् मारुते सौरभलोभं मा अमंस्था: is interpreted in two ways (1) Don't think that the wind is greedy after your fragrance (like the bee), (2) Don't be greedy in giving your fragrance to the wind, as you feel when you give it to the bee. Both these are correct and supported by commentators. मुद् (noun) pleasure. महित:- greatly honoured आत्मा-self. अर्थितानी to reduce to the condition of a beggar.

Appli. (1) A donor should not hesitate to give money to a self-less person. (2) Disgusted with selfish persons donors sometimes bar their door even to the unselfish.

19. वदान्येषु गुरव: (स. त.) The best of the generous. 'स्युर्वदान्यस्थूललक्ष्यदानशौण्डा बहुप्रदे' मिलिन्दे मञ्जु गुञ्जति loc. abso. Construction. मौनं मा उपयासी: Don't become silent सुरतरव:- desire-yielding trees. They are enumerated in the verse पञ्चैते देवतरवो मन्दार: पारिजातक:। सन्तान: कल्पवृक्षश्च पुंसि वा हरिचन्दनम्।। Bearing the bees on the head is the highest honour that can be given to them and hence it would be improper for Mālati to treat them with indifference.

Idea :—O मालति! don't treat the bee with indifference.

Appli :—It is not proper to treat a distinguished guest with indifference.

20. द्वे जिह्वे येषां तै: (बहु). According to the Indian Mythology the tongue of the snake was cut into two when he liked the *Darbha* grass on which the pot of ambrosia was

placed. (vide Mbh. Adi. 27-34) गुण-गुण-वान्-possessed of multitudes of merit. सतां असेव्यतां नीत: rendered useless for being the shelter of the good. औन्नत्यं-greatness. किं कथयाम: we cannot adequately describe. "द्विजिह्वौ सर्पसूचकौ" द्विजिह्व- a serpent, a traducer.

Idea :—O sandal! how should we describe your goodness?

Appli :—It is suggested by the meaning of द्विजिह्व. Even though traducers ruin the reputation of good persons, they are not chastiseA by them, which is indeed, an indication of their extra-ordinary goodness.

21. मधु पिबतीति (उप. त.) गहनम्-a forest विटपिन् lit. one having branches i.e. a tree "विटपी पादपस्तरु:" प्रपेदे is pass. perf. 3rd per. sing. of प्र+पद्

Appli :—This refers to persons who are paragons of excellence and hence whose equal cannot be found out.

22. अन्य परिमल: परिमलान्तरम् (कर्म) अपनीता परिमलान्तरकथा येन-तस्मिन् (बहु.) which does not suffer even the mention of other fragrance. धन्योऽसि is used ironically here and is equivalent in sense to धिक् त्वाम्. The meaning which is exactly contrary to the meaning of the word is to be indicated by the modulation of voice, this called काकु: in Sanskrit. Another fine example where this occurs in two places is seen in the opening stanza of the दशरूपक of धनञ्जय, आनन्दनिस्यन्दिषु रूपकेषु व्युत्पत्तिमात्रं फलमल्पबुद्धि:। योऽपीतिहासादिवदाह **साधुस्तस्मै नम:** स्वादुपराङ्मुखाय।। (The bold-typed words mean exactly their opposite in sense) The कल्पतरु is the source of the sweetest fragrance and hence the bee is playing a fool in searching for another flower.

Idea :—The bee is a fool if he wants to leave even the flower of the celestial tree.

23. विन्ध्यात् भवति- विन्ध्यभू: having its origin in the mountain विन्ध्य. रथ्याया: उदकस्य आदानं Receiving the water on the road. शुष्यन्ती-pres. parti. fem. of शुष्, getting dried up. चिराय for a long time.

Idea :—O river! don't take street-water.

Appli :—It is not indeed proper for highly dignified persons to stoop to low means even in their adversity.

24. पत्राणां फलानां पुष्पाणां च लक्ष्म्या by the beauty of leaves, fruits and flowers. "शूकोऽस्त्री श्लक्ष्णतीक्ष्णाग्रे" शूक: a thorn. उप+ सृप् to approach.

Idea :—O बर्बुर! what is there in you to attract us ?

Appli :—This applies to a wicked man who has nothing attractive, but much that is repulsive.

25. "गहनं काननं वनम्" गहन- forest. कलं a sweet note. समाना जाति: यस्य तस्य भाव:-belonging to the same species; hence साजात्यशङ्कया- mistaking you for one of their own species. निर्गता दया येभ्य: ते निर्दया: (बहु.) merciless.

Idea :—O कोकिल! do not utter a note, lest you will be killed.

Appil :—where ignorance is bliss, it is folly to be wise. or मूर्खाणां च समाजेषु वरं मौनं हि धीमताम्।।

26. भवस्य स्त्री भवानी by इन्द्रवरुण &c. (Pan 4-1-49) तरूणां कुलानां (clusters) सुषमां (beauty) अपहरति-सा. जीवानां जातं ष. त. everything that can be classed under the category of जीव. cf. तमध्वरे विश्वजिति क्षितीशं नि:शेषविश्राणितकोषजातम्। उपात्तविद्यो गुरुदक्षिणार्थी कौत्स: प्रपेदे वरतन्तुशिष्य:।। R. V. 5. 1. "हिमानी हिमसंहति:" महद् हिमं हिमानी (Pan वार्तिक 4-1-49) Himālaya is

always coverd with snow which mars the beauty of the trees. आर्ति: pain-जीवजातस्यार्ति:-ताम् जनयन्ती

Idea :—What good, O Himālaya, do you see in the snow that you bear it on your head ?

Appli :—This applies to persons who give shelter, for no reason, to people who are a source of constant trouble to society.

27. कलभ-a young elephant-'धूर्वहे धुर्यधौरेयधुरीणाः सधुरं धराः' धुरं वहति सः धुर्यः formed by sūtra धुरो यढडकौ (Pan. 4-4-77) दानेन सुन्दरः (तृ. त.) beautiful on account of ichor. द्वाभ्यां पिबन्ति ते द्विपाः - तेषु धुर्याः best of elephants. शिरसा धार्यः worthy of being borne on the head.

Idea :—O Young elephant! don't disrespect the bee.

Appli :—Same as in Bh. V. I-19.

28. बिडम्बना- making oneself an object of ridicule. अमराणां (of Gods) तरूणां कुसुमानां सौरभस्य (fragrance) सेवनेन संपूर्णाः (fulfilled) सकलाः कामाः (all desires) यस्य (बहु.) adj. to भ्रमर. for the use of बिडम्बना in this sense read, इयं च तेऽन्या पुरतो बिडम्बना यदूढया वारणराजहार्यया। विलोक्य वृद्धोक्षमधिष्ठितं त्वया महाजनः स्मेरमुखो भविष्यति।। K. S. 5-70 अन्यत् पुष्पं पुष्पान्तरम् (कर्म.)

Idea :—The bee is an object of ridicule if he resorts to another flower.

Appli :—This applies to persons who, although on the pinnacle of prosperity are longing for baser pleasures and thus make themselves objects of ridicule.

29. परैः (काकैः) पुष्टा Cuckoos. This is referred to in कालिदास'ऽ शाकुन्तल in the verse प्रागन्तरिक्षगमनात्स्वमपत्यजातमन्यैर्द्विजैः परभृताः खलु पोषयन्ति (Sak.5-22). उपमा means उपमान is generally superior to उपमेय- the thing that is compared. (in this case

आस्र). But here there can be no उपमान found and hence the mango is matchless in its qualities.

Idea :—O माकन्द! the bee did not find your equal.

Appli .:—This applies to some person who is unparalleled in the possession of excellent merits.

30. मालाः करोतीति- a gardener. भीमः भानुः यस्मिन् सः (बहु.) adj. to निदाघ or भीमाः भानवः (the rays) यस्मिन् सः धाराणां आसाराः the showers of rain. भानु-(1) the sun (2) the rays. "निदाघ उष्णोपगमः" निदाघः-the summer. प्रावृषेण्य belonging to the rainy-season, formed irregularly by adding the termination एण्य by the सूत्र "प्रावृष एण्यः" (Pan. 4-3-17) विश्वः everywhere. विकिरता Instr. 3rd person sing. of the pre. par. of कृ with वि. व्यरचि pass. aor. 3rd pers. sing. of वि+रच् पुष्टिः nourishment.

Idea :—The nourishment brought by the water of the gardener cannot be rendered by the amply pouring cloud.

Appli :—Even a little help counts a great deal, when proffered at the opportune moment तदनघ्यं यदवसरे दत्तम्।

31. आरामस्य अधिपतिः the master of the garden. "आरामः स्यादुपवनम्" विवेकेन विकल (तृ. त.) void of thought. रसा-earth. निर्गतः रसः यस्याः सा नीरसा (बहु.) adj. to रसा in which there is no life-giving juice, i.e. barren. परुषीकृताः-च्वि formation are hardened वात्याभिः वातसमूहैः by gusts of wind. चण्डः आतपः terrible heat. संहारस्य हेतुः the cause of destruction. धन्वन्-a country without moisture, barren land. "समानौ मरुधन्वानौ।। आविस्+ कृ to manifest. कुतः अपि from some unknown, unexpected quarter. अमृत water, nectar. vl. धुन्वति for धन्वनि and शकले for सकले. const. चंपकस्य शकले धुन्वति. Not so happy.

Idea :—O cloud! you have manifested yourself unexpectedly.

Appli :—This refers to a person whose very life is endangered owing to the presence of various fatal causes when suddenly a succour is sent by God.

32. VI. स्खलन्मुक्ताभारे भवति परलोकं गतवति (सति) अतिभयेन भ्रान्तानि नयनानि येषां ते (बहु.) with their eyes tremulous owing to excessive fear. गलद् दानं-तस्य उद्रेकः (अतिशयः) तेन भ्रमन्तः अलिकदम्बाः (समूहाः) येषु ते (बहु.) with multitudes of bees hovering around owing to the excess of trickling ichor. परलोकं गम् to die. शिव शिव alas ! स्थेमानं धा to stand steadily. लुठन्तः मुक्ताभाराः यस्मिन् तत् (बहु.) adj. to द्वारम् with myriads of pearls from the temples of the slain elephants rolling here and there. This is referred to in परं तुषारस्रुति धौतरक्तं यस्मिन्नदृष्टाऽपि हतद्विपानाम्। विदन्ति मार्गं नखरन्ध्रमुक्तैर्मुक्ताफलैः केसरिणां किराताः। K. S. I. 6. शिवा-a female jackal. v. l. for first line as given above takes it as a loc. absolute when you, who rolled (i.e. caused to roll) multitudes of pearls, have gone to the other world. For भ्रान्तनयनाः the v. l. is भ्रान्तहृदयाः which does not make much change.

Idea :—Now female jackals are howling where formerly even big elephants dared not stand.

Appli :—A place which people are afraid of approaching when the master is living, becomes condemned after the owner breathes his last.

33. समभावेन doing equal justice to all विपुलां करुणां न अकृत Did not show ample pity towards it, i. e. did not take special notice of it. द्राक्-immediately (adv.) " दगाङ्मंक्षुस-पदिद्रुतम्" द्राक् उद्यन्तः कुसुमनिकराः (collection of flowers) तेषाम्। दिशां अन्ताः (ष. त.). मधुपानां कुलानां (clusters of bees) झंकारेण भरितान् filled with the buzzing of bees.) आतेने Rendered. Perhaps a contrast is intended by the poet between the words तरु-बाल

बकुल, तरु meaning a big extensive tree. v. l. विपुलं to be taken with प्रेमाणं but this does not seem happy.

Idea :—Though neglected by the gardener, the बकुल plant rendered all directions fragrant.

Appli :—One who is many times neglected as insignificant, rises to an incredible prominence by his unique intrinsic qualities.

34. बन्धनैः दृढम् strong owing to the roots. मांसलाः strong दुःखेन गम्यते इति दुर्गः-मह्याः धरः महीधरः a mountain which is hard to ascend ज्वालानां आलयः collections of flames. ताभिः वलयीभवन् forming into circles. आधिः एव ज्वरः fever in the form of mental agony. नास्ति करुणा यस्मिन् सः—void of mercy. घस्मरः voracious "भक्षको घस्मरोऽद्मरः" मनाक् a little. "किञ्चिदीषन्मनाक् अल्पे" शतं is an उपलक्षण and means "many".

Idea :—O tree! you are all safe, excepting from the voracious forest-conflagration

Appli :—Even the strongest have to be afraid of something, that will cause their destruction.

35. भीष्मतरैः Comparative of भीष्म terrible. दिनं करोति इति दिनकृत् the sun. द्राघीयस is the comparative of दीर्घ. वासरान् days. कथमपि-कथं with चन्, चित् and अपि means "with great difficulty". Compare तस्य स्थित्वा कथमपि पुरः कौतुकाधानहेतोः (etc. Megh. 3) लोचनयोः गोचरः visible by the eyes करकाणां निपातनं shower of hailstones. "वपलस्तु करका" सा एव कृपा-here used ironically means cruelly. It is the convention of Sanskrit poets that the चातक longs for rain drops, of the स्वाती constellation. cf. कोप्याग्रहो गुरुरयं बत चातकस्य पौरन्दरीं यदभिवाञ्छति वारिधाराम्। The propriety of द्राघीयसः lies in the fact that the days are longest in summer.

Idea :—O cloud! when should we complain, if you now shower hailstones upon the चातक ?

Appli :—If that very person from whom we expect protection turns against us, where shall we seek for safety ?

36. दव: दहन: forest-conflagration "दवदावौ वनारण्यवह्नी" दवदहनस्य जटाला: ज्वाला: तेषां जालेन आहतानां भूरुहाणाम्-of trees which are besieged by the cluster of accumulated flames of the forest-conflagration. भुवि रोहन्ति भुरुहा: trees. परिगलिता: लता: येभ्य: तेषाम् with creepers dropped down. Here is the genitive absolute construction. vide Apte's Guide Sec. 122, also षष्ठी चानादरे (Pan. 2-3-34) cf. नन्दा: पर्यायभूता: पशव इव हता: पश्यतो राक्षसस्य (मुद्रा. ३-२७) शैलानां श्रेणीनां श्रृङ्गेषु on the peaks of the rows of mountains, where rain is not so vitally needed. वि+तृ to impart, although used in the sense of संप्रदान is sometimes used with the loc. cf. वितरति गुरु: प्राज्ञे विद्यां यथैव तथा जडे etc. (Uttara. 2-4). श्रिय: मद: the pride of wealth in the form of the abundance of water.

Idea :—Improper indeed is the pride of the cloud in pouring rain on the mountain summits neglecting the trees parched in the conflagration.

Appli :—This refers to persons offering abundantly to the already rich, neglecting those who badly want it.

37. पुर: in front of हन्त alas ! "हन्त हर्षेऽनुकम्पायां वाक्यारम्भविषादयो:" परुष च तत् गर्जितं च harsh thundering. विह्वलं मन: यस्य स: विह्वलमना: grieved at heart, विश्वस्य आर्ति: तस्या: वारणं-तस्मिन् समर्पितं जीवनं येन who has devoted his life (water-here) in the sense of doubt or uncertainty; vide Apte's Guide sec. 267 obs. अम्बुन: वाह: the vehicle of water i.e. cloud.

Idea :—O traveller! don't grieve at the thundering, it is merely a cloud, remover of all distresses.

Appli .:—This refers to a person whose harsh external bears behind it, an excessively sympathetic heart.

38. सौरभ्यं fragrance. भुवनानां त्रयम् the triad of worlds. शैत्यं coldness. लोकेभ्य:उतरम्-uncommon. दिश:एव अङ्गना: तेषां अङ्गणं गता reached the courtyard of the ladies in the form of quarters. निगिरति=निगिलति swallows completely. श्रीखण्ड–a sandal tree. गरलस्य ज्वाला the flame of poison. द्विजिह्वानां आवलि: the line of serpents.

Idea :—O sandal! you have all possible lofty merits but only one drawback that nullifies them all.

Appli .:—This refers to a person who is useless owing to one fault, inspite of his possessing hundreds of merits.

39. अपेक्षा expectation of reciprocal kindness. दाक्षिण्यं courtesy-politeness. सङ्गति: a sense of duty to a companion formed through long acquaintance. उन्नत (1) High up in the sky (2) Noble-minded, magnanimous. Like this cloud, the magnanimous person also removes the pains of the people, irrespective of a return and unimpelled by any other motives like love, courtesy etc.

Appli :—This points to the disinterestedly obliging nature of the magnanimous souls.

40. अम्बुन: जायते इति lotus-born of water. Each of the several qualities described above heighten the value of a lotus. निवास: the abode of लक्ष्मी because she is known as पद्मालया v. 1. विलास:-विलासस्थानम् a place of enjoyment. सुराणां हृदयानि हरति इति that which captivates the minds of Gods द्विजेषु उत्तंस: the best or the ornament of the birds i.e हंस. रति:—liking.

Idea :—The lotus will reach an extremely high position if it remains attached to the swan.

Appli :—The greatness of great men is greatly enhanced when they cherish love for the best of persons.

41. ग्राव्णां गणा:-तै: with multitudes of stones साकम् with. अर्कबिम्बं उपमा (उपमानं) येषा ते adj. to मणय:-jewels which are as lustrous as the orb of the sun. उन्नते: प्रौढि: the excess of greatness. The अविवेक deserves निन्दा and उन्नते: परा प्रौढि: deserves स्तुति. नारायण: is termed भगवान् i. e. possessed of the great qualities. These are supposed to be six-ऐश्वर्यस्य समग्रस्य वीर्यस्य यशस: श्रिय:। ज्ञानवैराग्ययोश्चैव षण्णां भग इतीरणा।। The author says that he is at a loss to make out whether the milk-ocean deserves praise or blame, because the principle of equality that the ocean follows is wrong. The commentator अच्युतराय says "तत्तद्योग्यतातारतम्यं विवेकेनैव" or even as Kālidạsa says" "भवन्ति साम्येऽपि निविष्टचेतसां वपुर्विशेषेष्वतिगौरवा: क्रिया: (K.S. 5-31).

Idea :—O milk-ocean! I cannot decide whether to praise you or to blame you.

Appli :—It is not easy to decide whether the actions of great persons are censurable or praiseworthy.

42. अर्णव-the sea. किम्-what is the use of ? अभ्रमिवाचरति अभ्रायति the past passive participle is अभ्रायित formed from the denominative verb from अभ्र by the sūtra उपमानादाचारे (Pan. 3-1-10). The body of the sea acts like the sky inasmuch-as it extends over a long distance and possesses blue colour " अभ्रं व्योम" पुष्करमम्बरम्, सलिलं-water.

Idea :—O sea! all your wealth is useless.

Appli :—This refers to a person who is a repository of immense wealth, but does not utilize even a farthing for doing good to others.

43. इयती so much—संपत्ति here refers to the copiouness of water. अधुना perhaps refers to the rainy-season when the

lake abounds in water. चण्डाः अंशवः (rays) यस्य सः the sun. अङ्गाराणां निकराः collection of burning charcoal. अंगार means the rays which are as scorching as the living coal. कृशीभूतः-च्वि formation, lean-emaciated, the water being dried up by the heat of the sun. अहह-alas ! 'अहहेत्यद्भुते खेदे' ताम्-तृष्णाम्.

Idea :—O lake! whose thirst will you be able to remove when you are dried up ?

Appli :—Charity should be practised while in prosperity because it is impossible in adversity.

44. रोषं उरीकरोषि &c. if you do not have recourse to anger. What the author means is this: "O sea! great as you are, it is unbecoming on your part to accept water that is given to you by those clouds that begged the same water from you. अर्थयते इति अर्थिन्-a beggar-a mendicant.

Idea :—O sea! do not accept water which has been once given in charity by you.

Appli :—This refers to those miserly persons who are not ashamed of accepting what has once been given in charity.

45. वर्षानदि O river in the rainy-season i.e. a rivulet which is so short-lived that it flows only in the rainy-season. जह्नोः जाता-जह्नुजा-जह्नु, the son of king होत्रक, who hid the Ganges under his thigh, finding her troublesome to him. Hence the Ganges is named after him. (vide वा. रा. बालकाण्ड सर्ग 43), The Ganges is decidedly a far greater river in comparision with the वर्षानदी. स्रोतस् a stream. तरुङ्गाणां भङ्गः the dashing or breaking of waves. प्रकटीकृ, च्वि formation, to manifest.

Idea :—O वर्षानदि! it is unbecoming for you to manifest breaking-waves, before the Ganges.

Appli :—It is not proper for an insignificant person to make an ostentatious dislplay of one's pride before the great.

46. पौलोम्याः पत्युः कानने In the garden of the lord of पौलोमी i.e. of Indra. गीर्वाणानां भूमीरुहः the trees of gods i.e. the desire-yielding trees. "गीर्वाणा दानवारयः" for कल्पवृक्ष see note on Bh. V. I. 28. आदौ आघ्रातानि पश्चात् समुज्झितानि first smelt and then given up. निर्गता जरा येभ्यः ते निर्जराः the unageing i.e. Gods. मधु एव व्रतं यस्य सः मधुव्रतः the bee. मधुव्रते माध्वीकमाकांक्षति &c. is the loc. absolute construction. विधिवशात् through the force of his ill-luck as he has to resort to an earthly lotus for seeking for honey—he who has once tasted celestial flowers. माध्वीकं-honey. लोभं अंचसि lit. goes to greed i.e. become greedy in giving honey to the bee.

Idea :—O lotus! do not be greedy in giving honey to the bee who has tasted the celestial trees.

Appli :—Same as in Bh. V. I. 19.

47. मृणालानां पटली ष. त. The cluster of lotus fibres. The swans live on the lotus fibres; vide Megh. the latter half of verse 11. नितरां पीतानि drunk to the heart's content. कृतः उपकारः येन सः (बहु) one who has done obligations in return.

Idea :—O swan ! how will you repay the obligation ?

Appli :—This refers to a person who is asked how he would show his gratitude towards one who has conferred upon him a number of obligations.

48. कुसुमानां आकरः (ष. त.) the vernal season. उल्लसन्तीनां मञ्जरीणां पुञ्जे on the cluster of the blooming sprouts. मञ्जुलानि गुञ्जितानि (कर्म.) the sweet hummings रचयन् producing. उत्सवान् आतनोः enjoyed excessively तान्-refers to the event of the past. cf. उन्मत्तः स च राजपुत्रनिवहस्ते बन्दिनस्ताः कथाः। सर्वं यस्य वशादगात् स्मृतिपथं कालाय तस्मै नमः।। तस्मिन् रसालशाखिनि कृशां दशां अञ्चति (सति) loc. absolute construction, showing time. When that

mango-tree is shorn of leaves. दैवात्-through ill-luck. विनय— gratitude, modesty.

Idea :—It is worst meanness that a bee should show ingratitude towards a leafless mango tree.

Appli :—It is the height of ingratitude to forsake our benefactor who is in adversity, with whom we have passed our best days.

49. कलय Know. कृष्णसार— a black antelope. हरि here means a lion. It is used to mean many more animals. यमानिलेन्द्र चन्द्रार्क विष्णु सिहांशुवाजिषु। शुकाहि कपिभेकेषु हरिर्ना कपिलेत्रिषु।। गर्वेण निमीलिते अक्षिणी येन सः (बहु.) Whose eyes are closed through pride. हरेः विहारस्य वसुंधरा the play-ground of the lion. भिन्नानां करीन्द्राणां कुम्भेभ्यः (गलिताभिः) मुक्ताभिः पूर्णा Filled with pearls dropping down from the temples of the best of elephants which are torn open. (by the lion) मय is the termination added according to तत्प्रकृतवचने मयट् (Pan. 5-4-21) in the sense of अधिकरण., "Subsisting therein". मुक्तमयीं full of pearls. एणी female of a कृष्णसार deer.

Idea :—O deer! don't enjoy thoughtlessly, you are in the vicinity of death.

Appli :—A man should not remain immersed in enjoyment, when danger is imminent.

50. जठरे ज्वलनः-The gastric fire तेन ज्वलता adj. to हरिणा अपगता शंका (scruples) यथा स्यात् तथा-unscrupulously. हरिणानां आली a herd of deer.

Idea :—Even though starving a lion will never attack deer.

Appli :—The great never stoops to base means even in adversity.

51. भिन्नाः करिणां कुम्भाः तेभ्य विस्खलतां मौक्तिकानां आवलिभिः मही अंचिता—The earth is covered with the rows of pearls dropping from the temples of elephants torn open. हरिणानां अन्तिके near the deer.

Idea :—The lion should not speak about his valour to the deer.

Appli :—The great should never speak about their greatness to the insignificant persons.

52. मदेनान्धे ईक्षणे यस्य—Whose eyes are blinded owing to rut. गजानां श्रेणीनां नाथः-the leader of the herds of elephants. जटिल formed by adding the term इलच् (इल) in the sense of censure according to सूत्र (लोमादि पोमादि) पिच्छादिभ्यः शनेलचः (Pan. 5-2-100) (lit-intermixed) dense. If no censure is implied it assumes the form जटावान्. स्थितिं धा—to stand. कुम्भिनां भ्रान्तिः तया-mistaking (the rocks) for elephants. खराश्च ते नखराश्च तैः विद्रावितः महान् गुरुणां ग्राव्णां ग्रामः येन (बहु.) adj. to हरिपतिः-The lion who has torn with his pointed nails a collection of big rocks. "ग्रावाणौ शौलपाषाणौ".

Idea :—O lord of elephants! the lion is sleeping now, so leave this place if you want to save your life.

Appli :—The weak ones should not stay at all even when their strong enemies are asleep.

53. गजानां राजा गजराजः formed by राजाहः सखिभ्यष्टच् (Pan. 5-4-91) तस्य पोतः the young one of the lord of elephants. "यानपात्रे शिशौ पोतः" गुरु गर्वः (कर्म) तेन गुम्फितः तृ. तः Being puffed up with great pride. गिरिगह्वरेषु in the caves of the mountain. स्तनं धयति-Sucking the (mother's) breast. This shows that the cub of the lion is so very young. हरिशिशुः-The cub of a lion. करेणवः परिशेषिताः यस्यां सा (बहु.) adj. to मही-with only

the female elephants remaining. "करेणुरिभ्यां स्त्री". The Idea is that the moment the cub of the lion is roused, he will slay all the elephants and only the female ones will be remaining as they are the objects of pity. cf. करिण्यः कारुण्यास्पदं Bh. V. 1-1 भविता-भविष्यति. cf. सिहः शिशुरपि निपतति मदमलिनकपोलभित्तिषु गजेषु।।

Idea :—The cub of the elephant is asked not to stir about arrogantly lest the cub of the lion might awake.

Appli :—The fiery, though young, are capable of vanquishing mighty enemies.

54. निसर्गात्-naturally. कृती-well-versed. आराम:—a garden. तरूणां कुलस्य समारोपे सुकृती—ingenious in planting myriads of trees. कोणस्य अन्तरम् (ष. त.) तत्र गतः-planted in some corner. जगतः जालं-the net of the world i. e. the whole world. कुसुमानां भरस्य सौरभ्येण भरितं-filled with the fragrance of the multitude of flowers.

Appli :—The great are sure to shine out though neglected by the thoughtless.

55. राघव is an excessively big fish. परिचलतां कल्लोलानां कोलाहलैः-By the loud uproar of huge waves moving here and there. हरित्सु (तिष्ठन्तः) दन्तावलाः-elephants standing at the quarters. "दिशस्तु ककुभः काष्ठा आशाश्चहरितश्च ताः" There is a mythological reference here to the eight guardian elephants that are supposed to support the earth, they are enumerated in the following verse, ऐरावतः पुण्डरीको वामनः कुमुदोऽञ्जनः। पुष्पदन्तः सार्वभौमः सुप्रतीकश्च दिग्गजाः। They preside respectively over the eight cardinal points. पूर्वाग्नेयी दक्षिणा च नैर्ऋती पश्चिमा तथा। वायवी चोत्तरैशानी दिशा अष्टविमाः स्मृताः।। मन्थाश्चासौ आद्रिश्च, तस्य भ्रमणं तस्य भ्रममापेदिरे-mistook it (the movement of waters)

for the revolving of the mountain that was made to work as the churn. When Gods and demons churned the ocean for getting nectar, they are said to have made the मन्दर mountain the churning handle. हृदि is optional locative sing of हृदय formed according to पद्दन्नोमास् हृद् etc. (Pan. 6-1-63) 'दन्ती दन्तावलो हस्ती' दन्तावले is formed by the affix वलच् (वल) after दन्त when a name is formed. See Sūtra दन्तशिखात् संज्ञायाम् (Pan. 5-2-113) and the final of the word दन्त is lengthened according to the Sūtra वले (Pan. 6-3-118) तुङ्गश्चासौ तिमिङ्गिल: तस्य अंगस्य कवलीकार: (the action of swallowing) एव क्रिया तस्यां कोविद:। "सन्सुधी: कोविदो बुध:"—An expert in the work of swallowing the body of a lofty तिमिङ्गिल fish. तिमि-तिमिङ्गिल-तिमिङ्गिलगिल and राघव is the order, the succeeding one swallowing the preceding one. कवल-a mouthful. Hence कवलीकृ—to swallow. " क्रोडं भुजान्तरम्" (bosom). द्रवकेलिपरिहासा: क्रीडा खेला च नर्म च। केलि (सबन्धी) कलह: तेन त्यक्त: अर्णव: येन स:-who quitted the sea due to the quarrel in sport.

Idea :—where will a राघव fish-whose movements strike terror in the heart of smaller fish, play ?

Appli :—If everyday actions of great persons strike terror in the heart of the smaller ones, while in their homes, where are they to go then ?

56. "मतङ्गजो गजो नाग:" मत्तै: मतङ्गजै: लूनं broken by intoxicated elephants. तुषारेण अर्दिता: तै:-Afflicted by frost. "तुषारस्तुहिनं हिमं " ग्रीष्मजस्य भीष्मस्य भानो: किरणै:-by the rays of the terrible summer sun "दारुणं भीषणं भीष्मं" भस्मीकृ-to reduce to ashes, कोणं गता (द्वि. त.) lying in the corner. मुहु:-frequently. "मुहु: पुन: पुन: शश्वदभीक्ष्णमसकृत् समा:" लवङ्गस्य लतिका-The clove plant.

Idea :—When the whole forest is destroyed the poor tender clove plant also has to yield to destruction.

Appli :—When the very master, who is resorted to, meets with destruction, the servants also who seek his shelter must naturally die along with him.

57. स्वरलोक: स्वर्लोक:-सुप्सुप्समास: स्वलोकस्य शिखायां मणि: The crest jewel of the celestial world. सुराणां तरूणां ग्रामस्य धाम—The abode of the collections (ग्राम) of the celestial trees. "वृन्देऽपि ग्राम:" पौलोमीपुरुहूतयो: "पुरुहूत: पुरन्दर: " पौलोमी-इन्द्राणी (पुलोम्न: अपत्यं स्त्री) पुलोमन् was the name of a demon. पुण्यानां आवलि:—a series of merits or meritorious acts. परिणति:—a noun from परि+नम्-fulfilment. नन्दन is the name of the garden of इन्द्र "हय उच्चैश्रवा:, सूतो मातलि:, नन्दनं वनम्" खाण्डवरङ्गताण्डवनट: "ताण्डवं नटनं नाट्यं लास्यं नृत्यं च नर्तने" खाण्डवं एव रङ्ग: तत्र ताण्डवं तस्मिन् नट:—The actor, dancing on the stage in the form of the खाण्डव forest. खाण्डव The name of a forest in कुरुक्षेत्र, dear to Indra and burnt by अग्नि with the assistance of अर्जुन and कृष्ण. रङ्ग:-a stage. "रङ्गो नृत्यरणक्षितौ" इति मेदिनी. "अग्निवैश्वानरो वह्नि:" वैश्वानर:-विश्वे नरा: अस्य इति विश्वानर:- विश्वानरस्य अपत्यं वैश्वानर:—God fire. (Pan 4-1-114).

Idea :—Although the celestial garden (नन्दन) is great in many respects yet it has dread from fire.

Appli :—Although a person maybe inconceivably great yet there does exist dread for him from some quarter at least.

59. स्वस्यां स्वस्यां व्यापृतौ (occupation) मग्नं मानसं येषां ते तेषां भाव: तया-Because there mind would be engaged in their respective occupation. चञ्च्वा: कोटिना विपाटितं अररस्य पुटं येन स:-one who has broken open the panes of a door (of the cage) with the point of the beak. "कपाटमररं तुल्ये" मनोरथमयं

पीयूषं= "पीयूषममृतं सुधा"—nectar in the form of the desire. वारणस्य करस्य इव आकार: यस्य स: बहु.-having the form of the trunk of an elephant, "करो वर्षोपले रश्मौ पाणौ प्रत्यायशुण्डयो:। इति मेदिनी. फणिषु ग्रामणी:-the best of serpents. "ग्रामणीर्नापिते पुंसि श्रेष्ठे" ग्रामं नयति-उ. त. Leader of men.

Idea :—While the parrot is planning his escape from the cage, the unforeseen peril of the serpent creeps in.

Appli :—Man proposes but God disposes or "मनसा चिन्तितं कार्यं दैवमन्यत्र चिन्तयेत्।"

59. चाञ्चल्यं जुषन्ते इति चाञ्चल्यजुष: (उ. त.) Those who like fickeeness (i.e. those who cannot remain steady.) श्रिता: नगा: यै: ते (बहु.) who are residing in mountains. कल्लोलानां मालाभि: आकुला: (तृ. त.)-Agitated by lines of surging waves. अंबुधे: कामिनी-A river. गाह् 1 A. to bathe in , The verb implying motion governs the acc. or the dat. of the place to which the motion is directed. "गत्यर्थकर्मणि द्वितीयाचतुर्थ्यौ चेष्टायामनध्वनि" (Pan. 2-3-12). व्यवसित is the p. p. p. of वि+अव्+सो (4 P.) यद् means ' since' in as much as उच्छलत: अम्बुन: निर्भरेण महद्भिरावर्तै: (स्यादावर्तौभसां भ्रम:) समावर्तित:-tossed by the great whirlpools of surging volume of waters. गजेषु ग्रामणी: (स. त.) the best of elephants. रसाया: तलं-the bottom of the earth. 'ग्रावाणौ शैलपाषाणौ'

Idea :—O deer! do not venture to bathe in the surging river in which even an elephant has been drowned.

Appli :—Why should pigmies try to achieve that in accomplishing which even persons of strength have met with destruction.

60. पोत:-child. 'यानपात्रे शिशौ पोत:'-मद. (युक्त) दन्तावल: तस्य धी: तया-thinking it to be an elephant in rut. हरितां अन्ता: (ष. त.) ends of quarters. किम् Joined with इति has the sense

of "why" cf. किमित्यपास्याभरणानि यौवने धृतं त्वया वार्धकशोभि वल्कलम्। K. S. 5-44. दृशः अन्ता. ष. त. side-glances. नवश्चासौ नीलश्च- new and dark. जलस्य धरः (ष. त.) the holder of water (cloud).

Idea :—O cub! do not cast angry side-glances at the thundering of the cloud, mistaking it for an elephant in rut.

61. नीरं ददाति (उ. त.) a cloud. अलं "enough" governs the instru. cf. अलं महीपाल तव श्रमेण प्रयुक्तमप्यस्त्रमितो वृथा स्यात्। न पादपोन्मूलनशक्ति रंहः शिलोच्चये मूर्च्छति मारुतस्य। R. V. 34 and the Sūtra पर्याप्तिवचनेष्वलमर्थेषु (Pan. 3-4-66) धीराश्च ते ध्वनयः (कर्म) तैः-धीरध्वनिभिः with sonorous rumblings. मासिकः- "मासमात्र-कालिकः" one month old. उन्मदः च असौ वारणः च तस्य बुद्ध्या-thinking it to be an intoxicated elephant. जठस्य मध्ये-मध्ये-जठरम्-अव्य. acc. to Pan. पारे मध्ये षष्ठ्या वा (Pan. 2-1-18).

Idea :—Even the foetus of the lioness, one month old, is moving at the thundering.

Appli :—तेजसां हि न वयः समीक्ष्यते। R. V. 11-1 or तेजसा सह जातानां वयः कुत्रोपयुज्यते। Heroism depends upon pre-natal impressions and not on age.

62. वेतण्डानां (गजानां) गण्डानां कण्डूत्यां पाण्डित्यं-तस्य परिपन्थी-तेन being the obstacle in the skill of the rubbing of the temples by the elephants. परिपन्थी an obstacle "अरातिप्रत्यर्थिपरिपन्थिनः" cf. अकरिष्यदसौ पापमतिनिष्करुणैव सा। नाभविष्यमहं तत्र यदि तत्परिपन्थिनी।। Malt. 9-51.

Idea :—The same as in the 51st verse.

Appli :—Timid persons do not deserve the heroic exploits of the brave to be related to them.

63. "जनुर्जननजन्मानि जनिरुत्पत्तिरुद्भवः" निर्मलतः=निर्मलात्। It is born of clear water. 'वामा वनिता महिला तथा' वामायाः मुखेन स्पर्धते इति-competing with the face of the woman. The word वामा does not mean an ordinary woman here but a woman with bewitching beauty. Bhanuji Dixita, the commentator on *Amarakoa* derives this as वमति स्नेहम् i.e. that which exhibits love and as such becomes an object of reciprocal affection. It is customary with the poets to utilize the lotus as the standard of comparison. Vide चकितहरिणलोललोचनायाः क्रुधि तरुणारुणतारहारि-कान्ति। सरसिजमिदमाननं च तस्याः सममिति चेतसि संमदं विधत्ते।। K. P. 10-2 गीर्वाणानां चेतः हरति इति (उप) that which captivates the minds of Gods. "गीर्वाणा दानवारयः" The lotus is indispensable for the speech of the great poets; for it is frequently used as a standard of comparison and the cupid cannot do anything without a lotus because it is his arrow. See अरविन्दमशोकं etc. Cupid is shown as boasting of the prowess of these arrows of his, which in his opinion are more potent than even thunderbolt of Indra. प्रसीद विश्राम्यतु वीर वज्रं शरैर्मदीयैः कतमः सुरारिः। विभेतु मोघीकृतबाहुवीर्यः स्त्रीभ्योपि कोपस्फुरिताधराभ्यः । K. S. 3-9 and hence जगन्नाथपण्डित calls अरविन्द to be the सर्वस्व of काम. मधुप (1) a bee (2) a drunkard.

Idea :—A lotus-repository of all greatness, containing a feeling of love for a bee-is condemnable.

Appli :—It is a stain on the character of a person endowed with supernatural qualifications to entertain love for mean minded persons.

64. लीलायां मुकुलिते नयने यथा स्याताम् तथा (अव्ययी.) with your eyes half closed in amorous sport. लीला is an amorous sport. 'हेला लीलेत्यमी हावाः क्रियाः श्रृङ्गारभावजाः'। सुखे शयनं-sleeping at ease. परिणामे विषमः हरिः-the lion who is terrible in

the end. (result.) (i.e. entering into enmity with this lion will lead to a grave catastrophe.

Idea :—O elephant! do not be engrossed in sport. You are thereby aggravating the enmity with the lion.

Appli :—Treating the mighty lightly kindles their wrath.

65. द्वौ रदौ येषां ते-तेषाम् elephants. "द्विरदोऽनेकपो द्विपः" पराञ्चन्ति from परा+अञ्च-are withdrawn, are taken back.

Idea :—"सकृज्जल्पन्ति पण्डिताः" The wise keep their own counsel.

66. "संभूतिः noun from सं+भू birth. दातृणां गुरुः-तस्य the preceptor i. e. best of donors. लोकेषु उत्तराः-Extra-ordinary. अर्थिषु प्रवराः तेषां यदर्थितं तस्य अर्पणविधौ. In the act of granting the solicitations of the best of solicitors. v. l. अर्थिप्रकरार्थतर्पणविधौ-In the act of satisfying the desires of the multitude of supplicants. (अर्थिनां प्रकारः तस्य अर्थाः-तेषां तर्पणविधौ).

Idea :—Had the celestial tree been discriminate in granting the requests of the supplicants, all its merits would have been extra-ordinary.

Appli :—Sometimes persons possessed of a number of extraordinary merits, have one serious defect.

67. अपगता घृणा यस्मात्-सः-relentless. अनुतापः-remorse. मा (अ) कृथाः imperative sense of the aorist; see note on the verse Bh. V. 1-6. विमलानि च तानि क्षेत्राणि (कर्म) तेषु-In sacred places. गूढः आशयः येषां ते-whose motives are concealed i.e. hypocrites. "अभिप्रायच्छन्द आशयः" कति न वसन्ति-सहस्त्रश एव वसन्ति। त्वया तुल्या कक्षा (गणना or अवस्था) येषां ते-whose state resembles yours or who are considered similar to you (in point of wickedness). कक्षा-गूढ-हिंसनादिकल्पना इति अच्युतरायाः.

Idea :—The fowler is asked not to feel remorse at heart as there are thousands of wicked persons like him.

Appli :—Here the poet intends to bring to light the secret hypocritical nature of the courtiers and so-called holy persons in holy places. In his opinion they resemble the fowler who slays those creatures that confide in him.

68. विश्वस्य-Gerund of the causal of श्वस् with वि, Having inspired confidence in. काश्यपि-O earth. "क्षोणिर्ज्या काश्यपी क्षितिः" कश्यपस्य इयं-she ought to be discriminate as she is related to the great sage.

Idea :—The earth has lost discretion. Hence she gives a resort to the cheaters.

Appli :—The same as that of the verse 13 in this Vilāsa.

69. जगद्धितमयी-beneficial to the world. अन्या has a typical meaning-extra-ordinary. आर्याणां हृद्या-captivating the noble. v.l. आर्तहृद्या—captivating the hearts of the distressed. "हृदि स्पृश्यते मनोज्ञत्वात्" दवीयः-comparative from दूर.

Idea :—Everything belonging to the learned beggars description.

70. आपदं गतः द्वि. त.-fallen into adversity. महान् आशयः येषां ते महाशयाः (बहु.) तेषां चक्रे वर्तते इति-the foremost of the high-souled or magnanimous. विस्तारयति-extends-causal of स्तृ with वि. पूर्वं अकृतं-अकृतपूर्वं-not shown (lit. done) before. उदारः भावः-तम-generosity-broadmindedness. कालागुरुः-a kind of sandal.

Idea :—Sandal when cast into fire emits greater fragrance.

Appli :—The great people shine more luxuriantly in adver-sity.

cf. कर्पूरः पावकस्पृष्टः सौरभं लभतेतराम्।।

71. विश्वस्य अभिरामाः गुणाः, तेषां गौरवेण गुम्फिताः (तृ. त.) तेषां adj. to निर्मलधियाम्-Filled with abundance (गौरव) of qualities agreeable to the whole world. निर्मला धीः येषां ते (बहु.) Those whose minds are pure i.e. free from jealousy etc. लोकं पृणन्ति ते (द्वि अलुक्) adj. to परिमल-The fragrance that brings satisfaction to the people. काश्मीरदेशे जायते-saffron is so called because it is produced in काश्मीर, नितान्तं रम्यां-excessively pleasing.

Idea :—Saffron though bitter is very agreeable.

Appli :—Even the wrath of persons who are selfless is pleasing. cf. रोषोऽपि निर्मलधियां रमणीय एव।

Compare:—

ये ये हताश्चक्रधरेण राजंस्त्रैलोक्यनाथेन जनार्दनेन।
ते ते गता विष्णुपुरीं प्रयाताः क्रोधोऽपि देवस्य वरेण तुल्यः।।

पाण्डवगीता

72. लीलया लुण्ठितः शारदायाः पुरस्य महत्याः संपदः भरः यैः तेषाम् (बहु.)-who in (mere) sport have plundered the excess of great wealth in the city of शारदा-the goddess of learning. विद्यायाः सद्मनः विनिर्गलतः कणान् मुष्णन्ति ते-adj. to पामराः-those who steal (of course hence very little of) particles dripping from the house of knowledge. "विवर्णः पामरो नीचः"-an insignificant person. अद्य वाश्वो वा इति अद्यश्वः सुप्सुप् समास to-day or tomorrow. v.l.-अद्यश्वः It is explained as अद्य वर्तमानदिने श्वयन्ते वर्धन्ते which means very recently born and is to be taken with शकुन्तशिशवः, शशाः and शालावश्काः मूर्ध्नि पदं धा-lit. to place a foot on the head i. e. to disparage, to defeat, to subdue, to overpower. "कुण्डली गूढपाद् चक्षुश्रवाः काकोदरः फणी" फणी-One possessing a hood. शालावृकाकपिक्रोष्टुश्वानः" Here it is better to take क्रोष्टु leaving the other two meanings.

Idea :—If persons with little knowledge were to prattle before the wise, impossible things will occur.

73. गुरूणाम्-of great persons. "गुरुस्तु गीष्पतौ श्रेष्ठे गुरौ पितरि दुर्भरे." परुषाणि अक्षराणि यासु-adj. to गीर्भिः containing harsh (words) letters. महत्वं यान्ति Attain greatness. न लब्धानि शाणे उत्कषणानि यैस्ते (बहु.) adj. to मणयः-That have not undergone the scratching on the touchstone 'चूडा किरीटं केशाश्च संयता मौलयस्त्रयः'। मौलिः-the head. 'कदाचिज्जातु.'

Idea :—Unless privations at the hands of great persons are put up with, none should hope to achieve greatness.

74. क्षितेः इन्द्राः (तत्पु.) Lords of the earth. 'पिशुनौ खलसूचकौ' पिशुनः जनः (कर्म.) a wicked man. विषस्य धरः-a repository of venom-a snake. मसीपटलं (शी) (षि) (सि)-the coat of soot. विधुः-the moon. 'विधुर्विष्णौचन्द्रमसि' "भजतेतराम् अत्यन्तं सेवते." तराम् is affixed of the verb in order to express the comparative degree. The verse perhaps brings to the world's notice that not only the earthly things like पटीरजन्मा or दीप but even celestial things like the moon, imitate the actions of the king, and hence the necessity of the king's character being a pattern of good conduct.

75. "पुरुषाः पूरुषा नराः" हितैः आचरणैः—by charitable conduct (कर्म). अमन्दं adv. without growing dull i.e. incessantly "उदारो दातृमहतोः" Here उदार means "generous" (in giving pleasure to the clusters of कैरविणीs) कैरव is a night lotus described as white in colour and blooming at the appearance of the moon. "सिते (कमले) कुमुदकैरवे"

Idea :—The good by their very nature are engaged in the work of doing good to others. cf. प्रकृतिरियं विमलानां क्लिश्यन्ति यदन्यकार्येषु।

76. महान् चासौ उपकारः च—great obligation. निर्गतः आतङ्कः यस्मात् सः निरातङ्कः-fearless. "रुक्तापशङ्कास्वातङ्कः" पीत्वा (1) Having drunk (milk) (2) Having swallowed i.e. forgotten (the obligation.) प्रत्युत-on the contrary. अपि is sometimes replaced by प्रत्युत. cf. अयं वत्सो न केवलं ध्रियते प्रत्युत प्राञ्जलिना गरुडेन पर्युपास्यमानस्तिष्ठतिः (Nag 5) "काकोदरः फणी" समानं उदरं यस्य सः-सोदरः-a brother. काकोदरस्य सोदरः-the brother of a serpent.

Idea :—A wicked man is as ungrateful as a serpent who bits the person who nourishes him with milk.

77. पाण्डित्यं परिहृत्य-Setting aside cleverness learnedness बंदित्वं—the duty of a bard or panegyrist. "बन्दिनः स्तुतिपाठकाः" दुःखेन प्राप्यते-दुष्प्रापं-difficult to be obtained, unobtainable. The Idea in the first line is, for whom flattery has been resorted to after setting aside love for lore and truth. तत्र रूढः-when he is established there-firmly-rooted there. निगीर्य has the same force as पीत्वा in the preceding verse. पूर्वेषां उपकाराणां आवलिं-series of previous obligations. प्रत्यवतिष्टते-स्था with प्रति and अप-("stand as an obstacle") becomes Atm. समवप्रविभ्यः स्थः (Pan. 1-3-22.)

Idea :—"पयःपानं भुजङ्गानां केवलं विषवर्धनम्"-Obligations shown to a wicked fellow result in ingratitude.

78. अपायं शङ्कन्ते इति-Those who suspect harm. कापय्यं एव दोषः-The defect of fraud. This तृतीया here shows हेतुः दूरेण is used adverbially at a distance. " आशीविषो विषधरः" serpent- "आश्यां (दंष्ट्रायां) विषं अस्य". विसृज्-to abandon, to leave.

Idea :—Those shrewd persons who apprehend fear from the deceitful, give no chance to them even to approach them.

79. आसङ्गः-आसक्तिः-Attachment, विशेषः आसङ्गः व्यासङ्गः- परस्य अर्थे व्यासङ्गः (तत्पु.)-Extreme attachment for doing good

to others, स्वार्थः एव परः यस्य सः (बहु.) तत्ता स्वार्थपरता-selfishness. उपजहत् is the nom. sing. of the present participle of उप+हा. The ending त् is not changed to न् (vide rule 23 lesson 16-Bhandarkar's second book of Sanskrit). गुणभूतेषु-between the three guṇas-सत्व, रजस् and तमस् and beings. (भूतs). v. l गुरुभूतेषु-गुरु is an adv. अभेद-(जातं) एकत्वम्(शाकपार्थिवादिः) अन्तः is an adverb-in the interior. ललितश्चोदात्तश्च महिमा (कर्म)-the beautiful and generous greatness. स्फुरति lit. throbs, manifests itself voluntarily. " समर्थस्त्रिषु शक्तिस्थे " समर्थः powerful. कोऽपि-indescribable. cf. तत्तस्य किमपि द्रव्यं यो हि यस्य प्रियो जनः। जयतितराम्-comparative from जयति.

Idea :—The man who is void of partiality and benevolent is the one who is victorious.

cf. अयं निजः परो वेति गणना लघुचेतसाम्।
उदारचरितानां तु वसुधैव कुटुम्बकम्।।

There is another interpretation also that has been given in many commentaries, which pertains to grammar. The कोऽपि पुरुषः in the last line refers to the तत्पुरुषसमास to which all the adjectives mentioned in the verse apply. (1) परार्थव्यासङ्गात्स्वार्थ-परतां उपजहत्. It abandons the meaning of itself (स्वस्थः अर्थः) by its attachment to the other meaning (परार्थ). In a तत्पुरुष compound the two members give up their individual meaning and form some different meaning e.g. in the compound. राज्ञः पुरुषः, the whole compound राजपुरुष points to a meaning different from that denoted either by राजन् or पुरुष taken individually. Thus the first line can be applied to the तत्पुरुष compound. There is अभेदैकत्व i.e. unity born from non-difference between the two members which are the components (गुणभूत) whereas the compound is the गुणी or the whole. Before the formation of the तत्पुरुष compound there is भेद between the two members but after the compound is formed there is absolute unity in the meaning. The third adjective is स्वभावाद्यस्यान्तः सकलोदात्त-महिमा स्फुरति. सकलोदात्तमहिमा is adj. to अन्त-सकलः उदात्तस्य महिमा यस्मिन्-with all glory of an उदात्त accent; The अन्त of a तत्पुरुष compound possesses all the greatnees of an उदात्त accent, whose end by its very nature throbs, whose last syllable (अन्तः) is always उदात्त. According to vedic grammar the last letter of a Tatpuruṣa compound is always accented or उदात्त. That तत्पुरुष is always able i.e. the words in the compound are capable of forming a समास i.e. they are capable of always giving one connected meaning.

This twisted sense shows too much mania for puns. Thus the natural beauty of a poem is marred, it becomes dull, insipid and artificial. मंम्मट also voices the same opinion when he says "शब्दचित्रं वाच्यचित्रमव्यङ्ग्य त्ववरं स्मष्टतम्" K. P.1-5.

80. "द्वौ वंशौ कुलमस्करौ" वंशः-Bamboo, गुण-a rope, a quality. सङविशेष in the case of पुरुष means "good company", in the other case it means "being fixed to." "तुम्बीफलेन विकलः (त.)-void of a तुम्बी fruit. वंशभवः and गुणवान् are to be construed both with पुरुष and वीणादण्डः. In the first instance वंशभव will mean "born of a noble family," in the second, "born of a bamboo."गुणवान् in the first case means" possessed of good qualities" in the second "possessed of strings."

Idea :—Inspite of the possession of a number of noble qualities, men are valued from the company they keep.

81. निखिलेषु रसायनेषु महितः (स. त.)-रसायन is the elixir of life. It is a medicine that prolongs life and prevents old age, similar to अमृत. महितः-honoured, prominent. The धन्वन्तरीय निघण्टु in the 4th (करवीरादि) वर्ग enumerates the qualities of

this कन्दलशुन. The various names that have been given there show its unique position in the sphere of medicine. रसोनो लशुनोऽरिष्टो म्लेच्छकन्दो महौषधम्। महाकन्दो रसोनः etc. The peculiar qualities are स्वादुरसोऽतिबल्यः। वृष्यश्चमेधा खरवर्णचक्षुर्भग्नास्थि-सन्धानकरः सुतीक्ष्णः-pungent excessively--It gives great strength and vitality, it is used in joining fractures, developes memory, sweetens voice, improves the colour of the body and gives a cooling sensation and improves the eye-sight. It is called रसोन because it contains all the five main tastes (रसs) with the exception of अम्ल (sour). अमिताः गुणाः यस्मिन् सः (बहु.) possessed of innumerable qualities.

82. सन्तः गुणाः यस्य (बहु.) One possessed excellent qualities. विपदम् गतः (द्वि. त.) reduced to adversity. मूर्च्छा गतः-fallen in swoon. The मूर्च्छा and मरण are to be construed with पारद also. It cannot be utilized unless it is संस्कृत i.e. operated upon. राजनिघण्टु in (सुवर्णादि) 6th वर्ग mentions-संस्कारहीनं खलु सूतराजं (पारदं) सेवेत यस्तस्य करोति बाधाम्। देहस्य नाशं विदधाति नूनं कुष्ठादिदोषान् जनयेन्नराणाम्-when मूर्च्छित it removes all diseases (मूर्च्छित-मूर्च्छितो हरते व्याधीन्) if मारित-it gives all Siddhis (सर्वा सिद्धिकरो लीनः,) it achieves all objects. मूर्च्छना and मरण are two chemical processes of treating quick-silver corresponding to calcination and purification respectively. The two processes of मूर्च्छना and मारण have been explained in detail in the शार्ङ्गधरसंहिता, मध्यमखण्ड अध्याय 12 verses 4 to 12 and 35-37 and we leave the critical study of these verses for students more particularly interested in that science.

83. वनस्य अन्तः (ष. त.) the boundary or skirts of a forest. (Here it is उपवन). खेलन्ती-Present Participle femin. of खेलृ. शशकस्य शिशुः (त.) a young hare. चकिता-विस्मिता startled.

सपदि immediately "सद्यः सपदि तत्क्षणे" भयस्य हर्ता भयहर्ता (त.) the remover of danger. भुजयोः प्रान्तः The space between the two hands (bosom) i.e. embraces her husband through fear. दश वदनानि यस्य सः-तेन नीता (त.) The ten faced i.e. Ravana. हलानि इव रदाः येषां ते (ब.)-whose teeth were as big as ploughs. परि+इ to surround-परीता surrounded. विवशा-विगतः वशः (control) यस्याः सा-helpless. कामपि दशाम् to an indescribably (pitiable) plight.

Idea :—सुखत्तु यो याति नरो दरिद्रतां धृतः शरीरेण मृतः स जीवति। (मृच्छ. १-१०.) The only difference between the two is that the result of adversity succeeding prosperity is expressed in the quotation, whereas in the verse under consideration it is suggested by the words कामपि etc.

84. "गीर्वाणा दानवारयः" गीर्वाणाः-Gods. पुरः governs the gen. of that with reference to which the direction is shown (vide Apte's guide sec. 112.) cf. तिष्ठन् भाति पितुः पुरो भुवि यथा (Nag. 1-6). निजभुजबलस्य आहोपुरुषिकां self-conceitedness of strength of one's own arms. अहं पुरुषः इत्यहंकारवान् अहोपुरुषः-तस्य भावः आहोपुरुषिका-egoism, pride, आहोपुरुषिका दर्पाद् या स्यात् संभावनात्मनि अहो-Alas ! "अहो धिगर्थे शोके च, [करुणार्थविषादयोः। संबोधने प्रशंसायां विस्मये पादपूरणे॥] कारं कारं- "अभीक्ष्णं कृत्वा" doing again and again. It is a Ṇamul form or gerund in अम् (vide Apte's guide sec. 162) पुराणि भिनत्ति इति पुरभिद्-God Śiva. The असुरs led by मयासुर prepared three big walls and remained in them safe from their enemies, the Gods. But महादेव, accompanied by other Gods, overcame them and destroyed these three पुरs and thus brought the demons to ruin. This episode has been described in many places, the above is common to all the places. (भागवत. ७-१०)

संमुखयतः–संमुखं कुर्वतः-presenting before, aiming gen. sing. from denominative participle from संमुख. स्मरस्य-of the god of love. स्वर्बालानां (देवाङ्गनानां) नयनानि एव सुमानि तेषां मालाः तासां अर्चनपदं (पूजास्थानम्)-The abode of worship or reverence by the garlands of flowers in the form of eyes of celestial damsel. भाले अनलः तस्य भसितजालं तस्य आस्पदम्-The receptacle of the mass of ashes of the fire on शिव's forehead. The reference is to the fire of the third eye on the forehead of God Śiva.

Idea :—The evil done to great persons returns on its author, (Here the God of love tried to make the great God Śiva the butt of his arrows, but was himself reduced to ashes by the fire on his forehead.)

85. मृदुलानि आसनानि-soft seats. चीत्कृतिः-refers to the particular cry of monkeys. अतिथेयी–(अतिथिसत्क्रिया)-hospitality. विपाटितानि refers to the scratches made by the monkeys in sport and in the act of greeting.

Idea :—Etiquettes of people vary according to their civilization. Herein are described those of monkeys.

86. In this verse a series of questions are put and poetically answered. The answers are ingenious enough so as to illustrate what is technically called परिसंख्या-Poetic exclusion. It consists of excluding general things that arise as natural answers to the questions asked. On account of some poetic cause e. g. here, what is a holy place ? the natural answer expected may be any holy place, like Benares. But the answer हरिपादपद्मभजनं excludes the possibility of all such answers and thus establishes its own prominence. Similarly other answers there. हरेः पादौ पद्मे इव तयोः भजनं-devotion to

the lotus-like feet of हरि. अच्छा—pure. द्वैतं एव अन्धकार: तस्य उत्कर:—The multitude of darkness in the form of dualism (considering परमात्मा different from जीवात्मा). सततं उपकारेषु रसिकं—always fond of obliging (others)-always taking pleasure in obligations. तत्त्वस्य अवबोध:-knowledge of the truth (viz. identity of परमात्मा and जीवात्मा-तत् (परमात्मा) त्वं (जीवात्मा) असि (छां VI-1-2) खेदस्य दाने कुशल:-clever in giving pain.

87. नितरां स्नात: निष्णात: lit. deeply bathed in i.e well-versed. वेदान्ते-वेदानां अन्ते-In the lore at the end of vedas i.e. philosophical lore. This is chronologically the latest portion of the Vedic literature. मैनाक:-(मेनकायां भव:) son of the Himālayas from मेनका. Formerly mountains were winged. Once it so happened that Indra was blocked by these mountains. Consequently he became angry and chopped of their wings. मैनाक whose friend was the ocean plunged himself into it in order to save himself from the fury of Indra. Thus he retained his wings. The same story is referred to in क्रुद्धेऽपि पक्षच्छिदि वृत्रशत्राववेदनाज्ञं कुलिशक्षतानाम् K. S. 1-20.

Idea :—न यत्नकोटिशतकैरपि दुष्ट: सुधीर्भवेत्। किं मर्दितोऽपि कस्तूर्यां लशुनो याति सौरभम्।। सु. निर्गता: गुणा: यस्मात् स: (ब.) तस्य भाव: नैर्गुण्यम् साधीयस् is the comparative in ईयस् from बाढ well. धिक् governing the accusative here. गुणानां गौरवम् (ष. त.) a multitude of virtues, शाखिन्-शाखा: सन्ति अस्य-a tree-lit. one that has branches. The verse voices the experience of the world where persons void of virtue enjoy freely while the virtuous are always labouring in the harness. A similar idea is expressed in the verse: गुणानामेव दौरात्म्यात् धुरि धुर्यो नियुज्यते। असञ्जातकिणस्कन्ध: सुखं स्वपिति गौर्गडि:।। or शुक पञ्जरवासस्ते मधुराणां गिरां फलम्।

89. परं प्रति उपसर्पणं (approaching) तेन अनन्ता या चिन्ता (the unending or interminable anxiety) सा एव अनलः तस्य शिखाः तासां शतानि तैः- by hundreds of flames of fire in the form of endless anxieties caused by approaching others (for begging for one's livelihood). न चुम्बितं (kissed, touched) अन्तःकरणं येषां ते (बहु.)-whose heart is not touched by that. साधु-happily. पादैः पिबन्ति इति (उप.).The trees are so called because they suck water through the roots. The poet aims at pointing to the pitiable condition of a householder in-as-much-as he is less happy than even an insentient tree.

For a similar idea compare:

दक्षिणाशाप्रवृत्तस्य प्रसारितकरस्य च।
तेजस्तेजस्विनोऽर्कस्य हीयतेऽन्यस्य का कथा।।

90. शून्ये (1) A place which is void of fibres. (ii) निर्गुणेऽपि- a man who is void of virtues. गुणवत्ता-the qualities of being (1) possessed of fibres (ii) Possessed of merits. स्वकीयानां गुणानां जालैः (ष. त.)-(1) by the network of its own threads. (ii) by the network (stock) of his own qualities. विवराणि मुद्रयन् (1) filling up the gaps (defects) of others. स्वकीयगुणजालैः is to be construed both with गुणवत्तामातन्वानः and विवराणि मुद्रयन्. The good man is here compared to a spider. It is well-known that this insect prepares a cob-web, out of threads drawn out from its own body. A good man transforms a dunce

lso into one possessed of good qualities and hides his shortcomings. "द्राङ्मङ्क्षु सपदि द्रुतम्"। The word ऊर्णायु (spider) has been formed by adding the term युस् to ऊर्णा in the sense of possession, by ऊर्णाया युस् (Pan. 5-3-123.)

91. सज्जनः एव कार्पासः तस्य रक्षणे एकः (अद्वितीयः) हुताशनः। The fire matchless in the protection of cotton in the form of

a good man. एक is used in the sense of अद्वितीय. Vide न केवलं तद्गुरुरेकपार्थिवः क्षितावभूदेकधनुर्धरोऽपि सः।। परेषां दुःखं एव अग्निः तस्य शमने मारुत:-the wind in cooling the fire in the form of the pain of others. In this verse by लक्षणा the words रक्षण and शमन mean exactly the opposite of the ordinary sense viz. भक्षण and प्रवर्धन respectively. This sense is to be followed because the expressed meaning is irrelevant here. लक्षणा consists in the superimposing of another meaning, when the primary meaning is not applicable; for details see-मम्मट's काव्यप्रकाश २. मुख्यार्थबाधे तद्योगेरुढितोऽथ प्रयोजनात्। अन्योर्थो लक्ष्यते यत्सा लक्षणारोपिताक्रिया।। There is another reading also in the सुभाषितरत्नभाण्डागार which reads धक्षण or भक्षण for रक्षण and धमन for शमन thus leaving no necessity of resisting to any लक्षणा at all. The fire burning the cotton is proverbial cf. न खलु न खलु बाणः संनिपात्योऽयमस्मिन्मृदुनि मृगशरीरे तूलराशाविवाग्निः। Sak-I-10, so is the constant companionship of fire and wind and hence the aggravation of fire. cf.

मधुश्च ते मन्मथ साहचर्यादसावनुक्तोऽपि सहाय एव।
समीरणो न दयिता भवेति व्यादिश्यते केन हुताशनस्य।।

K. S. III 21

92. The epithets in the first line have a double meaning and the comparisons are made effective on account of puns. परेषां यद्गुह्यं तस्य गुप्तिः तस्मिन् निपुणं well-versed in protecting the गुह्य (1) secrets in the case of सज्जन & (2) private parts in the case (of ललिताम्बर) of others "रहस्योपस्थयोर्गुह्यम्" गुणमयं (1) full of merits (2) full of threads. नितरामखिलैः समीहितं—p.p.p from सम्+ईह्. desired this is applicable to both-greatly desired by all. ललितं च तदम्बरं च a fine garment दूषयन्ति (1) spoil, blame (2) tear, gnaw. Instead of खलाः some read खराः। But

"रलयोः अभेदात्" खल and खर (an ass) need not be distinguished from each other.

93. यश एव सौरभ्यं तम्य लशुनः-a garlic to the fragrance in the form of fame. Here the wicked man is compared to a garlic poetically. A garlic is sure to destroy any fragrance, so also a wicked man is sure to sully fame. शान्तिरेव शैत्यं तस्य हुताशनः-fire to the cold in the form of tranquillity or calmness of mind. "शमथस्तु शमः शान्तिः" हुतं अश्नाति इति हुताशनः-fire Just as a fire is the enemy of cold so also a wicked man becomes the enemy of calmness of mind i. e. he will be ever perturbed, कारुण्यं एव कुसुमं तस्य आकाशः-the sky to the flowers in the form of compassion i.e. Just as आकाश will never produce flowers so also a wicked man will never put forth compassion. The idea suggested by "कुसुमाकाश" refers to the well-known अत्यन्ताभावs (absolute impossibility) in the following verse, मृगतृष्णाम्भसि स्नातः खपुष्पकृतशेखरः। एष वन्ध्यासुतो याति शशशृङ्गधनुर्धरः॥ He is ever merciless. सज्जनानां दुःखं-ददाति (v. l. दुःखलः-दुःखं लाति संपादयति) giving pain to the good.

94. कुसुमानि च पत्राणि च फलानि च तेषां आवलीनां भरं-The burden of clusters of flowers, leaves and fruits. घर्मस्य व्यथां pangs of heat. "घर्मो निदाघः" शीताद् भवां रुजं pangs arising from cold. "स्त्री रुग्रुजा चोपतापरोगव्याधिगदामयाः" वदान्येषु गुरुः तस्मै-the foremost among the donors. "मां याचस्वेति वदति वदान्यः" "स्युर्वदान्यस्थूल-लक्ष्यदानशौण्डा बहुप्रदे." नमस् requires the dat. of the person to whom salutation is offered. cf. हरचूडानिहितात्मने नमस्ते। V. K. 3)

Idea :—The tree is bowed down because he is the foremost among all those sacrificing their self for others.

c. f. स्वसुखनिरभिलाषः खिद्यसे लोकहेतोः
प्रतिदिनमथवा ते वृत्तिरेवं विधैव।
अनुभवति हि मूर्ध्ना पादपस्तीव्रमुष्णं
शमयति परितापं छायया संश्रितानाम्।। S. 5-7.

Appli :—The best of self-sacrificers deserve salutations.

95. हालाहलं-deadly poison-one of the fourteen jewels churned out of the ocean described in the well-known verse, लक्ष्मीःकौस्तुभ etc., and later on drunk by the God Śiva. पिपासति-3rd sing. of the desiderative verb formed from पा to drink-desires to drink. कालानलः-(कालरूपः अनलः)। This is the fire at the final deluge supposed to possess the greatest power of burning. cf. दग्धुं विश्वं दहनकिरणैर्नोदिता द्वादशार्काः। Ve. 3-8. परिचुचुम्बिषति desiderative 3rd per. sing. from परि+चुम्ब्-to touch-to kiss. व्यालानां अधिपः-the lord of serpents. परिरब्धुं-to bind. अद्धा. (adv.) actually, really, manifestly. वशयितुं-ing. of the causal from वश्—to persuade—to win over. मनीषा—a desire.

Idea :—It is absolutely impossible to win over a wicked man.

96. "दीनो दरिद्रो दुर्गतोऽपि सः" दुःसहः मदः यस्य सः (बहु.) दुर्मदः तस्य-one who is unbearably haughty or proud. शुष्काणि सस्यानि-crops dried up owing to drought. औदार्यं प्रकटयतः-displaying generosity. It refers to the profuse pouring of the rain by the cloud on the mountains. मह्याः धराः ष. त. तावकः विवेकः-त्वदीयः विवेकः Here by ironical sense विवेक means अविवेकः. For the use of such लक्षणा See Bh. V. 1-91.

Idea :—Here the profuse charity of the cloud to the mountains, setting aside dry fields, is ironically condemned.

Appli :—Charity shown to the rich setting aside the poor deserves condemnation. cf. दवदहनजटाल. Bh. V. 1-(36).

97. गुरवः-Great. जगदण्डम् (जगद्रूपं अण्डम्)-the whole universe. This universe is supposed to be the egg first created by the creator and then it produced this earth. प्रलयेऽप्यचलाः-firm-undaunted-even at the time of the world deluge. cf. अपि स्फुटति विन्ध्याद्रौ वाति वा प्रलयानले। गुरुशास्त्रानुगो मार्गः परित्याज्यो न धीमता।। (योगवासिष्ठः).

Idea :—The magnanimous are the greatest of all.

98. बीजाकृ-to sow seeds. पवने चित्रं निर्माति etc.-Sowing seeds in the sky is equivalent to no-sowing; drawing pictures in the wind and lines in water are as good as not doing so; similarly paying respect to the wicked is as good as not paying it.

Idea :—Respect paid to the wicked is fruitless. v. l. व्योमनि वासं कुरुते (or शम्बां कुरुते), चित्रं निर्माति यत्नतः सलिले। स्नपयति वासं सलिलैर्यः क्षुद्रे चरति सत्कारम्।।

शम्बां कुरुते-He ploughs the fields (in the sky.) शम्बां "क्षेत्रभक्तिं-कृषिविभागम्"

स्नपयति-Caus. 3rd. Sing. from स्ना to bathe cf. हालाहलं खलु Bh. V. I-98.

99. लेढि is present 3rd. per. sing. of लिह् to lick and जिघ्रति of घ्रा to smell. आसनं उन्नतं करोति-means, raises his seat (of course by placing the necklace below its haunches). This aims at showing that pearls cast before swine are not valued. In the present case the necklace of jewels is immensely valuable but what of that to an ape ? When he finds that it cannot be eaten, he throws it away; because it is worthless from his viewpoint. cf. किं मिष्टमन्नं खरसूकराणाम्।

Idea :—A monkey does not realise the value of a necklace of jewels.

Some editions read आननम् for आसनम् in line 4. This is also a good reading. This enables one to form a mental picture of the monkey. When it first licks the necklace, then smells and throws it away (finding it of no use) and then raises its head as if to express that it is worthless in his opinion in the act of mocking.

अनल्पं जल्पते इति-who is very talkative. विकसितं वदनं यस्याः—with a blooming face. The above is the expressed meaning wherein the action of a bee leaving a lotus plant that loves it inspite of its shortcomings is condemned for its faithlessness. This verse is also to be understood in another sense viz. as advice to a fickle lover who loves his lady who is attached to him inspite of his numerous shortcomings. This अलंकार is known as समासोक्ति in Sanskrit rhetoric and is defined by मम्मट as परोक्तिर्भेदकैः श्लिष्टैः समासोक्तिः (The description of another thing [परोक्ति] by paranomastic (श्लिष्टैः) adjectives (भेदकैः) is called समासोक्ति). Hence besides the one interpretation that has been given, there is also another explanation possible. Here a भ्रमर will mean a truthless, dishonest lover, whereas the सरोजिनी will mean the lady who is in love with him and tries to please him in all possible ways. In that case मलिनेऽपि रागपूर्णा etc., will mean that she is attached to you although you are truthless, deceitful. She looks smilingly at you although you are very talkative. (Talkative persons are supposed to be insincere in love-matters), she loves you, though you are fickleminded. How would you then, O lover, abandon your lady?

adjecti-ves	as applied to the bee.	applied to the lover	adjecti-ves	as applied to सरोजिनी	as applied to the lady.
मलिन	black	faithless	रागपूर्णा	red-coloured	full of love
अनल्प-जल्पे	Constantly humming	very talkative (indication of fickle mindedness)	विकसित-वदनां	with blooming lotuses	with smiling face.
चपले	active (physically)	unstable in mind	सरसां	full of honey	full of amorousness or affection.

101. मलिनतां भज्—to be blackened, to be disgraced. इदं किं विचित्रम् what wonder is there ? परस्मै इदं परार्थं (च. त.) स्वस्मै इदं स्वार्थम्. कालिमानं. Here the illustration is based on the pun on the word कालिमन्.

Idea :—Begging money of rich peolpe for selfish purposes brings infamy.

102. जनक: सानुविशेष:। The father of sandal is a particular सानु (summit) of the mountain मलय i.e. it has a low descent. जाति: काष्ठम्-Its caste is wood which is not so honourable. It keeps company with the serpents and hence this is also a serious defect. Thus all the three ways by which a man attains greatness viz. descent, position and companionship being absent in the case of sandal, naturally its greatness is

retarded, but it reaches greatness only through its intrinsic greatness not withstanding the presence of the above-mentioned three serious defects.

Idea :—Sandal is great only because of its intrinsic merits.

103. "हन्त हर्षेऽनुकम्पायाम्" here it shows अनुकम्पा. गुणानां ग्राम: (multitude) तस्य अर्जमन् obtaining a multitude of virtues. चेत्-if स्वात्मन: उपस्करणं ornament to oneself. भावा: qualities, things. शोभाभरै: संभृता: (lit. nourished) full of great beauty. सज्जसि-from the root सस्ज् to get ready. तैरेव कले: वर्तनम्। (वृत्ति:)-quarrels maintain themselves on these beautiful qualities. The idea is that quarrels grow in this world on account of the possession of merits. कलेवरं पुष्णाति-तस्य adj. to कलि: whose body is day by day growing robust and hence the quarrels in the world increase daily. The कलि is said to be waxing stronger because it is being powerful day by day as it advances. This is based on the belief that the कलि age began on the day when Śrī Kṛ—ṇa breathed his last and since that day it has been growing more and more powerful. Here कलि is personified and hence is described as कलेवरपुषू [The कलि is said to have begun on the day on which श्रीकृष्ण went to वैकुण्ठ when the great Bear entered the constellation मघा. It consists of 4,32000 years of men and it began on the 13th of Feb. 3102 B. C.]

Idea :—Do not cultivate any merits for it is the root of all dissensions.

The reading वर्धनं for वर्तनम् is not so happy because कलेवरपुष: already has the idea of वर्धन, वर्तनम् is much better because, although the body of कलि is fat, if its source of livelihood वर्तनम् (वृत्ति:) is stopped it will wane immediately.

Our deliberate negligence in acquiring merits is the only way of emaciating Kali.

104. धूमायिता:-P. P P. of the denominative from धूम-Turned smoky. दलितानि (bloomed) अरविन्दानि यासु ता: (adj. to दिश:) in which the lotuses are blown open. v. l. ललितारविन्दा:-in which there are charming lotuses; of course this reading is inapplicable as without the spring there can be no charm in lotuses. गन्धस्य वाहा:-गन्धवाहा:-winds. अन्तरेण "without" requires the acc. e.g. तत्त्वं किमपि काव्यानां जानाति विरलो भुवि। मार्मिक: को मरन्दानामन्तरेण मधुव्रतम्। Bh. V. 1-117. मृदूनि ताम्राणि दलानि येषां, ते आम्रा: तेषु मञ्जु गुञ्जन्त: मधुव्रता: (bees) यस्मिन् स:-एतादृश हे मधो-(मधु व्रतं भक्ष्यं येषां ते मधुव्रता:)-spring in which the bees are humming melodiously on the mango trees whose leaves are tender and red. v. l. मृदुताम्रदलाम्र मञ्जु गुञ्जन् मधुव्रत मधो. मृदुताम्रदलाम्र and मञ्जु...मधुव्रत quallify मधो-the meaning will be simuarly taken. v. l. मृदुलालकलाम्र Here आम्र after मृदुल is superfluous. v. l. मृदुजाम्रदलाम्र-(मृदुजालकल-आम्र) मञ्जुगुञ्जन्मधुव्रत मधो—This ‑eading yields a far fetched meaning मृदु जालक (कलिकाजाल) तद् लाति (आदत्ते) एतादृश आम्र-i.e. a tree, putting on the cluster of tender blossoms. मञ्जु व्रतम् qualifies त्वां कोकिलस्य is to be construed with देह in the 2nd line. Here there is दूरान्वय-दोष.

Idea :—Spring is a great pleasure-giver, without him lotuses and cuckoos will be scorched on account of summer heat.

Appli :—The value of a really deserving man is known only in his absence.

105. भिन्ना-P. P. P. from भिद् to break. करे जायन्ते इति करजा: (nails) तेषां अग्राणि तेषा जाग्रत: (active) उद्दामा: शौर्यस्य निकरा:

तैः—with a great deal of valour, active and prominent at the ends of their nails. "करटः करिगण्डे स्यात्" हेमः। करटिभ्रमेण—Mistaking rocks for elephants. दैवे पराचि-when fate is adverse. पराच् adj. unfavourable. कुत्रापि नापि खलु हा पिशितस्य लेशः। Here नापि=न+अपि passive 3rd per. sing. aorist from आप i. e. did not obtain. "पिशितं तरसं मांस" v. l. लिलिहे-Pass. Perf. of लिह् was licked.

Idea :—Under adverse circumstances even though a lion puts forth the best of his valour yet he does not get even a bit of an elephant's flesh.

Appli :—प्रतिकूलतामुपगते हि विधौ विफलत्वमेति बहुसाधनता।

106. गर्जितम् refers to the thundering of clouds. मनाक् means ईषद्-a little. "किञ्चिदीषन्मनागल्पे." निशायः अर्ध जातस्य अस्य-though half a night old. (Pan. कालाः परिमाणिना 2-2-5) द्राक्-at once, quickly. v. l. अतिभृशम् greatly निभृतम्—secretly. आकुंच्य-gerund of आ+कुञ्च् 6. P-Having contracted.

Idea and **Appli** :—cf. Bh. V. I-61.

107. दिव्या मतिः यस्य सः (बहु.) of divine (celestial) intellect (said ironically.) गुणेषु पक्षपातः (स. त.) Partiality for qualities (said ironically). अहनि च निशायां च अहर्निशम्-always, constantly. शालिन्-adj. generally used at the end of a compound meaning possessed of. Hence गुणशालिनः means men possessed of good qualities. The intended meaning is that the wicked always trouble the meritorious persons. This is technically known as व्याजस्तुति i.e. praise resulting in censure.

108. अग्र in front of वि+विच् (3-7 U) to separate, divide. Gerund of this root is विविच्य पापः आत्मा यस्य सः-whose self is sinful. हत-wretched अलम् used with instrumental in the

sense of निवारण. "अलं भूषणपर्याप्तिशक्तिवारणभूमसु" [This is an example of an आक्षेपालंकार, which consists in denying what is intended with the object of intimating something in particular. (see का. प्र. X)] "अथवा" is used to correct or modify the former statement. (vide Apte's Guide Sec. 245 a) दीर्घे किं न सहस्रधाहमथवा रामेण किं दुष्करम् (U. 6-40). Here the author leaves aside his first thought of relating the biography of a wicked man intimating that it is horrible and hence he is desisting from doing so.

109. खलानां समागमः-companionship with the wicked. आनंदः एव मृगः (कर्म.) तस्य दावाग्निः, दावश्चासौ अग्निश्च "दवदावौ वनारण्यवह्नी" forest conflagration to the deer in the form of joy. शीलं एव शाखी (कर्म.)-a tree in the form of character मदयुक्तः द्विपः-(शाखपार्थिवादि स.) like a rutting elephant to the tree form of one's character. ज्ञानं एव दीपः (कर्म.) तस्य महावायुः like a hurricane to the lamp in the form of knowledge.

Idea :—The companionship with the wicked, mars our joy, destroys our character and extinguishes our knowledge. आनन्द is metaphorically supposed to be a मृग, so also शील to be a शाखिन् and ज्ञान to be a दीप.

110. साधूनां हितं तस्य प्रत्यूहकर्म-तस्मिन् कुशलाः "विघ्नोऽन्तरायः प्रत्यूहः"-clever in the act of putting impediments in the welfare of the good. निर्गतं आगः यस्मात् सः-निरागाः तेषाम् (बहु.) "आगोऽपराधो मन्तुश्च।" प्राणान् is used in the plural, (Apte's Guide Sec.6,) because they are five in number-प्राण, अपान, व्यान, उदान and समान and are said to occupy the following places in the body. हृदि प्राणो गुदेऽपानः समानो नाभिमण्डले उदानः कण्ठदेशस्थो व्यानः सर्वशरीरगः॥

111. "रसज्ञा रसना जिह्वा" रसनायाः मिषेण in the guise of the

tongue. विनिवेशित is the p. p. p. of वि+नि+विश् cau. अवलीढ is p. p. p. of अवलिह-licked, bit. नास्ति मन्त्रः येषा ते (बहु.) (1) who are not cured by magical charms. (2) Unless good counsel is given to them.

112. (This whole verse is ironical). उन्नतम्-noble, here by व्यंग्यार्थ means "base." अमलम्-clear, unstained, by व्यंग्यार्थ notorious. आशिषः-blessings, here curses. यावज्जीवम् so long as life lasts, is a ṇamul form formed by the Sūtra यावति विन्दजीवोः (Pan. 3-4-30) (यावाञ्जीवः तावन्तं कालम्) सखे also then means शत्रो.

113. अविरतं परकार्यकृतां सतां वचः मधुरिमातिशयेन अमृतं (इव) अपि च मानसं अम्बुनिधिः (इव) यशः विमलशारदचन्दिरचन्किा। परेषां कार्याणि कुर्वन्ति ते पराकार्यकृतः-तेषां obligers of others. मधुरिम्णः अतिशयः तेन excess of sweetness. शरदि भवः शारदः by the Sūtra संधिवेलाद्यृतुनक्षत्रेभ्योऽण् (Pan. 4-3-16) विमलश्च असौ शारदः चन्दिराः (चन्द्रः) तस्य चंद्रिका-the moonlight of the clear autumnal moon. मानसं (mind) is like the sea-in its expanse, greatness. This points to the magnanimity of the man. The autumnal sky is typically clear.

114. कुसुमानां आकरः—mine of flowers i.e. spring. सञ्जीवयिता-1st future 3rd per. sing. from the causal of जीव् with सम्-will restore to life. समधायि—Pass. Aorist 3rd per. sing. from धा with सम्-was aimed at-i.e. discharged. शौभिकेन-by a fowler.

This is an example of how man proposes and God disposes.

115. निर्गताः गुणाः यस्मात् सः निर्गुणः-devoid of merits विपुलः आडम्बरः यस्य सः विपुलाडम्बरः-of ample ostentatious display i.e. set off by fine (outward) display. आपाते रम्या पुष्पाणां श्रीः

तया शोभित:-adorned by the beauty of flowers charming for the present moment.

116. सद:-An assembly-a meeting. "आस्थानं...सद:" कटुवर्णै:-Harsh alphabets. (कटवश्च ते वर्णाश्च तै:) विषयै:-sensual objects. पङ्कै:-the plural does not denote anything in particular. Perhaps it is used for euphony with जनै:, वर्णै: and विषयै:। Here in this verse the verb भाति is to be construed with every idea.

117. Exp. किमपि-indescribable. मार्मिक:-an appreciator. मरन्द:-honey. For अन्तरेण and मधुव्रत see Bh. V. 1-104.

118. निर्गता त्रपा (shame) यस्मात् स: निस्त्रप:-Shameless. In this verse the word निस्त्रप is the most important one as it is the root cause of the double meanings of the following words. सरजस्कां-रजसा सह-(1) full of pollen (applicable to the केतकी creeper) (2) a woman in menstruation (applicable in the case of a shameless man who is intended to be condemned.) पाण्डुवर्णा-पाण्डु: वर्ण: यस्या: सा (1) of dusty yellowish complexion, (2) of pale colour (It shows palour and consequent weakness of a woman who is therefore not proper for enjoyment.) कण्टकानां प्रकरै: अन्वितास्-(1) accompanied by a number of thorns. (The केतकी possessed of the thorns.) (2) possessed of rough hair. (in the case of a woman.) रोलम्ब-O bee.

Idea :—It refers to a shameless man who enjoys a woman in menstruation and to a bee who enjoys a केतकी of the type described above.

119. Four woethless things are pointed out in this verse. तान:-variation in notes in a song. राग: refers to any variety of a song. दानं-means "rut" "intoxication," "Ichor."

120. स्वत: of their own accord. परत: through the medium of others. "आमोद: सोऽतिनिर्हारी." हि-indeed. The idea in the

last line is-we are not required to take an oath to prove the existence of musk. विभाव्यते-Is made known; present causal passive 3rd per. sing. of भू with वि.

The good qualities of men come to light of their own accord and not through (the medium of) others. The fragrance of musk is not indeed made known by oath.

121. गर्वं मा (अ) यासी:-Do not be proud. मौलि:-the best (lit. the head) because 'head' is the best limb of the body. गिरे: गहने गुहायां in the den in the forest on the mountain. स्वजनक:—the father of musk i.e. the कस्तूरीमृग which possesses the musk and hence is hunted by the fowlers, his existence being made known everywhere by the diffusion of its fragrance.

Idea :—O कस्तूरि! do not be proud of your fragrance which brings death to your father.

Appl :—People should not feel proud of that wealth which they have obtained at the sacrifice of their near and dear ones.

122. दूरीकृ-विमलीकृ-चुलुकीकृ-बहुलीकृ are all च्वि formations in the sense of अभूततद्भाव i.e. changing a thing into that, which was not before. कुत्सिता मति: (कर्म.) विगत: मल: यस्मात् तत् (बहु.) adj. चेत: to चिरन्तन adj. of long standing. चुलुकीकरोति-(चुलुक-a mouthful) swallows i.e. destroys. cf. सत्संगति: कथय किं न करोति पुंसाम्. सतां संग: is to be construed with every clause.

123. अनवरत: य: परोपकार: तेन व्यग्रीभवति अमलं चेत: येषाम् तेषाम् (बहु.) adj. to महताम्-of the great whose pure mind is always engrossed in the incessant (performance of) charitable actions. आपाते काटवं येषं तानि adj. to वचनानि-whose bitterness (unpleasantness) is felt only in the beginning (afterwards it is

whole some as the medicine). The adjectives can be beautifully interpreted to refer to वचन as well as भेषज.

124. व्यागुञ्जन्तः ये मधुकराः तेषां पुंजैः मजुं (adv.) गीता. (adj.) to स्तुति-the praise that is sung by the clusters of sweetly humming bee उदयन् यो नयः (विनयः) तस्य अतिरेकः-Excess of modesty resulting from it (the praise) अवनौ रोहन्ति ते-trees. आभूमीतलं नताः कन्धराः येषां तानि-bending their necks to (reach) the ground.

Idea :—The trees (which are personified) bend down their neck and touch the ground by their branches through modesty on hearing their praise sung by the bees. This is a fine example of उत्प्रेक्षा.

In मृतस्य लिप्सा-मृतस्य is कर्मणि षष्ठी i.e. मृत is to be the कर्म of लिप्सा-लब्धुं इच्छा-लिप्सा a desiderative noun.-the desire of getting back a dead man. कृपणस्य दित्सा-Here कृपणस्य is कर्तरिषष्ठी i.e. कृपण is to be an agent of the action of giving-दातुं इच्छा-the desire to give, in the mind of a miserly man. (शास्त्र) विरुद्धो मार्गः विमार्गः तेन गच्छति सा विर्मागगा-a wanton woman. विधातुः सृष्टिः ष. त. तस्यां पूर्वं दृष्टा दृष्टपूर्वा सुपसुप्समास.

126. राज्ञः प्रियाः-राजप्रियाः favourites of the king i.e. the moon i.e. loved by the moon. कैरविण्यः-night lotuses. "सिते कुमुदकैरवे" कैरवाणि सन्ति येषां—the night-lotus-plants. मधुपैः-with the bees-drunkards. The poet hints at the second meaning by the word मधुप. Perhaps he thereby desires to have a glimpse at the contemporary court life. cf. यथा स्त्रीणां तथा वाचां साधुत्वे (शुद्धत्वे) दुर्जनो जनः। U. 1-5

127. उद्‌गता शृंखला यस्य सः-unruly-unchained.

128. This verse is a fine example of the heroic sentiment. दोर्दण्ड......मण्डलं adj. to त्वां. दोषौ दण्डौ इव–दोर्दण्डौ तयोः द्वयं तेन

कुण्डलीकृतं यद् लसत्कोदण्डं तस्य चण्डाशुगैः (terrible arrows) ध्वस्तं उद्दण्डविपक्षमण्डलं येन सः बहु.-तं [कुण्डलीकृतं-turned into a circle by drawing the string i.e. bent round. लसत्कोदण्डं-brilliant bow. "धनुश्चापौ धन्वशरासनकोदण्डकार्मुकम्" आशु गच्छन्ति-आशुगाः-quick goers i.e. arrows. उद्दण्ड-उद्गतौ दण्डौ येषां ते-Poweful bow. विरुद्धः पक्षः-विपक्षः enemy.]-Who has destroyed the circle of his mighty foes by the terrible arrows discharged from his shining bow bent round by his arms. रणस्य मध्ये-मध्येरणम् अव्य-In the battle. [वल्गद् गाण्डिवाद् मुक्तं यत् काण्डवलयं तस्य ज्वालानां आवलीनां ताण्डवेन भ्रश्यत् यत् खाण्डवं तस्मिन् रुष्टः (angry) पाण्डवः (i.e.अर्जुनः)-तं [वल्गद् गाण्डिव-noisy bow of अर्जुन named गाण्डिव-Mythological allusion:-Agni once approached Kṛṣṇa and Arjuna and begged of them the खाण्डव forest by eating which he hoped to be cured of the disease caused by eating too much of sacrificial food. The boon was granted by them and Agni was cured of his disease. Being thus pleased with Kṛṣṇa and Arjuna, he gave them as presents the वज्रनाभ चक्र and the गाण्डिव bow respectively.

Mbh. Adi. 224-225 adhyāyas.

काण्डानां वलयं circle of arrows. "काण्डोऽस्त्रीदण्डबाणार्व" ज्वालावलीताण्डव.-dance of the series of flames. भ्रश्यत्-being destroyed-perishing] अर्जुन who was indignant in the खाण्डव forest which was destroyed by the movement (lit. dance) of the series of flames (arising) from the circle of arrows discharged from the twanging bow.

Idea :—Your sight reminds one of अर्जुन.

129. खण्डितानां नैत्राणि एव कञ्जानि तेषां आलयः तेषां मञ्ज रञ्जने पण्डिताः-Expert in (giving) sweet amusement, in giving charm to the rows of lotuses in the form of the eyes of insulted

ladies. A खण्डिता is that woman whose husband's love is privately directed to another lady. She is very indignant at her husband for his infidelity. But her husband propitiates her and falls at her feet at sunrise. Hence the rays of the sun are said to cheer up the spirits of a खण्डिता lady. cf. मेघ. 39. खण्डिता is defined in साहित्यदर्पण as follows:-पार्श्वमेति प्रियो यस्या अन्यसंभोगचिह्नितः। सा खण्डितेति कथिता धीरैरीर्ष्या कषायिता॥ S. D. 114. के (in water) जायन्ते-कञ्जानि (Ir-reg. समासः) मण्डिताः अखिलदिक्प्रान्ताः (दिग्भागाः) यैः ते- who adorned all the nooks and corners of the quarters.

II

ŚṚṄGĀRAVILĀSA

1. मनाक्—a little, "किञ्चदीषन्मनागल्पे" इत्यमरः। राहुरोधशङ्का — danger of Rāhu's wrath. राहुणा रोधः (राहुरोधः) राहुरोधस्य शङ्का राहुरोधशङ्का। रुर्णाद्ध इति रोधः आवरणमित्यर्थः। रुधिर् आवरणे+घञ् or अच्। 'शङ्का वितर्कः सन्देहः।' इति हलायुधः। कलङ्कानुगमः—कलङ्कस्यानुगमः कलङ्कानुगमः। 'कलङ्कोऽलङ्केऽपवादे च कालाये समलेऽपि च' विश्वप्रकाशः (अनु+गम्+अच्=अनुगम contamination.

2. परुषा–rough, परुषं कर्बुरे रूक्षे स्यान्निष्ठुरवचस्यपि–विश्व-प्रकाशः, सरोजमाला—Lotus garlands. सरसि जातं सरोजम् (सरस्+जनि प्रादुर्भावे+ड)। सरोजानां माला सरोजमाला। माल्यं माला स्रजौ मूर्ध्नि इत्यमरः। मृणालानि—lotus stalks, मृणालं स्याद् बिसं कन्दः इति हलायुधः। विचारपेशलानि–विचारे पेशलानि विचारपेशलानि। 'पेशलो रुचिरे दक्षे' इति विश्वप्रकाशः। अङ्गकानाम्–अङ्गान्येवाङ्गकानि (अङ्ग+स्वार्थे कन्) तेषामङ्गकानाम्।

3. स्वेदाम्बुसान्द्रकणशालिकपोलपालीदोलायित–श्रवणकुण्डल-वन्दनीया–स्वेदाम्बूनि 'स्वेदस्तु स्वेदने धर्मे' इति विश्वप्रकाशः। सान्द्राः कणाः सान्द्रकणाः। 'निरन्तरं धनं सान्द्रं बहुलं विरलेतरम्' इति हलायुधः। स्वेदाम्बूनां-सान्द्रकणाः स्वेदाम्बुसान्द्रकणाः। तैः शालेते इति स्वेदाम्बुसान्द्र- कणशालिन्यौ। कपोलयोः पाल्यौ कपोलपाल्यौ। स्वेदाम्बुसान्द्रकणशालिन्यौ कपोलपाल्यौ। तत्र दोलायिते श्रवणकुण्डले स्वेदाम्बुसान्द्रकणशालिकपोलपालीदोलायित-श्रवणकुण्डलवन्दनीया।

मदिरेक्षणाया–मार्घात आभ्यामिति मदिरे मदकारके हर्षकारके वेत्यर्थः 'मदो हर्षे इषि मादि मुदिखिदीछिदिति मिदिमन्दिचन्दिनिनिमिहि मुहिमुचि

रुचिसधिबन्धि शुषिभ्य: किरच् (उणादिपूर) इति सूत्रेण किरच् प्रत्ययेऽनुबन्धलोपे विभक्तिकार्ये तत्सिद्धि:। मदिरे ईक्षणे यस्या: सा मदिरेक्षणा।' 'लोचनं नयनं नेत्रमीक्षणं चक्षुरक्षिणी' इत्यमर:। तस्या मदिरेक्षणा अङ्कुरयति-अङ्कुरं करोतीति (अङ्कुर+णिच्)।

4. कस्तूरीकातिलकम्–कस्तूरी एव कस्तूरिका (कस्तूरी+स्वार्थे कन्+टाप्) 'मृगनाभिर्मृगमदाप्रोक्ता कस्तूरिका बुधै:' हलायुध:। 'कस्तूरिका कटुतिक्ता क्षारोष्णा शुक्रला गुरु:। कफवातविषच्छर्दिशीतदौर्गन्ध्यशेषहृत्।' आलि–friend 'आलि: सखी इत्यमर:। स्मेरमाननं यस्या: सा स्मेरनना सस्मितवदना। सपदि'—Immediately, स्राग् झटित्यञ्जसाऽह्नाय द्राङ्मङ्क्षु सपदि द्रुते' इत्यमर:। सौधमौलिम्-सौधस्य मौलि: सौधमौलि:। तम् सौधमौलिम्। सौधोऽस्त्री राजसदनम्। कुमुदानि—lotuses, 'कैरवं कुमुदमिति हलायुध:।'

5. मधुराननश्री:–मधुरं (मनोहरम्) आननमिति मधुराननम्, मधुराननस्य श्री: मधुराननश्री:। or आननस्य श्री: आननश्री: मधुरा मनोहरा आननश्री: मधुराननश्री:। सायन्तनाब्जसहोदरलोचनाया:-सायम्भवं सायन्तनम्।

6. प्रातस्तराम्, अतिशयेन प्रात: प्रातस्तराम्, दयितया 'दयितं वल्लभं प्रियम्' इत्यमर:।

7. गुरुजनभयमद्विलोकनान्त: समुदयदाकुलभावम्-आकुलस्य भाव: आकुलभाव:। 'व्यस्ते त्वप्रगुणाकुलौ।' इत्यमर:। समुदयन्नाकुलभाव: समुदयदाकुलभाव:। अन्त: (अभ्यन्तरे) समुदयदाकुलभाव: अन्त: समुदयदाकुलभाव: मत्सम्बन्धि विलोकनं मद्विलोकनम्। मद्विलोकनाय अन्त: समुदयदाकुलभाव: मद्विलोकनान्त: समुदयदाकुलभाव:। गुरव: जना: गुरुजना:। गुरुजनेभ्य: भयं गुरुजनभयम्। गुरुजनभयेन हेतुना मद्विलोकनान्त: समुदयदाकुलभाव: गुरुजनभयमद्विलोकनान्त: समुदयदाकुलभाव:। तत् तथोक्तम्।

दलदरविन्दसुन्दरे–दलद् अरविन्दं दलदरविन्दम्। तस्य द्विवचने दलदरविन्दसुन्दरे। हरिणदृश:–

पश्यत्यनेनेति दृक् (दृश+करणे क्विप्) नेत्रमित्यर्थः। लोचनं नयनं नेत्रमीक्षणं चक्षुरक्षिणी। दृष्टी च इत्यमरः। द्विवचने दृशौ। हरिणस्य दृशाविव दृशौ यस्याः सा हरिणदृक्। 'सप्तम्युपमानपूर्वस्य' इति भाष्यवार्तिकेन समासः उपमानपदलोपश्च। तस्या हरिणदृशः।

8. बदरामलकाम्रदाडिमानाम्-बदरञ्च आमलकञ्च आम्रश्च दाडिमश्चैतेषामितरेतरयोग: बदरामलकाम्रदाडिमाः। तेषां बदरामलकाम्रदाडिमानाम् 'कोलं कुवलफेनिले सौवीरं बदरं घोण्टा' इत्यमरः। 'तिष्यफलात्वामलकी त्रिषु अमृता च वयः स्था च' इत्यमरः। करिशावकुम्भलक्ष्म्याः-करिणः शावः करिशावः। 'बालः पाकोऽर्भको गर्भः पोतश्च पृथुकः शिशुः। शावो डिम्भश्च इति हलायुधः। करिशावस्य कुम्भौ करिशावकुम्भौ। मूर्धपिण्डौ स्मृतौ कुम्भौ' इति हलायुधः। करिशावकुम्भयोः लक्ष्मीः करिशावकुम्भलक्ष्मीः। तस्याः करिशावकुम्भलक्ष्म्याः।

9. जम्बीरश्रियम्-जम्बीराणां श्रीः जम्बीरश्रीः। तां जम्बीरश्रियम्।

व्यानम्रीकृतकमनीयहेमकुम्भौ-हेम्नः कुम्भौ हेमकुम्भौ। कमनीयौ हेमकुम्भौ कमनीयहेमकुम्भौ। अनम्रौ नम्रौ कृतौ इति नम्रीकृतौ। अभूततद्भावे च्विः। वि विशेषेण आङ् समन्तात् नम्रीकृतौ इति व्यानम्रीकृतौ। व्यानम्रीकृतकमनीय हेमकुम्भौ। नीलाम्भोरुहनयने–नीलेऽम्भोरुहे नीलाम्भोरुहेते इव नयने यस्याः सा नीलाम्भोरुहनयना। तत्सम्बुद्धौ हे नीलाम्भोरुहनयने। कनकाचलेन–कनकमयः अचलः कनकाचलः। सुमेरुपर्वतः। तेन कनकाचलेन।

10. लावण्यधन्ये—oh you of slender body. लवणस्य भावः लावण्यम्। beauty. Jīvānanda gives the following definition of लावण्य in his commentary : मुक्ताफलेषु छायायास्तरलत्वमिवान्तरा। प्रतिभाति यदङ्गेषु तल्लावण्यमिहोच्यते। Rajānaka Ruyyaka has defined it in his Sahṛdayalīlā : तरङ्गिद्रवस्वभावाप्यायिनेत्रपेयव्यापिस्निग्धमधुर इव प्रीतिमौत्कर्षैकसार इव पूर्णेन्दुवदाह्लादको धर्मः संस्थानमुग्धिमव्यङ्ग्यो लावण्यम्। "लावण्येन हेतुना धन्या लावण्यधन्या तत्सम्बुद्धौ लावण्यधन्ये। सुकृती पुण्यवान् धन्यः" इत्यमरः।

ललितालकायाम्—ललिता: अलका: यस्या: सा ललितालका, तस्यां ललितालकायाम्-'अलकं कुटिला: केशा:' इति हलायुध:। In the sense of North direction the samāsa will be as: ललिता अलका (city of Kubera) यस्यां सा ललितालका। तस्यां ललितालकायाम्। 'अलका नगरी ज्ञेया' इति हलायुध:। वैश्रवणस्य of Indra.

It has double meaning. वै+श्रवणस्य। स्युरेवन्तु पुनर्वै वेत्यवधारण-वाचका:।' इत्यमर:। श्रवण means ear. 'कर्ण: श्रोत्रं श्रुति: श्रव: श्रवणमिति हलायुध:।' And in the sense of North, वैश्रवण is one word and it means Kubera. कुबेरस्त्र्यम्बकसखो यक्षराड् गुह्यकेश्वर:। किन्नरेशो वैश्रवण: पौलस्त्यो नरवाहन:' इत्यमर:।

11. नीवीम्–navel. 'परिधानांशुकग्रन्थि: प्रोक्ता नीवीतथोच्चय:'। इति हलायुध:। वारिजदृश:–of the lotus-eyed one. वारिणि जातं वारिजं कमलमित्यर्थ:। वारिजमिव दृक् यस्या: सा वारिजदृक्। तस्या: वारिजदृश:। or वारिजे इव दृशौ यस्या: सा तस्या:। जिहासो:–being desirous of हातुमिच्छु: जिहासु: (ओहाक् त्यागे+सन्+'सनाश सभिक्षड:' (3/2/168) इति उ:। तस्या: जिहासो:। मानसात्–from mind. 'चित्तन्तु चेतो हृदयं स्वान्तं हृन्मानसं मन:' इत्यमर:। सरसिजोदरसोदराया:–सह समानमुदरं यस्या: सा सोदरा (सह+उदरम्, 'सहस्य स: सञ्ज्ञायाम् (6/3/78) इति सहस्य स:। सरसि जातं सरसिजम्। (सरस्+जनि प्रादुर्भावे+ड' सप्तम्यां जनेर्ड: (3/2/97) तत: तत्पुरुषे कृति बहुलम्–resembling in complexion the interior of the white lotus.

12. मुधैव–in vain. 'व्यर्थके तु वृथा मुधा' इत्यमर:। नक्तम्–in night. 'अथ दोषा च नक्तञ्च रजनाविति' इत्यमर:। मृषैव–False 'मृषा मिथ्या च वितथे' इत्यमर:। उदश्रुचञ्चन्नयना-tears rising in her eyes. उद् उद्गता अश्रूणि ययोस्ते उदश्रुणी च चञ्चती च नयनं यस्या: सा उदश्रुचंचन्नयना नताङ्गी-नतमङ्गं गात्रं यस्या: सा नताङ्गी one whose body is bent. उररीचकार accepted.

14. हरिणकिशोरदृश:–the eyes of the faun-eyed one. हरिणस्य किशोर: हरिणकिशोरस्य दृशाविव दृशोर्यस्या: सा हरिणकिशोरदृक्।

15. मृगेक्षणा–deer-eyed one. मृगस्येक्षणे इवेक्षणे यस्याः सा मृगेक्षणा। 'सप्तम्युपमानपूर्वस्येति' समासः। शिशिरीकरिष्यते-अशिशिरे शिशिरे करिष्यते इति शिशिरीकरिष्यते (अभूत्तदभावे च्विः) कौमुदीव–like the moon-light.

16. दिवसावसानकाले–in the evening अवधि–'अवधिस्त्ववधाने स्यात् सीम्निकाले विलेऽपि च' इति विश्वप्रकाशः। विकसन्मुखी–She whose face will be brightened up. रामा–lovely lady.

17. वक्षोजाग्रम्–वक्षसि जातः वक्षोजः (वक्षस्+जनी प्रादुर्भावे+उ) breast. आननाब्जम्–She whose face is like a lotus. शोणाग्राभ्याम्–शोणे अग्रे ययोस्ते शोणाग्रे। ताभ्यां शोणाग्राभ्याम्।

18. परिवेष्टिता–surrounded, गण्डस्थल-कण्डूयनचारुकैतवेन–under the happy pretext of scratching the surface of her neck. दरदर्शितहेमबाहुनाला slightly discovered her golden stalk like arm.

19. गुरुमध्यगता-गुरूणां मध्यं गुरुमध्यम्। गुरुमध्यगता–in the midst of elderly persons. दरकुण्डलताण्डवम्–कुण्डलयोः ताण्डवं कुण्डल-ताण्डवम्। दर (ईषत्) कुण्डलताण्डवं यस्मिन् तद् यथा स्यात्तथा दरकुण्डल-ताण्डवम्। ear-ring dangling slightly.

नतभ्रूलतिकम्–लते एव लतिके (स्वार्थे कन्) इति भ्रुवौ एव लतिके भ्रुलतिके। नते भ्रुलतिके यस्मिन् कर्मणि तद् यथा स्यात् तथा नतभ्रू लतिकम्।

20. नयनारुणप्रसारः–become radiant.

अरुणस्य प्रसारः अरुणप्रसारः। नयनयोः अरुणप्रसारः नयनारुणप्रसारः।

निरन्तराश्रुधाराः–continuous streams of tears flow from eyes.

जीवितसंशयः– life is in danger.

जीवितस्य संशयः जीवितसंशयः। 'असवो जीवितं प्राणाः' इति हलायुधः।

21. अकरुण–करोति मन आनुकूल्यायेति करुणः। न करुणः अकरुणः तत्स:बुद्धै अकरुणा hard hearted. मृषाभाषासिन्धो–Ocean of false words मृषा (मिथ्या) भाषा मृषाभाषा मृषाभाषायाः सिन्धुः मृषाभाषासिन्धुः। 'मृषा मिथ्या च वितथे' इत्यमरः। उदन्वानुदधिः सिन्धुः सरस्वान् सागरोऽर्णवः' इति चामरः। तत्सम्बुद्धौ मृषाभाषासिन्धो। अविरलगलद्वास्पाम्–न विरलम-विरलम्। गलन्ति वास्पाणि गलद्वास्पाणि। अविरलं यथा स्यात्तथा गलद्वास्पाणि यस्याः सा अविरलगलद्वास्पा। ताम्-अविरलगलद्वास्पाम्। Who having tears continuously flowing from her eyes. निरस्तविभूषणाम्–विशिष्टानि भूषणानि विभूषणानि। निःशेषेण अस्तानि क्षिप्तानीत्यर्थः। (अनुक्षेपणे+क्त) निरस्तानि। निरस्तानि विभूषणानि यया सा निरस्तविभूषणा। ताम् निरस्तविभूषणाम् 'भूषणं स्यादलङ्कारः' इति हलायुधः। who is stripped off here ornaments.

22. वदनम्–Face, सहासम्–हासेन सहितं सहासम्, with smile. मुग्धा–मुह्यतिस्म इति मुग्धा (मुहवैचित्ये+क्त+टाप्) मूढेत्यर्थः। वैचित्यम-विवेकः (सिद्धान्तकौमुदी) and 'मुग्धः सुन्दरमूढयोः' इति विश्व प्रकाशः। अलिकिशोरमाला–the swarm of the silly young bees. अलीनां किशोराः अलिकिशोराः। अलिकिशोराणां माला अलिकिशोरमाला।

23. विपक्षकामिनीहारलक्ष्म–the impression made by the necklace of a rival woman. विरुद्धः पक्षः यस्याः सा विपक्षा। विपक्षा चासौ कामिनी च विपक्षकामिनी। विपक्षकामिन्या हारः विपक्षकामिनीहारः। विपक्षकामिनीहारस्य लक्ष्म विपक्षकामिनीहारलक्ष्म। तत् तथोक्तम्। दयितस्य–of lover, 'वल्लभो दयितः प्रियः इति हलायुधः। अंसदेश- विनिवीशिताम्–अंसस्य देशः अंसदेशः।' स्कन्धो भुजशिरोंऽसोऽस्त्री इत्यमरः। विशेषेण निवेशिता विनिवेशिता। अंसदेशे विनिवेशिता अंसदेशविनिवेशिता। तामंसदेशि-विनिवेशिताम्। निजबाहुवल्लरीम्–बाहुरेव वल्लरी बाहुवल्लरी 'वल्लरिर्मञ्जरिः स्त्रियौ' इत्यमरः निजा (स्वकीया) बाहुवल्लरी निजबाहुवल्लरी।

24. ईषन्निमीलितस्निग्धविलोचनाब्जम्–lotus like loving eyes partially closed, विलोचनेऽब्जे इवेति विलोचनाब्जे। ईषत् निमीलिते इति ईषन्निमीलिते। ईषन्निमीलिते च स्निग्धे विलोचनाब्जे यस्मिन् तत् ईषन्निमीलितस्निग्धविलोचनाब्जम्। अनल्पनिश्वासभरालसाङ्गम्–निश्वासस्य भरः निश्वासभरः। न अल्पः अनल्पः। अनल्पः निःश्वासभरः अनल्पनिःश्वासभरः अनल्पनिश्वासभरेण अलसानि अङ्गानि यस्मिन् तत् अनल्पनिःश्वासभरालसाङ्गम्, Limbs had grown lanquid owing to heavy breathings.

25. रोषावेशात्–रोषस्य आवेशः रोषावेशः। तस्मात् रोषवेशात्। यामयुग्मात्यामानां युग्मं यामयुग्मम्। तस्मात् यामयुग्मात्, एत्य–इण गतौ+ल्यप् कातराक्षी कातरेऽधीरे अक्षिणी यस्याः सा कातराक्षी, इन्दिरेव–Like Lakṣmī 'इवेन सहसमासो विभक्त्यलोपश्च' इति समासः।

26. कृतशैवलानुषङ्गा–शैवलानामनुषङ्ग सम्पर्कः शैवलानुषङ्गः। कृतः शैवलानुषङ्गः यया सा कृतशैवलानुषङ्गः अनुषङ्गः प्रलेप इति यावत्।

प्रियनामपरे–प्रियस्य नाम प्रियनाम। तत्परं प्रियनामपरम्। तस्मिन् प्रियनामपरे।

27. परिवर्तितकन्धरम्–परिवर्तितः कन्धरो यस्मिन् तत् परिवर्तितकन्धरम्

नतभ्रु-नते भ्रुवौ यस्मिन् तत् नतभ्रु।

28. मलयभुजगवान्ताः–मलये जाताः भुजगाः मलयभुजगाः।

कृतान्तः–'कृतान्तो यमुनाभ्राता शमनो यमराड्यमः इत्यमरः। कृतः अन्तः नाशः येन स कृतान्तः। cruel like Yama, the God of death. माकन्दमौलो–माकन्दस्य (आम्रस्य) मौलिः माकन्दमौलिः। तस्मिन् माकन्दमौलौ। चुलुकयति–चुलुक्+क्यच्+लट् (टिप्)

चञ्चरीकाः–चरति पुनः पुनरिति चञ्चरीकः bee.

30. कूजत्कपोतस्य–कूजन् कपोतः कूजत्कपोतः। तस्य कूजत्कपोतस्य। 'पारावतः कलरवः कपोतः' इत्यमरः।

स्मितार्द्रम्–स्मितेन आर्द्रं स्मितार्द्रम्।

वदनारविन्दम्–वदनमरविन्दमिव वदनारविन्दम्।

31. तिमिरम्–darkness, 'अन्धकारञ्च तिमिरं तमः' इति हलायुधः। हरिताम्–quarters, तापशालिनाम् तापेन शालते इति तापशाली। तेषां तापशालिनाम् those who suffer from affliction.

वदनत्विषः–(त्विष् दीप्तौ+सम्पदादित्वात् क्विप्+जस्=त्विषः) वदनस्य त्विषः वदन त्विषः the luster of face. चकोरलोचने–चकोरस्य लोचने इव लोचने यस्याः सा चकोरलोचना तत्सम्बुद्धौ चकोरलोचने–cakora-eyed one सरसीरुहश्रियः-सरस्यां रोहतीति सरसीरुहम् (सरसी+रुह+क्विप्). सरसीरुहाणां श्रीः सरसीरुहश्रीः। ताः सरसीरुहश्रियः। the beauty of lotus.

32. कुचावेव कलशौ कुचकलशौ। कुचकलशयोः युगं कुचकलशयुगम् कुचकलशयुगस्य अन्तः कुचकलशयुगान्तः। the interval between the two jar-like breasts, सपुलकतनुपुलकेन सहिता सपुलका। सपुलकतनुः यस्मिन् तत् यथा स्यात्तथा सपुलकतनु–body horripulated. गवाक्ष–window, चकिततनु–चकिता तनु यस्मिन् तद् यथा स्यात्तथा चकिततनु–limbs startled, सद्म–house

33. मद्वदनानुकूलम्–मम वदनं मद्वदनम्। मद्वदनस्यानुकूलं मद्वदना-नुकूलम्–conveniently near my mouth, बलारेः-बलस्य अरिः बलारिः, of Indra. अधरीचकार (अभूततद्भावे च्विः) अहीनाम् हीनामकरोत् इत्यर्थः।

34. बत–Alas, खेदानुकम्पासन्तोषविस्मयामन्त्रणे बत। सुदृशः-शोभने दृशौ यस्या सा सुदृक्। तस्याः सुदृशः- of the beautiful eyed one.

35. भूयः–frequent, हन्त–in happiness, सन्तापशान्तिम्–सन्तापस्य शान्तिः सन्तापशान्तिः। तां तथोक्ताम्, सपदि–suddenly.

36. कवलीकुर्वति–अकवलां कवलां कुर्वति इति कवलीकुर्वति। अभूततद्भावे च्विः। devouring or excelling, कोमलत्विषा–कोमला

त्विट्-कोमलत्विट्। तया कोमलत्विषा–tender lustre परिपाण्डुर-पुण्डरीकषण्डे– groups of white lotuses, महाधयः-महान्तः आधयः महाधयः–great anxiety, 'आधिस्तु मानसो पीडा' इति हलायुधः।

37. यौवनोद्गमनितान्तशङ्किता–यौवनस्योद्गमः यौवनोद्गमः। नितान्तं यथा स्यात्तथा शङ्किताः नितान्तशङ्किताः। constrained by the advent of youth, शीलशौर्यबलकान्तिलोभिताः–शीलञ्च शौर्यञ्च बलञ्च कान्तिश्चेति शीलशौर्य्यबलकान्तयः। शीलशौर्य्यबलकान्तिभिः लोभिताः शीलशौर्य्यबल-कान्तिलोभिताः। लोभः सञ्जातः आसामिति लोभिताः तदस्य सञ्जातः तारकादिभ्य इतच् (5/2/36) इतीतच् प्रत्ययः। attracted by effulgence, strength and prowess, जानकीनयननीरजश्रियः–जानक्याः नयने जानकीनयने। त एव नीरजे जानकीनयननीरजे। तयोः श्रियः शोभाः जानकी-नयननीरजश्रियः–the beauty of the lotuslike eye of Jānakī.

38. निरपायम्–निर्गतः अपायः यस्मात् तद् यथा स्यात्तथा निरपायम् निर्विघ्नमित्यर्थः। without any obstacle, मिथिलाधिनाथपुत्रीम्–अधिकः नाथः इति अधिनाथः। मिथिलायाः अधिनाथः मिथिलाधिनाथः। जनकः इत्यर्थः। मिथिलाधिनाथस्य पुत्री मिथिलाधिनाथपुत्री। ताम् मिथिलाधिनाथपुत्रीम्। सीतामित्यर्थः।

39. भुजपञ्जरे–भुजे एव पञ्जरं भुजपञ्जरे। case of hand, बालकुरङ्गीव–बाला चासौ कुरङ्गी च बालकुरङ्गी। तदिव बालकुरङ्गीव। like a female deer, वेपते trembles.

40. परिपीता–digested, विधुवदना–the moon-faced one, मानससदनात्–मानसं हृदयमेव सदनं मानससदनम्। तस्मात् मानससदनात्–from the house of mind.

41. अकरुणहृदय–न करुणमकरुणम्। अकरुणं हृदयं यस्य सः अकरुणहृदयः। तत्सम्बुद्धौ हे अकरुणहृदय–the distracted one कराम्बुजम्–करमम्बुजमिव कराम्बुजम्। hand is like a lotus.

42. वराटिकानाम्–of cowries, 'वराटकः स्थूलरज्जौ पद्मबीजे कपर्दके' इति विश्वप्रकाशः। तक्रम्–butter-milk, अटन्त्या–while moving मध्येरथ्यम्–रथ्यायाः मध्ये मध्येरथ्यम्–in the midst of street.

43. सकलेवरे–कलेवरेण सहितं सकलेवरम्। तस्मिन् सकलेवरे। with body.

44. मुग्धतया–मुग्धस्य भावः मुग्धता। तया मुग्धतया–foolishly, हुताशे–in fire.

45. औत्सुक्यात्–out of curiosity, त्रपया–by bashfulness or shame.

46. लघिमानम्–levity, लघोर्भावः लघिमा। तम् लघिमानम्, गरिमाणम्–gravity निर्विवेकाय–निर्गतः विवेकः यस्मात् तत् निर्विवेकम्। तस्मैनिर्विवेकाय–to the indescriminate fortitude.

47. न्यञ्चति–goes away completely

समुदञ्चति–sets in, मधुरिमाणम्–मधुरस्य भावः मधुरिमा। तं मधुरिमाणम्। sweetness, गतयः–walking, विभ्रमाः–gestures, 'स्त्रीणां विलासवि०वोक विभ्रमा ललितन्तथा होला लीलेत्यमी हावाः स्त्रियाः शृङ्गरभावजाः'। इत्यमरः।

48. निःसीमशोभासौभाग्यम्–निर्गता सीमा यस्मात् तत् निःसीमम्। शोभनं भगं (श्रीः) यस्य तत् सुभगम्। सुभगस्य भावः सौभाग्यम् शोभायाः सौभाग्यं शोभाभोभाग्यम्। निःसीमं शोभासौभाग्यं यस्मिन् तत् निःसीमशोभासौभाग्यम्। —possessing the bliss of measureless beauty. अन्योऽन्यालोक-नानन्दविरहादिव–as if through a lack of delight of beholding each other.

49. मृर्त्तिकाशकलैः–मृत्तिकायाः इदं मार्त्तिकम्। मार्त्तिकस्य शकलानि (खण्डानि) मार्त्तिकशकलानि। तैः मार्त्तिकशकलैः–pieces of clod रदयन्त्रितरसनाग्रम्–रदैः यन्त्रितं रदयन्त्रितम्। रसनायाः अग्रं रसनाग्रम्। रदयन्त्रितं रसनाग्रं यस्मिन् तद् यथा स्यात् तथा रदयन्त्रितरसनाग्रम्। pressing the tip of tongue between teeth. तरलितनयनम्–तरलिते नयने यस्मिन् तद् यथा स्यात् तथा तरलितनयनम्।

50. नयनाञ्चलावमर्शम्–नयनयोः अञ्चले (प्रान्तभागे') नयनाञ्चले तयो अवमर्शः नयनाञ्चलावमर्शः। तं नयनाञ्चलावमर्शम्। कटाक्षपातमित्यर्थः।

51. मानपराञ्चद्वदना–परा अञ्चद् पराञ्चद्। मानेन पराञ्चद् मानपराञ्चद्। तथाभूतं वदनं मुखं यस्याः सा मानपराञ्चद्वदना

शयानेव–शयनं कुर्वाणेव।

करकमले–करः कमलमिव करकमलम्। तस्मिन् करकमले।

उद्वेल्लद्भुजम्–उद्वेल्लन् सञ्चलन् भुजः बाहुः यस्मिन् तद् यथा स्यात्तथा उद्वेल्लद्भुजम्।

अलसग्रीवाबन्धः ग्रीवायाः बन्धः ग्रीवाबन्ध। अलसः ग्रीवाबन्ध यस्मिन्। तद् यथा स्यात्तथा अलसग्रीवाबन्धम्।

53. अधिरजनि–रजन्यामिति अधिरजनि। In night.

54. चिन्तामीलितमानसः–चिन्तया मीलितं चिन्तामीलितम्। चिन्तामीलितं मानसं यस्य सः चिन्तामीलितमानसः।

मनसिजः–मनसि जातः मनसिजः।

विहीनप्रभाः–विशेषेण हीनाः विहीनाः। विहीनाः प्रभाः यासां ताः विहीनप्रभाः। राकापतिः–राकायाः पतिः राकापतिः।

55. तिर्यग्वलितवदनायाः–तिर्यक् वलितं वदनं मुखं यस्याः यया वा सा तिर्यग्वलितवदना तस्याः तथोक्तायाः।

कराब्जव्यापारान्–करौ अब्जे इव कराब्जे तयोः व्यापाराः कराब्जव्यापाराः। तान् तथोक्तान्।

अतिसुकृतसारान्–अति अत्यधिकं सुकृतं पुण्यं अतिसुकृतम्। तस्य सारान् तत्त्वभूतानित्यर्थः।

रसयतः–आस्वादयतः

ललितोत्तंसः–ललितः उत्तंसः (कर्णपूरः) ललितोत्तंसः। तत्सम्बुद्धौ हे ललितोत्तंस।

56. भामिनी–अवश्यं भामते इति भामिनी। 'कोपना सैव भामिनी'

इत्यमरः। बालमृणालतः–बालं मृणालं बालमृणालम्। तस्मात् बालमृणालतः (बालमृणाल+तसिल्)

57. माङ्गलिकीः–मङ्गलाय हिता माङ्गलिकी (मङ्गल+ठक्)। ताः माङ्गलिकीः। प्रयाणस्य समयः प्रयाणसमयः। (प्र+या+ल्युट्+ प्रयाणम्) तस्मिन् प्रयाणसमये 'यात्रा प्रयाणम् प्रस्थानम्' इति हलायुधः। 'जने जल्पति' इत्यत्र 'यस्य च भावेन भावलक्षणमिति सप्तमी। अनल्पम्–न अल्पं यथा स्यात्तथा अनल्पम्। क्रियाविशेषणमेतद्। केलीमन्दिरमारुतायनमुखे–केल्याः मन्दिरं केलीमन्दिरम्। मरुदेव मारुतः। मारुतस्य अयनम्। अय् गतौ ल्युट्, गमनागमनमार्गः मारुतायनम्। गवाक्ष इत्यर्थः। केलीमन्दिरस्य मारुतायनं। केलीमन्दिरमारुतायनम्। तस्य मुखं केलीमन्दिरं मारुतायनमुखम्। तस्मिन् तथोक्ते'।

विन्यस्तवक्त्राम्बुजम्–विशेषेण न्यस्तं विन्यस्तम्। वक्त्रमम्बुजमिवेति वक्त्रमेवाम्बुजमिति वा वक्त्राम्बुजम्। विन्यस्तवक्त्राम्बुजम्। निः श्वासग्लपिताधरम्–निःश्वासेन ग्लपितः निःश्वासग्लपितः। निः श्वासग्लपितः अधरः यस्मिन् तद् यथा स्यात् तथा निःश्वासग्लपिताधरम्। परिपतद्बाष्पार्द्रवक्षोरुहा–वक्षसि रोहतीति वक्षोरुहः स्तन इत्यर्थः। परितः पतन् परिपतन्। परिपतन्, वाष्पः परिपतद्बाष्पः तेन आर्द्रैः परिपतद्बाष्पार्द्रैः वक्षोरुहो यस्याः सा परिपतद्बाष्पाद्रवक्षोरुहा।

58. सहचरि–सह चरति या सा सहचरी (सह+चर्+अच्+ङीप्) तत्सम्बुद्धौ सहचरि। सखि इत्यर्थः। शिथिलीकृतः–अशिथिलः शिथिलः कृतः इति शिथिलीकृतः (अभूततद्भावे च्विः)।

59. रसं जानाति रसज्ञा (रस+ज्ञा+क+टाप्), रसज्ञा रसना जिह्वा इत्यमरः।

60. नयननीलाब्जम्–नीलमब्जं नीलाब्जम्। नयनेन नीलाब्जम् (इति रूपकसमासः) नयनम् नीलाब्जमिव (इत्युपमासमासो वा) नयननीलाब्जम्।

मृगीदृशः–मृग्याः दृशौ यस्याः सा मृगीदृक्। तस्याः मृगीदृशः। हरिणीनयनायाः इत्यर्थः।

61. मृगेक्षणा–मृगस्येक्षणे इवेक्षणे यस्याः सा मृगेक्षणा। मृगनयनीत्यर्थः। मदीक्षासरणिम्–ईक्षणमीक्षा (ईक्ष+अ+टाप्) ईक्षायाः सरणिः ईक्षासरणिः। दर्शनमार्ग इत्यर्थः। जडजीवितेन–जडं जीवितम् जडजीवितम्। तेन जडजीवितेन।

62. करुणावती–करुणा अस्त्यस्या इति करुणावती (करुणा+मतुप्+ङीप्) 'कृपायां करुणा मता' इति विश्वप्रकाशः। विशन्ती–विश्+प्रवेशने+शतृ+ङीप्)। विलोचनेऽब्जमिव विलोचनाब्जम्। तयोः माला विलोचनाब्जमाला। तां विलोचनाब्जमालाम्।

64. प्रतिपक्षकामिनीसदनात्–प्रतिकूलः पक्षः यस्याः सा प्रतिपक्षः। प्रतिपक्षा चासौ कामिनी च प्रतिपक्षकामिनी। सपत्नी इत्यर्थः। प्रतिपक्षकामिन्याः सदनं प्रतिपक्षकामिनीसदनम्। तस्मात् प्रतिपक्षकामिनीसदनात्। नयनाब्जकोणयोः–नयनेऽब्जमिव नयनाब्जे। नयनाब्जयोः कोणौ नयनाब्जकोणौ। तयो नयनाब्जकोणयोः। अरुणद्युतिः–अरुणा द्युतिः अरुणद्युतिः।

67. वासदानविधानतः–वासस्य दानम्। वासदानस्य विधानं वासदानविधानम्। तस्मात् वासदानविधानतः।

69. कालागुरुद्रवम्–कालमगुरुकालागुरुं। सुगन्धिकाष्ठविशेषः। तस्य द्रवः कालागुरुद्रवः। तं कालागुरुद्रवम्। हालाहलवत्–विषमिवेत्यर्थः व्यालावलिम्–व्यालानामावलिः व्यालावलिः। तां व्यालावलिम्।

75. मृगदृशाम्–मृगस्य दृशाविव दृशौ यस्याः सा मृगदृक् तासां मृगदृशाम्। उन्निद्रम्-उद्गता निद्रा यस्यात् तत् उन्निद्रम्। विगतनिद्रमित्यर्थः। कामनृपातपत्रसुषमम्–कामः नृपः कामनृपः। कामनृपस्यातपत्रं कामनृपातपत्रम्। कामनृपातपत्रेण सुषमा यस्मिन् तत् कामनृपातपत्रसुषमम्।

77. उन्मीलत्पुलकनिकुरम्बौ–पुलकानां निकुराम्बानि। पुलकनिकुरम्बानि उन्मीलन्ति पुलकनिकुरम्बानि ययोस्तौ उन्मीलत्पुलकनिकुरम्बौ।

78. राजानम्–The king and the moon.

जैवातृक–The moon, मदन– Cupid

धाता–The creator Brahmā. The metre is Sārdulavikrīḍita. In this verse we have vyatirekālaṁkāra dhvani.

79. In this verse the poet has presented the description of vipralambha Śṛṅgāra.

मधुस्यन्दिनी–मधु स्यन्दतेऽस्या इति मधुस्यन्दिनी, मधुवर्षिणी, मनोहारिणीत्यर्थः। कार्म्मणज्ञा–कार्म्मण वशीकरणकर्म जानातीति कार्म्मणज्ञा। पाण्डिमा–पाण्डोः भावः पाण्डिमा Metre is Mandākrāntā.

80. यदुपतेः–यदूनां पतिः यदुपतिः। तस्य यदुपतेः। कृष्णस्य। स्विद्यत्पुलकितकपोला-स्विद्यन्तौ पुलकितौ च कपोलौ यस्याः सा स्विद्यत्पुलकितकपोला। विषज्वालाजालम्-विषस्य ज्वाला विषज्वाला विषज्वालायाः जालं विषज्वालाजालम्। 'जालं समूह आनाय गवाक्षक्षम-केष्वपि' इत्यमरः। The metre is Śikhariṇi.

81. कैशोरे–किशोरस्य भावः कैशोरम्। तस्मिन् कैशोरे। (किशोर+ष्यञ्)

कौमारं पञ्चमाब्दान्तं पौगण्डं दशमावधि।

कैशोरमापञ्चदशात् यौवनञ्च ततः परम्।।

तनुताम्–तनोः भाव तनुता। ताम् तथोक्ताम्।

आगामिनि–आगमिष्यति सतीत्यर्थः। पूर्णशशाङ्कतापूर्णः शशाङ्कः। तस्य भावः पूर्णशशाङ्कता।

82. शैवलशयने–शैवलनिर्मितं शयनं शैवलशयनम्।

तस्मिन् शैवलशयने–On the bed of moss.

नवेन्दुलेखेव–Like a digit of the new-moon.

83. सुभ्रुवः–of the beautiful-eye browed one.

असतपल्लवा–surpasses the beauty of the foliage leaf. शशिकान्तिलंघिनी-शशिनः कान्तिः शशिकान्तिः। शशिकान्तिं लंघते इति शशिकान्तिलंघिनी–surpasses the beauty of the moon. The metre is Vaitālīya.

84. व्यत्यस्तम्–incoherently, निरालम्बनाम्–Vacantly, वैदेहीविरहव्यथाविकलितः–overpowered with the pangs of separa-

tion from Vaidehī. The figure of speech is Kāraka-dīpaka alaṁkāra and the metre is Śārdulavikrīḍīta.

85. Here the Alaṁkāra is samuccaya.

99. पंकेरुहाक्षि–oh lotus-eyed one.

मृगनाभिपङ्कम्–the tilaka mark of musk

उलासपल्लवितकोमलपक्षमूला:–spreading through joy the tender pinion-roots.

102. सुधैकमयमूर्ते:–the embodiment of nectar, शतकोटि-कठिनचित्त:–of an adamantine heart.

III

KARUṆAVILĀSA

1. दैवं– Fate, दैवं दिष्टं भागधेयं भाग्यम् स्त्री नियतिर्विधिः इत्यमरः। 'यस्य च भावेन भावलक्षणम्' (२/३/३७) इति सप्तमी। पराग्वदनशालिनि–परा अञ्चतीति पराक् (४२१+अञ्च+क्विप्) पराक् वदनम् पराग्वदनम्। तेन शालते इति पराग्वदनशाली तस्मिन् पराग्वदनशालिनि।

हन्त–विषादे 'हन्त हर्षेऽनुकम्पायाम् वाक्यारम्भविषादयोः' इत्यमरः। दिवम्-स्वर्गम्। आधिम्-mental pain, 'आधिर्मानसी व्यथा' इत्यमरः।

2. प्रत्युद्गता–(प्रति+उत्+गम्+क्त+टाप्)

स्मेरैः–with sweet smile, स्मरस्य-of cupid, सचिवैः-associates, सरसावलोकैः-अवलोकनमवलोकः, (अव+लुक्+घञ्)। रसेन सहितः सरसः। सरसाः। अवलोकाः सरसावलोकाः। तैः सरसावलोकैः।

मञ्जुरचनैः-मञ्जु (मनोरमम्) रचनं (रचना) येषां तानि मञ्जुरचनैः। बाले-'बालेति गीयते नारी यावत् षोडशवत्सरम्'। तत्सम्बुद्धौ। बाले। शिशिरी करोषि-अशिशिरं शिशिरम् करोषि इति शिशिरीकरोषि। अभूततद्भावे च्विः। शीतलीकरोषि।

3. विस्मृतिपथम्–वि+स्मृ+क्तिन्= विस्मृतिः। विस्मरणम्। विस्मृते पथः विस्मृतिपथः। तं विस्मृतिपथम्। विषयाः-'विषयः स्यादिन्द्रियार्थे देशे जनपदेऽपि च। गोचरे च प्रबन्धाद्ये यस्य ज्ञातस्तु तत्र च।' खेदकलिमा-खेदेन कलिता। खेदः परिश्रमः। कलिता प्राप्ता अभ्यस्ता वा।

विमुखीबभूव–वि (विरुद्धं विपरीतं वा) मुखं यस्याः सा विमुखा। अविमुखा विमुखा बभूवेति विमुखीबभूव। हरिणशावकलोचना–हरिणस्य शावकः हरिणशावकः। Baby deer. हरिणशावकस्य लोचने इव लोचने यस्याः सा हरिणशावकलोचना।

4. निर्वाणमङ्गलपदम्–मङ्गलस्य पदं मङ्गलपदम्-निर्वाणं एव मङ्गलपदं निर्वाणमङ्गलपदम्।

त्वरया–विशन्त्या- विश+शतृ+ङीप्) मुक्ता-free, भामिनी-angry lady. निभालयसि-look at. त्वरया-in haste कटाक्षैः-with glances. कटं गण्डम् अक्षति व्याप्नोतीति कटाक्षः। कट+अक्षुव्याप्तौ+अण्।

5. पदस्खलनभीतिवशात्–through the bear of slipping of foot. शिलाशकलम्-a slap of stone.

विहाय–leaving

6. निर्दूषणा–निर्गतं दूषणं (दोषः) यस्याः सा निर्दूषणा faultless. गुणवती-possessed of good qualities सालङ्कृतिः-अलङ्कृतिभिः सहिता सालकृतिः। with ornaments. श्रवणमङ्गलवर्णराजिः-वर्णानां राजिः वर्णराजिः। श्रवणे मङ्गला (सुखदा) इति श्रवणमङ्गला। श्रवणकोमलाः वर्णराजयः यस्यां सा श्रवणकोमलवर्णराजिः-charming.

7. शशाम–subsided इन्दोः-of moon. असमाम्-not comarable. कलकलः-melodious notes.

8. सौदामिनी–Lightening. महेन्द्रभोगान्–महानिन्द्रः महेन्द्रः महेन्द्र-योग्या भोगाः महेन्द्रभोगाः। तान् महेन्द्रभोगान्। मन्त्रोज्झितस्य–मन्त्रेण उज्झितः (वर्जितः) मन्त्रोज्झितः। rejected by mantra. राज्यलक्ष्मीः-राज्यस्य लक्ष्मीः-the regal deity of a King.

9. विलसितेन–sportive actions. वि+'लस'+क्त-विलसितम्। समुद्गतस्य-produced of करभोरु-करभाविव ऊरू यस्याः सा करभोरुः। तत्सम्बुद्धो हे करभोरु-Lady having things like the inner edge of the palm of the hand वशंवदा-वशीभूता। पतिव्रता-पतिः एवं व्रतं यस्याः सा पतिव्रता। devoted wife. मुक्तरमणीसदनम्–मुक्तानां मुक्तदेहानां रमण्यं मुक्तरमण्यः। तासां सदनं मुक्तरमणीसदनम्। abode of liberated ladies.

10. काव्यात्मना–काव्यस्यात्मा काव्यात्मा तेन काव्यात्मना। in the

form of poems परिणता:-developed, पीयूषसारसदृशा:-पीयूषस्य सार: पीयूषसार:। तस्य सदृशा: पीयूषसारसदृशा:। sweet as the essence of nectar. रमणीरमणीयशीला-रमणीयं शीलम् रमणीयशीलम्। रमणीनां रमणीयशीलम् रमणीरमणीयशीलम् रमणीरमणीयशीलं यस्या: सा रमणी-रमणीयशीला।

11. तावकीनम्–तवेदं तावकीनम्। भूमण्डले-भुव: पृथिव्या: मण्डलं भूमण्डलम्। तस्मिन् भूमण्डले। कातराक्षि-कातरे अक्षिणी यस्या: सा कातराक्षी। तत्सम्बुद्धो। राका-full moon-night- 'पूर्णे राका निशाकरे' इत्यमर:। इन्दिराया:-of Lakṣmī.

12. सुधया–by nectar. परिषिच्य-परि+षिच् क्षरणे+ल्यप्-having sprinkled. नेत्रोत्पलै:-नेत्राण्येव उत्पलानि नेत्रोत्पलानि। तै: नेत्रोत्पलै:। blooming lotuses in the shape of her eyes. नित्यमङ्गलमयी-ever auspicious गृहदेवता-household deity, कामेश्वरी-कामानामीश्वरी कामेश्वरी-the desire fufilling goddess. दयिता-beloved.

13. एणशावाक्षि-एणस्य शाव: एणशाव: एणशावस्य अक्षिणीव अक्षिणी यस्या: सा एणशावाक्षी। Swan-eyed one.

14. लावण्यम्–beauty. अपास्ततुलम्-अपास्ता (निरस्ता), शीलम्० लोकोत्तरम् अर्थमयम् अशरणान्-न विद्यते शरणं येषान्ते अशरणा:। तान् अशरणान्। 'शरणमगारं निवसनम्' इति हलायुध:। त्रिदिवम्।

15. कान्त्या सुवर्णवरया-सुवर्णादपि वरा सुवर्णवरा। तया सुवर्णवरया। परया-by best. स्विका:-स्वस्य इमा: स्विका: आत्मीया। शिखा:- Flames, कुशेशयलोचने-कुशे जले शेते इति कुशेशयम्। कुशेशये इव लोचने यस्या: सा कुशेशयलोचना। तत्सम्बुद्धौ हे कुशेशयलोचने। कोपकलुष:-कोपेन कुलष: कोपकलुष:।

16. कर्पुरवत्तिरिव–कर्पूरनिर्मिता वर्त्ति: कर्पूरवर्त्ति। सेव कर्पूरवर्त्तिवि। वर्त्ति नयनाञ्जनम्।

स्वप्नान्तरे-स्वप्नस्य अन्तरं स्वप्नान्तरम्। तस्मिन् स्वप्नान्तरे।

लोचनतापहन्त्री–लोचनयोः तापः लोचनतापः। हन्ति नाशयति इति हन्त्री। लोचनतापस्य हन्त्री लोचनतापहन्त्री।

फुल्लाम्बुजस्रगिव–फुल्लमम्बुजं फुल्लाम्बुजम्। अम्बुनि जातमम्बुजम्। फुल्लं विकसितम्। फुल्लाम्बुजानां स्रक् फुल्लाम्बुजस्रक्। सेव फुल्लाम्बुजस्रगिव।

कण्ठसुखैकहेतुः–एकः अद्वितीयः हेतुः एव हेतुः। कण्ठस्य कण्ठसुखम्। कण्ठसुखस्य एक हेतुः कण्ठसुखैकहेतुः।

चेतश्चमन्कृतिपदम्–चेतसः चमत्कृतिः चेतश्चमकृतिः चमत्कृतिः लोकोत्तराह्लादः। तस्य पदं (स्थानं) चेतश्चमकृतिपदम्।

रम्या-रन्तुं योग्या। नम्या-नमितुं योग्या।

17. अनुस्मरन्ती– शयने-in bed. कृशाङ्गी–कृशानि अङ्गानि यस्याः सा कृशाङ्गी।

19. रीतिम्– गिराम् of speech अमृतवृष्टिकिराम्–अमृतस्य वृष्टिः अमृतवृष्टिः। तां किरति वर्षतीमि अमृतवृष्टिकिरा। तां तथोलान् सुधावर्षिणी-मित्यर्थः।

अभिनन्दनीयाम्–अभिनन्दितुं योग्या अभिनन्दनीया,ताम् अभिनन्दनीयाम्। लोकोत्त्राम्-लोकादुत्तरा लोकोत्तरा। तां लोकोत्तराम् extra-ordinary. करुणारसार्द्राम् करुणायाः रसः करुणारसः। तेन आर्द्रा। तां करुणारसार्द्राम्।

IV

ŚĀNTAVILĀSA

1. विशाला या विषयाणां (objects of sense) अटवी (forest) तस्याः वलयं (circle) तस्मिन् लग्नः यः दावानलः (forest conflagration) तेन प्रसृत्वरा (spreading) या शिखानां (flames) आवली तया विकलितम् (afflicted) adj. to मनः। प्रसृत्वरा-प्रसरणशीला. The word is formed by adding the affix क्वरप् to प्र+सृ in the sense of agent, possessing that habit, by Sūtra इण्नशजिसर्तिभ्यः क्वरप् (Pan 3-2-163) अमन्दन् (incessantly) मिलन्ती इन्दिरा (beauty) यस्मिन् सः (बहु.) adj. to चन्दिनः। निखिलायाः माधुर्या (loveliness) मन्दिरं-तस्मिन्। मुकुन्दस्य मुखं एव चन्दिरः (कर्म.) तस्मिन्। 'चन्दिरोऽनेकपे चन्द्रे' इति विश्वः। चकोरायताम् is the potential 3rd pers. sing. of the denominative from चकोर showing "acting like" hence meaning 'may it act like a चकोर' i.e. long for the moon in the form of the face of श्रीकृष्ण. This is formed by the Sūtra उपमानादाचारे (Pan 3-1-10). The चकोर is conventionally supposed to long for the appearance of the moon, so that it might drink her nectar. This idea has also been referred to in Bh. V. 1-4.

Idea :—May my mind long for a vision of मुकुन्द.

2. जलधेः नन्दिन्याः (Lakṣmī) नयने एव नीरजे (lotuses) तयोः आलम्बनं (support) तत्संबोधनम्। Lakṣmī is only delighted at the sight of विष्णु. ज्वलन् (burning) यः ज्वलनः (fire) तस्य जित्वरः (conqueror-i.e. more scorching than fire) यः ज्वरभरः (excess of pain) तस्य त्वरा (keenness) तेन भङ्गुरः (fragile) adj. to अहम्। जित्वर is formed like प्रसृत्वर. See notes on the above stanza. भङ्गुर also shows "the habit of breaking" and has been formed

by the Sūtra भञ्जभा समिदां घुरच् (Pan. 3-2-161) प्रभाते (विकसतः) जलजस्य उन्नमन् (appearing) यः गरिमा (expanse) तस्य गर्वस्य सर्वंकषैः (नाशकैः) adj. to लोचनैः The eyes remove the pride of the bigness of the lotus i.e. they are even bigger than the lotus. जगतः त्रितयं (a collection of three worlds) तस्य रोचनैः (pleasing) adj. to लोचनैः। शिशिरय= make me cool. The plural लोचनैः is justified when it is interpreted as glances and not "the eyes".

Idea :—Consol me because I am immersed in worries. "कादम्बिनी मेघमाला " It literally means a row of clouds. Here however by लक्षणा (for लक्षणा vide notes on verse 91 of प्रा.वि.) it should mean Kṛṣṇa himself who is always described as being possessed of the श्याम colour. The incident described in the poem is the one dealing with the गोपिकावस्त्रहरण when Śrī-Kṛṣṇa seated himself on a कदम्ब tree and played with the Gopis. cf. तासां वासांस्युपादाय नीपमारुह्य सत्वरः। हसद्भिः प्रहसन् बालैः परिहासमुवाच ह।। Bhag.-X. 22-9 तरुणातप meaning scorching heat, here of course of the worldly affairs. Krishna is supposed to remove the distresses of his devotees, even when remembered once. Cf. यस्य स्मरणमात्रेण जन्मसंसारबन्धनात्। विमुच्यते नमस्तस्मै विष्णवे प्रभविष्णवे।। Kṛṣṇa, like other Gods, is always described and painted as being possessed of a halo of lustre round his head and this is referred to in the second line. विद्युतां शतैः hundreds of lightnings. अभङ्गुरा तनूनां त्विट् येषां तानि adj. to विद्युतां शतानि. The lustre of whose bodies is not transitory like that of the lightning. Mark here the आधिक्य of उपमेय i.e. तनुत्विष् over उपमान the विद्युत्, resulting into what is termed in rhetorics as the व्यतिरेक. There is also अतिशयोक्ति clearly visible herein. कलिन्द-नगस्य नन्दिनी-तस्याः तटे (वर्तमानः) यः सुरद्रुमः-तस्मिन् आलम्बते-सा-Resorting to the celestial tree on the bank of the daughter of the mountain कलिन्द "कालिन्दी सूर्यतनया यमुना शमनस्वसा". The कदम्ब tree on which Kṛṣṇa seated himself is here called the celestial tree because of its unparalleled luck in being the resort of कृष्ण. This verse vividly pictures before our mind's eye the scene on the bank of the Yamuna where on the नीप tree कृष्ण is sitting with an object of joking with garments left on the bank by the गोपीs who are taking naked bath in the Yamuna. Jagannātha in various places associates the blue line of clouds with Śrī Kṛṣṇa. (Cf. Stanzas 5,8 etc of this विलास) मदीयां मतिं चुम्बते सा lit. one that touches my intellect i.e., becomes an object of my contemplation. का अपि means indescribable. This word suggests that the present कादम्बिनी is infinitely superior to the ordinary कादम्बिनी (row of clouds.) inasmuch as the latter possesses only one lightning with transitory lustre but the former is encircled by hundreds of lightnings with everlasting lustre. Hence such a कादम्बिनी is nothing except श्रीकृष्ण himself. This is the opening stanza of the रसगंगाधर.

Idea :—May I contemplate over Lord Śrī Kṛṣṇa.

4. कलिन्दगिरिनदिन्याः (यमुनायाः) तटे यद् वनस्य अन्तरं (the interior of the forest) तत्। भासयन् filling with lustre. Śrī Kṛṣṇa is supposed to have sanctified the regions surrounding Muttra by his divine presence there. प्राणिनां पथि गतागतश्रमभरं हरन्- Removing the burden of the exhaustion due to the (frequent) going and coming in the journey. पथि here means the worldly path." and गतागत to "the Cycle of births and deaths" and then the whole meaning aptly applies to श्रीकृष्ण who liberates his devotee from the "Cycle of births and deaths." लतावलीनां शतेन आवृतः-Encircled by hundreds of rows of creepers. लताः refers to the gold-complexioned गोपीs who encircle श्रीकृष्ण

at the time of the famous रासक्रीडा. See (Bh. 10=33) आशु-instantly. रुचा संभृत:-enhanced by splendour. तमालदुम:-a tree named तमाल with a dark bark; here inwardly it refers to श्रीकृष्ण whose complexion is like that of a तमाल tree. Who else can be instataneous remover of the fatigue but श्रीकृष्ण ?

5. नवीन: i.e. लोकोत्तर:. Here in this verse all the epithets are not applicable to the जलधर. Hence it is called the नवीनो जलधर; but on the other hand it can be said that no जलधर has power to bring about any of the actions referred to in the verse. So, naturally, all the actions referred to their only agent i. e. श्रीकृष्ण. Hence जलधर refers to श्रीकृष्ण. His dark complexion which resembles that of a cloud also points to the same. Besides the word नवीन (जलधर) is also significant. ज्योत्स्नामय्य: या: नवसुधा: ताभि:-with new nectar full of moon light-splendour. ज्योत्स्नामयी-full of moonlight जटिलयन् Pres. Parti. of the denom. from जटिल lit. making matted i.e. pervading, filling. जगज्जालम्-the net of the world i.e. the surface of the earth.

त्रय: विधा: यस्य स: तम्— of three kinds-त्रिविधसन्ताप refers to the three-fold trouble of the worldly people i. e. आधिभौतिक-Elemental troubles of the transmigratory existence. आधिदैविक-Godly-pertaining to Gods. आध्यात्मिक spiritual-pertaining to the soul. When a person is liberated from the clasp of three troubles he acquires final beatitude प्रशमयन्-Pre. Past. from the caus. of शम् with प्र. removing-putting a stop to नता: निखिल-वृन्दारका: (all Gods) तै: वृत:-surrounded by all the Gods that bowed down (to him)-"वृन्दारका दैवतानि" स्वान्तस्य ध्वान्तम्-the darkness i.e. (ignorance) of my heart. तिरयतु-may destroy.

6. ग्रीष्मे यः चण्डकरः तस्य मण्डलं (disc), तस्य भीष्मज्वालाः इव संसरणं (worldly existence) तेन तापिता मूर्तिः यस्य सः एवं विधस्य मे। चण्डाः कराः यस्य सः the Sun. भीष्मज्वालाः-the terrible heat flame. संसरण noun from सृ with सम्— transmigratory existence. It is so called because a person is required to move form one birth to another according to his merits and demerits (thus through 8400000 existences) until he gets मोक्ष. प्रावृषेण्यः प्रावृषि भवः, वृष्णिषु वरेण्यः (श्रेष्ठः) the best of वृष्णिs i. e. यादवs-श्रीकृष्ण. वृष्णि is the name of the ancestor of श्रीकृष्ण.

The idea is that just as the cloud in the rainy season allays the heat of the tormenting summer-sun so also may श्रीकृष्ण liberate me from this transmigratory existence.

7. न विद्यते पारः यस्य सः shoreless-unlimited-difficult to be crossed. विषमं विषयरूपं अरण्यं तस्य या सरणिः तस्याम्-In the path leading to the uneven forest in the form of the worldly pleasures. भ्रामं भ्रामं-णमुल् having frequently wandered. Repetition shows frequency. विगलित विरामः यस्मिन् कर्मणि तत्तया-in a manner in which rest is lost i.e. restlessly. जडा मतिः यस्य सः तस्य मम— dull minded. तरणेः 'द्युमणिस्तरणिर्मित्रः' तनया (यमुना) तस्याः तीरे निलयः (home) यस्य सः- adj. to हरिनवतमालः। हरिः एव नवतमालः।

8. जलधेः कन्यका-The daughter of the Ocean i. e. Goddess लक्ष्मी. लक्ष्मी is one of the fourteen jewels churned out by Gods and demons from the Ocean. Cf लक्ष्मीकौस्तुभपारिजातकसुरा-धन्वन्तरिश्चन्द्रमाः etc. लीलया सह यथा स्यात् तथा इति सलीलम्-Sportively. लग्न. P. P. from लग् (attached to or embraced) प्रियंगुलता is a tender-creeper. It is the convention of the Sanskrit poets that सहकार (a mango tree) and अतिमुक्तलता, तमाल and प्रियंगुलता are the types of loving couples and hence the

significance of the simile in the present verse. देहस्य अवसानसमये at the time of the end of the body. अवसान-Termination-noun from सो with अव to finish (4. P.) अरविन्दं नाभौ यस्य सः-one who has a lotus in his naval. Mythology says that a lotus rose from the naval of विष्णु and from it, came out the four-faced God, Creator-ब्रह्मदेव.

9. नयनयोः आनन्दस्य सन्दोहः (mass) तस्य तुन्दिलीकरणे क्षमा (able)-able to increase (तुन्दिलीकरणे) the mass of joy to the eyes. (तुन्दिल lit. means corpulent). तिरयतु may it remove. आशु means immediately.

10. सुधा इव मधुरा Sweet like ambrosia. निर्गतः मलः यस्याः सा, तया वाचा-pure. This वाक् is nothing but the वेद्s which are supposed to be the breath of God. शिक्षा consists of the realization of the non-difference between God (सः) and ego. (अहम्) viz. तत्त्वमसि Ch.VI-12. अहंभावः the notion of considering oneself as different from the Supreme Being. अदाः Aorist 2nd pers. sing. of दा to give.

अहंभावावृतः-overwhelmed by ego. निर्गता त्रपा यस्मात् सः shameless. आगसां शतम् hundred faults. स्वीयेषु men favoured by God. त्वत्+तः (ablative) मत्तः (ablative). मत्तः arrogant.

11. सुरपुरी the city of Gods i.e. अमरावती which is supposed to be the place of unmixed joy. मेरु is supposed to be the highest mountain of gold (see Bhāgavata 5-16-7) पारावाराणां परम्परा line of oceans. 'पारावारः सरित्पतिः' the oceans are supposed to be seven in number encircling the seven द्वीप्s surrounding the मेरु mountain.

According to "*Bhāgavata Purāṇa*" (5-20) मेरु is in the centre. Surrounding this mountain there is the country known as जम्बुद्वीप (on which we are living surrounded by क्षीरोद. Surrounding this क्षीरोदधि there is the प्लक्षद्वीप surrounded by इक्षुरसोद. This will be made clear by the following diagram:- आधि is mental trouble whereas व्याधि is physical pain. पराहत: overwhelmed. रसायनं medicine. रस्य taste. शून्यै: fruitless v. l. आधिव्याधिजरापराहत. overpowered by mental and physical pain and old-age.

12. गणिका-a prostitute. The story of the गणिका पिङ्गला has been narrated in Bhāgavata 11-8 Verses 22-43. She attained to the knowledge of her "Self". According to her profession she was waiting for a customer but till late at night she got none and through despondency she realized the truth, the real पुरुष was her own "Self" and none else.

cf- सन्तं समीपे रमणं रतिप्रदं, वित्तप्रदं नित्यमिमं विहाय।
अकामदं दु:खमयादिशोकमोहप्रदं तुच्छमहं भजेऽज्ञा।।
Bhāg. 11-8-31

अजामिल was a sinner. He was a man of impure conduct but was ultimately saved, when he saw three persons with nooses in hands coming to kill him, knowing that Death would soon overtake him he called aloud his dearest son Narayana (Bhāgvat 6-Adhy. 1-2) Immediately the servant of Viṣṇu arrived and drove away those (servants) of यम. He was then filled with remorse for his evil way of leading life and obtained मुक्ति.vide हैमं विमानमारुह्य ययौ यत्र प्रिय: पति:। भव: एव मरुगर्त: the desert in the form of the worldly existence. सीयन् drooping-desponding सर्वथा न उपेक्ष्य:. It does not become you to neglect me altogether i.e. lend some help to me to raise myself from this worldly existence.

13. "मृद्वीका गोस्तनी द्राक्षा" रस् to taste. सिता sugar. सम्+अश to eat and समशिता eaten (to my heart's satisfaction) स्फीतं-

ample. स्वर्यातेन कतिधा सुधा अपि अधायि स्वर्यातः i.e. स्वःयातः- gone to heavens कतिधा many a time. अधायि passive aorist of धे to suck. रम्भायाः अधरः खण्डितः lit. bit the lower lip of रम्भा (कतिधा taken with both) रंभा is "the wife of नलकूवेर and considered as the most beautiful woman in the paradise of India" कतिधा because of the manifold births. "खण्डितो रतिरभसवशाच्चुम्बनावसरे कदाचिद्दन्तेनापि क्षत इति यावत्." भ्राम्यत् wandering in the world मधुरिम्णः उद्गारः the stream of sweetness.

14. कृष्णेति वर्णद्वयं विजयते। Here are series of metaphors and कृष्ण is poetically indentified with so many things.

वज्रं पापमहीभृतां-पापानि एव महीभृतः i.e. mountains in the form of sins. तेषाम् वज्रम्- Mythology: The demon हिरण्याक्ष by his magical powers endowed mountains with wings and they used to pound down the cities on which they would rest at their sweet will. God Indra, being touched by the feeling of humanity for the people of those cities clipped the wings of those mountains with his thunderbolt (वज्र). Hence the वज्र strikes terrors to mountains. (हरिवशं)] महीं विभ्रति इति महीभृतः। भवः (संसारः) एव गदः (disease) तस्य उद्रेकः (excess) तस्य। 'रोगव्याधिगदामयाः' सिद्धं च तद् औषधं च। Specific medicine or antedote. मिथ्याज्ञानं-Erroneous Knowledge; it consists of considering the Supreme Being as different from the individual soul (जीवात्मा)

तिग्माः अंशवः यस्य सः। तिग्मांशुः तस्य बिम्बस्य उदयः one whose rays are hot i.e. The Sun. मिथ्याज्ञानं एव निशा तस्या यद् विशालं तमः तस्य। मह्यां रोहन्ति इति महीरुहः (trees) क्रूराः केल्शाः एव महीरुहः तेषाम्। उरुतराः (gigantic) ज्वालाः ताभिः जटालः (increase-dencircled) "शिखावानाशुशुक्षणिः" शिखावान् means शिखी (शिखिन्) i.e. fire. निवृत्तिः refers to the final beatitude निर्वृतेः सद्म, तस्य (house of final beatitude.)

15. चारयन् Per. Pass. from the caus. of चर् grazing, feeding. गवां वृन्दं (1) the multitude of Kine (2) the group of senses (गो) नवः अम्बुदः तस्य निभा यस्य असौ (श्रीकृष्णः) like the new cloud-this refers to श्रीकृष्ण on account of his dark complexion. सौन्दर्यस्य अमृत-nectar of his beauty. उद्गिरद्भिः Vomitting-giving out-emitting-संमोह्य gerund of the caus. of सं+मुह Having tempted or enticed. v.l. संयोज्य-having joined to, it is not so happy. मन्दस्मितैः-by his slow smiles i.e, charming smiles. वल्लभ-dear. क्षयं नेष्यति-will lead to ruin.

The poet here resorts to the out of the way but at the same time the most telling poetic device in order to give vent to his devotion to श्रीकृष्ण.

By "बन्धुर्नकार्यः" he means "स एव बन्धुः कार्यः" because the reason which he asserts is that he will give you मोक्ष final beatitude and a giver of मोक्ष (मोक्षदः) is not to be neglected. Thus the poet intends to bring out the positive meaning by the emphatic negative expression.

16. अव्याख्येयां-Inexplicable-indescribable वितरति प्रयच्छति-gives, imparts. अन्तर्निमग्ना-when it occupies the interior of the heart. कण्ठे लग्ना-when it is attached to the throat i.e. when it is repeated. आन्तरं ध्वान्तस्य जालम्-the mass of the internal darkness. This refers to the मिथ्याज्ञान of the अद्वैतवेदान्तिन्-Some may construe this as अन्तरस्य (अन्तःकरणस्य) ध्वान्तस्य (अज्ञान-तमसः) जालं i.e. the mass of the darkness of the heart. द्राक्षाद्यैः by the grapes etc. द्राक्षाः आद्याः येषां ते-तैः। V. l. द्राक्षार्थैः=द्राक्षामौल्यैः (अर्थ means wealth and hence price) v.l. द्राक्षोद्यैः by the clusters of the grapes. द्राक्षाद्यैरपि बहुमतां. Highly regarded even by the grapes etc., i.e. superior to even the grapes in sweetness. आख्या-name. "रसज्ञा रसना जिह्वा" रसं जानाति इति रसज्ञा.

17. रम्यं रूपं येषा ते Having beautiful forms. अधिगताः अक्षं अक्षेण वा, अध्यक्षाः तैः-fallen in the range of sight (अक्ष= sense) v. l. उर्ध्वाक्षैः-ऊर्ध्वं अक्षिणी येषां ते तैः with their eyes raised up. अध्यक्षः-'प्रत्यक्षेऽधिकृतेऽध्यक्ष' निजस्य सखा-निजसखः-तम्-one's own friend " राजाहःसखिभ्यल्टच्" (Pan. 5-4-91.) नीरद नीरं जलं ददाति इति-that which gives water, a cloud. किमपि indescribable "कृष्ण" अभिधानं यस्य तत् whose name is "कृष्ण" चितं आरूढं-चिन्तारूढ-rising to own mind.

18. विष्वद्रीच्या formed irregularly by विष्वग्देवयोश्च (Pan. 6-3-92) (original word विष्वद्यच-fem. from विष्वद्रीची) pervading everywhere.

विष्वद्युत्या विष्वग्समंततः and रूचिः lustre i. e. brightening all around. भासते etc. cf.: तमेव भान्तमनुभाति सर्वम्। तस्य भासा सर्वमिदं विभाति (मुं. 2-2-10) v. l. अहमिति प्रत्ययालंबनं अहंवृति-स्फुरणाश्रयः—the support of the consciousness of 'I'ness. or "अहं ब्रह्मा". It is said "अहंवृत्तिरिदंवृतिरित्यन्तः करणं द्विधा। विज्ञानं स्यादहंवृत्तिर्मनोभवेत्। "अहं" इति अहंकारः-Ego. v.l. स्वहृदयमतावेदिनः-स्वहृदयस्य मतं न विदन्ति not knowing the opinion of their own hearts. v. l. स्वहृदयतलावेदिनः Here, तलं=Real form. नावेदिनः i. e. not knowing their own hearts. अन्यायोऽयं शिव शिव ! Alas ! this is impropriety, the injustice referred to is fully expressed in the following couplet.

"योऽन्यथासन्नमात्मानमन्यथा प्रतिपद्यते।
किं तेन न कृतं पापं चोरेणात्मापहारिणा"।।

This verse brings in a nutshell the whole philosophy of the "Upaniṣads" in unambiguous expressions. The first line points out that the whole universe depends upon that Brahman for lustre i.e. life. The second line shows that the जीव has no existence apart from ब्रह्मन् and the third states that one's heart is the receptacle of ब्रह्मन् as expressed in "(एष मे आत्मा अन्तर्हृदये") Ch. 3-14 and "ईश्वरः सर्वभूतानां हृद्देशेऽर्जुन तिष्ठति" Bhāgavata. G. 18-1.

19. This is an advice of the poet to his mind सेवा service. चिन्ता means not "anxiety" as is generally taken but here it means "contemplating over." चक्रम् आयुधं यस्य सः (बहु) i.e. Viṣṇu. आलापः means conversation. स्मरस्य रिपुः i.e. शङ्करः v.l स्मरगुरोः i.e. the father of Cupid (प्रद्युम्न) i. e. श्रीकृष्ण and therefore, this reading is better to suit this reading "गाथा" meaning "Bhagvat Gītā." स्मररिपोर्गाथा i.e. verses dealing with शिव स्वापः sleep. निर्गता अर्गला (chain-limit) यस्मात् तत् adj. to सुखम् i.e. happiness, unlimited or unbounded. सुप्यताम् is the Imperative 3rd person sing. of the passive of स्वप् (2nd conj.p.) "to sleep".

20. "कलुषं वृजिनैनोऽघमहो दुरितदुष्कृतम्" दूरिकृतं कलुषाणं जालं यैः (बहु) who have removed the bondage of sin " सुकृती पुण्यवान् धन्यः " भवः एव ग्रीष्मः तस्य प्रौढ. आतपः तस्य निवहः (mass) तेन संतप्तानि वपूंषि येषां ते i.e. whose bodies are heated by the mass of excessive heat of the summer in the form of this worldly existence. निगड=chain. अविवेकस्य व्यतिकरः (आधिक्यं)-the contact of thoughtlessness (आत्मनात्मविवेकशून्यता) उन्मूल 10 v. to uproot. आत्मा एव अमृतं तस्य सरः the lake of the nectar of Ātmā. नैराश्येनशि शिरं तस्मिन्-cool on account of hopelessness for as long as hopes are there none can enjoy the bliss of आत्मन् cf. आशा हि परमं दुःखं नैराश्यं परमं सुखम्। (Bhagvat. 11-8-44)

21. बन्धात् उन्मुक्तिः freedom from bondage (of this worldly existence) मखाः मुखे येषां ते adj. to कर्मपाशाः (पाश at the end of a compound expresses) "abundance, mass." Hence कर्मपाश-

myriads of कर्मs "मखमुखा: कर्मपाशा: i. e. the myriads of कर्मs of which the sacrifice is the most important. मुनीनांशतानि तेषां मतानि तेषां अनल्पा (बहुधा) चिन्ता (चिन्तनं)-deep contemplation of the opinions of hundreds of sages. All these sages claim that their opinion alone is the one which leads to final beatitude-for example the सांख्य of कपिल, वेदान्त of बादरायण, मीमांसा of जैमिनी and many others. अशुभानि एव जलधि: the sea of sins. मज्जन्ति bathe (मस्ज् 1 P.) तीर्थ a holy place of pilgrimage, a place of water. निपानागमयोस्तीर्थं ऋषिजुष्टजले गुरौ" भवे भ्रान्ति (perplexion) भजन्ते-who have missed their right way (getting ब्रह्मज्ञान) in this world. प्रामादिकं Erroneous.

Here जगन्नाथपण्डित condemns (1) the rites as being instrumental in bringing about freedom from bondage. cf. इष्टापूर्तं मन्यमाना: वरिष्ठं नान्यच्छ्रेयो वेदयन्ते प्रमूढा: Muri.3-2-3.

Thirdly, he has no faith in the religious merits produced by pilgrimages for surmounting sins (cf. शुचिमनो यद्यस्ति तीर्थेन किम्। Bh. 2-55).

22. चुम्बितौ चरणौ यया सा resting on the feet; जंघ च (legs from ankle to the knee) जानू च (the two knees) ऊरू च (the thighs) नाभि: च हृदयं च=जङ्घा...हृदयानि आश्लिष्य embracing (i. e. contemplating over) मुखं अब्जं इव. It is customary to begin the contemplation over God from the leg, proceeding upwards to the head.

23. भूयात् is the benedictive third pers. of भू may I reside in the great soul (परमात्मा); this soul described as being free from all dualism (द्वैत) परमात्मनि स्थिति: that परमात्मा is not different from जीवात्मा one who has reached this stage does not differentiate between likes and dislikes cf:-दु:खेष्वनुद्विग्नमना:

सुखेषु विगतस्पृहः वीतरागभयक्रोधः-B. G. 2-56 निर्दोषं हि समं ब्रह्म (B G 5.19) निरन्तरा-निर्गतं अन्तरं यस्यां सा adj to स्थितिः a condition of mental equipoise where one does not see any difference between himself and any other thing and between the things themselves. The great Śaṅkarācārya very aptly says.

कल्यार्णव इवात्यन्तपरिपूर्णैकवस्तुनि।
निर्विकारे निराकारे निर्विशेषे मिदा कुतः। विवेकचूडामणि. 403

मलयानिलश्च कालकूटश्च तयोः between the breeze coming from the मलय mountain (which is very cool because it comes form sandal trees there on) and the deadly poison. रमण्याः कुन्तलाः the hair of a beautiful woman. भोगिनः भोगः the body of a serpent "अहेः शरीरं भोगः स्यात्" "उरगः पन्नगो भोगी जिह्मगः पवनाशनः"श्वानं पचति सः one who cooks a dog i. e. the चण्डाल who is generally seen to be ugly. आत्मभूः one who is born of himself i.e. cupid "पुष्पधन्वा रतिपतिर्मकरध्वज आत्मभूः" who is the ideal of beauty in the world. Such a condition of mind alone is capable of giving the ब्रह्मानन्द, the everlasting joy.

24. नश्वरं momentary-perishable; कलेवरं-शरीरं-Body. "अथ कलेवरं गात्रं वपुः संहननं शरीरं" तस्य कृते-for its sake. " कृते " "for" governs the genitive. कियान् how great ?

25. पले पले=प्रतिपलं At every moment. विरमति-रम् by itself is Ātmanepadi but with वि becomes Parasmaipadi. See "व्याङ्परिभ्यो रमः" (Pan. 1-3-83) "वि+रम्" "to desist from" in the latter sense it governs the ablative cf. 'न निश्चितार्थाद् विरमन्ति धीराः Bh. 2-80.

26. सपदि-at once. कृपाणस्य धाराः blades or edges of swords. अपहरतुतरां may much more take away. तराम्-Comparative termination is appended to verbal forms. cf. जयतितराम्,

गच्छतितराम्. कृतान्तः-God of Death. "कृतान्तो यमुनाभ्राता शमनो यमराड् यमः मनाग् a little.

27. This should be supposed to be the speech of one who deliberately restrains from talking anything that is offensive even to his enemy.

निरन्तरं incessantly; बहलः च असौ दहनः च तस्य जालम् a net of excessive fire. धमतु may blow. Imperative third pers. sing. from 'ध्मा' to blow. अप+भाष् to talk ill of.

28. This is the sum and substance of the poet's भक्ति philosophy.

ताम्यसि-Pres. 2nd per. sing. of तम् 4. to pine, to be afflicted. तरणस्य उपायः-A remedy-means to cross (the sea of mortal existence.) The poet means that his जीव need not worry if it does not yet find any means, because only the remembrance of Lord Kṛṣṇa at the time of death is sufficient to give it eternal freedom: Vide अन्तकाले च मामेव स्मरन्मुक्त्वा कलेवरम्। यः प्रयाति त्यजन्देहं स याति परमां गतिम्। (Bh. Gītā 8-5)

चेतःसरणौ-चितवृत्तौ न आगन्ता 3rd pers. sing. of the first future of आ+गम्.

29. माद्यन्ती (full of rut) या गजघटा (a crowd of elephants) तस्याः मदः तस्मिन् भ्राम्यन्ती (hovering) या भृङ्गाणां आवलिः (row of bees) तस्याः मधुरः, झंकारः तेन सुभगाः adj. to श्रियः द्रविणं एव मदिरा तेन घूर्णिता (rolling) दृक् (sight) येषां-तेषाम्-with the eyesight rolling-unsteady-owing to the wine in the form of wealth. अय्=to go. सपर्या-facility. Very adequately; here the devotee prays that he should never grow rich lest he will forget the worship of his favourite deity. With this compare what कुन्ती says in the पाण्डवगीता-"विपदः सन्तु नः शश्वत् यासु संकीर्त्यते हरिः"।।

30. This is an address of the poet to his own soul. वयस: शेषे-in the remnant of life, (since the poet is uttering this perhaps in old age.) नि:शंकं-निर्गता शंका यथा स्यात् तथा (अव्ययी०) without any fear of the catastrophe (Death) impending upon him. जागर्ति-is awake. The poet has extreme faith in the unique purifying influence of the Ganges and he has composed a number of memorable verses called the-गङ्गालहरी in praise of the divine river. His utter faith in गङ्गा as his sure saviour is manifested in the following verse:-

त्रपन्ते तीर्थानि त्वरितमिह यस्योध्द्तिविधौ
करं कर्णे कुर्वन्त्यपि किल कपालिप्रभृतय:।
इमं ते मामम्ब त्वमियमनुकम्पार्द्रहृदये
पुनाना सर्वेषामघशमनदर्पं दलयसि।। गङ्गा० 28
सुखं शेते मातस्तव खलु कृपात: पुनरयं
जगन्नाथ: शश्वत्त्वयि निहितलोकद्वयभर:।। गङ्गा० 36

Hence he does not fear even though death overtakes him since the Ganga is sure to save him. Tradition attributes to first-half of this verse to अप्पयदीक्षित, the author of कुवलयानन्द,- a work on rhetorics and a famous Pandita of Dravida Country; and a contemporary of जगन्नाथ. Once when he visited Benares (वाराणसी), while returning home from the river Ganges, he chanced to see some person lying on the steps (घाट) leading to the river, embracing his young wife, and could be judged as old from his white hair on the head, which were visible, although all his body was covered with a garment; overcome by anger, astonishment and pity, simultaneously he exclaimed:-

"किं नि:शंकं शेषे वयसि त्वमागते मृत्यौ"। At this पण्डितराज raised his garment and saw the adviser. But seeing that the person was जगन्नाथ-himself lying there अप्पयदीक्षित added the second line अथवा...जननी because he was conversant with

Jagannātha's immense faith in the river and her reciprocal favour for जगन्नाथ.

31. धावं धावम्-णमुल् from धाव् to run, to struggle; धावं धावं i.e. running frequently-struggling after everything in this world. v. l. सम्पादयामि यदयं for सन्तापयामि हृदयं. The reading does not seem to be so important.

32. मनसः भवः यस्य सः-मनोभवः (cupid-mind-born). तस्य शासनस्य (i. e. शिवस्य) पादौ एव अम्बुजे तयोः द्वयम्। अनारतं-Incessantly-संसृतिः (संसारः) एव गर्तः (pit) तस्य मध्ये। v. l. आमनन्तं—Thinking of or contemplating over, instead of आनमन्तम्.

Idea :—The poet means that his mind would not forget its grief for its child (Cupid) by throwing him (the poet) into the worldly existence as a punishment for his act of bowing to the feet of the burner of its son (Cupid).

Here the reference is to the incident of burning of मदन by शंकर when the former undertook the work of bringing about the union of शंकर and पार्वती in order to beget a son to kill the demon तारक (see कुमार cantos 2 & 3).

33. मरकतमणीनां मेदिनीधरः-मेदिन्याः धरः-the mountain of emeralds. ऋषीणां निकरैः—By the multitudes of sages. प्रपेदे Pass. Perf. 3rd pers. Sing. from प्र+पद्.

Idea :—Here various doubts arise in the minds of sages at the sight of Rāma of dark blue complexion in the "Daṇḍaka forest." Of course these doubts are based on poetic comparison.

34. तरणेः (सूर्यस्य) तनया=यमुना, तोयमयी-full of water. मरकतमणिः (an emerald) तस्य ज्योत्स्ना its lustre. बिलोकने तत्परैः engrossed or absorbed in seeing. उदितं कुतुके येषु ते-तैः curious. कायस्य च्छाया-the complexion of the body. "कायोदेहः क्लीवपुंसोः"

सन्दिदिहे is the pass. perf. of सम्+दिह् to be in doubt, to mistake for.

35. तरुषु मुख्य: the best of trees i.e. कल्पद्रुम मनीषिन्- Intelligent, wise "धीरो मनीषी ज्ञः प्राज्ञः" अथ here shows आनन्तर्य i.e. after he entertained so many misconceptions. गुरुभिः निश्वसितैः long deep sighs. वियोगोऽस्ति यस्याः सा वियोगिनी one who is separated from her husband; निरणैषीत् Aorist 3rd per. sing of निर्+नी to ascertain.

36. दारिद्यस्य कोलाहलः-uproar of poverty. भूतिः-prosperity. असतः पथः जुषः-Resorting to an evil path. समा=year "हायनोऽस्त्री शरत्समाः" कोषः एव दहनः तस्य ज्वालाभिः जटालाः-filled with flames of the fire in the form of anger. जगतः ईशः-the ruler of the world

37. रत्नानि सानौ यस्य सः रत्नसानुः "मेरुः सुमेरुर्हेमाद्री रत्नसानुः सुरालयः"। The mountain मेरु is the northern-most mountain on the earth according to Indian mythololgy. आ is used सीमार्थे cf. सोऽहमाजन्मशुद्धानाम् Raghu 1-5. मलयेन वलयिताद्-encircled by the Malaya mountain (which is in the south and known as the Home of Sandals) कूलम्—shore "कूलं रोधश्च तीरं च"

पयांसि धीयन्ते यत्र इति पयोधिः i. e. the ocean. काव्यानां प्रणयने पटवः-well versed in composing poems. विगता शङ्का यस्मिन् कर्मणि तत्तया-निःशंकं i. e. undoubtedly-without any doubt. मृद्वीकायाः मध्यः तस्माद् निर्यन्ती (coming out) या मसृणा (soft, delicate) रसस्य झरी (a stream-let) तस्याः माधुरी तस्य भाग्यं भजताम् (adj. to वाचाम्) v. l. काव्ये प्रणयनपटवः and v. l. ० झरीभाग्यभाजां नृपाणां-this reading is not very happy, we shall have to supply 'सभायां' after नृपाणां and ०भाजां becomes the adj. to नृपाणाम्.

Idea :—This poem and also the next two serve as a

challenge of our poet in the art of writing poems. His are the most melodious poems and conesquently he is the only blessed poet. Taking into consideration the worth of his poem, we can assert this much that his is not an empty boast. He has a remarkable command over Sanskrit Language. He means to say that sweetness of his poems surpasses that of even grapes as he has repeated elsewhere in this book.

38. गिरां देवी-Goddess of speech-the deity presiding over speech. गुण:-string-Here it refers to the string of the lute. रणनं-playing upon (वादनं) v. l. रसनं (tune or sound). हीनादर:. हीन: आदर: यस्य स: adj. to कर: i. e. having no regard for; and वीणाया: गुणानां रणने हीनादर: कर: यस्या: सा-whose hand lost (quitted) its fondness for playing upon the strings of a lute (वीणा) v.l. हीनादरकला-whose art is inferior-not so happy. यदीय like मदीय (mine) त्वदीय (thine) अस्मदीय, युष्मदीय, तदीय-is an adjective and hence it qualifies वाचाम्. अमृतमयम्-full of nectar. श्रवणयो: सुभगं charming to ears. पण्डितानां पति:-तस्य-it refers to जगन्नाथराय himself who considers himself to be the lord of the poets. अधुन्वन् i. e. न धुन्वन् not nodding (his head) v. l. अमृतमथम्. for मयम् अमृतं मथ्नाति इतिऽsurpassing nectar. नृपशु: अथवा पशुपति: नृपशु: i.e. नृषु पशु: or ना एव पशु: means the beast among men, or a beast in the form of a man. He means to say that the non-appreciator of his poem must be either a beast or he must be above everything. i.e. he must be a मुक्त like पशुपति i.e. entirely liberated from this transmigratory existence-he who has lost all charms for poems. पशुपति: i.e. God Shiva who is supposed to be a मुक्त (य: पुरस्ताद्यतीनाम् Malavikā 1-1)

सुभाषितेन गीतेन युवतीनां च लीलया।
यस्य नो द्रवते चित्तं स वै मुक्तोऽथवा पशु:।।

39. साक्षाद् अमृतम्-nectar incarnate i.e. nectar itself अथ and also cf. गणितमथ कलां कौशिकीम्" (Mk.1.) वामानां (सुन्दरस्त्रीणां) अधरे या सुधा सा— nectar on the lower lips of lovely ladies. वामं सव्ये प्रतीपे च द्रविणे चातिसुन्दरे" इति विश्व:-विदधीरन्-Pot. Atm. 3rd per. plu. from of धा with वि. to do "3rd conj. V." मुद्-joy-अहह ! alas ! "अहहेत्यद्भुते खेदे परिक्लेशप्रकर्षयो:" cf.-अहह कष्टमपण्डितता विधे: (Bh. III-110) मन्दा मति: येषां ते-मन्दमतय: Dullards-the sluggish persons. जगन्नाथस्य भणिति: the words of Jagannāth i.e. His poems.

40. This verse should be supposed to be a piece of advice given by जगन्नाथ to one of his brothers in profession. यदि (त्वं) अत्यन्तपाक द्रवन्मृद्वीकामधुमाधुरीमदपरीहारोद्धुराणां गिरां निर्माणे नितरां मार्मिकोऽसि, तर्हि, सखे, त्वं मादृशां सम्मुखे काव्यं कथय, नो चेत्, आत्मना कृतं दुष्कृतं इव (स्वकाव्यं) बहि: मा (अ) कृथा:।

अत्यन्त: पाक: (full ripening) तेन द्रवन् यद् मृद्वीकामधु (the pride juice dropping from grapes) तस्य माधुर्या: मद: (the pride of sweetness) तस्य परीहारे (removing) उध्दुरा: adj. to गिरा: उध्दुर=Victorious-successful; मार्मिक:-capable-able. संमुखे पुरत:, स्वान्ताद् बहि:-out of your own mind i.e. Don't show it to anybody lest it might be condemned. [माद्दशां संमुखे shows the immense confidence of the poet in his own unique capacity as a poet and the perusal of his works leads us to think that he is quite justified in his self-eulogy. See also verse 34.

41. This poem is addressed by जगन्नाथ to his own "speech" which is disheartened because of the deliberate disrespect shown towards it by the wicked through jealousy. हे मद्वाणि मात्सर्यमग्नमनसां खलानां अनादरेण विषादं मा कुरु। (यत:) (त्वं) काव्यारविन्दमकरन्दमधुव्रतानां आस्येषु कियतो विलासान् धास्यसितमाम्।

मात्सर्ये मग्नानि मनांसि येषां ते-तेषाम्-whose minds are full of jealousy; काव्यं एव अरविन्दं (lotus) तस्य मकरन्दस्य मधुव्रता: (bees) त्तोषम्, आस्येषु (on the faces) कियत: विलासान् धास्यतितमाम् i.e. the satisfaction arising from the approbation of your poetry. It points to a very general truth that a सहृदय alone can appreciate the beauty of a काव्य, none else irrespective of his immense intelligence or erudition. cf.-बोद्धारो मत्सरग्रस्ता: प्रभवस्मयदूषिता: (Bh. N. 2).

42. परेषां वचसां श्लाघ्या: Praising the words (poems) of others. वाचंयमा:-Restraining their own speech; the idea is that learned men, although they appreciate and realize the worth of the poetry, written by others, will be very cherry in expressing their admiration, through rivalry or jealousy. cf. प्राय: समानविद्या: परस्परयश: पुरोभागा:। Mal. Agni. 1-20. वाचं (नि) यच्छन्ति ते वाचंयमा:; कमलाया: (of Lakṣmī) विलासा: (sports) एव मदिरा तस्या: उन्मीलन् (produced) य: मद: (pride) तेन आघूर्णिता: (staggering, blinded). i.e. staggering or blinded by the intoxication (pride) of the wine in the form of sports of Lakṣmī; विपाक: the exuberance (of my speech) i.e. my best poetry. कामेन अलसा: (impassioned) या स्वर्वामा: (Heavenly damsels) cf. "वामा वनिता महिला तथा"-तासां अधरस्य माधुरी (the sweetness of the lower lip) तां अधरयन् i.e. exceeding the sweetness of the lower lip of the heavenly damsels. अधरयन् Pres. Part. from अधर (low) i.e. reducing them to a position of subsidiary importance. लास्यं—Dance (of pleasure).

43.धुर्य i. e. the best "धूर्वहे धुर्यधौरेय धुरीणास्तु धुरन्धरा:" इक्षु: sugarcane. माक्षिक—honey (मक्षिकाभि: कृतम्) v. l. माधुर्ये in sweetness; this reading is better and v. l. द्राक्षा...माक्षिकादीनाम्।

44. आकलीतानि P. P. P. कल् with आ, were mastered-

grasped-comprehended; नित्याः च ते विधयः च-usual duties (expected of a Brahmin); संभाविता:-P. P. P. from the causal of भू with सम्; were attended to-were performed. दिल्लया: वल्लभस्य पाणिपल्लवयोः पाणी एव पल्लवौ-कर्म.) तले i.e. under the kind patronage of the king of Delhi (lit. under the blossom-like hands of the king of Delhi) नवीनं वयः the prime of life or the flower of life i.e. youth उज्झिताः वासनाः यस्मिन् कर्मणि तद्यथास्यात्तथा In a manner in which all the desires are given up. मधुपुरी refers to the City of Muttra-it was formerly the city of the demon मधु. v.l. संप्रत्यन्धकशासनस्य नगरे तत्त्वं परं चिन्त्यते। (the punisher ot the Demon) अन्धक-vide मत्स्यपुराण 178. तस्य नगरम्= Benares. पण्डितराजानां राजिषु तिलकः—the foremost of the lines of princes of poets. अकारि-Pass. Aorist 3rd per. sing form कृ 8 U. to do-was done. लोकाधिकम्-more than (other) people.

45. जारेभ्य. जन्मानि येषां ते-Born of paramours. शङ्का-fear; पद्यानि एव रत्नानि-तेषां मञ्जुषा i.e. a box "पिटकः पेटकः पेटा मञ्जुषा" Jagannāth in this concluding verse gives the reason why he has locked up all his verses in this book called भामिनीविलास. He says that he has done so to guard himself against plagiarists (literary thieves). All the verses contained in the present book are scattered severally in his other works like the रसगङ्गाधर and hence, his apprehension of the fear.

APPENDIX A

१ प्रास्ताविकविलासः

दृढप्रेमा भग्नः सदसिरिव सन्धिं न लभते
लभेताभिप्रायः स्खलति बहुयत्नैरपि धृतः।
स्खलेन्नौ चेत्साम्यं न भजति भजेद्वा न पवति
च्युतं संगच्छेत स्मृतिमुपगतस्तु व्यथयति॥

This is what is given in Mr. Vaidya's edition. Herein some words are difficult to be construed and are perhaps misread and miswritten. As given in the सुभाषितरत्नभाण्डागार the verse runs thus—

दृढप्रेमा भग्नः सदसिरिव सन्धिं न भजते
भजेतापि प्रायः स्खलति खलु यत्नैरपि धृतः।
स्खलेन्नौ चेत् साम्यं भजति न भजेद्वा न भवति
च्युताशङ्कश्चेत्स्यात् स्मृतिमुपगतस्तु व्यथयति॥१॥

This verse describes how friendship once broken cannot be revived and made as strong or efficient as it originally was.

दृढः प्रेमा (यदि) भग्नः (चेत्) सदसिः इव संधिं न भजते, (संधिं) भजेत अपि यत्नैः अपि खलु धृतः प्रायः स्खलति, नो स्खलेत् चेत् (पूर्वप्रेम्णा) साम्यं न भजति; (साम्यं) भजेद्वा न (पूर्ववद्) भवति; च्युताशङ्कः चेत् स्यात् तु स्मृतिमुपगतः व्यथयति।

दृढः sincere, everlasting. प्रेमन् (m) love. सद्+असिः a good sword. संधिं न लभते cannot be joined. स्खलति breaks. साम्यं न भजति-does not reach the original standard. न भवति does not long, does not grow powerful. च्युता आशंका यस्मिन् सः adj. to प्रेमा where the distrust or apprehension due to the breach of friendship has disappeared because of the compromise that is brought about between two friends, तु-yet, even when the compromise is effected, व्यथयति-produces painrankles in the heart. i.e. the effect of the breach of friendship persists even then. The simile with असि may be sustained further, where applicable.

The staunch friendship when broken is not joined like a good sword even though it is joined, it becomes loose although it is maintained by endeavours, if it does not get loose, it does not approach the original sincerity, or if it is reached, it does not last for a long time, if the doubt disappears, the remembrance of lost friendship rankles in the heart.

(२)

कातराः परदुःखेषु निजदुःखेष्वकातराः
अर्थेष्वलोभा, यशसि सलोभाः, सन्ति साधवः॥२॥

कातराः grieved. नास्ति लोभः येषु ते-not covetous.

Good men feel distressed at the griefs of others, and are not distressed at their own griefs. They are not covetous of money but they covet fame.

(३)

विद्वत्सु विमलज्ञाना विरक्ता यतिषु स्थिताः
स्वीयेषु तु गरोद्गाराः नराकाराः क्षितौ खलाः॥३॥

क्षितौ नराकाराः खलाः विद्वत्सु विमलज्ञानाः (स्थिताः) यतिषु विरक्ताः स्वीयेषु तु गरोद्गाराः (स्थिताः)

नरस्य इव आकारः येषां ते-Having the form of human beings. विमलं ज्ञानं येषां ते. गरं इव उद्गाराः येषां ते whose words are like poison.

On this earth, wicked persons, disguised as men, show themselves as possessed of pure knowledge when they have to talk with learned persons, show themselves as free from all bondage, when they have to talk with Yatis, but when with their kinsmen, they eject venom in the form of their speech.

Additional verse in शान्तविलास.

सुरस्त्रोतस्विन्याः पुलिनमधितिष्ठन्नयनयोः
विधायान्तर्मुद्रामथ सपदि विद्राव्य विषयान्।
विधूतान्तर्ध्वान्तो मधुरमधुरायां चिति कदा
निमग्नः स्यां कस्यांचन नवनभस्याम्बुदरुचि॥१॥

सुरस्त्रोतस्विन्याः पुलिनमधितिष्ठन्, नयनयोः अतः मुद्रां विधाय, अथ सपदि विषयान्विद्राव्य, विधूतान्तर्ध्वान्तः (अहं) कस्यांचन नवनभस्यांबुदरुचि मधुरमधुरायां चिति कदा निमग्नः स्याम्।

सुराणां स्त्रोतस्विनी The river of gods i. e. the Ganges. पुलिनमधितिष्ठन् standing on the sandy bank. the acc. of पुलिन is according to अधिशीङ्स्थासां कर्म (Pan. 1-4-46) मुद्रां विधाय-Shutting or closing-closing the eyes inwards. The highest principle according to the Vedānta philosophy is visible only to those who look inwards, closing all communication with the outer world. This process of looking inwards with the object of getting परमात्मज्ञान has been referred to Kaṭha. 2-1 in the mantra परांचि खानि व्यतृणत् स्वयंभूः तस्मात्पराङ् पश्यति नान्तरात्मन्। कश्चिद् धीरः प्रत्यगात्मानमैक्षदावृत्तचक्षुरमृतत्वमिच्डछन्॥ विषयान् विद्राव्य is the gerund of the causal of वि+द्रु lit. causing the objects of senses to dissolve. i.e. when all the objects of sense are extinct or विषय may mean शब्द-स्पर्श etc. as in B. G. 18-51 शब्दादीन् विषयांस्त्यक्त्वा...ब्रह्मभूयाय कल्पते॥ Because as long as these विषयs are intact, the bondage persists. विधूतं अन्तः (वर्तमानं) ध्वान्तं येन सः who has shaken off the internal ignorance. चित् knowledge, one of famous Trinity सत्-चित्-आनंद existence, knowledge and bliss. The highest truth is often described as चित् cf. दिकङ्कालाद्यनव च्छिन्नानन्त चिन्मात्रमूर्तथे। स्वानुभूत्येकमानाय नमः शान्ताय तेजसे।। (भर्तृख १-१) नवः नभस्ये (भाद्रपदे) अंबुदः तस्य रुग् (शोभा) इव रुग् यस्य-तस्मिन्-whose lustre-complexion-is like the new cloud in the month of भाद्रपद i. e. bluish. 'स्युर्नभस्यः प्रौष्ठपदभाद्भाद्रपदाः समाः' मधुरमधुरा very sweet.

When shall I be merged in the extremely sweet knowledge (i.e. कृष्ण) whose complexion-lustre-resembles that of a new cloud in the month of भाद्रपद, I-with the internal ignorance completely shaken off, am standing on the bank of the celestial river, after closing my eyes inward, immediately dissolving the objects of sense.

APPENDIX B

Metres ocurring in the text with their definitions and schemes.

A stanza (पद्य) in Sanskrit Poetry is a combination of four quarters (पादs). A पाद is a combination of a certain number of syllables (अक्षरs) or of syllabic instants (मात्राs). A पद्य is either a वृत्त or जाति. A वृत्त is a stanza, the metre of which is regulated by the number and position of syllables in each quarter. A जाति is a stanza, the metre of which is regulated by the number of syllabic instants (मात्राs) in each quarter.

वृत्त

१. समवृत्त २. अर्धसमवृत्त ३. विषमवृत्त

१. समवृत्त is a stanza in which the पादs composing the stanza are all similar.

२. अर्धसमवृत्त is a stanza in which the alternate quarters are similar.

३. विषमवृत्त is a stanza in which the quarters are all dissimilar.

Sanskrit poems are generally written in the वृत्त metres and only occasionally in the जाति, of which only the आर्या variety is most commonly used.

A syllable (अक्षर) is so much of a word as can be pronounced at once, i.e. a vowel with or without one or more consonants.

अक्षर

लघु (short) गुरु (long)

A syllabic instant (मात्रा) is the measure of time required to pronounce a short vowel.

A syllable ending in a short vowel is called लघु e.g. अ, इ, उ, ऋ, ऌ

A syllable ending in a long vowel or ending in a short vowel, followed by a conjunct consonant or an अनुस्वार or a विसर्ग, is called गुरु. "सानुस्वारश्च दीर्घश्च विसर्गी च गुरुर्भवेत्। वर्णः संयोगपूर्वश्च तथा पादान्तगोऽपि वा।।" छन्दोमञ्जरी.

The last syllable of a quarter (पाद) may be लघु or गुरु as the metre requires it .

In metres regulated by the number of syllabic instants (मात्रा), a लघु vowel has one मात्रा and a गुरु one has two मात्राs.

For the purpose of scanning metres regulated by the number of syllables, each quarter (पाद) is divided into groups of three letters each. Each such group forms a syllabic foot and is styled as a गण. There are eight गणs, each being distinguished by the position of particular syllables, short or long, which it contains viz. य, र, त, भ, ज, स, म, and न "आदिमध्यावसानेषु यरता यान्ति लाघवम्। भजसा गौरवं यान्ति मनौ तु गुरुलाघवम्".

The sign for ल (लघु) is । and for ग (गुरु) ऽ

य । ऽ ऽ; र ऽ । ऽ ;त ऽ ऽ । ; न । । ।.

भ ऽ । ।; ज । ऽ ।; स । । ऽ; म ऽ ऽ ऽ.

Characteristics of the metres given above.

१. आर्या—12 मात्राs in the 1st and 3rd पाद, 18 मात्राs in the second पाद and 15 in the fourth.

(This is the general characteristic)

२. शिखरिणी—रसै रुद्रैश्छिन्ना यमनसभलाग: शिखरिणी।

य, म, न, स, भ, and one short and one long letter with stops at 6 and 11.

३. पृथ्वी—जसौ जसयला वसुग्रहयतिश्च पृथ्वी गुरु:

ज, स, ज, स, य, one short and one long letter with stops at 8,9.

४. शार्दूलविक्रीडितम्—सूर्याश्वैर्यदि म: सजौ सततगा: शार्दूलविक्रीडितम्।

म, स, ज, स, त, त, and one long letter with stops at 12,7.

५. मालिनी—ननमयययुतेयं मालिनी भोगिलोकै:।

न, न, म, य, य with stops at 8,7

६. पुष्पिताग्रा—अयुजि नयुगरेफतो यकारो
युजि तु नजौ जरगाश्च पुष्पिताग्रा।

न, न, र and य in odd quarters and न, ज, ज, र, and ग in even quarters.

७. प्रहर्षिणीयम्—त्र्याशभिर्मनजरगा: प्रहर्षिणीयम्।

म, न, ज, र, and one long letter with stops at 3, 10

८. वसन्ततिलका—उक्ता वसन्ततिलका तभजाजगौ ग:।

त, भ, ज, ज, and two long letters.

९. मन्दाक्रान्ता—मन्दाक्रान्ताम्बुद्धिरसनगैर्मो मनौ तौ गयुग्मम्।

म, भ, न, त, त, and two long letters.

१०. अनुष्टुप्— श्लोके षष्ठं गुरु ज्ञेयं सर्वत्र लघु पञ्चमम्।
द्विचतु:पादयोर्ह्रस्वं सप्तमं दीर्घमन्ययो:।।

११. वैतालीय— षड्विषमेऽष्टौ समे कलास्ताश्च समे स्यु निरन्तराः न।
समात्र परश्रिता कला वैतालीयेऽन्ते रलौ गुरुः।।

१२. उपेन्द्रवज्रा—ज, त, ज, and two long letters.

(same as इन्द्रवज्रा with the exception of the first letter, which is short here).

१३. रथोद्धता—रात्परैर्नरलगै रथोद्धता

र, न, र, and one short and one long letter.

१४. गीतिः—12 syllabic instants in I and III quarter and 18 in II and IV.

१५. मञ्जुभाषिणी—सजसा जगौ च यदि मञ्जुभाषिणी।

स, ज, स, ज and one long letter.

१६. उपगीतिः—12 syllabic instants in I and III quarter and 15 in II and IV.

१७. उद्गीतिः—12 syllabic instants in I and III, 15 in II and 18 in IV.

१८. उपजातिः—mixture of इन्द्रवज्रा and उपेन्द्रवज्रा both of which have been given above.

१९. प्रमिताक्षरा—सजससैः कथिता प्रतिताक्षरा। स, ज, स and स

२०. द्रुतविलम्बितम्—द्रुतविलम्बितमाह नभौ भरौ।

न, भ, भ, and र

२१. स्वागता—स्वागता रनभगैर्गुरुणा च।

र, न, भ, and two long letters.

२२. हरिणी—नसमरसलागः षड्वेदैर्हयैर्हरिणी मता।

न, स, म, र, स, one short and one long letter; stops at 6, 4, 7.

The following is the distribution of verses according to metres.

Name of Vṛtta.	*No. of verses in Vilāsa I.*
१. आर्या	१,७,१०,१३,२१,२२, २४,२६,२८,२९,५०,८१, ९०,९२,९७,९८,१०२, १०८,
२. शिखरिणी	२,३२,३३,४०,४३,५२, ५४,६०,७९,८३,८४,
३. पृथ्वी	३
४. शार्दूलविक्रीडितम्	४,१६,३१,३४,३५,३८, ४१,४६,४८,५५,५६,५७, ५८,५९,६३,६६,६७,७२, ७७,८६,१०३,१२८.
५. मालिनी	५,३६,१२१,
६. पुष्पिताग्रा	८,७४
७. प्रहर्षिणी	१५,९६,१२४
८. वसन्ततिलका	१७,३७,४७,४९,६९,७०, ७१,७५,९४,९५,१०१, १०४,१०५,१२२
९. मन्दाक्रान्ता	३०
१०. अनुष्टुप्	३९,६२,६५,७८,८७,८८, ८९,९१,९३,९९,१०९, ११०,११२,११५,११६, ११७,११८,११९,१२०, १२६,१२७,१२९
११. वैतालीयः वत वियोगिनी	४४,१११

१२. उपेन्द्रवज्रा	४५,१२५
१३. रथोद्धता	५१
१४. गीतिः	१२,६,९,१४,१८,२०, २५,२७,४२,६८,८०, १००,१०६,११४,१२३
१५. मञ्जुभाषिणी	५३
१६. उपगीतिः	६१,६४,७३,८२
१७. उद्गीतिः	११,१९,७३
१८. उपजातिः	७३,८५
१९. प्रमिताक्षरा	१०७
२०. द्रुतविलम्बितम्	११३
२१. स्वागता	
२२. हरिणी	

No. of Verses in Vilāsa II

१. आर्या	४०,४५,५२,५३,६८,८२,१०२,१०५,१११, ११९,१४५,१४९,१७०,१८३.
२. शिखरिणी	५५,७६,७७,८०,९०,१२५,१३७,१५३.
३. पृथ्वी	७५,१४०,
४. शार्दूलविक्रीडितम्	५४,६३,७२,७३,७४,७८,८१,९१,१६६.
५. मालिनी	२८,३२,३५,५६,५७.
६. पुष्पिताग्रा	७,१४.
७. प्रहर्षिणी	९
८. वसन्ततिलिका	३,४,५,६,११,८९,९२,९९,१३६,१५६,१५८,१६८.
९. मन्दाक्रान्ता	७९
१०. अनुष्टुप्	२९,४८,६०,६५,६७,८७,९३,९६,९८,१०१,१०३, १०४,१०६, ११२,११५,११७,११७,१२४,१२६,१३०, १३१,१३२,१३५,१५४,१५६,१५९,१७३,१७५.
११. वैतालीय	६४,१००,११६.
१२. उपन्द्रेवज्रा	१३,२४,२०८,१३४,१३८.
१३. रथोद्धता	१५,२३,३७.
१४. गीतिः	३१,४१,४२,४३,४४,४६,४७,४९,५१,६९,८३,८५, ९५, १४३,१४४,१५०,१५१,१६४,१६८,१८१.
१५. मञ्जुभाषिणी	११०
१६. उपगीतिः	१४६,१६३.
१७. उद्गीतिः	५०,७१,८६,७७,१२७.
१८. उपजातिः	१०,१२,२२,३०,३३,३६,६६,१०७,१२०,१२३,१३९, १४२,१४६,१६९,१७६,१७९.
१९. प्रमिताक्षरा	
२०. द्रुतविलम्बितम्	१२१, १५२
२१. स्वागता	१०९
२२. हरिणी	२९

२३. कालभारिणी	१,२,८,२७,३४,३८,६२,७०,१२२,१३३,१४८,१६०, १६१,१६५,१७२,१८०.
२४. मालभारिणी	१६,२८,१९,१७४.
२५. शालिनी	१७,२५.
२६. प्रबोधिता	३१
२७. औपच्छन्दसिकम्	५८,५९.
२८. सुन्दरी	१७,१४१,१६२,१७१,१६६,१८२.
२९. इन्द्रवज्रा	११३
३०. वंशस्थम्	११४,१२१,१५५.

No. of Verses in Vilāsa III

१.	वसन्ततिलका	१,२,३,४,५,६,७,८,९,१०,११,१२,१३, १४,१५,१६,१७,१९.
२.	कालभारिणी	१८

No. of Verses in Vilāsa IV

आर्या	२५,३१,४३,
शिखरिणी	५,७,२०,२९,३८,३९,
	App. ४
पृथ्वी	१,२,३,४
शार्दूलविक्रीडितम्	१०,११,१३,१४,१५,
	१९,३६,३७,४०,४२,
	४४
पुष्पिताग्रा	२६,३३
वसन्ततिलका	८,३२,४१
मन्दाक्रान्ता	१६,१७,१८,२१
	९,४५, App. २,३
वैत्तालीयः और वियोगिनी	३५,२३,२४
गीतिः	२२,२७,२८
उद्गीतिः	१२
स्वागता	६
हरिणी	३४

श्लोकानुक्रमणी